THEOLOGICAL NEGOTIATIONS

PROPOSALS *in* SOTERIOLOGY *and* ANTHROPOLOGY

DOUGLAS FARROW

Baker Academic

a division of Baker Publishing Group

Grand Rapids, Michigan

© 2018 by Douglas Farrow

Published by Baker Academic
a division of Baker Publishing Group
PO Box 6287, Grand Rapids, MI 49516-6287
www.bakeracademic.com

Printed in the United States of America

Library of Congress Cataloging-in-Publication Control Number: 2018014185
ISBN 978-1-5409-6039-9

18   19   20   21   22   23   24   7   6   5   4   3   2   1

for Anna,

who on our silver anniversary remains marital gold

Contents

Preface

Half a millennium ago, the Protestant Reformation created new and tragically bloody borders in Europe, fundamentally altering not only its already tumultuous political terrain but changing permanently its philosophical and cultural landscape. There are plenty of books about that, but this is not one of them. It is a book of theology, a book whose author is insufficiently embarrassed by the fact that theology contributed to the tumult and bloodshed to consign it to the margins of thought and culture, as the men of the Enlightenment proposed and pretended to have achieved. Of course, they achieved no such thing. What they achieved was a very different kind of theology, the kind that secularizes rational discourse about God to make it serve purely temporal ends. That such discourse perforce ceases to be rational, that it reverts to being mythological, either did not occur to them or failed to embarrass them. (Even Kant, to whom it did occur, was prepared to indulge in it or at least to excuse those who did, so long as they did it on his terms.) Which is one reason why what came after them was even bloodier than what went before them. But there are plenty of books about all that too, including some recent history-of-ideas books such as Michael Gillespie's *The Theological Origins of Modernity*, Brad Gregory's *The Unintended Reformation*, and (most recently) Carlos Eire's *Reformations*. This is not that kind of book either. It is a book devoted to certain contiguous theological loci that are of perennial interest to Christian thinkers and to the Church and that long before the Reformation, as well as during and after, have been sites of controversy.

At the heart of the book lies an interest in the dialectic of nature and grace, which is explored not only in its own right in chapter 2 but also in various epistemological (chap. 1), soteriological (chaps. 3 and 4), sacramental (chaps. 5

and 6), anthropological and ecclesiological (chaps. 7–9) dimensions. Running throughout these explorations there is a timely subtext that treats Catholic and Protestant differences and seeks to negotiate, not a set of compromises, but rather a fresh way of seeing the differences. It is certainly my hope that, where it succeeds, this book might contribute to advances in ecumenical theology. It is likewise my hope that Catholic and Protestant and even Orthodox theologians will find the book stimulating in itself, quite apart from any ecumenical concerns they might have before—or after—reading it.

Among the many books of my late mentor and friend, Colin Gunton, is one called *Theology through the Theologians*. The present book is somewhat like that, though it is less occasional and, in its way, a little more ambitious. Not that I fancy myself a proper scholar of any of the major figures who appear here: Anselm, Aquinas, and Luther especially, not to mention Calvin and Barth, or Ockham, Descartes, Kant, and the later nominalist thinkers (such as Mill and Raz) with whom I deal in passing, or indeed the author of Hebrews. Rather, this is just another case of someone learning as they write. Those who think I haven't learned well enough may wish to set me straight on any number of points, and I will not be ungrateful.

It is unusual to begin a book of original essays with one already published, especially if it appears with relatively minor modifications. But I think readers will agree that it belongs here, and of course most readers will not have read it where it first appeared, namely, in the English edition of *Nova et Vetera*; my thanks to that journal for allowing it to appear in both places. It is from this essay that I have taken both the inspiration and the title for this book, which reminds me to say that more than a few of its chapters, beginning with that one, had their origin in papers presented to the Fortnightly Philosophy and Theology Seminar here at McGill. To colleagues in that venture I am also grateful, as to the graduate and undergraduate students who have read with me and discussed Anselm, in particular, at some length.

In chapters 2 through 7 it is to Anselm and Aquinas that I keep returning. Aquinas, of course, is always indispensable, and often satisfying. Where he is not satisfying, however, I find myself driven back to biblical motifs better developed in earlier thinkers such as Irenaeus, Augustine, and Anselm. The last of these has come to play a larger role than I anticipated he would. Anselm was the first to encounter and to grasp the scope of the problem of nominalism, that philosophical and theological and political movement which has so dramatically altered Western civilization and continues, as chapter 7 observes, to do so today. Should any of my readers feel that chapter 7 should really have been a second volume, I will not demur; but events are moving so quickly now that delay seems ill-advised. Nominalism is Western civilization's wounded side, from which is flowing, not water and blood, but blood and fire. To stem that flow it is necessary to see in nominalism what Anselm saw, something the chapter's long arc attempts to reveal.

The central chapters treat the soteriological and doxological issues which, for the Church, have always been and must always be the most important. Of Luther, who features in chapter 3, it must certainly be said in his favor that he had a keen eye for what really mattered; against him, it may fairly be said that he got some of these things badly wrong and that his tongue was often sharper than his mind. I hope I haven't proven such an example of that myself as to put off his present-day admirers altogether. To contemporary representatives of views and practices Luther himself derided on the radical side of the Reformation, I express the same hope. More specifically, I extend thanks to Le Centre d'études anabaptistes de Montréal and to Regent College in Vancouver for hosting events in which earlier versions of chapter 5 were read and patiently heard, despite content controversial both to the Radical Reformation and to Calvinists. And here I want to say that I am especially grateful to Professor Alan Torrance of St Andrews, a longtime friend, for his willingness to respond to the version read in Vancouver. He is of course absolved of any and all responsibility for its claims, some of which he vigorously disputes.

As I looked back through his father's essays in that connection, I met once again thought after thought, motif after motif, that have governed my own subsequent work in theology. Many of them came to fruition in *Ascension Theology*, which (though decidedly Catholic) owes much to T. F. and J. B. Torrance. Yet anyone who has read that book will know that, in its own fifth chapter, I suggest that the problem of Pelagianism in ecclesiology, and more particularly in doxology, is not just a danger among Protestants, as it is among Catholics, but is rather deeply rooted in Protestantism as such. Readers who were puzzled by that claim will find it elucidated somewhat here. These two chapter 5s, together with my *First Things* article on the elder Torrance, form a kind of trilogy in which the question "Whose offering?" is pressed.[1]

Pressing that question inevitably raises the topic of transubstantiation, which is treated in chapter 6. Having already ventured something in *Ascension Theology* toward a better grasp of that doctrine, particularly in its eschatological dimensions, it seemed right to venture a little more here, this time by way of a sustained engagement with Aquinas. His recent expositors

---

1. Douglas Farrow, "T. F. Torrance and the Latin Heresy: Praising and Critiquing One of the Twentieth Century's Greatest Theologians," *First Things* (December 2013): 25–31. My subsequent essay, "Discernment of Situation," *First Things* (March 2017): 39–43, brings the same critique mutatis mutandis to bear on contemporary Catholicism.

(including friends whose essays appear in the text or notes) notwithstanding, I remain troubled by the difficulty of doing justice to the eucharistic *conversio* in its temporal aspect by a strict deployment of the substance/accidents distinction. Here, further negotiation may well be necessary, there being many unasked questions and unsolved problems. As for those, Protestant or Catholic, who are inclined to dismiss talk of transubstantiation as tangential to the real interests of Christianity today, I beg them to think again. What is more characteristic of contemporary Western culture than the resurgent gnosticism to which philosophical and liturgical forms of nominalism have brought us? As I try to show in chapter 7, our contemporary fascination with the will and its autonomy is very much at the expense of the body, and of course it is precisely to questions about the body that discourse about transubstantiation drives us.

A word about chapter 8: It too treats a soteriological issue that from the outset was crucial to the Church. In this case, however, that issue—the relation between Jew and Gentile in the body of Christ under the *berit hadasha*—was for a very long time sublimated and neglected, until in the nineteenth century it began to press for attention again. From the latter part of the twentieth century it has been a site of no small controversy in circles Protestant as well as Catholic. If the Jerusalem Council had to ask and answer the question about the place of Gentiles in what was then a Jewish Church, today we must ask and answer questions about the place of Jews in what is a decidedly Gentile Church. The requisite negotiations are as humanly delicate as they are theologically demanding. The approach taken here may please only a few, but the arguments, I hope, will garner the attention of many. To Matthew Levering, who helped shape them, and to the entire crew in Manhattan who first listened to them, some with a certain horror no doubt, a debt is due. This chapter too might better have been a book, but there are others more qualified to write it.

And chapter 9? I wrote this meditation on Hebrews for a session in San Antonio at the Society of Biblical Literature, after which a number of people asked me for it. It seems to fit in just here as an antidote to what is described in chapter 7 and as a word of warning to Jew and Gentile alike, made more urgent by signs that the times of the Gentiles may be drawing to a close. The misconstrual of autonomy that now prevails in our society, if not corrected, will certainly destroy society itself along with individual souls. The former, being a temporal loss only, is not as serious as the latter, but it is serious enough; and the only possible corrective, whether for the soul or for society, is a recovery of the fear of God. That, I think, is what theologians and preachers most need to say now, without neglecting their other tasks. When it comes to the fear of God, there can be no negotiation. God is God, and the border between man[2] and God is negotiable only by way of the mediation of the Holy One of God. That is the message of Hebrews, which is as much a tract for our times as for its own.

2. Throughout this book, as in all my books, I use gendered language freely, in the classical mode of my sources, whose anthropology I largely share. Those who will not acknowledge that God made "man" male and female are today legion, but I am not among them.

Abbreviations

General and Bibliographic

ANF   *The Ante-Nicene Fathers: Translations of the Writings of the Fathers down to A.D. 325*, ed. Alexander Roberts and James Donaldson, rev. A. Cleveland Coxe, 10 vols. (New York: Christian Literature, 1885–87; repr., Peabody, MA: Hendrickson, 1994)

CCC   *Catechism of the Catholic Church: With Modifications from the* Editio Typica, 2nd ed. (New York: Doubleday, 1997)

CD   Karl Barth, *Church Dogmatics*, ed. G. W. Bromiley and T. F. Torrance, trans. G. W. Bromiley, 4 vols. (Edinburgh: T&T Clark, 1956–75)

CDH   Anselm, *Cur deus homo* / *Why God Became Man*

CIC   *Codex Iuris Canonici*

Civ.   Augustine, *De civitate dei* / *The City of God*

DC   Anselm, *De concordia praescientiae et praedestinationis et gratiae dei cum libero arbitrio* / *The Compatibility of God's Foreknowledge, Predestination, and Grace with Human Freedom*

DCD   Anselm, *De casu diaboli* / *The Fall of the Devil*

De Pot.   Aquinas, *Quaestiones disputatae de potentia* / *On the Power of God*

DEC   Norman Tanner, *Decrees of the Ecumenical Councils*, 2 vols. (London: Sheed & Ward, 1990)

DS   Heinrich Denzinger, *Enchiridion symbolorum definitionum et declarationum de rebus fidei et morum*, ed. Adolf Schönmetzer (Freiburg: Herder, 1997) / Handbook of Creeds, Definitions, and Declarations on Matters of Faith and Morals

DV   Aquinas, *Quaestiones disputatae de veritate* / *On Truth*

DZ   Heinrich Denzinger, *The Sources of Catholic Dogma*, trans. Roy J. Deferarri from the 30th edition of the *Enchiridion Symbolorum* (Fitzwilliam: Loreto, 2002)

EQP   Benedict XIV, *Ex quo primum*

Haer.   Irenaeus, *Adversus omnes haereses* / *Against Heresies*

In Rom.   Aquinas, *In epistolam ad Romanos* / *Commentary on Romans*

LW	*Luther's Works*, ed. Jaroslav Pelikan and Helmut T. Lehman. American edition, 55 vols. (Philadelphia: Muehlenberg and Fortress; St. Louis: Concordia, 1955–86)
Mor.	Augustine, *De moribus ecclesiae catholicae* / *On the Morals of the Catholic Church*
NPNF[1]	*A Select Library of Nicene and Post-Nicene Fathers of the Christian Church*, 1st series, ed. Philip Schaff, 14 vols. (New York: Christian Literature, 1886–89; repr., Peabody, MA: Hendrickson, 1994)
NPNF[2]	*A Select Library of Nicene and Post-Nicene Fathers of the Christian Church*, 2nd series, ed. Philip Schaff and Henry Wace, 14 vols. (New York: Christian Literature, 1890–1900; repr., Peabody, MA: Hendrickson, 1994)
PG	*Patrologia Graeca*, ed. J.-P. Migne, 162 vols. (Paris, 1857–86)
PL	*Patrologia Latina*, ed. J.-P. Migne, 221 vols. (Paris, 1844–64)
Pros.	Anselm, *Proslogion*
Quod.	Aquinas, *Quaestiones quodlibetales* / *Miscellaneous Questions*
Sent.	Lombard, *Libri quattuor sententiarum* / *The Four Books of Sentences*
SCG	Aquinas, *Summa contra Gentiles* / *On the Truth of the Catholic Faith*
ST	Aquinas, *Summa Theologiae* (Benziger Bros. edition, 1947, trans. by Fathers of the English Dominican Province; available with other works by Thomas Aquinas at http://dhspriory.org/thomas)
Supp.	*Supplementum* / Supplement to the *Summa Theologiae*
Trin.	Augustine, *De Trinitate* / *On the Trinity*

Old Testament

Gen.	Genesis		Song	Song of Songs
Exod.	Exodus		Isa.	Isaiah
Lev.	Leviticus		Jer.	Jeremiah
Num.	Numbers		Lam.	Lamentations
Deut.	Deuteronomy		Ezek.	Ezekiel
Josh.	Joshua		Dan.	Daniel
Judg.	Judges		Hosea	Hosea
Ruth	Ruth		Joel	Joel
1–2 Sam.	1–2 Samuel		Amos	Amos
1–2 Kings	1–2 Kings		Obad.	Obadiah
1–2 Chron.	1–2 Chronicles		Jon.	Jonah
Ezra	Ezra		Mic.	Micah
Neh.	Nehemiah		Nah.	Nahum
Esther	Esther		Hab.	Habakkuk
Job	Job		Zeph.	Zephaniah
Ps(s).	Psalm(s)		Hag.	Haggai
Prov.	Proverbs		Zech.	Zechariah
Eccles.	Ecclesiastes		Mal.	Malachi

Deuterocanonical Books

Sir.   Sirach (Ecclesiasticus)

Wis.   Wisdom of Solomon

New Testament

Matt.	Matthew	1–2 Thess.	1–2 Thessalonians
Mark	Mark	1–2 Tim.	1–2 Timothy
Luke	Luke	Titus	Titus
John	John	Philem.	Philemon
Acts	Acts	Heb.	Hebrews
Rom.	Romans	James	James
1–2 Cor.	1–2 Corinthians	1–2 Pet.	1–2 Peter
Gal.	Galatians	1–3 John	1–3 John
Eph.	Ephesians	Jude	Jude
Phil.	Philippians	Rev.	Revelation
Col.	Colossians		

1

Theology and Philosophy

Recovering the Pax Thomistica

The theology included in holy teaching is different in kind from that theology
that is part of philosophy.

Aquinas, Summa Theologiae 1.1.1

For as soon as we allow two different callings to combine and run together, we
can form no clear notion of the characteristic that distinguishes each by itself.

Kant, The Conflict of the Faculties I.1.A

However legitimate or possible this other task may be, the task of dogmatics
is set aside when it is pursued.

Barth, Church Dogmatics 1.1 §2

With these opening aphorisms—the apparent agreement of which masks still
more fundamental disagreements—I may be suspected of stacking the deck,
having surrounded an eminent philosopher with two eminent theologians,
one on each side; but one of the latter is also an eminent philosopher, and
the latter in any case do not see eye to eye on the relation between theology
and philosophy. By considering the view of each, I hope to clarify my own
view just a little and perhaps yours as well, whatever disagreements we shall

discover between ourselves. I hope at all events that you will not have occasion to think (as Kant might) that I have leapt, "like Romulus's brother, over the wall of ecclesiastical faith" by meddling in reason; or indeed that I have only "meddled" with reason.[1]

If we mean to speak of the relation between theology and philosophy, however, we should begin with some highly provisional attempt at definition—highly provisional because nothing stacks the decks like definition! Philosophy, of course, is notoriously difficult to define, and its literal meaning does not suffice to distinguish it from theology. As a working definition I will offer this, cribbed in part from our philosophy department's website: Philosophy is the pursuit of clarity about ourselves, our world, and our place in it, for the sake of the good life;[2] in its academic dimension it involves inter alia the study of logic, epistemology, metaphysics, ethics, and aesthetics.

Of theology I will say: It is discourse about deity, and the creature in relation to deity, that is disciplined by metaphysics—this is so-called natural or philosophical theology, "in which divine things are considered not as the subject of the science but as principles of the subject," as Thomas has it—and/or by Scripture, liturgy, and dogma—this is revealed theology, in which divine things are themselves the subject.[3] In its academic dimension revealed theology demands, in addition to philosophical and cultural studies, careful study of what is contained in the sources of revelation.

1. Immanuel Kant, *The Conflict of the Faculties*, in *Religion and Rational Theology*, trans. and ed. Allen Wood and George di Giovanni (Cambridge: Cambridge University Press, 1996), 252.

2. What is missing on that site (www.mcgill.ca/philosophy) is direct reference to the good life, without which philosophy cannot be taken literally as a love of wisdom. Kant, as Gilles Deleuze notes in *Kant's Critical Philosophy: The Doctrine of the Faculties* (Minneapolis: University of Minnesota Press, 1985), 1, "defines philosophy as 'the science of the relation of all knowledge to the essential ends of human reason,' or as 'the love which the reasonable being has for the supreme ends of human reason' (CPR and Opus postumum, A839/B867)"; or, more fully, as "a science of the human being, of his representations, thoughts and actions" that "should present all the components of the human being both as he is and as he should be—that is, in terms both of his natural functions and of his relations to morality and freedom" (Kant, *Conflict of the Faculties*, 288).

3. Thomas distinguishes between knowledge of divine things "as their effects reveal them" and "as they reveal themselves." Hence there are "two kinds of divine science, one, in which divine things are not considered as the subject of the science, but as principles of the subject, which philosophers pursue and which is known as metaphysics, and another, which considers divine things themselves as the subject of the science, and this is the theology which is handed down in Sacred Scripture" (*Super Boetium De Trinitate* 3 q. 5, a. 4, co. 4). In his *Lectures on the Philosophical Doctrine of Religion*, Kant defines theology generically as "the system of our cognition of the highest being" (in *Religion and Rational Theology*, 342), but he also distinguishes between rational and revealed theology while subdividing the former into *theologia trancendentalum*, *naturalem*, and *moralem* (346).

Both natural and revealed theology aim at establishing sound speech about God (what Plato calls οἱ τύποι περὶ θεολογίας, *Republic* 379a), but the one works with what can be known of God by way of divine effects in creation, and the other devotes itself to the whole knowledge and counsel of God, as disclosed especially in God's redemptive self-manifestation.[4] Which is to say, revealed theology also pursues clarity about ourselves, our world, and our place in it, and does so precisely for the sake of the good life; but it knows quite concretely, from its own sources, what natural theology, on some accounts, also has an inkling of, namely, that "humanity is directed towards God as to an end that surpasses the grasp of its reason" and that the good life lies in the direction of God, who is goodness itself.[5] It knows this with a definiteness and a detail that natural theology lacks, and it speaks of God with a directness proper to itself.

I say "on some accounts" because of course this basically Thomist view is not everyone's view. Kant and Barth, for example, do not share it. Kant denies revealed theology both the independence and the superiority that Thomas ascribes to it while at the same time severely restricting the natural theology that Thomas inherited from Greek and Christian sources. Barth not only restricts natural theology but also denies its validity. He emphasizes the grandeur of revealed theology but thinks that grandeur greatly imperiled by natural theology:

> Of all disciplines theology is the fairest, the one that moves the head and heart most fully, the one that comes closest to human reality, the one that gives the clearest perspective on the truth which every discipline seeks. It is a landscape like of those of Umbria and Tuscany with views which are distant and yet clear, a work of art which is as well-planned and as bizarre as the cathedrals of Cologne or Milan. . . . But of all disciplines theology is also the most difficult and the most dangerous, the one in which a man is most likely to end in despair, or—and this almost worse—in arrogance. Theology can float off into thin air or turn to stone, and worst of all it can become a caricature of itself.[6]

4. Obviously it is only as revealed theology—theology that is happy to take direction from Scripture and tradition, to incorporate their claims into its arguments, and indeed to make their claims the focus of its arguments—that theology is a discipline distinct from philosophy rather than a mere subdivision of it. As Aidan Nichols observes, its special task is "the disciplined exploration of what is contained in revelation," an exploration that makes the highest demands on reason; for "the wonder, curiosity, and ever-deepening pursuit of truth implicit in the act of faith generate a variety of questions" that must be systematically addressed. *The Shape of Catholic Theology: An Introduction to Its Sources, Principles, and History* (Collegeville, MN: Liturgical Press, 1991), 33f.

5. *ST* 1.1.1 (F. C. Bauerschmidt, ed. and trans., *Holy Teaching: Introducing the "Summa Theologiae" of St. Thomas Aquinas* [Grand Rapids: Brazos, 2005], 32).

6. Quoted in Eberhard Busch, *Karl Barth*, trans. J. Bowden (Grand Rapids: Eerdmans, 1994), 244, from Barth's 1934 Calvin lectures in Paris.

It is most likely to do so, according to Barth, where it follows the path of those who "think first of cause and effect, of the infinite and the finite, of eternity and time, of idea and phenomenon," rather than of the self-determination of God for man in the person of Jesus Christ.[7] Natural theology, if by that we mean right reason and true speech about God based on something other than God's self-revelation in Christ, is beyond the capacity of fallen man and a repudiation of divine grace.

Thomas, for his part, was resident on both sides of the border between philosophy and theology, inhabiting the borderlands as one who sought consistency and coherence between their respective attempts to speak of God. If this distinguishes him from Barth and Kant, how much more from those who, at some distant extreme, shrink altogether either from philosophy, as Barth did not, or from theology, as Kant did not (or not quite)? The *pax Thomistica*, as we might call it, both respects the border and regards it as a friendly one. But let us look at Kant, then at Barth—for otherwise we cannot understand Barth—before returning to Thomas.

Kant's Philosophical Imperialism

We ought really to look first at the Franciscans; that is, at Ockham and the nominalist philosophers who set out on the trail that eventually led around to Kant.[8] But for brevity's sake we go directly to Kant, the mature Kant at that—the Kant who waited out King Frederick William II before issuing *The Conflict of the Faculties*, in which he tried to put these disciplines in their proper places.

Kant, as you know, drew certain distinctions between the higher faculties (medicine, law, and theology in ascending order) and the lower (philosophy). The former, in which people train for professions, are statute or canon based, while the latter is truth based. The former are regulated by the government with a view to generating effective public servants; the latter is free and self-regulating, insofar as it pursues truth for its own sake. The higher faculties

---

7. CD 2.2:148. Barth is thinking first, but not exclusively, of the tendencies of Reformed scholasticism, over against which he is offering a novel doctrine of election.

8. Like Ockham (see Gordon Leff, *William of Ockham* [Manchester: Manchester University Press, 1975], 359), Kant also knows that God is inscrutable and that theology is no science. But unlike Ockham, Kant refuses to take on authority truths either about God himself or about God's relation to the world; all that is left to him is the philosophical constraint of theology that was already operative in Ockham, though for Kant theology arises only as an inference from practical reason. On Kant's unsuccessful attempt to provide an answer to the nature/freedom problem posed by Ockham's nominalism, see Michael Gillespie, *The Theological Origins of Modernity* (Chicago: University of Chicago Press, 2008), 39ff. and 258–63.

must be scrutinized by the lower, then, as regards truth; but the lower is not scrutinized by the higher. With the help of the lower, the higher faculties can learn to interpret and deploy their respective canons to the maximum benefit of society by approximating more closely a rational view of their own subject matter. The professionals they train will in turn influence for the better the government that regulates them. Some day the government may even come to recognize that the lower faculty, by virtue of this role, *is* the higher, that its free and dispassionate counsel is most to be prized.[9]

On this scenario the biblical theologian (the one, that is, who deals with revealed theology or *theologia empirica*) must be contrasted sharply with the rational theologian (whose efforts are devoted to natural theology or *theologia rationalis*).[10] Likewise, "ecclesiastical faith," which expounds Scripture dogmatically, must be contrasted with the "pure religious faith" that is the product of natural reason. The one, as we know already from *Religion within the Boundaries of Mere Reason*, is the sum of "certain teachings regarded as divine revelations"; the other, "the sum of all our duties regarded as divine *commands*."[11] The one may vary from community to community or from culture to culture; the other, precisely as "a purely rational affair," is universal. Which is to say: there may be many churches or systems of worship, each more or less adequate in its way as a medium of the moral truth that underlies them all. But it is the typical mistake of the theology faculty, and of the biblical theologian, to suppose that the historical particularities to which it professes allegiance (or at least devotes scholarly attention) are somehow essential to pure religious faith. And it is philosophy's task to expose this error, as Kant himself sets out to do.[12]

Kant, in other words, reduces the study of revealed theology to a professional discipline in the service of public morality. He does not deny that it is scholarly; indeed, he allows that as an empirical study it is scholarly in a way that natural or rational theology (quite deliberately) is not.[13] He does not

9. Kant, *Conflict of the Faculties*, 261.

10. "A biblical theologian is, properly speaking, one *versed in the Scriptures* with regard to *ecclesiastical faith*, which is based on statutes—that is, on laws proceeding from another person's act of choice. A rational theologian, on the other hand, is one *versed in reason* with regard to *religious* faith, which is based on inner laws that can be developed from every human being's own decrees" (ibid., 262, italics original; cf. 346).

11. Ibid., 261.

12. Biblical particularities—the historical and ritual elements of Judaism and Christianity— are the husks that must be stripped from the kernel of authentic religion: *Nunc istae reliquias nos exercent* (ibid., 263, quoting Cicero).

13. The faculty of philosophy has an empirical branch, but here we are dealing with pure philosophy; more specifically, with the metaphysics of morals (ibid., 256).

deny either its utility or the loftiness of its aims. After all, it deals not merely with the body or the body politic (these belong to the faculties of medicine and law respectively) but with the citizen himself and his character, and may come even to a consideration of eternal life. But the biblical theologian must be made to understand that "the moral improvement of the human being is the sole condition of eternal life." Moreover, he must be made to understand that Scripture is at best an indirect guide to moral improvement and eternal life; indeed, that "the only way we can find eternal life in any Scripture whatsoever is by putting it there."[14] He must learn to discover the abiding rational kernel of morality (the true substance of religion) beneath the transitory historical husk (the accidents of tradition). He must recognize that faith invested in the historical particulars themselves, or in the dogmas that arise from those particulars, is irrational. Faith is a posture that reason may produce and adopt for itself in recognition of the limits of human conformity to reason and of reason's own limits; but this remains faith *in* reason. It invests nothing in supposed historical manifestations of the supernatural.[15]

Now for Kant the opposition between the higher and lower faculties is dialectical, inasmuch as they share a "final end" in the public good.[16] That opposition must therefore be adjudicated. But it is the lower faculty itself that will do the adjudicating, producing *concordia* from *discordia*, since it is the lower that is characterized by freedom and truth.

Where theology is concerned, a major conflict arises with philosophy over the public interpretation of Scripture; this above all must be adjudicated. Kant lays down firm ground rules, "philosophical principles of scriptural exegesis for settling the conflict." First, texts that "transcend all rational concepts . . . may be interpreted in the interests of practical reason," while texts that contradict practical reason *must* be so interpreted. There is to be no appeal, then, to dogmas such as the resurrection, the incarnation, and the Trinity (which, "taken literally, has no practical relevance at all"); nor to the putative supernatural events on which dogma is based.[17] Second, there is to be no denigration of doubt. "The only thing that matters in religion is *deeds*."[18] Third, there is to be no appeal to grace, if grace means the influence of an external cause in the performance of good deeds. Texts that seem to do so

14. Ibid., 263.
15. "But it is superstition to hold that historical belief is a duty and essential to salvation" (ibid., 285).
16. This final end, as regards theology, is the cultivation of "inner religion" (ibid., 264, though elsewhere Kant speaks, curiously, of "final aims"), which produces better deeds and better citizens (see note at 281).
17. Ibid., 264f.
18. Ibid., 267, italics original.

must be Pelagianized by the interpreter.[19] Fourth, if a "supernatural supplement" is sometimes required to quell the accusing conscience, the *possibility* of such may be allowed in the rational interpretation of Scripture so long as no attempt is made to specify its character or to make definite our knowledge of it—we may allow for *fides qua*, as it were, but not for *fides quae*.[20]

The price of peace between biblical and rational theology, then, or between the faculties of theology and philosophy, is the capitulation of the former to this philosophical policing of its sacred texts; and for such attention, Kant insists, theology should feel grateful. Alternatively, the following compromise is proposed: "*If biblical theologians will stop using reason for their purposes, philosophical theologians will stop using the Bible to confirm their* [own] *propositions.*"[21] A sharper rebuke is hard to imagine, and it leaves us certain that Kant's exercise in accommodation is based on practical necessity rather than on interdisciplinary respect. Biblical theology, revealed theology, has no credibility except what philosophy can lend it for the sake of its service to morality. The only contribution biblical theology can make from its own resources is to provide vehicles of the imagination that can be commandeered to philosophically determined ends. Religion itself has become in Kant a philosophical concept, and Christianity "the Idea of religion." Christianity in its historic manifestation, however, is a disposable object. As for Judaism, and the Judaizing sectarianism that still plagues Christianity, pure moral religion is its "euthanasia."[22]

What shall we say about all this? No doubt Kant encountered many a Euthyphro whom he wished, like Socrates, to cure of pious impieties.[23] But it will not do, I think, to give an account strictly in terms of the parlous state of Protestant (and Catholic) theology at the time; that would require a different kind of critique altogether, and a different kind of cure. Nor will it will do to reduce the whole business to a misunderstanding about Christian doctrine,

19. "Grace is none other than the nature of the human being insofar as he is determined to actions by a principle which is intrinsic to his own being, but supersensible—the thought of his duty" (ibid., 268; cf. Kant, *Grounding for the Metaphysics of Morals*, first section). Likewise, "Christianity is the Idea of religion" (Kant, *Conflict of the Faculties*, 269), rather than something supernaturally revealed; it is to be governed not by biblical theology but by rational theology.

20. Texts or dogmas that tend toward a "supernatural supplement" (Kant, *Conflict of the Faculties*, 268) must be consigned to discourse about the "vehicles of moral faith," not to discourse about moral faith itself. "The teacher should warn [the people] not to ascribe holiness to dogma itself but to pass over, without delay, to the religious faith it has introduced" (267).

21. Ibid., 270, emphasis original; cf. 251.

22. "The great drama of religious change on earth, the restoration of all things," will take place when there is "only one shepherd and one flock" (ibid., 276).

23. Some of these will have been housed in theology faculties known to Kant, though at Königsberg he seems to have had friends and collaborators on that side (F. T. Rink, e.g.).

though Kant permits himself a generous helping of such misunderstandings. Nor yet will it suffice to give an account that is primarily political or cultural. A glimpse of what is really happening here is available at the point where Kant apparently deploys the epistemology of the Meno dialogue (not the Euthyphro) against the biblical theologians: "For the concepts and principles required for eternal life cannot really be learned from anyone else: the teacher's exposition is only the occasion for him to develop them out of his own reason. But the Scriptures contain more than what is in itself required for eternal life; part of their content is a matter of historical belief, and while this can indeed be useful to religious faith as its mere sensible vehicle (for certain people and certain eras), it is not an essential part of religious faith."[24] One does not reason from inspiration, he insists,[25] nor is history "entitled to pass itself off as divine revelation." Only a moral interpretation of Scripture, a philosophical interpretation, "is really an *authentic* one—that is, one given by the God within us," who speaks to us only by way of our own moral reason.[26]

This reminds of the famous maxim of Lessing, indispensable to the Enlightenment, that "accidental truths of history can never become the proof of necessary truths of reason."[27] In Kant, as in Lessing, there is a Meno revival, we might say, that opposes itself to everything that has intervened in the meanwhile; that is, to all the tiresome "relics" of Jewish or salvation-historical modes of thought that have corrupted the exercise of reason and the idea or rational archetype of religion that is the true genius of Christianity. Kant is more concerned than Lessing to separate the epistemological from the onto- and cosmo-theological dimensions of Platonism, which indeed he rejects. He is not quite so committed, perhaps, as Lessing (or later, Hegel) to the substitution of universal history, the history of the race, for the particular histories of Israel and the Church.[28] But he is equally concerned to disestablish the latter. If there is to be theology at all, it cannot be allowed to root itself in that soil. Which is to say, it cannot be "revealed" theology in that sense,

24. "Now the faculty of biblical theologians," he continues, "insists on this historical content as divine revelation as strongly as if belief in it belonged to religion. The philosophical faculty, however, opposes the theology faculty regarding this confusion, and what divine revelation contains that is true of religion proper" (ibid., 263).

25. "One does not argue on the basis of an inspiration" (ibid., 265). Is this also an allusion to the Meno dialogue?

26. Ibid., 271. Hence he opines in *Religion within the Boundaries of Mere Reason* that one may do with the sacred text as one pleases, so long as it is made to serve moral reason.

27. *On the Proof of the Spirit and of Power*, in G. E. Lessing, *Theological Writings*, ed. and trans. H. Chadwick (London: Black, 1956), 53.

28. Though, in his treatment of the law faculty, Kant shows that he has his own way of doing this, through a "philosophical prophecy" about "the whole scope of all the peoples on earth" in their "progress toward the better" (*Conflict of the Faculties*, 304).

and it cannot be doctrinal. It cannot be taught, much less taught by authority. It is revealed only by and to reason. It is not *discovered* (as by Moses at the burning bush) but rather *un*covered, because it is not accidental or particular but necessary and universal.

I said that Kant reduced the study of revealed theology to a professional discipline in the service of public morality; *pace* St. Thomas it was not truly a science in its own right.[29] But at stake, then, was not simply the relation between the human faculties of faith and reason, or between the university faculties of theology and philosophy—though Kant tried, with no small success, to reverse their positions and influence. What was at stake (though Kant was probably not thinking of this) was almost everything contained or implied in the first question of the *Summa*. Providing a negative rather than a positive answer to the very first article of that question—"whether, besides philosophy, any further doctrine is required"—Kant also opposed most of the remaining articles. And it is worth observing that, like Thomas, he linked his answer to the doctrine of grace, a doctrine he was at pains to deny, even if it meant denying Luther as well as Thomas.[30]

Not to put too fine a point on it, for Kant (though his own language is juridical rather than military) the borderlands were a battle zone, and in the battle of the borderlands Kant's aim was to conquer and occupy: no *amicabilis compositio* can be permitted.[31] The mark of divinity for any purported revelation, he says, or "at least the *conditio sine qua non*, is its harmony with what reason pronounces worthy of God."[32] For Thomas, knowledge of God transcends reason's capacity to work things out for itself, and what reason can work out for itself, if only with great difficulty, is made plainer and more obvious by revelation; things uncertain (for example, did the world have a beginning or did it not?) are sometimes settled by revelation.[33] Whereas for

29. Kant takes Ockham's part, as already indicated. Should Scotus be mentioned in this connection as well? By prioritizing will over intellect, does Scotus already reduce theology to *scientia practica*, making metaphysics the new queen? Or does he make theology a still higher science precisely because it is practical—that is, relational—having as its end the possession of God? But this does not concern us here, since no such thing crosses Kant's mind.

30. See again *Religion within the Boundaries of Mere Reason*, which consciously reverses the Reformation scheme.

31. "This conflict cannot and should not be settled by an amicable accommodation" (*Conflict of the Faculties*, 260). By way of contrast, see D. C. Schindler, *The Catholicity of Reason* (Grand Rapids: Eerdmans, 2013).

32. "The kind of characteristics that experience provides can never show us that a revelation is divine; the mark of its divinity (at least the *conditio sine qua non*) is its harmony with what reason pronounces worthy of God" (*Conflict of the Faculties*, 270).

33. "It was necessary for man's salvation that there should be a knowledge revealed by God besides philosophical science built up by human reason" (*ST* 1.1.1).

Kant, substantive knowledge of God is not possible and the supposed science of revelation has no real content of its own at all, whether speculative or practical. The very idea of revelation is useful only in the form of a hortatory "as if": what reason demands of us in the moral sphere must be received *as if* it were a revelation from God, a command of God.[34]

Barth's Theological Totalism

Friedrich Schleiermacher, who just a few years later was charged with finding a proper place for theology in the new University of Berlin, tried to get around all this by locating religion and theology in the sphere of *Gefühl*. Religion, he proposed, would be deemed neither knowing *nor* doing, but feeling; theology, an attempt to articulate the deep sense of awe and dependence arising from an intuition of the unity of all things. This was in some sense a feint or at least a half measure, as Troeltsch later observed, since Schleiermacher refused to let go entirely of a historical redeemer and a historic redemption; christology was still to control theology. The likes of Ritschl and Harnack provided for subsequent generations something of a more Kantian character by directing historical scholarship into biblical criticism and a skeptical examination of the development of dogma, while making theology over into a moralistic discipline in the service of social progress. But Karl Barth, who had drunk deeply from both these streams in his formative years, became disenchanted by the latter in particular when, at the outset of the Great War, he discovered how easily a theology reduced to ethics could fail its great ethical tests. A theology committed to soundings of *Gefühl* did not seem to him adequate either, even where Jesus was proposed (per Schleiermacher) as the instrument of measurement. So Barth set about reviving revealed theology.

34. "The *divinity* of its moral content adequately compensates reason for the *humanity* of its historical narrative which, like an old parchment that is illegible in places, has to be made intelligible by adjustments and conjectures consistent with the whole. And the divinity of its moral content justifies this statement: that the Bible deserves to be kept, put to moral use, and assigned to religion as its guide *just as if it is a divine revelation*" (Kant, *Conflict of the Faculties*, 284f., italics original). It is worth remarking that this "as if" is the mirror image of Anselm's. Anselm, having discovered truth through revelation, attempts to display it for reason as if reason alone were discovering it. Kant, having discovered truth through reason, allows revelation to display it as if it were the property of revelation. But revelation cannot with authority say other or more than that; it is reason alone that speaks, as Benjamin Whichcote put it, with "the very Voice of God" (*Moral and Religious Aphorisms* [London: Mathews & Marrot, 1930], no. 76, p. 11). Kant, by the way, is mistaken in thinking that Anselm tried "to establish the necessity of a highest being through mere concepts" (*Philosophical Doctrine of Religion*, 349). Anselm tried only to show that reason's reach for God falls into incoherence if it tries to bracket out God's self-existence (see below, p. 204f.).

The way he went about that invites, in its totalism, analogy with Kant. Not that Barth thought that theology could take charge of philosophy; far from it. But Barth had no place at all for natural theology, or no place that he recognized as such.[35] God, argued Barth, *is* Revealer, Revelation, and Revealedness; that is, Father, Son, and Spirit. What is known otherwise, under the rubric "God," is not in fact God, whether this putative knowledge arises from religion or from first philosophy. For Barth natural theology cannot coexist alongside revealed theology, since the latter is all an affirmation of grace and the former all a denial. Natural theology is theology that wants to say in advance what God can or cannot be, to make God submit to what reason pronounces worthy of God. Revealed theology is *theologia relationis*, theology that reports what it has actually heard from God and so permits reason to be reasonable where God is concerned. The former is presumptuous, and in its presumption both artificial and misleading. The latter is obedient, and in its obedience enlightened and enlightening. Both, humanly speaking, are impossible enterprises, but the latter is (in Franz Overbeck's phrase) the impossible possibility.

A simple illustration of these competing totalisms: Kant thinks Paul's argument, "If Christ had not risen . . . neither would we rise again," invalid.[36] As for the premise that Christ himself rose, he proposes that moral considerations moved Paul to accept as true a tale otherwise "hard to credit"—the tale being made to serve moral purposes accidentally rather than essentially.[37] So even the question of the resurrection of Jesus is historically and theologically inconsequential; what can reasonably be said about the subject of resurrection is determined already by Kant's moral philosophy. Barth, on the other hand, takes the resurrection of Jesus to be a fact of the utmost

35. T. F. Torrance pointed out to Barth that there was room inside his theology for a form of natural theology, even if he rejected it as a *preambula fidei*; see the preface to his *Space, Time and Resurrection* (Edinburgh: T&T Clark, 1998) and the chapter on "Natural Theology in the Thought of Karl Barth," in *Transformation and Convergence in the Frame of Knowledge* (Grand Rapids: Eerdmans, 1984).

36. Kant (*Conflict of the Faculties*, 264) does not actually bother himself with this enthymeme, which contains a valid argument that can be construed as follows:

   Every gift of God to the people of God is a gift given first or pre-eminently to Jesus.
   Resurrection is not a gift given first to Jesus.
   Therefore resurrection is not a gift of God to the people of God.

Paul of course rejects the minor premise and accepts the major—just the reverse of Kant's view.

37. Cf. Lessing, *On the Proof of the Spirit and Power*, 55, where it is suggested that the resurrection reports may at least be worthy of deliberation and doubt, but for the purposes of establishing sound metaphysics and morals they can be ignored with the same impunity as "the old pious legend that the hand which scatters the seed must wash in snail's blood seven times for each throw."

consequence—ontologically, morally, and epistemologically too. The cross and resurrection of Jesus are a "bar" to every attempt of fallen man to penetrate the truth about either man or God; at the same time they are the "exit" or way of escape from man's dilemma. Just because of the resurrection, the truth about God and man that is concentrated in Jesus Christ is self-authenticating. It, or rather he, is capable of reaching back to embrace us even if we, from our own resources, are incapable of reaching out to find or embrace him.[38]

Barth thus sides with Kierkegaard, who recognizes exactly what the Enlightenment thinkers are up to and what is at stake in their return to the Meno epistemology. In his thought experiment at the outset of the *Philosophical Fragments*, Kierkegaard makes the point that what confronts us in the gospel of Jesus Christ, crucified and risen, is the possibility that the Greek philosophical tradition, and the Enlightenment with it, is working inside the wrong circle, so to say; that it has presupposed the essential divinity and truthfulness of the soul and consequently produced an epistemology that does not actually correspond to the human condition. What is more, it has understood truth and divinity in ways that effectively negate the value of time, matter, and individuality. Therefore it cannot take seriously what someone like Paul wants to say about the resurrection, a concept to which it is closed *a priori* and absolutely. Even to have conceived of working in some other circle, such as Paul's, is an impossibility for it—but it must nonetheless reckon with this "impossible" possibility.

Kierkegaard in turn is siding with a tradition extending back to Justin Martyr, who in his *Dialogue with Trypho* had already made the same basic point; or rather, the old man he encountered by the sea, who converted him from Platonism to Christianity, had made it. But I digress. My own point is that the Christian tradition can meet the kind of natural theology it encounters in Kant only with an equally totalizing claim; there is no middle ground here. Barth himself looks to Anselm rather than to Justin or Kierkegaard to explain how he thinks theology, rational theology, is to be done. Their circle comprises *fides, intellegere, probare, delectatio*, in that order. Faith explores its own inner *ratio* through an intellectual and aesthetic appreciation of what is grasped by faith—for example, the resurrection or the Trinity—which issues in demonstration or proof of its surprising propriety and beauty (its *convenientia, decentia, pulchritudo*, etc.) and hence also in joy, delight, and praise (*eucharistia*).[39] Theology, in other words, cannot survive on the crumbs falling

---

38. Any demand for *independent* proof of the resurrection ignores the Risen One methodologically and systematically, which he thinks futile and indeed perverse.

39. Karl Barth, *Anselm: Fides quaerens intellectum* (London: SCM, 1960), 13ff.

from Kant's table or from any other philosophical table. It has its own feast to enjoy, and in enjoying it may show philosophy something new, something philosophy did not know how to conceive for itself.

Think, for example, of Nicæa's notoriously controversial ὁμοούσιον, the implications of which pried apart οὐσία and ὑπόστασις so as to give ontological weight to the idea of personhood. Or Chalcedon's equally controversial exception to the Aristotelian principle that there is no φύσις ἀνυπόστατος, blind adherence to which had produced the Nestorian and Eutychian heresies, but the overcoming of which produced not merely two-nature orthodoxy but (inter alia) an unprecedented world of Christian art. Think of Augustine's *De Trinitate*, which comes to mind from a long list of examples because its marvelous thirteenth book took the doctrine of the resurrection of the dead and showed that, without it, human reason, human morality, and the human drive for happiness are deprived of real hope for fulfillment and must wither away in pointlessness and despair. Kant, of course, has his own worries about that and his own rather hesitant and, historically speaking, ineffective solution—pounding ever harder on his "as if," something we have long since ceased to do—but nowhere does he demonstrate any real grasp of the alternative presented to him by an Augustine, an Anselm, or an Aquinas, much less a Paul. In Kant we seldom encounter anything more than caricatures of these men or of their ideas, though here and there he expropriates something for his own purposes.

But what of Barth? Barth too is problematic, in that he seems to have no room for natural theology even where the latter does not mean to be totalizing. Barth finds the doctrine of God in Kant "quite intolerable," since Kant fails to respect the Thomist maxim, *Deus non est in genere*, and so does not learn from God how to be reasonable but vainly tries to teach God how to be reasonable (*CD* 2.1:310f.). Yet Barth balks at that other Thomist maxim, *gratia non tollit naturam sed perficit*, from which Aquinas draws the conclusion that "natural reason should minister to faith as the natural inclination of the will ministers to charity."[40] In Barth's mind, Kant and neo-Protestantism

---

40. *ST* 1.1.8, ad 2; cf. *Super Boetium* 1.2.3, co. 1: "I answer that it must be said that gifts of grace are added to those of nature in such a way that they do not destroy the latter, but rather perfect them [*dona gratiarum hoc modo naturae adduntur quod non tollunt, sed magis perficiunt*]; wherefore also the light of faith, which is gratuitously infused into our minds, does not destroy the natural light of cognition, which is in us by nature. For although the natural light of the human mind is insufficient to reveal those truths revealed by faith, yet it is impossible that those things which God has manifested to us by faith should be contrary to those which are evident to us by natural knowledge. In this case one would necessarily be false: and since both kinds of truth are from God, God would be the author of error, a thing which is impossible. Rather, since in imperfect things there is found some imitation of the perfect, though the

generally are no more than extensions of the Catholic error embodied in this *non tollit sed perficit*. Natural theology, even in the Christian tradition, is for those who think they already know what "God" and "man" are before encountering them concretely in Jesus Christ, where they are mutually interpreted and interpretable. Natural theology is for those who are certain, therefore, to impose on Jesus a false interpretation that prevents, rather than facilitates, any real knowledge of either God or man. It is for those who refuse to see in the Crucified One the death of their own miserable attempts to approach God.[41]

For Barth natural theology is a sin of the intellect that must, so to say, be nailed to the tree. We need to be clear, however, about what he means by natural theology. Natural theology not only posits knowledge of God by way of a general revelation given with creation and accessible to unaided reason (as Paul says in Rom. 1:20, "ever since the creation of the world his invisible nature, namely, his eternal power and deity, has been clearly perceived in the things that have been made"), it also employs this knowledge in a perverse attempt to control the knowledge that is possible through special revelation. It makes general revelation into a prolegomenon for special revelation in such a way as to establish in advance the conditions under which the latter can be received and understood. In doing so it seeks a path from anthropology to christology, and from a prior knowledge of God the creator to a posterior knowledge of God the redeemer—a path that no longer lies open to reason, if ever it did. In other words, it ignores the fall.[42] Indeed, it ignores the fact (as Barth has it) that the covenant of redemption is the inner basis for the covenant of creation. It reverses the ontological and epistemological relation between the two. "There is a way from christology to anthropology, but there is no way from anthropology to christology" (CD 1.1:131).

Natural theology therefore posits the *analogia entis*—an analogy of being between God and man rooted in the act of creation—as its own condition of possibility, when the only genuine analogy is an *analogia gratiae* rooted

---

image is deficient, in those things known by natural reason there are certain similitudes of the truths revealed by faith."

41. A message well represented, thought Barth, by the prodigious finger of John the Baptist pointing to Christ in Grünewald's Isenheim altarpiece.

42. Barth denies that "the turntable between philosophy and theology" is the man who can be analyzed "in the light of a divine revelation from creation." Natural theology wrongly thinks that this man, or rather this analysis, can serve "as the *introitus* to the inner circle of a true theology grounded in a *revelatio specialis*." Such an enterprise, however, is possible only "in the realm of Roman Catholicism, since this presupposes that God's manifestation in our creatureliness, the creation of man which is also the revelation of God, is in some place and in some sense . . . directly discernible by us." Whereas the truth of the matter is that "this direct discernment of the original relation of God to man . . . has been taken from us by the fall" (CD 1.1:130).

in the act of redemption. Even if it does so retrospectively, in the light of revelation, it nonetheless supposes that what revelation shows it is simply the truth about what already exists: man's capacity for God, a capacity that has survived the fall and manifested itself in countless expressions of human reason and culture, which grace now affirms, supports, and perfects. But for Barth this amounts to a denial of grace:

> Grace which has from the start to share its power with a force of nature is no longer grace, i.e., it cannot be recognised as what the grace of God is in the consideration and conception of that divine act, as what it is in Jesus Christ. And therefore revelation which has from the very outset a partner in the reason of the creature, and which cannot be revelation without its co-operation, is no longer revelation. At any rate, it is not the revelation which takes place in the act in which God opens Himself to man in pure goodness; in which He does not find an existing partner in man, but creates a partner; in which even the fact that God is known and knowable is the work of His freedom. (CD 2.2:531)

Barth thus "leaves no room for any knowledge of God apart from the knowledge of humanity's reconciliation in and through Jesus Christ."[43] Outside of that all is idolatry, whether open or subtle idolatry.

As severe as this sounds, it does not amount to a complete rejection of philosophy or of any positive relation between philosophy and theology, only of philosophical pretensions to independent knowledge of God or of the real truth about man, who must indeed be understood by analogy with God—the *analogia gratiae*. Taking up the gauntlet thrown down by Kant over the proper method of reading Scripture, Barth allows that no one reads Scripture without philosophical spectacles of one prescription or another. "We cannot basically contest the use of philosophy in scriptural exegesis," he says; "where the question of legitimacy arises is in regard to the How of this use."[44] Indeed, the use of philosophy "is not only unavoidable as such, but legitimate, just as it was not only unavoidable but legitimate when, just as he was, in his poverty and rags, the prodigal son arose and went to his father."[45] But this means that "there is no essential reason for preferring one of these schemes to another."

43. Keith Johnson, "Reconsidering Barth's Rejection of Pryzwara's *Analogia Entis*," *Modern Theology* 26.4 (2010): 645. Admittedly, my account here to some extent conflates the earlier and the more considered perspectives of Barth.
44. CD 1.2:729f. "It is no more true of anyone that he does not mingle the Gospel with some philosophy, than that here and now he is free from all sin except through faith." Note that Barth shares with Kant the view that the only border worth talking about is the interpretation of Scripture.
45. CD 2.2:729. "My mode of thought may not be of any use in and by itself, but by the grace of the Word of God why should it not be able to become useful in His service?" (CD 1.2:731).

In principle, any philosophy can be put to work, so to say, by the Word of God. "It can be elucidated and then elucidate" (*CD* 1.2:733–35).

Kant's challenge is met, then, not by a stubborn insistence on theology rather than philosophy as the dominant partner but by the relativization of both: "It is not really a question of replacing philosophy by a dictatorial, absolute and exclusive theology, and again discrediting philosophy as an *ancilla theologiae*. . . . In face of its object, theology itself can only wish to be *ancilla*. That is why it cannot assign any other role to philosophy. Scripture alone can be the *domina*. Hence there is no real cause for disputes about prestige."[46] Theology retains a certain primacy, however, for "in the philosopher-theologian it is not the philosopher but the theologian who will have to be criticized" in any encounter with the Word of God. This statement is made in good faith, apparently, unlike Kant's tongue-in-cheek proposal of a truce that would deprive theology of any right to appeal to reason. It nevertheless raises the question whether Barth's seemingly open border between theology and philosophy is really one sealed against philosophy, or sealed at least against any philosophy not content, so to say, with a tourist visa. "If we do not commit ourselves unreservedly and finally to any specific philosophy, we will not need totally or finally to fear any philosophy."[47]

Pax Thomistica

If we take Kant and Barth as champions for philosophy and theology respectively, the disciplinary lines seem to be drawn as battle lines. But Kant

---

46. *CD* 1.2:734. With this compare Kant's ironic concession: "We can also grant the theology faculty's proud claim that the philosophy faculty is its handmaid (though the question remains, whether the servant *carries her lady's torch before or her train behind*), provided it is not driven away or silenced" (*Conflict of the Faculties*, 255, emphasis original).

47. *CD* 1.2:735. We might illustrate Barth's approach from his use of Karl Jaspers. The two were colleagues at Basel from 1948 and lectured in close proximity. "Lecture room 2—the biggest which we have here—is the scene of his public activity," wrote Barth, "while mine is in the more modest Room 1, immediately and literally at his feet. There are plenty of gifted young men going up and down the steps linking the two rooms, like angels up and down Jacob's ladder" (quoted by Busch, *Karl Barth*, 351). It is no surprise, then, that in §44.2, "Phenomena of the Human," Barth allows "that in the existentialist philosophy of today we find in operation a new and serious philosophical concern with the religious question" (*CD* 3.2:113, quoting Martin Werner). He even allows that in Jaspers—for whom, "in philosophizing, a faith lacking all revelation reaches expression" (Karl Jaspers, *Philosophie* 1 [Berlin: Springer, 1948], v)—"recognisable traces of the proximity of the Christian Church" are to be found, and that these "are more relevant and important than those which with a little good will we can also find in the philosophy of Fichte or Hegel." Yet this stubborn difference remains: If such a philosophy "has seen a phenomenon of the human" it cannot be said "that it has shown us real man"! But in engaging the question of "real man," Barth is at his best when he takes on Nietzsche (see *CD* 3.2:231ff.).

and Barth are both, in their way, biblicists; that is, they are Protestant. And those fellow Protestants who stand between them, rather than on one side or the other, are exposed to some pretty deadly crossfire. Barth is right, I think, that their position is untenable, not least because they attempt *as* Protestants something that is viable only on Catholic principles.[48] But we have yet to consider Catholic principles, other than from Barth's point of view.

In keeping with those principles, Vatican I declared it an error, a morally culpable error, to deny that "by the light of natural reason" the existence of the one true God can be known with certitude.[49] Of natural theology Catholicism demands little more than this acknowledgment, but it does demand at least this. In practice of course—since it insists on "the mutual assistance of faith and reason," which "can never be at variance with one another"[50]—it expects much more and makes frequent appeal to philosophical lines of thought. It simply insists that divine faith exceeds the deliverances of unaided reason without thereby being or becoming unreasonable and that it is right and proper to believe things on account of the authority of God who reveals them, allowing what is so believed to inform reason in its rightful pursuits.[51]

So, for example, if I may add to my earlier list, the Church did not hesitate at Lateran IV to insist upon *creatio ex nihilo*, which theological doctrine (in excess of philosophy) helped lay the foundations of modern science. Or, on the other hand, to reject Abbot Joachim's exaggerated view of spiritual perfection by observing (in philosophical fashion) that "between the Creator and the creature so great a likeness cannot be noted without the necessity of noting a greater dissimilarity between them."[52]

This kind of thinking—the kind that has both philosophical and theological components, whether or not it is positing an *analogia entis*—was the kind that Thomas, aided by the recovery of Aristotle, brought to an astonishing level of sophistication, steering as it were between the Scylla and Charybdis that threatened to either side. As William Turner observes in *The Catholic Encyclopedia*: "John Scotus Eriugena, in the ninth century, by his

---

48. For Barth there is "no third alternative between that exploitation of the *analogia entis* which is legitimate only on the basis of Roman Catholicism, between the greatness and misery of a so-called natural knowledge of God in the sense of the *Vaticanum*, and a Protestant theology which draws from its own source, which stands on its own feet, and which is finally liberated from this secular misery" (*CD* 1.1:xiii).

49. DZ 1806.

50. DZ 1797–99. We should be careful here of a certain equivocation between *fides qua* and *fides quae*. Faith and reason as human functions *should not* be at odds but may be; the true deliverances of reason and of revelation *cannot* be at odds, even if they seem to be.

51. See DZ 1810–20.

52. DZ 431.

doctrine that all truth is theophany, or showing forth of God, [had] tried to elevate philosophy to the rank of theology, and identify the two in a species of theosophy. Abelard, in the twelfth century, tried to bring theology down to the level of philosophy, and identify both in a rationalistic system. The greatest of the Scholastics in the thirteenth century, especially St. Thomas Aquinas, solved the problem . . . by showing that the two are distinct sciences, and yet that they agree."[53]

Today the same threats still exist: on the one side in the form of Hegelianism, or perhaps even in the form of Continental philosophy's vaunted theological turn, which elevates phenomenology into a sort of *ordo salutis*; and on the other side in the form of those who make revealed theology rest entirely on natural theology, thus justifying Barth's worry that the *analogia entis* is "the invention of Antichrist."[54] (The latter often suppose themselves in harmony with Aquinas but are not; their approach may be Cartesian or it may be Hobbesian, but it is not Thomist.) A third threat is Barthianism itself, which does not concern itself as far as it should with whether theology and philosophy *ought* to agree. But from Leo XIII to Benedict XVI a concerted attempt has been made, with considerable success, to revive the *pax Thomistica*, in which philosophy *qua* philosophy and theology qua theology reason together, each respectful of the other. The theological foundation for this—and it can only have a theological foundation, if theology exceeds philosophy—is located especially in the doctrine of bodily resurrection, the very doctrine that Barth thought denied it. For it is that doctrine, more than any other, which insists upon the continuity of grace and nature and demands the *non tollit sed perficit*.

The *pax Thomistica*, rightly understood, does not entail any concession to philosophy respecting some privileged access to the being of God apart from God's works. Neither does it divide God, as Barth supposes, when it acknowledges access to God through the work of creation without prior

53. Turner continues: "They are distinct . . . because, while philosophy relies on reason alone, theology uses the truths derived from revelation, and also because there are some truths, the mysteries of Faith, which lie completely outside the domain of philosophy and belong to theology. They agree, and must agree, because God is the author of all truth, and it is impossible to think that he would teach in the natural order anything that contradicts what he teaches in the supernatural order" ("Scholasticism," *The Catholic Encyclopedia*, vol. 13 [New York: Robert Appleton, 1912]; www.newadvent.org). F. C. Copleston remarks that for Thomas "the distinction between philosophy and theology is a distinction between different ways of arriving at and viewing truths rather than primarily a distinction between propositions considered with respect to their content" (*Aquinas* [London: Penguin, 1955], 56). The same could be said of Anselm, I think, though Barth does not consider that.

54. CD 1.1:xiii. I will remark further on this below.

reference to the work of redemption—when it acknowledges "a general and confused" knowledge of God that belongs to man as such. It does do that, of course. It holds to a natural knowledge of God because it holds that man, even fallen man, is defined as man by his vocation to happiness, which is but another name for God.[55] It holds to the notion that creation itself is a form of grace, that man's nature is graced. Which is to say, it does indeed understand grace "doubly," as Barth charges. Or rather it understands grace triply: *gratia creans* (the gift of being, and of being ordered to God, and of being helped by God)[56] is exceeded by *gratia elevans* (making humans capable of deification, of participation in the internal economy of God), which in view of the fall requires also *gratia sanans* (the healing or redemptive grace that reopens the path to deification).[57] These three, though distinct, are all acts of the one true God with corresponding modes of the knowledge of God. The God who is known by man naturally is the same God who is known salvifically and perfectively, though he is not known with the same clarity or in just the same way. That he is known only by virtue of *gratia creans*, and

55. "For Man naturally desires happiness, and what is naturally desired by man must be naturally known to him" (*ST* 1.2.1, ad 1; cf. 1–2.3.1).

56. The term *gratia creans* may not be deployed by Thomas, but the concept is. That concept goes back at least to the fifth-century dispute over Pelagianism, in which St. Fulgentius distinguished between saving grace in Jesus Christ and the grace given man in and with his creation (cf. Adolf von Harnack, *History of Dogma*, 7 vols., trans. Neil Buchanan [Boston: Little, Brown, 1895–1900], 5:256); but in fact it belongs to the doctrine of *creatio ex nihilo* as we find it already in Irenaeus. The term itself is used by Bernard (*Aliae Sententiae*, no. 28; PL183, 0754A), who offers a fourfold scheme: *Gratia quadripartita est: gratia creans, gratia redimens sive miserans, gratia donans, gratia remunerans. Prima:* Omnia per ipsum facta sunt. *Secunda:* Verbum caro factum est. *Tertia:* Plenum gratiae. *Quarta:* Et veritatis (*Joan.* I, 14).

57. Cf. *ST* 1–2.109.1: "Man's nature may be looked at in two ways: first, in its integrity, as it was in our first parent before sin; secondly, as it is corrupted in us after the sin of our first parent. Now in both states human nature needs the help of God as First Mover, to do or wish any good whatsoever. . . . But in the state of integrity, as regards the sufficiency of the operative power, man by his natural endowments could wish and do the good proportionate to his nature, such as the good of acquired virtue; but not surpassing good, as the good of infused virtue. But in the state of corrupt nature, man falls short of what he could do by his nature, so that he is unable to fulfil it by his own natural powers. Yet because human nature is not altogether corrupted by sin, so as to be shorn of every natural good, even in the state of corrupted nature it can, by virtue of its natural endowments, work some particular good, as to build dwellings, plant vineyards, and the like; yet it cannot do all the good natural to it, so as to fall short in nothing; just as a sick man can of himself make some movements, yet he cannot be perfectly moved with the movements of one in health, unless by the help of medicine he be cured. And thus in the state of perfect nature man needs a gratuitous strength superadded to natural strength for one reason, *viz.* in order to do and wish supernatural good; but for two reasons, in the state of corrupt nature, *viz.* in order to be healed, and furthermore in order to carry out works of supernatural virtue, which are meritorious. Beyond this, in both states man needs the Divine help, that he may be moved to act well."

under the debilitating conditions of the fall, means that he remains to some extent "the unknown God" (Acts 17). It does not mean that he is not known at all or in any way whatsoever. For man would not be man at all if he did not know God at all.

So what is the specific contribution of philosophy to such a partnership, a partnership in which knowledge of God is acknowledged to be a, or rather the, *desideratum*? In a well-known passage from *Super Boetium* Thomas provides his answer. That is, he sets out his conviction that "in sacred doctrine we are able to make a threefold use of philosophy":

> First, to demonstrate those truths that are preambles of faith and that have a necessary place in the science of faith. Such are the truths about God that can be proved by natural reason—that God exists, that God is one; such truths about God or about His creatures, subject to philosophical proof, faith presupposes.
>
> Second, to give a clearer notion, by certain similitudes, of the truths of faith, as Augustine in his book, *De Trinitate*, employed many comparisons taken from the teachings of the philosophers to aid understanding of the Trinity.
>
> Third, to resist those who speak against the faith, either by showing that their statements are false, or by showing that they are not necessarily true.

To which he adds, to the comfort of Barthians:

> Nevertheless, in the use of philosophy in sacred Scripture, there can be a two-fold error: In one way, by using doctrines contrary to faith, which are not truths of philosophy, but rather error, or abuse of philosophy, as Origen did. In another way, by using them in such manner as to include under the measure of philosophy truths of faith, as if one should be willing to believe nothing except what could be held by philosophical reasoning; when, on the contrary, philosophy should be subject to the measure of faith, according to the saying of the Apostle (2 Cor. 10:5), "bringing into captivity every understanding unto the obedience of Christ."[58]

To ask and answer this question the other way around—what use is philosophy able to make of revealed theology?—is the task of the Thomist, or at least the cooperative, philosopher. The theologian may want to make some suggestions about particulars, however, just as the philosopher will within the present framing. As for Barthians, they may perhaps refuse to be comforted, having noted the apologetic bent of the first and third uses especially, and being wary of purported similitudes and *vestigia*. But Thomas's "nevertheless" surely puts paid to any notion that the *preambula fidei* are

---

58. *Super Boetium* 1.2.3, co. 3. In the biblical text "understanding" is νόημα.

what Barth fancies them to be—viz., creaturely constraints on the freedom of God to be who he is and to reveal himself as such—just as it puts paid to Kant's claim that one does not argue from inspiration. For holy teaching, says Thomas, "makes use also of the authority of philosophers in those questions in which they [are] able to know the truth by natural reason," albeit "only as inessential and probable arguments" (*ST* 1.1.8, ad 2).

On Thomas's view, then, as Servais Pinckaers observes, "theology does not destroy but perfects philosophy."[59] Likewise, faith does not destroy but perfects reason. It enables reason to overachieve, we might say, while also enabling the will to outrun the intellect in loving God, hence in finding the good life about which theology and philosophy both must speak. And this is just what is required if (as Augustine says) reason itself is not to end in despair.[60]

A Thomist Excursus on Barth

We may pause briefly to consider Barth more closely from a Catholic point of view. For in his admirable zeal not to concede to man any control over God or the knowledge of God, Barth is obviously much nearer to Thomas than to Kant, who denies such knowledge.[61] Yet Barth evades the question

59. "Far from being separate, much less in competition, these sciences work together through what we could call a vital integration of philosophy and theology. At the prompting of the theologian, the philosopher comes to reflect on the fundamental questions about the purpose and meaning of life, about good and evil, about happiness and suffering, about death and the afterlife, and he no longer thinks that only he can offer a complete answer to these problems. The theologian, for his part, needs the philosopher in order to learn how to use his reason with rigor and insight as he investigates the human dimensions of action and to provide him with the necessary categories and language for a sound explanation of the riches of the Gospel and the Christian experience. This sort of association between philosophy and theology is based on St Thomas' maxim: *Gratia non tollit, sed perficit naturam*, which could be rephrased: theology does not destroy, but perfects philosophy. In our opinion, however, the principle should not be understood in the sense that philosophy, as a work of reason, must first be constructed while saying to oneself that in any case it will be confirmed by grace, but rather in the opposite sense: we must have the boldness to believe in the Word of God and to abandon ourselves to grace, in the assurance that, far from destroying whatever is true, good and reasonable in philosophy, grace will teach us how to make it our own, to develop it and to perfect it, while revealing to us a broader and more profound wisdom than any human thought, the wisdom given by the Holy Spirit who unites us with the person of Christ and his Cross by teaching us to 'live in Christ'" ("The Place of Philosophy in Moral Theology," *L'Osservatore Romano*, June 16, 1999, 15).

60. Benedict XVI insists that faith is capable of protecting reason "from every temptation to mistrust its own capacities" ("On Aquinas, Philosophy and Theology," General Audience, 16 June 2010); cf. *Trin.* 13.11f.

61. Eugene Rogers argues in *Thomas Aquinas and Karl Barth: Sacred Doctrine and the Natural Knowledge of God* (Notre Dame, IN: University of Notre Dame Press, 1995) for the basic compatibility of the two, furthering the trajectory of Hans Urs von Balthasar in *The Theology*

of what fallen man can and should know. His refusal to see grace "doubly" as *gratia creans* and *gratia sanans*, with *gratia elevans* as the final cause of both, backs him into a corner. Either nature is a sphere outside of grace and therefore independent of it—whether in Catholic or Protestant form, this view is entirely untenable and can barely attain even to Kant—or nature is altogether absorbed by grace in supralapsarian fashion. While Barth whole-heartedly rejects the former error, he cannot escape the latter. Thus even his ecclesiology becomes prey to occasionalism, which helps to account for his readiness to oppose tradition.[62]

But did Barth really need to adopt the stance the *Vaticanum* anathematizes? The conciliar fathers, by declining to absolve fallen man of responsibility to acknowledge the existence of the one true God, did not thereby posit a God other than the one Paul identified as "the God and Father of our Lord Jesus Christ." Just the opposite. By holding fallen man accountable for such truth about God as can be perceived even "in the things that have been made," it maintained the unity of that man with the man whom Christ came to save. And no objection should be made here to their appeal to the natural light of reason, for it is not reason that is fallen but the man who reasons. In announcing the good news that he *may* reason rightly, it is also announced that he *is* reasoning wrongly when he denies the one true God, even when he is reasoning not from the gospel but in advance of it.

Barth of course was worried that any reasoning in advance of the gospel endangers the gospel by establishing conditions under which the gospel itself must be judged—a procedure epitomized in Kant's claim that talk of resurrection is simply morally useful fiction. It does not allow God to be God but requires him to be only such a God as man can conceive or construct for himself; in short, an idol. But Barth was mistaken. It does not follow from the fact that man can pervert knowledge of the one true God into idolatry

---

of Karl Barth, 3rd ed. (San Francisco: Ignatius, 1992). The latter observes, however, that "Barth never leaves the standpoint of pure theology and never sketches out a philosophy as such or a metaphysics that could bridge the divide between theology and philosophy" (36). Barth was concerned "with deflecting the constant threat of philosophy's encroachments into the field of theology. If he rallied behind Thomism, it was only on two specific points: (1) that there is an authentic creaturely freedom, but that (2) it remains subordinate to the all-determining freedom of God. But he immediately renounced these statements when they purported to be philosophical, for then they threatened to trap theology in a narrow pen. Why? Because then they became anticipatory determinations about things that only the revelation of grace can establish and determine" (130f.).

62. The root of the problem lies in Barth's conflation of ontology and soteriology, as I have argued elsewhere, not in what Ingolf Dalferth (*Theology and Philosophy* [Oxford: Blackwell, 1988], chap. 10) calls his "method of interiorisation" and "interpretive meta-discourse," admiration for which I share, the qualification implied by the present essay notwithstanding.

that he does not possess that knowledge in the first place. Nor does it follow that because God is triune, and known to be triune through his saving acts, that he cannot be known in his unity through his creative acts—albeit in a limited and no doubt dangerous way—by appeal to the *analogia entis*. That it is only under the conditions of the fall that such a dangerous way is attempted does not mean that the attempt itself is a perverse act. Quite the contrary. It is a perverse act when fallen man, not yet in full possession of the gospel of his triune Redeemer, or possessed by it, refuses even to acknowledge the existence and unity of God.

Again, it does not follow from the fact that God through word and sacrament produces an *analogia entis* based on *gratia sanans* that he has not produced—and maintained in spite of the fall—a lesser *analogia* based on *gratia creans*. It does not follow that to inquire after the lesser *analogia* is to posit an unreal distinction between the one God and the triune God. It does not follow from the fact that fallen man is sometimes inclined to do just that, with a view to avoiding the gospel, that the theologian is catering to this inclination by participating in a discussion of the lesser *analogia* (though of course he might be). And it is certainly not true that the lesser *analogia* is either lost or rendered inaccessible because of the fall; for God sends rain, literally and metaphorically, on both the just and the unjust.

This is the point at which Barth is most deeply entangled in the heresy of Luther, which is merely a permutation of the heresy of Ockham. Ockham thought that reason and revelation were fundamentally disparate sources of human knowledge and proposed to reconcile them by taking the latter as raw data received on authority from the Church but interpreted or rendered meaningful (so far as they were capable of meaning) by philosophical reason.[63] Luther, for his part, rightly sought the meaning of revealed truths within themselves but wrongly disparaged *both* the authority of the Church *and* the authority of reason. If the disparaging of the authority of the Church made possible Kant's radical extension and revision of Ockham's program, the disparaging of both (that is, of reason also) made possible Barth's adventure in theological totalism, which does not know how to grant philosophy its place, except as something which need not be feared because no final commitment

63. Ockham is unlike Kant in allowing that theology has real content, even if that content is the delivery of faith rather than of reason. He is unlike Barth because he does not allow for a mode of knowing in theology that is at once trustful, experiential, intellective, and scientific. He is unlike Thomas in that he isolates theology from philosophy and allows them to be, de facto if not de jure, in competition. On his relation to Thomas, see Alfred Freddoso, "Ockham on Faith and Reason," in *The Cambridge Companion to Ockham*, ed. Paul Vincent Spade (Cambridge: Cambridge University Press, 1999), 326–49.

is owed it. This may be an improvement on Luther—Barth after all was a Calvinist—but it is only a modest improvement.

We may however agree with Barth that God's embrace of human beings, so as to elevate them beyond their natural creaturely capacities, equipping them for communion with himself and for authentic personhood, is something that philosophical theology cannot know on its own, nor yet make its own, without passing over into the care of revealed theology. *Gratia elevans*, which in view of the fall proceeds by way of *gratia sanans* to the fulfillment of the divine purposes already operative in *gratia creans*, is accessible to human reason only as the latter is aided by revelation and by the faith it evokes.[64] Barth gets it about right—even if he does not get Thomas quite right—in the following passage, which is worth quoting at length:

> God takes up the cause of the creature, the reality distinct from Himself, in such a way that He accepts it as a reality and intervenes for it in recognition, not in suspension, of its reality. For it as such, He is severe with Himself. He suffers for it. He sacrifices His only Son for it. He does it for the creature as such— which means that God's mercy does not act in such a way as to overpower and blot out its object. God does not take the place of the creature in such a way as to annihilate it. That He takes its plight to His own heart does not mean that He robs it of its independent life, making the latter a mere potentiality or recollection in His own life. The encounter of His eternal love with the creature existing in space and time does not imply the utter dissolution of its space and time and therefore of its existence as such. The fact that God in His mercy intervenes for it must be understood in the full sense of the two words "for" and "it" in such a way, therefore, that this divine intervention for the creature does not exclude but includes its independent life—whatever the encounter with God may entail for that life—so that the atoning will of God maintains His

---

64. Not that Barth would put it this way. Balthasar quotes the early Barth to similar effect, however, noting that theology "holds the position 'toward which the true philosopher will necessarily point (his pointer is the culminating pinnacle of his own work, when he has reached the end of his legitimate reflections; this termination then points to the place occupied by theology) . . . even if as a philosopher he does not draw on theology for his own work'" (Balthasar, *Theology of Karl Barth*, 149; quoting *Zwischen den Zeiten* [1927]: 206). The later Barth, too, allows "that philosophy can legitimately pose the question of God as well as of the authentic created nature of the world and the problem of becoming that this entails"—that "this question 'at the very least lies at that unsettling periphery and borderline of its picture of the world'" (Balthasar, ibid., 149; quoting *CD* 3.1:341). Of course he also insists that any philosophical worldview "distinguished by a clear and genuine geneseology must necessarily cease to be a mere world-view. At the decisive juncture it must necessarily become identical with the Christian doctrine of creation." That is, it must "become theological at this point, and base itself on the datum of divine revelation"; while the doctrine of creation, for its part, "cannot itself become a world-view," nor "base itself on any world-view," nor "guarantee any world-view" (*CD* 3.1:343f.). We will return to this dialectic in a moment.

will and act as the Creator: "What our God has created He will also uphold, and sooner or later control by His grace." He will control it—but not in such a way that grace means the catastrophic destruction of nature. It means radical judgment upon nature. It means its radical transformation and renewal. But it does not mean its violent end. In this sense we must admit the truth of that maxim of Thomas Aquinas which is so often put to dangerous use and in the first instance was no doubt dangerously meant: *gratia non tollit (non destruit) sed (praesupponit et) perficit naturam*. (*CD* 2.1:411)

We ought not to concede, however, that it was "dangerously meant" in the first instance. If the *Summa* both allows and expects of pre- and even anti-Christian man a certain inalienable knowledge of God and of the natural order, it does not ever allow to such knowledge the final or controlling word on either. The *Summa*'s tripartite structure—*prima*: God, *secunda*: Man, *tertia*: the God-man—draws this general and confused knowledge, which philosophy already helps in small part to clarify, into the specific, lucid, and saving knowledge that is mediated by Christ and organized with philosophical as well as theological rigor. "The light of faith, which is gratuitously infused into our minds, does not destroy the natural light of cognition, which is in us by nature"; but it does indeed refract that light through the prism of revelation.[65]

Neither should we concede Barth's claim to find in Gottlieb Söhngen's use of the *analogia entis* "an important deviation" that proves, so to say, the Catholic rule (*CD* 2.1:81f.). Barth approves of Söhngen's insistence that *esse sequitur operari* noetically, even if ontically *operari sequitur esse*, and that the *analogia entis* must therefore be subsumed within the *analogia fidei*. But is Söhngen really the exception Barth thinks he is? And is it really true "that there is not a single word in the *Vaticanum* to suggest that the God referred to is engaged in a work and activity with man"—that it entirely overlooks the unity of the divine action whereby the creator is also the savior"? According to Barth, "the intolerable and unpardonable thing in Roman Catholic theology" is that "there is this splitting up of the concept of God, and hand in hand with it the abstraction from the real work and activity of God in favour of a general being of God which He has in common with us and all being" (*CD* 2.1:84). We have already observed that the charge is false. The

---

65. Balthasar tries very hard to read Barth in this Thomist light, notwithstanding the fact that "Barth's starting point is entirely different from that of Thomism" (*Theology of Karl Barth*, 131). Working with the theological anthropology of *CD* 3.2, he argues that "philosophy in this context is to theology as the abstract is to the concrete and [as] possibility is to reality" (151). "Theological anthropology can and may abstract as long as it comes from the concrete and returns to it" (155). "So long as it is really the abstraction of *this* concretion, the possibility of *this* reality, it is legitimate and has its own truth" (151).

Syllabus of Pius IX denies that the independence of philosophy should be construed in such a fashion.[66] Moreover, Vatican I, which in its chapter on God the creator commits itself to *creatio ex nihilo*, rules out the splitting up which Barth thinks he finds there: "Since man is wholly dependent on God as his Creator and Lord, and since created reason is completely subject to uncreated truth, we are bound by faith to give full obedience of intellect and will to God who reveals."[67] In other words, its "twofold order of knowledge," in which "we know in one way by natural reason, in another by divine faith,"[68] holds together—distinguishing without separating—the work of faith and of reason and the knowledge of God sought by both. Is it not rather Barth who splits up the knowledge of God by failing to allow that such knowledge as every rational creature has of the divine *operari*, precisely by virtue of being a rational creature, discloses something of the divine *esse*?

Barth's protest against those who wish to foreclose on the knowledge of God—by deciding in advance of revelation, or apart from faith, the limits of what can or should be said of the divine *esse*—is entirely legitimate, but against this the *Vaticanum* protests with equal vigor. Unlike Barth, it does not misconstrue Thomas, who knows no God who is one but not three, nor any reason that does not lead, if it is right reason, in the direction of the Trinity. Catholics, of course, are capable of making the mistake against which this protest is made, if they are not careful to render talk of preambles and presuppositions in a nuanced way. "Faith," says Thomas, "presupposes natural knowledge even as grace presupposes nature" (*ST* 1.2.2, ad 1). And Catholics today may be inclined to follow this up with what seems a fair question: "If human nature is unintelligible in its own right, what possible sense can be given to the doctrine of the incarnation of the Word? If being is unintelligible, then the revelation of God—who is perfect being—will be perfectly unintelligible."[69] But it must be asked in response how far, and to whom, being is intelligible in its own right, if "in its own right" means within the constraints of philosophy and natural theology. Likewise with human being in particular. Without conceding either that there is no such thing as human nature or that human nature is philosophically inaccessible, we ought to insist that it is only imperfectly accessible and that man has ultimately to learn from God who and what man is, if he really wants to know. This means (just as Barth says)

66. See e.g., *DZ* 1704, 1710, 1714, and 1757.
67. *DZ* 1789; cf. 1783.
68. *DZ* 1795.
69. Romanus Cessario, "Duplex Ordo Cognitionus," in *Reasons and the Reason of Faith*, ed. P. Griffiths and R. Hütter (London: Continuum, 2005), 330; quoted by D. Stephen Long, *Speaking of God* (Grand Rapids: Eerdmans, 2009), 72.

learning who and what man is from the incarnate One himself, in the Spirit and the Church, rather than from a mere overlay of theological concepts on philosophical ones. It means, therefore, conversion and salvation.[70]

Philosophia Christiana?

For Barth, philosophy has the basic questions asked and answered by theology as "its disturbing margin and border" (CD 3.1:341). Philosophy cannot cross that border without becoming theology, for what lies on the other side is not its own. But theology, apparently, can cross the border into the realm of philosophy—in much the same manner "as the Israelites did or should have done on their entry into Canaan: They had to invade Canaan, not as a foreign country which did not belong to them, but as the land of their fathers."[71] For Thomas, on the other hand, this militaristic image is foreign. He envisions rather a cooperative and peaceful cohabitation along a respected border. But if we may ask Barth whether he thinks philosophy is really failed theology—and theology the philosophy that ought to have been, or at least its substitute[72]—we may also ask Thomas a similar question: Is the peace he envisions really a peace maintained by independent disciplines, between which there is in fact a border, or has the need for a border all but disappeared? Does

---

70. DZ 1783, 1789, 1795. Cf. *Gaudium et spes*, 19; Pius XII, *Humani generis*, 2ff. On the other hand, Catholics are also capable of making the Barthian mistake, as Stephen A. Long observes in *Natura Pura: On the Recovery of Nature in the Doctrine of Grace* (New York: Fordham University Press, 2010). Long, however, in an otherwise convincing critique of De Lubac, Balthasar, et al., does not attend adequately to the primacy of the second Adam, in whom it is shown that human nature is precisely for communion with God and cannot be grasped properly in any lesser connection (see Irenaeus, *Haer.* 5.16.2, and Aquinas, *DV* 18.1, ad 5 and 6; cf. *ST* 1.62.2). Great care must be taken with the claim "that God might without injustice have created man *in puris naturalibus*" (Long, *Natura Pura*, 269n8), which is not the right way to protect the distinction between nature and grace (or *gratia creans* and *gratia elevans*), since it hypothesizes a "man" altogether unrelated to Jesus Christ and hence lacking any image-bearing capacity. Whether such a man might have existed is not knowable; certainly he does not exist.

71. CD 2.2:522. The port of entry here is ethics. How to square this with the rejection at CD 1.2:731 of "a dictatorial, absolute and exclusive theology" is not immediately clear.

72. Barth (CD 1.1:3ff.) indicates that there might in principle be *philosophia christiana*, though in practice it has never existed. Theology is a kind of substitute for it, or a necessary protest against the lack of it. Theology, as an academic enterprise distinct from the Church's doxological action, comes into existence not because it has its own proper object of study—"all sciences might ultimately be theology," by taking up "the criticism and correction of talk about God according to the criterion of the Church's own principle"—but rather because this job has to be done, and is not being done elsewhere. Theology "cannot think of itself as a link in an ordered cosmos, but only as a stop-gap in a disordered cosmos" (10). A Thomist *responsio* might begin by asking whether this is really adequate to what Barth attempts in the *Dogmatics*.

the *pax* or *pactum* between theology and philosophy mean that philosophy itself is somehow Christian? If so, is it still philosophy?

This brings us full circle to the question as to what philosophy is. We said that it is the pursuit of clarity about ourselves, our world, and our place in it, for the sake of the good life. It is important to say "for the sake of the good life," lest philosophy (with its broad reach) be indistinguishable from the more abstract dimensions of other disciplines that inhabit the lower faculty. But if it is for the sake of the good life that philosophy does its work, seeking to discover from the universe, from human society, from the human mind itself, what is good or what makes for good, and where it cannot see good nevertheless to pursue the good of clarity—if philosophy, or the ideal of philosophy, is a patient search for truth and understanding out of an abiding love of the good—then it cannot do without some intuited or inherited sense of the good, however provisional and open to revision. It is all fine and well to say that the love of wisdom (*philosophia*) is the love of the good, or of the way to the good (for it is wisdom that helps us on our way), and even to say that this is the way of happiness, which all men want. But if philosophy is not to be vain and empty, or utterly confused and incapable of helping us along the way, it must already know something of the good. How else can it hope to discern or disclose the good, and to speak of man "both as he is and as he should be"?[73]

Philosophy, viewed thus, cannot but have natural theology and natural law (or first philosophy and moral philosophy) as its proper horizons, for unless it is prepared to press its inquiry about the good and about its knowledge of the good through to first principles, its attempt to discern good and evil will be haphazard at best. Moreover, philosophy viewed thus will be open, not closed, to the kind of claim that arises from beyond those horizons in the form of revealed theology, even if it is not competent to judge everything that revealed theology has to say. Why? Because, especially at the level of first principles, it will be aware (if it is not Eunomian) of the fact that it does not know concretely but only abstractly; that its knowledge of the good, taken by itself, is deficient. Its approach to the good and to God, and so to man himself, requires to be augmented and corrected by a knowledge that is more adequate to God. As Thomas says: "In the system of philosophy, which considers creatures in themselves and from them leads on to the knowledge of God, the first study is of creatures and the last of God; but in the system of faith, which studies creatures only in their relation to God, the study is first of God and afterwards of creatures; and this is a more perfect view, and

73. Kant, *Conflict of the Faculties*, 288 (cf. n. 2 above).

more like to the knowledge of God, who, knowing Himself, thence discerns other beings."[74]

Much effort has been expended in modernity to argue otherwise, of course, often in the name of clarity, though perhaps more obviously out of resistance to Thomas's conclusion that philosophy "should be subject to the measure of faith." (We saw this in Kant, who denies that the "more perfect view" is possible.) But any attempt to isolate philosophy from theology is self-defeating. Far from assuring that philosophy retains its own vocation and liberty as an act of reasoning from and about the world, it forces philosophy to transgress its vocation and to lose its liberty by becoming a sort of *faux* theology. Philosophy then tries to discover, not only in the universe and in human society, but ultimately in the mind or will itself, something that is not actually there: the Good that is the source of goodness; or, at all events, something that is good in itself without qualification.[75]

This latter kind of philosophy leads sooner or later to despair, despair even of reason. For it cannot find what it is looking for, and it can never lead to that which all men want. In refusing to learn of God from God, it cannot know the mind or heart of man either. In declining to hear of man's redemption, it cannot reckon with his fall, which is fatal to the whole enterprise of philosophy. For the fall skews the proper relation between is and ought, and our perception of that relation; it corrupts our sense of what is true and right. Plato, for want of the requisite revelation, may be mistaken in his construal of the κόσμος νοητός and the afterlife of the soul, but he is correct in saying that "a man must take with him into the world below an adamantine faith in truth and right."[76] And whence arises this faith, if it is not merely blind, and therefore doubtful, but rather adamantine? It arises in response to what is known to be trustworthy. It arises in response to what has shown itself trustworthy. It arises, on the Christian account, in response to the God of Israel, the Father of Jesus Christ, who is indeed ready to make us able "to learn

74. *SCG* 2.4. The final clause (*qui seipsum cognoscens alia intuetur*) and the construct as a whole may be accused of "onto-theology," but only if what Thomas the theologian actually has to say about God is ignored.

75. When Kant says that "there is no possibility of thinking of anything at all in the world, or even out of it, which can be regarded as good without qualification, except a good will" (*Grounding for the Metaphysics of Morals*, first section), he is trying to avoid what he calls "misology"—hatred or distrust of reason. There is not room here to show why he does not succeed, but only to remark that reason is better served by saying with Jesus that "no one is good but God alone" (Mark 10:18). And to add that, if this were understood, the subsequent attempts by Fichte and Hegel et al. to put the human knower and willer where Thomas has the divine would be seen for what they really are: the impossible inflation of philosophy and the reason for its eventual collapse through despair of the good.

76. Plato, *Republic* 10, 619a (trans. Benjamin Jowett).

and discern between good and evil."[77] One burden of revealed theology is to explain how it arises and how it is maintained, and thus to perfect philosophy by bringing it—precisely as human reason that begins with man and the world—into communion with divine reason, the reason that was with God in the beginning and for our sake came into the world.

Now this perfection is not a sublation. Revealed theology does not substitute for philosophy, nor philosophy for revealed theology. But no philosophy, whatever it communes with, can evade its responsibility to take certain decisions about the Good and the good life, for philosophy that denies itself any attempt to rise to a clearer knowledge of the good ceases to be philosophy.[78] And as these decisions are taken, it will necessarily take on the character that corresponds to them. If with Thomas, in contrast to Aristotle or Averroes, for example, the world is understood not only as having God as its cause but as having *this* God—the holy Trinity—as its cause, philosophy's act of reasoning, both in its selection of problems to which to attend and in its way of attending to them, will change. Even the meaning of "cause" will change, as will the meaning of being, unity, truth, freedom, goodness, etc., under the impact of the *analogia gratiae* that reforms and perfects the *analogia entis*. Logic will not change, but epistemology, metaphysics, ethics, and aesthetics will change because new light will be cast upon them. To receive and reflect that light is what it means to be subject to the measure of faith.

So in that sense it is quite right to speak of Christian philosophy, even of Augustinian or Thomist philosophy, just as it is right to speak of Greek or Enlightenment philosophy, even of Aristotelian, Kantian, or Heideggerian philosophy—to say nothing of Hindu or Buddhist philosophy. There is no philosophy *povera et nuda*. Yet to speak of Christian philosophy does not elide the distinction between philosophy and theology; neither is deprived of its own vocation, tasks, and liberties. It does not even decide in advance between philosophies. "In itself the term is valid," says John Paul II, "but it should not be misunderstood: it in no way intends to suggest that there is an official philosophy of the Church, since the faith as such is not a philosophy. The term seeks rather to indicate a Christian way of philosophizing, a

---

77. Plato, *Republic* 10, 618c.

78. The attempt may be restricted or distorted by certain anti-metaphysical commitments, as in Kant's *Grounding for the Metaphysics of Morals* or, more dramatically, in Nietzsche's *Beyond Good and Evil*. It may even be almost entirely implicit, rather than explicit, in a given enterprise. But every exercise of reason is directed by and to some perceived good, and philosophical reason—though it is not by itself sufficient for it—has no more definitive or indispensable task than to learn the discernment of good and evil.

philosophical speculation conceived in dynamic union with faith."[79] Which means a way of philosophizing that in reasoning from the world benefits from the light shed on the world by special revelation, not a way of philosophizing that welcomes the unnatural and diseased hybrid (rejected by Thomas and Barth) that so often passes for theology today.

As soon as we speak of Christian philosophy, however, it becomes evident that what we are calling the *pax Thomistica* does not extend to every particular philosophy in the same way or to the same degree. How could it? The theologian will have both philosophical and theological reasons for preferring one to another, and will in any case have to insist on certain principles that make some partnerships impractical if not impossible; likewise the philosopher, who will not regard theology with indifference.[80] Yet the offer of peace can be extended from the side of theology to any philosophical endeavor insofar as it does not contradict, materially or methodologically, what (*pace* Descartes) is not for the Church actually in doubt; that is, what is known about man and the world through the knowledge of divine things, divinely revealed. And why should that offer not be welcomed, on the other side, by anyone who is not completely certain that it must be left to philosophy to determine the limits of human knowledge? Why indeed should it not be welcomed even by those who are certain? Whatever the illusions or misunderstandings of theology, whatever the vincible or invincible ignorance with which it may be charged, there is no denying that philosophy has frequently been in its debt and might become so again.

This peace is not merely a negative peace, a sort of toleration, but a positive and cooperative peace from which new possibilities emerge for both theology and philosophy. Witness again the subject of personhood, which (as I said) first emerged for theology and philosophy from discussion of the triune identity. Philosophy, in its various Græco-Roman forms, contributed terms or concepts such as οὐσία, ὑπόστασις, and πρόσωπον. Christian theology contributed an understanding of Father, Son, and Spirit, drawn from the economy of revelation, that required a new configuration of these terms and concepts—uniting ὑπόστασις more closely to πρόσωπον, so that being and personhood might be mutually defining in an ontology of communion. And this in turn was used

---

79. John Paul II employs "faith" here both in the sense of *fides qua* and of *fides quae*. Otherwise put, Christian philosophy has a subjective aspect, "in the sense that faith purifies reason," and an objective aspect, in that revelation "clearly proposes certain truths which might never have been discovered by reason unaided." These together "broaden reason's scope for action" (*Fides et Ratio* 76; cf. 103).

80. Regrettably, the task of showing how Barth and Aquinas agree and differ on the question of what theology is, and on what *philosophia christiana* is or might be—which ought to be pursued further just here—must instead be left to another occasion.

both for theological purposes (in ecclesiology, say) and for philosophical purposes (in thinking about language and psychology, rights and freedoms, and other anthropological issues that extend beyond the Church). The subject of being itself was transformed when it was understood that the being of God is irreducibly a being in communion.[81] For we do not learn from the study of being very much, perhaps, about what it means to be God; but from the study of God we learn a great deal about what it means to be. Or we may do so, by way of a christologically informed *analogia entis* that carries us beyond the apophatic and lends to the *via eminentiae* its rightful content.[82]

If we do so, we inhabit the borderlands where philosophy and theology are not isolated or even competing disciplines but semiautonomous members of an intellectual commonwealth. Since that commonwealth exists in service to "the supremely cooperative, supremely ordered association of those who enjoy God and one another in God,"[83] the high knowledge it pursues requires "angels ascending and descending"—men and women doing the work of philosophy as of theology, but united (to one degree or another) in faith as in reason. And if few there be who, like Thomas, move with equal facility in both directions without becoming confused or disoriented, that only makes more evident the necessity and benefit of working together.

81. It could hardly be otherwise, since the incarnation requires not only that ontology make room for real relations in God (Ockham, *In Sent.* 1.26.1; cf. Spade, ed., *Cambridge Companion to Ockham*, 104f., 343ff.) but also that it make room for real relations in creation.

82. Cf. *Fides et ratio*, 92: "The Truth, which is Christ, imposes itself as an all-embracing authority which holds out to theology and philosophy alike the prospect of support, stimulation and increase (cf. Eph 4:15)."

83. Augustine, *Civ.* 19.13 (trans. Oliver O'Donovan and Joan Lockwood O'Donovan, *From Irenaeus to Grotius: A Sourcebook in Christian Political Thought* [Grand Rapids: Eerdmans, 1999], 155).

2

Thinking with Aquinas about Nature and Grace

Thomas Aquinas has many friends who are confident they agree with Thomas and equally confident that the friend next to them does not. To say anything about Thomas, particularly on nature and grace, is to risk uniting this motley crew in disagreement with oneself. That is likely enough to happen here, particularly as I intend to honor the master by thinking, as far as I can, both with him and against him. With him, simply because he is the master; against him, because I think he himself (however rarely compared to the rest of us) has made mistakes.

The rubric under which I wish to think for and, if necessary, against Aquinas is "nature and grace." The context in which I do so is my readings in previous masters, in Thomas himself, and in disputatious friends of Thomas such as Henri De Lubac and (recently) Stephen Long. I will have something to say about their concerns in due course, but I must make my own way there. Like them, I am concerned with the relation between the natural and the gratuitous ordering of man to God.[1]

1. Anyone wanting a proper introduction to this debate should consult chapter 5 of Reinhard Hütter, *Dust Bound for Heaven: Explorations in the Theology of Thomas Aquinas* (Grand Rapids: Eerdmans, 2012). Regrettably, I did not myself discover it until after writing this essay. As will be evident, I agree with Hütter's assessment that "Thomas comes out far ahead of the alternatives that are predominantly considered in contemporary theology." I further agree that "the human call to glory" must be approached by "considering simultaneously . . . two constitutive principles, nature and destiny—or constitution and ordination—that remain irreducible to

Rendering Aquinas, Briefly and Perhaps Tendentiously

Aquinas believes that man, like the angels, is created by grace (i.e., freely and as the constant recipient of divine power to think, choose, and act) and in grace (i.e., that he is given already in the first instance a properly ordered soul, or original justice, by grace-that-makes-pleasing (*gratia gratum faciens*), such that his will is subject to God. All this, says Aquinas, can be attributed to his nature,[2] and it is not inappropriate for us to speak of it, in Bernard's rather than Thomas's expression, as *gratia creans*.[3]

Aquinas also thinks that man, in his original state (*natura integra*), is already the recipient of *gratia elevans* (which is also, though differently, *gratia gratum faciens*) in that he has, and knows he has, a supernatural end, which we can speak of as a will to happiness that includes the desire to see and know God *in se* and not merely as his creator and lord. This of course is just the beginning of elevating grace, not yet the *gratia consummata* required for him to achieve his supernatural end, and he knows that too: "In the state of innocence Adam desired to see God through His essence, but that desire of his was well ordered. For he strove to see God when it would be time for him to do so. Hence, he did not suffer at all at not seeing God before the proper time."[4]

---

each other" (14). The conclusions to which he comes in chapter 6, leaning on Marie-Joseph Le Guillou's article, "*Surnaturel*" (*Revue des sciences philosophiques et théologiques* 34 [1950]: 226–43), seem to me exactly right, and the case that is made goes into much detail that I have not attempted to master here. As my own readers will see, however, I am not entirely content with Thomas's intellectualism and angelomorphism, which understands the call to glory in terms of a *visio dei* that renders what is peculiarly human almost beside the point after all (the principle articulated at *De pot*. q. 5, a. 10, ad 5 notwithstanding; cf. e.g., *SCG* 3.25.10; 3.50.9; and Hütter, *Dust Bound for Heaven*, 214ff.). This concern is beyond the purview of Hütter's admirable work in these chapters.

2. *ST* 1–2.85.1 (emphasis added): "The good of human nature is threefold. First, there are the principles of which nature is constituted, and the properties that flow from them, such as the powers of the soul, and so forth. Secondly, since man has from nature an inclination to virtue, as stated above (60.1, 63.1), this inclination to virtue is a good of nature. *Thirdly, the gift of original justice, conferred on the whole of human nature in the person of the first man, may be called a good of nature.* Accordingly, the first-mentioned good of nature is neither destroyed nor diminished by sin. The third good of nature was entirely destroyed through the sin of our first parent. But the second good of nature, viz. the natural inclination to virtue, is diminished by sin." For a helpful discussion of original justice, see Jean-Pierre Torrell, "Nature and Grace in Thomas Aquinas," in *Surnaturel: A Controversy at the Heart of Twentieth-Century Thomistic Thought*, ed. Serge-Thomas Bonino, trans. R. Williams and M. Levering (Naples, FL: Sapientia, 2009), 163ff.

3. See chap. 1, n. 56.

4. *DV* 18.1, ad 6. That ultimate or supernatural end seems (as with the angels) to involve, for each rational intellect, a fixed degree of knowledge of God, and to be a point of permanent rest or actualization. There is no hint of *epektasis* in it, per *SCG* 3.48.3: "So, there is a natural desire of man to be established in felicity. Therefore, unless along with felicity such an unmoving

The continuity between *gratia creans* (including original justice)[5] and *gratia elevans*, in God, is simply God himself; for God's grace is always God himself in his free and generous action *ad extra*. The continuity in their effect on us is in the reality of our being ordered to God. But these two forms of divine goodness or grace, the creating and the elevating, order us to God in two distinct ways, so that it is necessary to speak of "a twofold ultimate perfection of rational or of intellectual nature. The first is one which it can procure of its own natural power; and this is in a measure [*quodammodo*] called beatitude or happiness.[6] Hence Aristotle says that man's ultimate happiness consists in his most perfect contemplation, whereby in this life he can behold the best intelligible object; and that is God. Above this happiness there is still another, which we look forward to in the future, whereby 'we shall see God as He is.' This is beyond the nature of every created intellect."[7]

The two ways in which man is ordered to God are compatible but incommensurable. For the latter ordering does not belong to his nature, whether as an inalienable possession, such as his will, or as an alienable endowment, such as original justice.[8] It belongs to him only as a further and distinct vocation beyond that inscribed in his nature. "To love God as the principle of all being pertains to natural love, but to love God as the object of beatitude pertains to the gratuitous love in which merit consists" (*Quod.* 1.4.3). However, his nature and his existence (*esse*) are given him precisely for the sake of this further gratuitous finality, which is eternal rather than temporal and unattainable by any unassisted exercise of his own powers, even when rightly ordered: "Now

---

stability be attained, he is not yet happy, for his natural desire is not yet at rest. And so, when a person attains felicity he likewise attains stability and rest, and that is why this is the notion of all men concerning felicity, that it requires stability as part of its essential character." But must stability exclude *epektasis*?

5. Original justice should not be confused with *gratia elevans*, at least not in the sense of the latter that leads to talk of *gratia consummata*. Original justice, to be sure, is a gift beyond that of mere existence with particular natural capacities and powers, but it is a gift directly connected to natural beatitude and only indirectly connected to supernatural beatitude; that is why it should be aligned with *gratia creans*.

6. *Ultima autem perfectio rationalis seu intellectualis naturae est duplex. Una quidem, quam potest assequi virtute suae naturae, et haec quodammodo beatitudo vel felicitas dicitur.*

7. *ST* 1.62.1; cf. Hütter, *Dust Bound for Heaven*, 154, 158f.

8. On the loss of original justice, cf. e.g., *ST* 1–2.109.3: "Hence in the state of perfect nature man referred the love of himself and of all other things to the love of God as to its end; and thus he loved God more than himself and above all things. But in the state of corrupt nature man falls short of this in the appetite of his rational will, which, unless it is cured by God's grace, follows its private good, on account of the corruption of nature. And hence we must say that in the state of perfect nature man did not need the gift of grace added to his natural endowments, in order to love God above all things naturally, although he needed God's help to move him to it; but in the state of corrupt nature man needs, even for this, the help of grace to heal his nature."

it was shown above, when we were treating of God's knowledge, that to see God in His essence, wherein the ultimate beatitude of the rational creature consists, is beyond the nature of every created intellect. Consequently no rational creature can have the movement of the will directed towards such beatitude, except it be moved thereto by a supernatural agent. This is what we call the help of grace."[9] Man's ultimate beatitude or well-being (*bene esse*) is not an afterthought, in other words, nor the grace that leads to it a later addition. There is no *natura integra* which is not already the object of *gratia elevans* or deifying grace. That is why man desires supernatural beatitude already from the beginning, though he has no claim upon it, and until it is promised to him explicitly he has not even the claim of faith in that promise.

Internecine Warfare among Thomists

The coincidence and coordination of *gratia creans* and *gratia elevans* that we find in Aquinas, deliberately argued over against some of his predecessors and contemporaries, has given rise to endless debates about what is or is not natural to man. It is not unreasonable to ask: If man is from the outset the recipient of *gratia elevans*, if in being called into existence he is at the same time called to the *visio dei*, is he not in some sense designed for this? And does design not imply nature? Of course he has already his existence, and therefore his created nature, and he has not the *visio dei*; his deiformity is as yet remote from him. But as the object both of *gratia creans* and of *gratia elevans*, is it not his nature both to be what he is and to be on the way to being what he is not yet?

We should not be surprised that some, like Pelagius or Baius—or even De Lubac and Balthasar, if we are to accept Stephen Long's rather harsh reading of them in *Natura Pura*—are inclined to conflate nature and grace, making "natural" even that which merits eternal life. Or that others are inclined to pull the two apart, as was already being done before Aquinas—and on De Lubac's reading was done after and to Aquinas by Cajetan and Suárez—making space for an anthropology in which man's purely gratuitous finality is, at least for some purposes, bracketed off and ignored. Or that still others, such as Teilhard, are inclined to swallow up nature in grace, such that the force of Aquinas's *non tollit sed perficit naturam* is lost.[10]

---

9. *ST* 1.61.2; cf. 1.1.1, where Thomas, defending the necessity of revealed theology, tells us that "man is directed to God, as to an end that surpasses the grasp of his reason."

10. The *perficit*—if it is also the *praesupponit et perficit*—requires both something to perfect and its preservation. But that something does not, for Teilhard, include the body; see my *Ascension and Ecclesia* (Grand Rapids: Eerdmans, 1999), 198ff.

Aquinas himself makes clear the fundamental unity of *gratia creans*, which produces human nature, and *gratia elevans*, which perfects and deifies it, when he says that "our intellect was made for the purpose of seeing God," or again, when he accepts that "man was made to see God" and to participate in his beatitude.[11] When he says that man has a passive capacity (*aptitudo passiva*) for the perfection that nevertheless lies beyond his natural powers, or that "the soul is naturally capable of grace" (*ST* 1–2.113.10), or that there is in man an innate desire to see God, he points to this same unity.

Does Aquinas regard rationality itself as ordered to the vision of God? There is some ambiguity here. Are we meant to understand that the rational creature, having its beginning and its end in God who is above nature, seeks God with the intellect naturally only insofar as it also does so supernaturally, by grace? And, if so, is there any such thing as "natural" reason that is not merely a moment within the process of revelation and deification?

When Aquinas says that above the beatitude appropriate to unaided reason there is another and higher beatitude, a supernatural beatitude, he seems to be arguing both that there *is* a natural beatitude and that there is no rational animal for whom it would be proper to seek that natural beatitude exclusively—as if it had never been invited to, or at all events were not interested in, the supernatural vision. He even goes to some lengths to show that the former is unsatisfactory and as such not really a beatitude at all, that in the last analysis there is really only one beatitude. "The vision of God itself is essentially the final end of the human soul, and its beatitude."[12] Of natural knowledge of God, it is said: *non est autem possibile hanc cognitionem Dei ad felicitatem sufficere.*[13]

What can all this mean, asks De Lubac, if not that man is so constituted as to seek his true happiness in the *visio dei*, though he has not, in or of himself, the means to do so? "Although man is naturally inclined to this end, he cannot pursue it naturally, but only through grace," as Aquinas says.[14] Scotus likewise asserts (in De Lubac's paraphrase) "that man's end is natural to him if considered in terms of his desire, but supernatural in terms of how it is attained, or by whom it is brought about."[15]

11. *DV* 10.11, ad 7; *DV* 18.1.
12. *In 4 Sent.*, dist. 49.2; quoted in Henri de Lubac, *The Mystery of the Supernatural*, trans. Rosemary Sheed (New York: Crossroad, 1998), 117.
13. "It is not possible for this knowledge of God to suffice for felicity" (*SCG* 3.38.2).
14. *Expositio in librum Boethii De hebdomadibus* 6.4.
15. See *Mystery*, 115f., where De Lubac associates Aquinas also with the words of another Franciscan, Pierre Olivi: "It is most natural for every mind to strive for the eternal and highest beatitude." De Lubac leaves us in some doubt, however, as to the exact sense in which the desire to see God is natural, speaking as he does of a "twofold call," both natural and supernatural (130f.).

It is not always obvious, then, how we should read or understand Aquinas on this point. The likes of De Lubac will read him one way, the likes of Long another.[16] According to the former, "the desire to see [God] is in us, it constitutes us, and yet it comes to us as a completely free gift."[17] According to the latter, not so. We must reject this distinction between end and means and deploy instead a distinction between end and end. Man has two ends, not one; for no creature can be inclined by nature to what is beyond nature, though (by virtue of the *potentia obedientialis* unique to the rational soul) both men and angels can be inclined by nature to their respective natural ends while simultaneously being inclined by grace to what is beyond them; viz., to a supernatural end that is the same for the one as for the other.

As far as I can tell, all seem to agree that there is no man who is not made for the purpose that he should know God and also that, had God willed it, there might have been such a man, though there is not. But the dispute nevertheless remains: Does man have both a natural end in God and a supernatural end, hence (in principle) both a natural or imperfect beatitude and a supernatural or perfect beatitude? Or does he have but a single supernatural end—God, or happiness in God—toward which he strives both by natural and by supernatural means?[18]

What makes this dispute so important is its bearing on the question, What is man? This is what both sides are concerned with. On De Lubac's side are

16. Take, as a further example, *De virtutibis in communis* 10: "But just as man acquires his first perfection, that is, his soul, by the action of God, so too he has his ultimate perfection, which is his perfect happiness, immediately from God, and rests in it. Indeed this is obvious from the fact that man's natural desire cannot rest in anything else save in God alone. For it is innate in man that he be moved by a desire to go on from what has been caused and inquire into causes, nor does this desire rest until it arrives at the first cause, which is God. Therefore, it is necessary that, just as man's first perfection, which is the rational soul, exceeds the capacity of bodily matter, so the ultimate perfection to which a man can come, which is the happiness of eternal life, should exceed the entire capacity of human nature."

17. De Lubac, *Mystery* 167. Which is to say: it is in us, naturally and constitutively, as a call to the supernatural; yet this very call that determines our nature and our constitution is extended gratuitously, since things might have been otherwise.

18. No one thinks that man has only a natural end. At *ST* 1–2.5.5, ad 2, Thomas plainly states that man has an end that transcends nature: "The nature that can attain perfect good, although it needs help from without in order to attain it, is of more noble condition than a nature which cannot attain perfect good, but attains some imperfect good, although it need no help from without in order to attain it, as the Philosopher says (De Coel. ii, 12) . . . And therefore the rational creature, which can attain the perfect good of happiness, but needs the Divine assistance for the purpose, is more perfect than the irrational creature, which is not capable of attaining this good, but attains some imperfect good by its natural powers." At *ST* 3.1.3, ad 3, we read: "A double capability may be remarked in human nature: one, in respect of the order of natural power, and this is always fulfilled by God, Who apportions to each according to its natural capability; the other in respect to the order of the Divine power, which all creatures implicitly obey . . . [though] God does not fulfil all such capabilities."

those who, like John Paul II, believe that an eclipse of the sense of God has led to an eclipse of the sense of man and that what must be restored above all is a sense of man's supernatural vocation. On the other side are those who think that the best response to the eclipse of the sense of man is to recover our sense of nature as ordered by God—what Long calls the theonomic principle of nature—and that this cannot be done by focusing on man's supernatural end at the expense of attention to his natural end.

"Does human nature receive its proper definition from the ordering to supernatural beatitude?" asks Long. "No." For, if it did, there would be no difference between man and angel, or for that matter between angel and angel—already a sign of the loss of nature. Rather, human nature "receives its species from the proportionate, proximate natural end, which is further ordered in grace to the *finis ultimus* of supernatural beatitude."[19] Both/and is the only solution, in other words. For the proper recognition of human dignity and the right ordering of human life, it is just as necessary to recognize the natural end as to recognize the supernatural. And to grasp the natural end we must, so to say, prescind from grace and think about mere nature: *natura pura*, human nature as ordered to God even apart from the *gratia elevans* that orders it to an end that transcends nature. We must think about natural human capacities, and about the gifts that belong to *gratia creans*, including the original justice by which the goods of the body are ordered by and to the goods of the soul, and those of the soul to those of the intellect, and those of the intellect to God as first and final Cause.[20]

What worries De Lubac, of course, is that in this prescision man disappears for want of grace, the *gratia elevans* in which and for which he was created. What worries Long is that man disappears if he is not allowed his natural end, the lesser end that is logically though not chronologically prior to the greater end, because without it grace has nothing on which or with which to work in moving toward that greater end. What worries me, if I may say so,

19. Long, *Natura Pura*, 91.
20. Cf. André-Mutien Leonard, "The Theological Necessity of the Pure Nature Concept," in *Surnaturel: A Controversy at the Heart of Twentieth Century Thought*, ed. Serge-Thomas Bonino, trans. R. Williams and M. Levering (Naples, FL: Sapientia, 2009), 329f.: "God did not create man in the state of pure nature, whom he would afterward destine for the beatific vision . . . But it is true that within this wholly unique being [already destined for God] there is a zone, discernible with great difficulty, that must correspond to man's essential nature and that could have had a real integrity outside of grace. That is exactly what theologians call 'pure nature,' an expression that therefore designates a wholly hypothetical condition of man." Leonard wants both this—"The grace of divinization fulfils man from within without violating his nature. Thus one avoids extrinsicism."—and this: "Even if it were not destined to the grace of divinization, human nature would have an authentic meaning. Thus one maintains the gratuitousness of grace and the integrity of human nature." It sounds good, but it is not quite right, as we shall see.

is that neither side is working with a sufficiently robust christology. Indeed, it is not clear to me that Thomas himself, whom both sides claim as their champion, is doing so.

Querying Both Thomas and Thomists

Let me begin with his friends, who are united in the struggle to retain both nature and grace but divided in their analysis as to how the threat to man has arisen and in their response to that threat. Several questions come to mind, among them the following.

First, a set of questions to those on Long's side: If by man's natural end we mean God as creator, God as first principle or first and final cause, and if we mean to say that the natural beatitude of man rests on recognition of this end, are we speaking of man's knowledge of God as one in prescision from his knowledge of God as triune? That is, of man qua philosopher rather than qua theologian, though he is in fact both? Or are we speaking of man as ordered to God rationally but not yet relationally? Hence of man who knows that he ought to pray but does not know how or through whom he should pray?

The latter category is empty, apart from lapsed man lacking *gratia sanans*.[21] And this man, alas, is by no means the philosopher that he ought to be. He does not have a clear conception of man because he does not have a clear (if limited) conception of God. Though he is not excused thereby for falling into skepticism, either about God or about himself, he is subject to much confusion about both. His nature is still intact, in a certain sense, yet for him natural beatitude is not realizable or even fully conceivable.[22] So how can we be talking about him, save indirectly, as the beneficiary (if he is willing) of the philosophical clarity of which redeemed man is capable?

But if we are talking about the man who is both philosopher and theologian— insofar as he is philosopher and can speak intelligently of human life as ordered to the one God without ignoring or denying or even restricting what must also

21. It is otherwise empty because Adam was not such a man in the state of integrity if he was indeed created as the object of *gratia elevans*, and because the lapsed but redeemed man is not such a man either. He too is both a philosopher and a theologian, though it may be that, like Adam, he can recognize the difference between philosophy and theology.

22. I say "in a certain sense" because it is not right, in repudiating those who misunderstood the relation of nature and grace before the fall and who therefore attributed to the fall a loss of nature as well as of grace, to overlook the teaching of the fathers, especially of Irenaeus and Athanasius, that by sin man was "turned away backwards" and even in danger of disappearing. The wounds of sin, though they are indeed wounds and (contra certain Reformation or Baian or Jansenist ideas) do not remove man's nature or supplant it with some other nature, are fatal to man if left untreated.

be said theologically about this God as holy Trinity and man as the friend of God in supernatural charity—then we are talking about the man Adam was on his way to being and that we ourselves, in Christ, are on the way to being. And this means that we are talking about the man who is not actually aiming at natural beatitude in prescision from supernatural beatitude, but only in connection with supernatural beatitude. For to aim at natural beatitude alone, or to be a philosopher without also being a theologian, would ipso facto be to fall from grace. That indeed is what it means to fall.[23]

Thus we may inquire of Long whether the malaise of post-Christian man (so-called) does not have more to do with the nominalist abstraction of nature from grace than with any putative lack of attention to nature; whether in fact the eventual lack of attention to nature does not follow from the attempt to bracket it from grace. We may nevertheless agree that a recovery of grace without attention to nature is no real recovery at all.

Second, and to both parties: Could we not have more clarity in our discussion of ends and means? And might this not go some way toward resolving the dispute?

If we say that there are two ends—proximate and final, natural and supernatural—we can be speaking only of our relation to one and the same God in two different ways: of "a twofold ultimate perfection" of our rational nature, including "one which it can procure of its own natural power," which we may call happiness only *quodammodo*, and one that it cannot, which may without reservation be called happiness.

If we prefer to say rather that God, or beatitude in God, is our one final end, adding that (given *gratia elevans*) we approach this one final end through the use of both natural and supernatural means, we are not implying that natural means carry us part of the way and supernatural the rest of the way, but rather that our proper end is attained only by a concurrent operation of natural and supernatural gifts, each enabling our happiness in their proper way.[24]

The question remains whether it is right to say with Scotus that this one end is natural to us even though it can be achieved only supernaturally (that is, by the addition of gratuitous gifts). Here also there is danger of obfuscation. For surely it is natural in one sense and not in another. If we

---

23. To attempt to achieve by nature what can only be achieved by grace: that is an Augustinian view of the fall that Aquinas takes up in *De malo*. There are questions and nuances that ought to be considered—what exactly is it that the devil is trying to achieve, or that man is trying to achieve, when he falls?—but it is not necessary to pursue that here.

24. We cannot say that natural knowledge of God, and natural ordering to God, is the basis of a beatitude proper to this life only, while its counterpart is proper to the eschaton, for that would destroy all continuity between life in this world and life in the world to come.

are viewed as being made for God, it is natural. If we are viewed simply as made, then it is supernatural. Would Thomas himself have lingered long over this question?

The problem, however, is not merely perspectival. When we ask whether we desire naturally to see God as he is, or only supernaturally, we are asking whether that desire is constitutional. De Lubac wants to hold in dialectical tension the claim that it is constitutional and the claim that it is always elicited by a gratuitous offer, not abandoning either assertion.[25] He tries to suggest that one claim is ontological, the other ethical, for we are both nature and freedom; and God himself is utterly free, so that his offer is not subject to any necessity even though it corresponds to our nature and our nature depends upon it.[26] But all this is question begging. If we are constituted by a call and a corresponding desire, and the call is entirely gratuitous, then we are constituted gratuitously. Are *gratia creans* and *gratia elevans* not indeed conflated, then, as those on the other side charge?

We will return to this, but here is a third question, again for both sides: Is it actually right to say that God might have made a universe in which there was no gratuitous offer of deification, just *natura pura* with no supernatural end, *gratia creans* without *gratia elevans*? De Lubac qualifies this idea, of course, by adding that this would entail another kind of humanity altogether, a qualification to which Long understandably objects as negating any meaningful reference to *natura pura*. For Long it is important to say that God might have made precisely our humanity without extending his grace to it.[27] For grace perfects nature; it does not substitute one nature for another. But we must ask Long also, would not this hypothetical humanity be pointless? If no creature were called to see and enjoy God as God really is, would that not reduce the whole of creation, and each of its parts, to a mere spectacle for God? And would it not be unfitting to say of God that he might have created such a spectacle? Can this really be the right way to defend either the gratuitousness of grace or the concreteness of human nature?

25. De Lubac, *Mystery*, 183.
26. Rahner's "supernatural existential" is another attempt to resolve the difficulty, as David Coffee observes in "The Whole Rahner on the Supernatural Existential," *Theological Studies* 65 (2004): 95–118. Perhaps the most satisfactory and least objectionable rendering of that concept is to think of it terms of a vocation, a *gratia vocans*, that comes to every man.
27. Thus *Natura Pura*, 142, e.g.: "the doctrine of *natura pura* is the double doctrine (1) that even here and now, in the concrete order, there is impressed upon each human person a natural order to the proximate, proportionate, natural end from which the species of man is derived, which is distinct from the final and supernatural end; and (2) that this ordering *could have been* created outside of sanctifying grace and without the further ordering of man to supernatural beatific vision." Cf. Hütter, *Dust Bound for Heaven*, 242f.

But now a fourth question, aimed at Aquinas as well as his disputatious friends: Is it right to say that man is distinguished from angels according to his natural end but not according to his supernatural end? Or does this reveal a false intellectualism and angelomorphism that actually diminishes our conception of both the natural and the supernatural end?

According to Aquinas, the rational soul or intellect is created immediately by God. This is the case for men as for angels. The implications of this claim are not altogether clear. Does it compel us to admit that, having created the soul immediately and for himself, God does indeed have a debt to the soul, to lead it to the *visio dei*, just as he has a debt to the body and to the rest of nature, to sustain it by his providence? Thomas does not seem to think so, and all seem to shun this as Baian heresy, though generally without explaining why we should worry about God owing what he chooses to owe, whether in *gratia creans* or in *gratia elevans*, even if we understand that the soul can no more give itself eternal well-being than it can give itself being in the first place.[28]

Now it may be that the immediate creation of the soul implies no more than that the soul is the kind of thing that can recognize that God is and what God is, the kind of thing that can articulate the honor owed to God as first principle. Angels and men, considered as souls, are both this kind of thing, just because they are (in that respect) created by God without the deployment of secondary causes.[29] But we must attend to the fact that this approach, which lumps together angels and men under the genus "rational soul" or "created intellect," puts a great deal of weight on the composite nature of man in order to distinguish him from the angels according to his natural end, yet it fails to recognize that his supernatural end also differs, in its way, from that of the angels.[30] Moreover, we should acknowledge straightaway that Thomas does not give a satisfactory account of the body in relation to the human experience of beatitude in God. Indeed—let those Thomists who expend so much energy defending *natura pura* as a vital feature of Thomism take note—it is never quite clear why or how being human enhances rather

28. The condemnation of Baius by Benedict XII is a repudiation of any confusion of nature and grace, but not of the faithfulness of God to freely made promises, or indeed of God's faithfulness to himself, to which Athanasius appealed in positing the fittingness, even the necessity, of *gratia sanans*. Cf. Anselm, who distinguishes "a necessity which removes graciousness" from "a necessity whereby the debt of gratitude owed for a benefaction is increased" (*CDH* 2.5, which takes up the Irenaean motif that God stands in need of nothing).

29. We may set aside here the problem of the role of parents in the creation of human souls and of the relation of subsequent human souls to the (in some sense parentless) first humans.

30. See e.g., *ST* 1.75.7, ad 1, which distinguishes angels and men according to their natural ends but not their supernatural. (Cf. Long, *Natura Pura*, 17; however, he is not clear what the natural end is or how it distinguishes according to species.)

than impedes the *visio dei*. Thomas is no Origenist, but neither (as we shall see) does his vision of the heavenly city, or the role of embodiment in that city, rise to that of the fathers.[31]

Which leads to the final and most important question: Where is the christology, and how far is it controlling the construct or the debate, either in Aquinas or in his interpreters? Who is taking full and proper account of the incarnation in setting out the relation between nature and grace?[32]

Christ the Mediator

Long criticizes De Lubac on this point; or at least he appeals to Nicaea and Chalcedon to chide De Lubac for not recognizing any definite human nature for the Son to assume. It is indeed remarkable that De Lubac's defense of *Surnaturel* in *The Mystery of the Supernatural* is so devoid of christological reasoning. But Long himself does not employ christology in any meaningful way in *Natura Pura*. He does not even pause to ask whether the doctrine of the incarnation, with its uniting of two natures in one person, has any significance for interpreting human nature as such. It is almost as if the whole tradition from Irenaeus onward has faded from view: "He became what we are that we might become what he is." If this is soteriological, it is also ontological; if it speaks of *gratia sanans*, it speaks also of *gratia elevans*. What is more, it makes nature (as all agree) a preamble to grace in the sense that nature is *for* grace,

31. Jesus says there will be no marrying or giving in marriage, from which it is rightly understood that there will be no sexual intimacy or reproduction, the former being redundant in true communion and the latter being excluded by the particular perfection of that communion. Thomas adds that there will be no eating and drinking, activities he sees (together with sex and reproduction) as signs of imperfection, as indeed they are. But this addition runs counter to what Jesus says about the kingdom, and to the embodied nature of resurrected humanity as shown by Jesus.

32. Thomas Joseph White ("Imperfect Happiness and the Final End of Man: Thomas Aquinas and the Paradigm of Nature-Grace Orthodoxy," *The Thomist* 78 [2014]: 288) argues "that the natural desire for the vision of God is a rational, philosophical desire that arises from man's reaching an imperfect beatitude of the natural contemplation of God, and as an outcropping of that beatitude." Hence, "when grace promises us a yet higher beatitude of seeing God face to face, it does not act extrinsically to our natural end." *Pace* Barth, "there exists a natural point of contact in us such that grace is not alien to human nature and can lead human nature without violence through the ascent upward into the supernatural life of God . . . in profound accord with nature's own highest inclinations and through an accomplishment of those aspirations that nature cannot realize for itself." Yet *pace* De Lubac, "nature is not intrinsically ordered toward the objects of supernatural revelation as such, but is surpassed by the higher order of divine life even as it is fulfilled by it." But surely this attempt to solve the problem only brings us back to the question of how we *know* nature and recognize this point of contact. Must we not allow grace, in its incarnational concreteness, to revise our understanding of nature itself?

elevating and deifying grace, from the very outset. But does it also make human nature itself something wanting its true definition until it finds it in Christ? The question as to whether the incarnation would have occurred even if sin had not is obviously important here. To give an affirmative answer is to underline that nature is for grace, and it was almost certainly a mistake on Thomas's part to decline to do so.[33] What must be insisted upon, however, is that all things are created in and for Christ and that in him all things hold together. That includes angelic nature, to be sure, but a fortiori human nature, which is not stabilized until it is also *his* nature. About this Irenaeus is very clear: "For in times long past, it was *said* that man was created after the image of God, but it was not [actually] *shown*"; not until man was assimilated "to the invisible Father through means of the visible Word."[34] But to think along these lines, reckoning all the while (as Thomas also does) with the fact that the Son of God does not lay hold of angels but of men, that he does not assume to himself and perfect in himself angelic natures but human nature only, is to grasp the fact (which Thomas doesn't) that deification in the proper sense belongs to men rather than to angels.

The supernatural beatitude of angels, in other words, is not altogether like that of men, or even of other angels, just as the natural beatitude is not. There is more to it in the beginning and less to it in the end, as Irenaeus explicitly says:

> For there is one Son, who accomplished His Father's will; and one human race also in which the mysteries of God are wrought, "into which the angels desire to look." And they are not able to search out the wisdom of God, by means of which his handiwork, confirmed and incorporated with his Son, is brought to perfection: that his offspring, the first-begotten Word, should descend to the creature, that is, to what had been moulded, and that it should be contained by him; and, on the other hand, that the creature should contain the Word and ascend to him, passing beyond the angels, and be made after the image and likeness of God. (*Haer.* 5.36.3)

On this approach, the call to the supernatural, if we want to use that expression, is our created openness to the company of God fulfilled in the

---

33. His reasoning—viz., that Scripture presents the incarnation as atonement in a soterio-logical rather an ontological sense and that it is best to stick with that—is adequate neither to Scripture nor to reason. If this principle were consistently applied, Aquinas could not say a great deal that he does say.

34. *Haer.* 5.16.2; see 5.14–16 (*ANF* 1:541–44). He who is *consubstantialem Patri secundum deitatem* is also *consubstantialem nobis eundem secundum humanitatem*, as Chalcedon puts it, and this double solidarity not only effects redemption but also completes the creation of man, informing and qualifying everything to be said about man. This, by the way, is not to make the cross of no effect; quite the contrary, the cross now shows up all the better as a truly free act of the incarnate one in response to the contingency of sin.

incarnation. The offer of grace *is* the incarnation, in which God is both utterly free and completely bound, as ever, by his own faithfulness. Moreover, in the incarnation man is at once utterly dependent and wholly free. It is only in this way that the problem of nature and grace, of *gratia creans* distinguished but not separated from *gratia elevans*, can be resolved. In the advent of man, *gratia creans* operates, as Thomas taught, with *gratia elevans* already in play and *gratia consummata* in view. It does so precisely because Jesus Christ is already in play and his glorification already in view.

Human nature is a gift given in connection with Jesus Christ. What it actually is depends upon, and is revealed by, what happens in the incarnation. Hence it cannot be known in its integrity in prescision from him; which is to say, in abstraction from or in denial of grace. As *Gaudium et spes* says at §19: "The dignity of man rests above all on the fact that he is called to communion with God. This invitation to converse with God is addressed to man as soon as he comes into being. For if man exists it is because God has *created* him through love, and through love continues to hold him in existence. He cannot live fully according to truth unless he freely acknowledges that love and entrusts himself to his Creator." But the call in question is concretely given in the person of Jesus Christ and not apart from him.[35] Creation is christocentric and christological. It is one and the same Jesus Christ who in the Spirit reveals to man what God is, and to man what man is, however and whenever he does it, whether in the garden of Eden with Adam or in the garden of Gethsemane with his disciples, or even in the midst of those who scarcely recognize him at all, though they are in fact learning from him.

If all that is true, however, then it is also true that man does naturally desire a supernatural end—and supernaturally desires a natural end—insofar as he desires Jesus Christ. In Jesus, man is for God and therefore also for himself and his neighbor. In Jesus God is for man, though God is for God even before Jesus.

Does this make nonsense of Thomas's claim that "to love God as the principle of all being pertains to natural love, but to love God as the object of beatitude pertains to the gratuitous love in which merit consists"?[36] Not at all.

---

35. Cf.§22. Let us call this *gratia vocans* and say that this is what it means to be created immediately by God.

36. *Quod.* 1.4.3. Nature's powers (*naturalia*) properly exercised are not meritorious as regards eternal life except in connection with *gratia gratum faciens* in the form of elevating or deifying grace. What fallen man does by his natural powers alone (*naturalia puris*) may help him in this life only; and after the fall they do not help him as they used to. For with the lapse from original justice man becomes subject to ignorance, loss of appetite for the good, and concupiscence; he therefore finds it harder to develop virtuous habits. Moreover, he is plagued by the sorrow and anxiety of no longer being able to achieve his supernatural end, since elevating grace is also withdrawn.

That also is true, as far as it goes. It's just that it doesn't go far enough, until it comes to Christ, the mediator between the natural and the supernatural.

It does, however, make nonsense of any angelomorphic construal of human beatitude. Deification is not the dissolution or even the marginalization of human nature but rather its coming to be as a real creaturely existence for and with God. The perfection or happiness attained *quodammodo* by nature is finally dependent on the happiness attained by grace. Natural gifts require transcendent gifts to sustain them—reason, for example, requires supernatural love in order to be and remain reasonable, as Augustine showed.[37] Nature, being made for grace, is deliberately incomplete and as such not to be considered fully explicable or viable on its own terms and in prescision from grace.[38] Irenaeus says rightly that this world was formed according to a provisional and temporary mode of being. It was formed, in other words, with a view not only to the grace of the incarnation but to that eventual perfection which the incarnate one would achieve. This is not the perfection of angels, though angels too will be perfected in it. It is the perfection of "real men," who precisely as such will pass beyond the angels into the true glory of God.[39]

Reckoning with Angelomorphism

This line of thought is quite foreign to Aquinas, who perhaps is too steeped in the angelomorphic assumptions of his era to grasp or develop it. He knows, of course, that human nature is changeable. At *ST* 3.1.1 (ad 1) he

---

37. With *Trin.* 13, cf. *SCG* 3.48.1: "If, then, ultimate human felicity does not consist in the knowledge of God, whereby He is known in general by all, or most, men, by a sort of confused appraisal, and again, if it does not consist in the knowledge of God which is known by way of demonstration in the speculative sciences, nor in the cognition of God whereby He is known through faith, as has been shown in the foregoing; and if it is not possible in this life to reach a higher knowledge of God so as to know Him through His essence, or even in such a way that, when the other separate substances are known, God might be known through the knowledge of them, as if from a closer vantage point, as we showed; and if it is necessary to identify ultimate felicity with some sort of knowledge of God, as we proved above; then it is not possible for man's ultimate felicity to come in this life."

38. Cf. *De caritate* 1, ad 16: "Through created charity the soul is raised up above nature, so that it is more perfectly ordered toward the end that the faculty of nature has." And at *Quod.* 1.7.2: "Now human perfection consists in the charity which joins a man to God." For it is indeed charity, as created grace within man and as consummating grace transcending man—both being mediated by Jesus Christ—that joins the soul to God and so perfects man.

39. *Haer.* 5.36.3; cf. Aquinas, *DV* 18.1, ad 5: "Man was made to see God, not in the beginning but in the last stage of his perfection [*non in principio, sed in ultimo suae perfectionis*]. Therefore, that he did not see God through His essence at the beginning of his existence was not the result of being hindered by some obstacle, but only the result of his own imperfection, because he did not then have that perfection which is needed to see the divine essence."

says: "The mystery of the Incarnation was not completed through God being changed in any way from the state in which He had been from eternity, but through His having united Himself to the creature in a new way, or rather through having united it to Himself. But it is fitting that a creature which by nature is mutable, should not always be in one way. And therefore, as the creature began to be, although it had not been before, so likewise, not having been previously united to God in Person, it was afterwards united to Him." Aquinas admits that "this taking hold of human nature unto the unity of the person of the Son of God exalts our nature beyond measure."[40] He says that "Christ was greater than the angels, not only in his Godhead, but also in his humanity, as having the fulness of grace and glory," though "in regard to his passibility he 'was made a little lower than the angels'" (*ST* 3.22.1, ad 1). Unfortunately, he does not draw from these facts the Irenaean conclusion. They do not alter his basic understanding of the relative dignity of human and angelic natures.[41]

In the *Prima pars* Aquinas distinguishes humans and angels as having a common intellectual nature but different modes of knowing. While this enhances the diversity and beauty of the cosmos and makes possible the perfection of knowledge, the rationality of man is in important respects inferior to that of the angels. "The very fact that the soul in a certain way requires the body for its operation, proves that the soul is endowed with a grade of intellectuality inferior to that of an angel, who is not united to a body."[42] Man and angel are alike in having a vocation to know God as first principle, in the different ways they do know God as first principle; and alike, too, in having a supernatural vocation to know God *in se*, God's self-knowledge being shared with them by grace in the manner appropriate to each. Yet to be lower than the angels seems to belong to man, even as fully graced. "Man is said to be 'a little less' not in regard to the kind of knowledge, because both man and angel share the same kind of knowledge, but according to the manner, because

---

40. *Super epistolam ad Hebraeos* 148 (re: Heb. 2:14–18).

41. He quotes Chrysostom: "'It is a great and marvelous thing for our flesh to be seated above and to be adorned by angels and archangels. As I turn this over in my mind, I experience excessive joy, imagining great things about the human race.'" Far from developing this joyous thought, however, Aquinas proceeds in the next paragrapah (§149) to argue that the incarnation would be more fitting were it to involve rather the assumption of an angelic nature, but for the fact that it depends not only on the dignity but on the need of the nature; apart, that is, from the fact that it is aimed at the reparation of sin, which in an angel is not possible.

42. *ST* 1.75.7, ad 3; cf. 1.51.1, ad 3 ("an intellectual substance which is not united to a body is more perfect than one which is united to a body") and 1.89.1. In Aquinas's "hierarchy of higher and lower liberties" (G. K. Chesterton, *Saint Thomas Aquinas* [New York: Doubleday, 1956], 164) this imperfection fixes man beneath the angels. Cf. Ps. 8:5; Heb. 2:7.

the angels know in a more excellent way than men."[43] This ought to undergo modification in the *Tertia pars*, but it does not.

For his part, Irenaeus understands man as "a little less than the angels" only for a little while. That is, man starts out lower than the angels but finishes higher, just because human nature itself isn't finished until it is vested with God in the incarnation and perfected in the ascension, something that never happens to angels or angelic nature. Hence man in due course surpasses the angels. But this "surpassing" Aquinas cannot conceive. The angels (as separate substances) already inhabit the highest place, the changeless empyrean, from their creation. Man is not fitted for that, inasmuch as he has a corporeal body that enmeshes him in the "necessities of the corruptible life." Nevertheless he will come there in the end, as God intended from the beginning, to join the angels in an everlasting beatitude when "all the business of the active life" has come to a halt.[44] "In this final consummation of things the lower spirits will receive the properties of the higher spirits, because men will be as the angels in heaven: and this will be accomplished by conferring the highest degree of perfection on that in which the human spirit agrees with the angelic."[45] The body will then share in the glory of the soul, which will be fixed in contemplation of God. Body and soul will be resplendently at rest. Man will be with the angels and like the angels, who in their simplicity are naturally more like God. Man (as an embodied soul) will retain what is proper to himself, but his life will consist in beholding God and not in anything else that we now associate with the human.[46] Indeed, it is not at all evident that the human qua human is of any great import in heaven, apart from the fact that the Son himself still wears the nature in which he redeemed humans.

43. "Although an angel and a soul are of one nature, namely, intellectual, nevertheless, the soul is united to a body . . . ; in this he [man] is a little less, because though the dignity of the soul is not destroyed by this union it is dulled and impeded from higher contemplation: 'The corruptible body is a load upon the soul' (Wis. 9:15) . . . Man is a little less not as to gratuitous gifts, in which 'they will be as the angels in heaven' (Mt. 22:30), but as to natural gifts" (*Sup. epis. ad Heb.* 110, trans. adapted).

44. *SCG* 4.82.24; cf. *Supp.* 91.1, ad 3 (emphasis added): "I say then that *the future renewal of the world preceded in the works of the six days by way of a remote likeness, namely in the glory and grace of the angels.* Moreover it preceded in the obediential potentiality which was then bestowed on the creature to the effect of its receiving this same renewal by the Divine agency."

45. *Supp.* 91.4. With this qualification he does not even go as far as Augustine, who at *CD* 21.24 has perfected men as "the equals of God's angels." At *ST* 3.1.2, however, Aquinas quotes Augustine from *Trin.* 13.17: "Since human nature is so united to God as to become one person, let not these proud spirits [fallen angels] dare to prefer themselves to man, because they have no bodies."

46. *ST* 1–2.3.5: "the last and perfect happiness, which we await in the life to come, consists entirely in contemplation."

That is a serious charge, requiring much elaboration, but it is warranted by Aquinas's notion of man's ultimate happiness. Happiness is that which man enjoys upon entering heaven and experiencing the *visio dei*. This heaven (the empyrean that stands above the stars) is a place of rest for both body and soul. There, "through the divine vision, intellectual substances obtain true felicity, in which their desires are completely brought to rest and in which is the full sufficiency of all the goods which, according to Aristotle, are required for happiness."[47] These goods include the peace of the body, but they are ultimately intellective goods, contemplative goods, including the highest of all goods, the good of seeing God through God, and therefore (with and like God) of having all knowledge all at once.[48] When God himself passes into the intellect to enable it to see God, the intellect is absorbed in God's eternity. It remains distinct from God and retains the knowledge of itself as a created self, and it does not comprehend God as God does; for this is not a Eunomian sort of felicity but a felicity that passes all understanding, whether it is the felicity of a man or of an angel. The point, however, is that it is not a specifically human felicity but rather the kind of felicity that belongs to the angels or "separate substances"—or perhaps we must say: which Aquinas, going well beyond Scripture and tradition, supposes to belong to them.[49]

Here in the world below there is no real analogue to be found other than that which appears in the spiritual life of the philosopher or the scholar-monk. In Thomas's own words, "there is nothing in this life so like this ultimate and perfect felicity as the life of those who contemplate truth, to the extent that it is possible in this life . . . [T]he contemplation of truth begins in this life, but reaches its climax in the future; whereas the active and civic life does not go beyond the limits of this life."[50] The heavenly, as he understands it, both as a place and as a condition of bliss, excludes everything animal and political, just because it is life in God. Though it does not (as in gnostic or Origenist heresies) exclude the body of flesh and bone, it does exclude time and motion and bodily activity. Its Edenic features are all features of the mind and

---

47. *SCG* 3.63.9.

48. *SCG* 3.60.1; cf. 3.60.3, 5; 3.61.2–5; and 3.62.2 ("the aforementioned vision, which makes intellectual creatures happy, is not in time but in eternity").

49. *ST* 1–2.5.5; cf. 1.12.4. In the state of true felicity "the soul will understand in the way that separate substances understand" (*SCG* 3.48.15). "And so, man's ultimate felicity will lie in the knowledge of God that the human mind has after this life, according to the way in which separate substances know Him. For which reason our Lord promises us 'a reward in heaven' and says that the saints 'shall be as the angels . . . who always see God in heaven,' as it is said" (*SCG* 3.48.15, which indulges in the worst sort of prooftexting with this appeal to Matt. 5:12, 18:10, and 22:30).

50. *SCG* 3.63.10.

not of the body. Biblical texts suggesting otherwise must be read not literally but metaphorically.[51]

Now this take on our future felicity creates a number of difficulties, even for Thomas, with respect to the humanity of man. The *Supplementum*, at 91.1, provides a window through which we can view the big picture as he sees it. It also affords some understanding of the justification he offers for minimizing our engagement with the corporeal creation while not doing away with it altogether (something Scripture, no matter how it is read, will not permit). Referring us again to Psalm 8, Thomas says:

> We believe all corporeal things to have been made for man's sake, wherefore all things are stated to be subject to him. Now they serve man in two ways, first, as sustenance to his bodily life, secondly, as helping him to know God, inasmuch as man sees the invisible things of God by the things that are made. Accordingly glorified man will nowise need creatures to render him the first of these services, since his body will be altogether incorruptible, the Divine power effecting this through the soul which it will glorify immediately. Again man will not need the second service as to intellective knowledge, since by that knowledge he will see God immediately in His essence. The carnal eye, however, will be unable to attain to this vision of the Essence; wherefore that it may be fittingly comforted in the vision of God, it will see the Godhead in Its corporeal effects, wherein manifest proofs of the Divine majesty will appear, especially in Christ's flesh, and secondarily in the bodies of the blessed, and afterwards in all other bodies. Hence those bodies also will need to receive a greater inflow from the Divine goodness than now, not indeed so as to change their species, but so as to add a certain perfection of glory: and such will be the renewal of the world. Wherefore at the one same time, the world will be renewed, and man will be glorified.

The first difficulty to be noted is that this picture offers a much too simple account of the way in which corporeal things serve man and of the way in which man relates to the world in which he is embedded. Moreover, it errs simply by virtue of being too pictorial. The faculty of vision entirely dominates. God will be seen immediately by intellective vision[52] and mediately by carnal vision,

---

51. "Therefore the last and perfect happiness, which we await in the life to come, consists entirely in contemplation" (*ST* 1–2.3.5). "These goods that [presently] serve for the animal life are incompatible with that spiritual life wherein perfect Happiness consists. Nevertheless in that Happiness there will be the aggregate of all good things, because whatever good there be in these things, we shall possess it all in the Supreme Fount of goodness" (1–2.4.8, ad 2; on the metaphorical reading of contrary texts, see ad 1).

52. "Thus, then, shall we see God face to face, in the sense that we shall see Him without a medium, as is true when we see a man face to face" (*SCG* 3.51.5; but cf. 3.61.5).

aided by the interior light in each creature that results from the greater inflow of the divine goodness. The entire universe will stand, motionless yet glimmering, like a grand portrait revealed and, in an eternal moment, revealing its Creator.[53] Think Moses and the seventy elders, feasting with God on Sinai but transfixed by the *visio dei* in such a fashion that all merely human forms of feasting cease. Or a Eucharist in which, at the moment of consecration, the divine substance is seen, and seen in such a fashion that the liturgy itself ceases—neither word nor gesture nor music nor temporal measure of any kind remaining. Think a world in which all lesser ends are done away with now that the final end has been reached; a world in which man is so absorbed with God, and all things so ordered to God, that no further ordering is required or even possible.

Is this unfair to Thomas? Let us fill it out a little, lest we misrepresent him. Besides the angels, the new creation will comprise the heavenly bodies, the elements, and man; for only such are "subjects of incorruption." The heavenly bodies will not move at all, and neither then will there be any "mutual action and passion" in the lower elements. There will, however, "be some movement in glorified bodies." After all (and here is some welcome christology), "Christ's body was moved in His ascension." In the general resurrection the saints' bodies will likewise "arise from the earth [and] ascend to the empyrean."[54] And "even after they have climbed the heavens," he says, "it is likely that they will sometimes move according as it pleases them; so that by actually putting into practice that which is in their power, they may show forth the excellence of

---

53. I am put in mind here of a passage from Barth, who in *CD* 3.3 presses still further the logic of a creation in which "time shall be no more." This, he says, is how the creature will persist: "In all the unrest of its being in time it will be enfolded by the rest of God, and in Him it will itself be at rest" (90). For Barth, of course, temporality belongs to the creature and cannot be removed from it. Hence in eternity the creature "will only *have been*" (89, emphasis added). What will abide in eternity is essentially the light of revelation, the light that is the glory of God himself. This becomes a starkly heterodox claim: "In the final act of salvation history, i.e., in the revelation of Jesus Christ as the Foundation and Deliverer and Head of the whole of creation, the history of creation will also reach its goal and end. It will not need to progress any further, it will have fulfilled its purpose. Everything that happened in the course of that history will then take place together as a recapitulation of all individual events. It will be made definitive as the temporal end of the creature beyond which it cannot exist any more. Its life will then be over, its movement and development completed, its notes sounded, its colours revealed, its thinking thought, its words said, its deeds done, its contacts and relationships with other creatures and their mutual interaction closed, the possibilities granted to it exploited and exhausted. And in all this it will somehow have a part in that which Jesus Christ has been and done as its Foundation and Deliverer and Head. It will not need any continuance of temporal existence. And since the creature itself will not be there, time which is the form of its existence will not be there" (87f.). I do not mean to confuse Barth and Barth—who sounds a great deal more orthodox elsewhere—much less Barth and Thomas. Reading Barth, however, may send us back to Thomas with new questions.

54. See *Supp.* 74.5, 84.2, and 91.5.

Divine wisdom, and that furthermore their vision may be refreshed by the beauty of the variety of creatures" in which that wisdom is displayed. The motion of these godly tourists, in other words, will both demonstrate the power of the soul over the body and make for a better view of things created; "for sense can only perceive that which is present, although glorified bodies can perceive from a greater distance than non-glorified bodies." As a change of place it will also entail a form of temporality. "Although after the resurrection the time which is the measure of the heaven's movement will be no more, there will nevertheless be time resulting from the before and after in any kind of movement."[55]

These concessions to our creaturehood do not amount to much, however, since they rule out most of what we know as creaturely. The creatures to be viewed, we should remark, will not include anything organic, for the organic will have no place in the new creation. There will be no plants, no animals, no wheeling stars above or pulsing quarks below.[56] The creatures in question are all things to be seen, not things with which to engage. There will be no lesser ends to be hierarchically arranged by man under God. There will be no bodily effort; no building or constructing; no political life, the only purpose of which, according to Aquinas, is to compensate for the fall.[57] There will be no stories to live or to tell. For the spiritual eye will be wholly absorbed in the vision of God, and the carnal eye will view the creatures of God only so that it may in its fashion share in that vision. There will be refreshment of our carnal vision—though why it might be needed remains obscure—but there will be no progress in knowledge or felicity, no *epektasis*.[58]

Will the World Still Turn and Man Still Be Man?

The difficulties we are presently considering are bound up with his view of the location and nature of the empyrean, but Thomas binds his eschatology

55. *Supp.* 84.3, ad 5. The time he has in view here appears to be continuous with the time we already know; moreover, the space is the very same that we already know. How this local motion involves no decay is not easy to say.

56. Plants and animals and organic processes "will altogether cease after the renewal of the world" (*Supp.* 91.5); "for whatever remains after the world has been renewed will remain for ever, generation and corruption being done away."

57. Cf. *SCG* 3.37.7.

58. "Again, the ultimate end of man brings to a termination man's natural appetite, in the sense that, once the end is acquired, nothing else will be sought. For, if he is still moved onward to something else, he does not yet have the end in which he may rest" (*SCG* 3.48.2; cf. 3.48.3). By contrast, Irenaeus taught that it belongs to the creature to make progress (*proficere*) by constant reception of the goodness of God in which it perfectly abides; see my *Ascension Theology* (London: T&T Clark, 2011), 130.

far too closely not only to the pre-Copernican cosmology but also to other problematic features of the Greek worldview, including a view of movement inadequately revised by trinitarian insights and a view of change too tightly tied to entropy. "In every change there is an element of decay," he insists[59]— but is that a necessary characteristic of change, or only of change under the conditions of the world that now is? Should we agree with Thomas that human nature, directed to its proper end, is directed toward a condition of changelessness, or with Irenaeus that it is directed only toward a condition exclusive of decline or decay?[60] Should we follow Thomas in his projection from the laws of physics, as he mistakenly supposed them to be, to a belief that "immobility is simply nobler than movement," that space can exist time-lessly, luminosity without energy, the human body without any connection to other organic life, etc.?[61] The new heavens and earth, transformed by the very power of God that created the cosmos in the first place, will no doubt operate according to revised laws that we cannot as yet anticipate. All eschatology therefore requires at once the modesty, together with the certainty, exhibited by Paul in 1 Corinthians 15. But Thomas violates this modesty by way of his projections and extrapolations.

A simple question suffices to make the point. When creation has been renewed and the whole man, as the Church believes, wholly enjoys God, will the world still turn? Aquinas did not know, of course, that it turns now, and we perhaps cannot know whether it will turn then. What we do know is that there will be no more "night" (that is, nothing in which sin may hide or evil lurk) and no more "sea" (no consequent chaos of the nations) and no more curse upon nature, with its attendant suffering and tears (Rev. 22). But Aquinas thinks he knows something more than that. He thinks he knows that the world will stop; or rather, from his perspective, that the movement of the heavens will cease, and he thinks he knows why. Taking up Aristotle's maxim that "all movement is for some end" and coupling it with the premise that

59. The sensible creation "'will be delivered from the servitude of corruption,' i.e., change-ableness: because in every change there is an element of decay, as Augustine says and the Philosopher too in *Physics* VIII" (*In Rom.* C.8 L.4, 668, quoted from *Commentary on the Letter of Saint Paul to the Romans*, trans. F. R. Larcher, Latin/English Edition of the Works of St. Thomas Aquinas: Biblical Commentaries [Lander, WY: Aquinas Institute for the Study of Doctrine, 2012], 37:223). At §672 Aquinas adds that by the "groaning" of creation (8:22) "is understood decay, which is an element of local motion, inasmuch as a body ceases to be in one place and begins to be in another." At §674 he excludes angels from this groaning, "because they already have the glory, the likeness of which we await" (per Matt. 22:30).

60. Irenaeus too was ignorant of these things, naturally, but drew no such conclusions. He knew better than to practice the kind of natural theology into which Thomas sometimes strayed.

61. *Supp.* 91.2 (cf. *sed contra* and ad 10).

"all movement for an end ceases when the end is obtained,"[62] he draws his conclusion that the heavenly movements will cease, and a great many other things with them, including cosmic time. The creation is for man, and man is for God, and when man is found in God, it all comes to a halt. Misreading the *tempus amplius non erit* of Revelation 10:6 ("there shall be no more delay") as "time shall be no longer," Thomas posits a cosmos in which man will then exist pretty much as he supposes the angels now to exist.

Thomas's conclusion that the heavenly movements will cease is true enough, if the heavens, like the earth, are indeed to "pass away with a loud noise" before being renewed.[63] But his argument about ends is not sound. It ignores the fact that many movements have multiple ends, that the movements of love (if the love is God's) never cease, and that the movements of creatures, including heavenly creatures, will persist precisely insofar as they serve the purposes of love.[64] It fails indeed to notice that there are movements besides those of the eye that serve the purposes of love, including the very vibrations of the air.

"My soul thirsts for God, for the living God," exclaims the psalmist. "When shall I come and behold the face of God?" And he adds: "I will go to the altar of God, to God my exceeding joy; and I will praise thee with the lyre, O God, my God."[65] The lyre serves music, and music serves love. It serves joy, too, along with sorrow. If there are men in heaven—that is, in the world to come—surely there will be music in heaven, and it will be the music of men in glorious counterpoint to the music of angels, who at the foundation of the world sang for joy. What and how that music shall be, when all is renewed and there is no sorrow, eschatological modesty forbids us to say; yet it will certainly be a curious sort of music if it lacks not only the lyre but any analogy in the movement of the heavens and of the elements themselves.

Again, are we being too hard on Thomas if we say his eschatology has still an Origenist hue? That human destiny tends here to the angelomorphic, or more precisely to the seraphic, in that it makes contemplation of God (both in himself and in the reflected light of creation) the *only* feature of eternal life rather than its quickening and governing feature? That his view of finality itself is flawed because it cannot readily accommodate the active life except

---

62. *Supp.* 91.2.

63. Though that is not how Aquinas reads 2 Pet. 3:10. See *Supp.* 74.4, which claims that only the atmosphere or "aerial heavens" shall be cleansed by fire; no mention is made of passing away.

64. These purposes cannot be reduced, as claimed in *Supp.* 91.1, to two: the sustenance of man while he begets (until the number of the elect is complete) and the showing of the invisible through the visible. Neither can it be assumed that the latter is entirely redundant in glory.

65. Pss. 42:2; 43:4; cf. Job 38:7.

as a faint analogue (sending oneself here or there to view this or that) of the contemplative life?[66]

It may be said in reply that, since nothing can compare with God, to pine for anything other or "more" than the pure vision of God—"I would have nothing but You, Lord!"—is to pine for man's imperfect past rather than for man's perfect future. It may even be said that it is to affirm our fall into sin rather than our rise into grace. It may also be pointed out that what Thomas intends is a proper baptism of the *exitus/reditus* grammar of the Greeks, yet without prejudice to the principle that grace perfects nature. But does grace really perfect nature if the organic is rejected as such, if progress is as much to be overcome as regress, if a plurality of lesser ends is incompatible with a final end, if for man to reach his final end, to have God himself, means that he must leave off with every lesser end? Is that not really just to make the old Greek and pagan mistake, which the grammar in question can never resolve, of supposing that the One and the many, or God and the creature, are somehow inherently opposed?

I will concede that Thomas's eschatology is more Christian than Greek, more Augustinian than Platonist or Aristotelian. But its effect, nonetheless, is to render the biblical grammar of Eden, of Sinai, of Zion—of walking and talking, hearing and obeying, receiving and stewarding, going out and coming in—a lost language, articulating things belonging only to the beginning but not to the end. In the end there are no ends (at least none to be actively pursued) but God himself, the End who in surpassing even our intellect reduces us to a purely intellective form of life: that of our highest faculty contemplating, without distraction, its highest object.[67]

What Thomas fails to consider, unlike Irenaeus or Augustine, is that Christian eschatology has an obligation to show that the final end of man is not the dismissal of all distractions but the dismissal of distraction itself, that the perfecting of nature does not mean the cessation of the active life but its true harmony with the contemplative.

To ask another simple and pointed question: Is man really man if he is merely a seraph with (unused) muscle and bone? And does Jesus really teach

66. Indeed, it is not clear how it can accommodate it at all. If "man's ultimate felicity consists only in the contemplation of God" (*SCG* 3.37.9), and "if that knowledge of God . . . , when acquired, leaves no knowledge of a knowable object to be desired" (3.39.6), and if indeed the mind or intellect is fulfilled in a single eternal act, how then does it either desire or direct the bodily movements that serve the refreshing of the carnal eye?

67. Cf. *ST* 1–2.3.5 with *Supp.* 91.4: "Now in this final consummation of things the lower spirits will receive the properties of the higher spirits, because men will be as the angels in heaven: and this will be accomplished by conferring the highest degree of perfection on that in which the human spirit agrees with the angelic."

what Aquinas frequently asserts, viz., that man shall be, in all important respects, like the angels? Jesus, to be sure, teaches that men shall be like the angels in not marrying or giving in marriage. It is quite safe to assume that this means also not copulating or multiplying, since man, like the angel, will not die. Of course this means a fundamental change in the nature of organic life—so fundamental that it is at present incomprehensible to us. But Jesus teaches no such doctrine, even as regards angels, as that everything belonging to the active life shall cease.[68] When he says, "Blessed are the pure in heart, for they shall see God," he says no such thing as that the contemplative and the active are ultimately incompatible or that perfection and pursuit are incompatible. Were that so in God himself, we would be forced to ask how God came to be our creator in the first place—unless after all it was in the Greek rather than the Christian sense, viz., without deliberation or intention. And were it so in man, we would be forced to ask what point there was to Jesus's promise that the meek shall inherit the earth.

The psychology and sociology of the world to come cannot be based primarily on the seraph, or even on the scholar-monk in corporate or solitary meditation on God and the works of God. It must be based more fundamentally on the *agape* feast and the eucharistic liturgy. What Augustine undertakes to show in the nineteenth book of *The City of God*, namely, that the Christian can, with much greater consistency than the pagan, affirm that "the wise man's life is social," Aquinas unfortunately shies away from. Not entirely, of course—he allows that Christ is present, the friend is present,[69] indeed all the angels and saints are present—but nonetheless noticeably. If he can affirm with Augustine, he is much more reticent in affirming, that the

68. Nor does Jesus say that the glory of the human body will be only a reflection of the glory of the soul. Thomas seems to lean in that direction when he addresses the (supposed) native inferiority of the female body: "In the ultimate state, however, such is the subjection [of body to soul] that the quality of body follows the virtue of the mind; whence according to the diversity of merits one soul will be more worthy than another soul, and the body more glorious; whence there will not be a difference on account of diverse sex." (*Scriptum super Sententiis* II, 21, qu. 2, art. 2) We must do better than that if we think the human body, both male and female, something with eschatological (hence supra-reproductive) value in its own right.

69. *ST* 1–2.4.8 makes a qualified allowance for society in the form of friendship: "But if we speak of the perfect happiness which will be in our heavenly Fatherland, the fellowship of friends is not essential to Happiness; since man has the entire fulness of his perfection in God. But the fellowship of friends conduces to the well-being [*bene esse*] of happiness. Hence Augustine says (*Gen. ad lit.* viii, 25) that 'the spiritual creatures receive no other interior aid to happiness than the eternity, truth, and charity of the Creator. But if they can be said to be helped from without, perhaps it is only by this, that they see one another and rejoice in God, at their fellowship.'" Note once again an emphasis on the faculty of vision, here shared by Augustine; cf. *ST* 1–2.4.2.

life of the world to come will be that "of the supremely ordered, supremely cooperative, association of those who enjoy God and one another in God."[70] If he can say it at all, he has much more difficulty saying that the peace of the heavenly city, in which man shall see God and live, is a peace at once personal and political, contemplative and active—that it is not all contemplation completed by vision, that it does not all reduce to the stillness of vision.[71]

Now we have already seen that it does not all reduce to the stillness of vision. The saints in the resurrection shall move their bodies here and there for the sake of a better view of God's works. Aquinas even quotes the saying, "They shall run to and fro like sparks through the stubble."[72] But this only leads him into contradiction, something one can rarely say of Aquinas. How is it that the mind that has all its knowledge at once, that is wholly absorbed in eternity, turns without prejudice to its eternity to the directing of these tours of the body, determining the places to be visited and creating the time that is the consequence of local motion, with its before and after? On the traditional view this is not the kind of problem that it is in Aquinas, because the tradition has not committed itself to the particular view of eternity that Aquinas adopts—a view that makes his language about eternity problematic, if not incoherent, at several other points as well.[73] Of course his remarks about time and space are not only problematic, they are often simply wrong, though he can hardly be blamed for that. And his notion of a body not only fully subservient to the soul, but acted upon by nothing but the soul, calls into question the very meaning of the word "body."

Surely we ought not to follow him in such things or on the path that leads to them. Not only because of the reductionism, the incoherence, or the contrariety to Scripture but also because of the constraint imposed on our eschatological vision—a constraint that sets grace *against* nature. Thomas tells us that "all human functions may be seen to subserve the contemplation of truth," and perhaps that is so. But how do things look if we substitute for the contemplation of truth "the love of God and of neighbor"?[74] Does that

70. *Civ.* 19.13.

71. Or rather that the vision in question is the sort of vision that one finds in the final chapters of the Apocalypse.

72. *Supp.* 84.2 ("among the reeds"), after Wis. 3:7.

73. See again n. 66 above, which queries the notion that the mind caught up in an eternal simultaneity can or should or would descend to govern bodily movements. There are also inconsistencies in his notion of incorruptibility, for example, and some confusion between simultaneity and sempiternity (evident in *SCG* 3.60 and elsewhere).

74. Of course he accepts the "of God" but has difficulty with the "of neighbor," which cannot be subsumed so readily under the contemplation of truth.

not open up a different way of thinking about fulfillment and felicity? At all events, it points us to the underlying problem, which is not cosmological but christological.

Aquinas's Christological Deficit

It is one thing to say that God alone is our happiness and another to say that we are happy in no other way than by a timeless act of the speculative intellect. Again, it is one thing to say that we are made to be happy through direct knowledge of God and another to say that, since we are made to be happy, we are made ultimately for contemplation and for the intellective vision alone.[75] To think of felicity like that makes it very difficult to think of felicity in terms of a life mediated by Jesus Christ, the incarnate Son of God, because what we are trying to think of is something by nature *im*mediate. That we find in Aquinas's treatment of felicity, and in his vision of human destiny, a striking paucity of christology and ecclesiology should not surprise us. He is wonderfully clear about the fact that Christ is the way to the *visio dei* and that this way leads through the Church and her sacraments. But for him the *visio dei* itself, in which lies our perfect felicity, is something we arrive at only at the end of the way—through it and because of it, certainly, but only in some sense after it. The *visio* includes awareness of the mediation of Christ but includes it intellectively and eternally, all at once. To behold God face to face is to know him all at once, directly and not indirectly.

The question must therefore be raised: When Jesus delivers up the kingdom to the Father, that God may be all in all, does he cease to be our ruler, our mediator, our great high priest? Does he or doesn't he continue (if continue is the right word) to communicate to us the effects of his priesthood? Does the active life altogether cease for Jesus also?

We know that Jesus came to us not as a contemplative but as an itinerate preacher and prophet and wonder-worker and messianic claimant. We know that he went home to his Father as our great *leitourgos* and high priest and indeed as the triumphant messianic king, that he sits in heavenly session and will come again as lord and judge of the world. We know that he wept with us, suffered with us, shared our sorrows, yet somehow was happy even in his unhappiness. We know that he is happy, with the full felicity possible for man, and that he is not in his heavenly session inactive. And what are we

---

75. These are all things that Thomas does say, and we should note that he thus correlates man's natural and supernatural ends in the tightest possible way. Unfortunately he does not correlate them with his christology.

to say of his felicity in the world to come? If we try to grasp it in Thomistic terms it does not so much appear to us as escape us. Will the active life cease for Jesus? Will his kingdom and priesthood come to an end?

Thomas insists that the saints in heaven require "consummation through Christ himself, on whom their glory depends."[76] He confesses with St. Paul, and with the entire Church, that his kingdom shall have no end. However, he does not make clear what this means. Nor does he treat the happiness of Jesus Christ. He turns far too readily from his humanity to his divinity, insofar as he considers his consummating role at all. The *Supplementum* follows suit, looking to the humanity only for evidence of the divinity. What the outer eye beholds of Christ will aid the inner eye in its contemplation of God; but it is the divinity beheld by the inner eye that beatifies, and this latter beholding is all that really concerns Aquinas.[77]

This failure to analyze happiness christologically, or to consider the role of Jesus in the life of the world to come, suggests that Thomas's view of heavenly felicity is not a product of the evangel but by and large an inference from questionable philosophical and faulty cosmological premises. It seems no accident that he reads Christ out of some of the key biblical texts to which he appeals. Take 1 John 3:1–3, for example, which is a favorite both in the *Summa contra Gentiles* and in the *Summa Theologiae*: "See what love the Father has given us, that we should be called children of God; and so we are. The reason why the world does not know us is that it did not know him. Beloved, we are God's children now; it does not yet appear what we shall be, but we know that *when he appears we shall be like him, for we shall see him as he is*. And every one who thus hopes in him purifies himself as he is pure." The italicized clauses Thomas takes as references to God and to the vision of God,[78] not (as is plainly demanded in the context of the letter) to Jesus and hence to our entrance into his kingdom. Something similar happens in his use of Titus 2:13, to offer another example.[79]

---

76. *ST* 3.22.5, ad 1. He alludes here to the Day of Atonement ritual as a type, and to Heb. 9:11, which speaks of Christ as "a high priest of the good things that have come." See also *ST* 3.57.6. Cf. Paul O'Callaghan, *Christ Our Hope* (Washington, DC: Catholic University of America Press, 2011), 184–86.

77. This tension between the outer and the inner eye is exacerbated in the spirituality of the *Theologica Germanica*, especially in chap. 7.

78. See *ST* 1.12.1 and *SCG* 3.51.6. Thomists (see, e.g., White, "Imperfect Happiness," 271) often take this up uncritically.

79. Perhaps it is just by way of economy that *In Rom.* 8, §658 truncates its quotation of Titus 2:13, such that *expectantes beatam spem et adventum gloriae magni Dei* is not completed by *et salvatoris nostri Iesu Christi*. But I am arguing that the economy seems to extend to the whole analysis of the new creation, such that it never becomes properly christological.

It may be observed, parenthetically, that the uncertain relation between the mediatorial work of Christ and the beatific vision is somewhat exacerbated by *Benedictus deus*, in which Benedict XII declares that

> since the ascension of our Lord and Saviour Jesus Christ into heaven, already before they take up their bodies again and before the general judgment, [purified souls] have been, are, and will be with Christ in heaven, in the heavenly kingdom and paradise, joined to the company of the holy angels. Since the passion and death of the Lord Jesus Christ, these souls have seen and see the divine essense with an intuitive vision and even face to face, *without the mediation of any creature by way of object of vision*; rather the divine essence immediately manifests itself to them, plainly, clearly and openly, and in this vision they enjoy the divine essence. Moreover, by this vision and enjoyment the souls of those who have already died are truly blessed and have eternal life and rest.[80]

Thomas himself is cautious about the fullness of human felicity before the resurrection of the body and about the soul's perfection in its intermediate state, since (as Augustine says) it naturally desires to rule the body.[81] But Benedict's declaration of the saintly soul's ability to "see" God even when absent from the body, much as the blessed angels see God, invites questions about the further necessity or utility of the mediator apart from his role in raising the body.[82] Given Benedict's reckoning with the cross, resurrection, and ascension as the *conditio sine qua non* for this blessedness, however, "without the mediation of any creature by way of object of vision" cannot be taken to mean without the mediation of Christ. Christ himself is not seen or heard or touched bodily until the general resurrection. (How could he be, since the saints in question lack bodily capacities?) Yet he is heard and seen in the intuitive fashion that the soul may "hear" and "see" at all, and God is "heard" and "seen" in, with, and through him. It is no purpose of this papal constitution, nor indeed would it be orthodox, to suggest that the blessed see

---

80. *Benedictus deus* (1336), emphasis added. "Such a vision and enjoyment of the divine essence do away with the acts of faith and hope in these souls," faith and hope being virtues required only *in via*.

81. See *ST* 1–2.4.5. "Happiness belongs to man in respect of his intellect," says Thomas (*ST* 1–2.4.5, ad 3); "and, therefore, since the intellect remains, it can have Happiness. Thus the teeth of an Ethiopian, in respect of which he is said to be white, can retain their whiteness, even after extraction." That is, the rational soul of a man, in respect of which he can be said to be like (as well as unlike) an angel, can retain its rationality even after the death of the body and the cessation of the activity of the brain. Yet there is more to man than his rational soul, and this has a bearing on the extent, though not the intensity, of his happiness.

82. Benedict, being less cautious on this point even than Aquinas, runs this risk—if not indeed the risk that people will mistake the Ethiopian's teeth for the Ethiopian himself!

God in and with Christ but no longer through Christ. But if through him, then of course still, in that sense, corporeally (for Christ is corporeal) and indeed ecclesially, and only so intuitively and directly, as those who have departed to be with Christ, "absent from the body and at home with the Lord" (2 Cor. 5:8).

If it be asked what is added in the resurrection to this heavenly beatitude, a fuller answer must be given than is found either in Thomas or in *Benedictus deus*: the restoration and perfection of the soul's rule over the body, yes, and with it every blessing that belongs to the race to which God has joined himself in the incarnation; the blessedness of the properly *human* race, into which even the angels long to look. For however the latter see God, and however exalted their place in the new creation and in the eternal city of God, they never have or will see God in the same way, or with the same intimacy, as those who see God ecclesially through, with, and in Jesus Christ.[83] It is Thomas's failure to consider the unique dignity of the human race in Christ, and its unique felicity in and with Christ, that constitutes his christological deficit.

On Not Distorting, or De-naturing, Nature

In his commentary on Romans, Thomas indicates that creation waits in two ways for its end: naturally for its natural end (to be free from servitude to corruption) and supernaturally for its supernatural end (to be clothed with the glory of the children of God). But does freedom from servitude to corruption mean that motion and change must cease? Why not say instead that motion should fulfill, and keep on fulfilling, rather than deprive or vacate? And that this it will do, when the curse is removed and the Spirit adorns man with the natural powers proper to him as well as with the supernatural gifts that will make all his creaturely motions, whether physical or psychical, proper analogues (in their fashion) of the divine motions of the Trinity itself?[84] Is there not more christological and theological justification for the latter than for the former?

83. Cf. Eph. 3:14–19: The Father, "from whom every family in heaven and on earth is named," grants through the Spirit an indwelling of Christ and with it the power "to comprehend with all the saints what is the breadth and length and height and depth," and so to be "filled with all the fulness of God."

84. As the Apocalypse declares, the holy city comes down "out of heaven from God, having the glory of God," and "by its light shall the nations walk." The vision is plainly Edenic, on the one hand—replete with references to the water of life and the tree of life—and civic or Zionist on the other. It is messianic and covenantal, like the whole prophetic tradition that it recapitulates. "The throne of God and of the Lamb shall be in it, and his servants shall worship him; they shall see his face, and his name shall be on their foreheads . . . And they shall reign forever and ever." Of course it is possible to take all this imagery and distill it into the faculty of carnal vision, on the one hand, and (more essentially) into the intellectual vision that man

God is self-moved and moving in love. And the movement of God toward man is just that: "Behold," says the great voice from the throne, "the dwelling of God is with men. He will dwell with them, and they shall be his people, and God himself will be with them" (Rev. 21:3). The world, as he will then establish it, and the man who beholds his glory in it, will be eternal but not time-less, fixed in and on God but not motionless. For time, when not corrupted by sin, is not the opposite of eternity, or movement the opposite of eternal rest, any more than the creature is the opposite of the Creator, who in the incarnation becomes a creature.

The movement of the divine love that through Christ enlightens and sustains man, and the fire of judgment that purifies the creation of which man is a part, will not mean the cessation of the movement of the heavens or the cessation of life on earth. It will mean only the cessation of sin and mourning and death. It will not mean even what Paul Griffiths, in *Decreation*, thinks it will mean: a repetitive stasis in which motion and time loop back upon themselves in liturgical "folds" lacking directionality or progress.[85] Griffiths's vision is more christocentric and anthropocentric than Aquinas's; but his rejection of *epektasis* bespeaks the diminishment and not, as he supposes, the perfection of creaturehood. He, too, falsely restricts the options in eschatology by seeing "metronomic" motion and time as strictly fallen—not suffering the curse, but part and parcel of the curse. Hence he follows the angelic doctor to a largely seraphic end for man, albeit one described with a more Dante-like dynamism (and more attention to the body) than Thomas himself manages. Grace does not perfect nature but again divests it of things proper to it.[86]

"Behold, I make all things new!" Unless we give full weight to this "all things," we are likely to engage eschatologically in a truncation of our humanity

shares with the angels. But that would be a misappropriation of the imagery—a reading at odds with the whole tradition from Genesis to Revelation that the latter brings to fruition. It would be to mistake the seeing of the seer for the thing itself.

85. See Paul Griffiths, *Decreation: The Last Things of All Creatures* (Waco: Baylor University Press, 2014), 21ff., 25f., 95ff., 215ff.

86. To make good on this charge would require much more space than I can allot to it here. Griffiths asserts that "a creature with an endlessly novel future lacks a *novissimum*" (ibid., 25) but that is not so if God, in and through Christ, makes himself the creature's final habitation and, as such, his *novissimum* (or the condition for his *novissimum*) in both senses of that word. "Endlessly novel" is in any case a prejudicial way to state the concept of *epektasis*, since it does not allow for the possibility that resurrection time is neither something that simply goes on and on nor something that goes "systolically" in and out or back and forth or round and round. And at the end of the day it isn't altogether clear that Griffiths's repetitive, "internally complex" stasis is so very different from "simple stasis." The one is a kind of liturgical dance, so to say, and the other a kind of eucharistic adoration, but does either do full justice to biblical visions of redeemed and fulfilled humanity?

that requires also a truncation of the biblical and patristic tradition, famously captured by Irenaeus: "For since there are to be real men, so must there also be a real establishment [*plantationem*], that they vanish not away among non-existent things, but progress [*proficere*] among those which have an actual existence. For neither is the substance nor the essence [*substantia neque materia conditionis*] of the creation annihilated—for faithful is he who established it—but 'the fashion [*figura*] of the world passes away'; that is, those things among which transgression has occurred, since man has grown old in them."[87]

The relevance of all this to our earlier discussion should be obvious. For if we treat "human nature itself, which is the substratum of the goods of grace,"[88] as something that is aimed (and by grace arrives) at a point of rest in which the only remaining distinction between man and angel is that the soul of man makes resplendent a body the angel does not have, then this very substratum begins to look rather thin and pale. Which exacerbates the tension between those who wish to say that nature is *for* grace and those who worry that nature may be *lost* to grace, rather than perfected by grace. But we ought to be able to say that nature is for grace without fearing that grace will eliminate nature. I would contend that we cannot do so, though Thomas would have us do so, without correcting his eschatology, which to a serious extent de-natures nature. Grace and nature are bound to collide once they quit their christological orbit.

It remains only to ask whether Thomas's eschatology *can* be corrected without other quite fundamental adjustments to his project. I confess that I am not sure how to answer. Plainly there are weaknesses in his view of nature that he has not allowed christology to correct. But that the requisite adjustments might be made (if we confine ourselves to the *Summa Theologiae*) along the trajectory of the unfinished *Tertia pars* seems to me a reasonable working hypothesis. No doubt its proper completion, which the *Supplementum* certainly did not achieve, would require significant conversions in Thomas's thought. I will refrain from joining those who suggest that some of these conversions may have occurred already in the mystical experience that, according to legend, led him to leave off working on the project, and say only that I would like very much to see what he would afterward have written, had he written. Of course I am hardly alone in that!

---

87. *Haer.* 5.36.1 (*PG* 7.2, col. 1221).
88. *In Rom.* 8, §659.

3

Thinking with Luther about Justification and Sanctification

As we mark the 500th anniversary of the Protestant Reformation, which some date to the posting of Luther's ninety-five theses in AD 1517, we may do so in a spirit of chastened humility for the rending of Christ's ecclesial body, and for the subsequent decimation of Christianity in the West, or in some more pugnacious fashion. It is even possible to combine the two approaches, and when dealing with Luther, whose own character and legacy are full of contradictions, that is pretty much necessary. What I'd like to deal with here, however, is a text of the Reformer at his systematic best and, indeed, his gentlemanly best. I will do so as generously as I know how, reserving pugnacity for a more suitable occasion. The text in question is *The Freedom of a Christian*, which treats the relation between justification and sanctification—more specifically, between justification and good works—a relation which had been a problem throughout the entire history of the Church but never quite so compelling a problem, at least not since the original Pelagian controversy, as Luther here helped to make it.[1]

---

1. Jaroslav Pelikan, *The Christian Tradition: A History of the Development of Doctrine*, 5 vols. (Chicago: University of Chicago Press, 1984), 4:253, observes that the doctrine of justification, in Augustine and throughout the intervening period, "was not the primary focus

The Freedom of a Christian was accompanied by a respectfully disrespect-ful letter to Leo X, dated 6 September 1520. *Exsurge Domine* had been issued on 15 June of that year, and a copy of it was publicly burned by Luther on 10 December, after the previous month saw both the publication of *Freedom* (penned without reference to the bull) and of much more bellicose texts written in response to rumors and controversies surrounding the bull. So we have in *Freedom* the last, and perhaps the most important, of Luther's major pre-excommunication theological writings.

Exsurge Domine—even by the standards of the day a poorly judged response to the dissident German theologian—spoke of foxes in the vineyard and "the wild boar from the forest." Looking back from our vantage point, it is perfectly plain that there were such. Some would say that Luther, others that Leo, was among the foxes; many would finger both, if for quite different reasons. But the present document, as I said, represents Luther at his theological best: a theologian still in and of the Church, albeit one already working out a line of thought and action that, amid many complicating circumstances, would contribute to the rending of the Church. It is a shame, those circumstances notwithstanding, that *Freedom* did not become the centerpiece of a theological debate capable of preventing the rending. Perhaps today, pursuant to the 1999 Joint Declaration on the Doctrine of Justification, which limits the force of sixteenth-century anathemas in the present state of affairs,[2] we can put it in such a light as to permit it somehow to contribute to the healing of the Church. To help with that is one object of the present exercise. The other is to make some advance in understanding the problem itself and related problems, such as the doctrines of penance and purgatory, though these latter stand only in the background of the text.

Luther's Gambit

The first thing to be said, pursuant to both objects, is that in this document Luther looks to the gospel of Jesus Christ as the Christian's true mandate for authentic moral existence. That is the vision that unites Luther to Paul and to Augustine, as well as to Barth, say, or to John Paul II. That is what unites him to every serious moral theologian of the Christian tradition. The gospel

---

of the presentation of the mode and content of salvation" and that it remained a remarkably flexible one that afforded many different angles of approach, leaving plenty of unasked or unanswered questions.

2. I put the matter cautiously. §41 states, somewhat incautiously perhaps, that "the teaching of the Lutheran churches presented in this Declaration does not fall under the condemnations from the Council of Trent."

liberates man for the good life. Which means, on the one hand, that no talk of "the gospel" that fails to orient man to the good life has actually engaged the gospel; and, on the other, that no discourse about the good life that refuses the light of the gospel is capable of staying the course.

The opening lines of *Freedom* lay this out in the form of a paradox to be overcome. Luther confronts us with two seemingly contradictory theses, which it will be his task to reconcile: (1) "A Christian is a perfectly free lord of all, subject to none." (2) "A Christian is a perfectly dutiful servant of all, subject to all."[3] The reconciliation or synthesis of these theses will be attained by interpreting both of them evangelically, such that sanctification, no less than justification (or, as some would have it, the ethical no less than the ontological), is considered as a feature of the gospel.

Before elaborating, it is necessary to remark on the pastoral problem that motivated the argument, which was no mere exercise in speculative theology. Under the influence of teaching shaped by the early penitential manuals, conscientious Christians had learned to think of themselves as living in a kind of oscillation between the state of grace and a state of sin, the former state being induced by the infused grace of the sacraments and the latter being induced by their spiritual lapses, which required rectification by confession, penance, and absolution. Alas, this rectifying process was sometimes abused by manipulative clerics who cultivated belief in an angry God, much of whose energy was spent firing the furnaces of purgatory and of hell. Various means of appeasement were proffered, some of which amounted not to genuine penance but rather to a kind of trade, a lucrative trade, in divine goods. The combination of the spiritual burden of an uneasy conscience and this corruption of the ecclesial channels of grace had become intolerable not only to Luther but to many Christians. It was of course the appearance of Tetzel in Wittenberg, for the purpose of peddling indulgences, that prompted the posting of Luther's theses,[4] which constitute (if we pass over their flaws) a powerful and altogether necessary *cri de coeur* against the corruption of the gospel.[5]

---

3. Timothy E. Lull, ed., *Martin Luther's Basic Theological Writings* (Minneapolis: Fortress, 1989), 596. The text is drawn from *LW* 31:333–77.

4. "Theses" is not really the right word for the numbered sentences of this document. While many could become articles for debate in a *disputatio*, others are simply exclamations (cf. 15–19, e.g., with 90–95).

5. Under the circumstances it was a grave theological and pastoral duty, in which the Church was dangerously derelict, to insist that "Christians are to be taught that he who gives to the poor or lends to the needy does a better work than buying pardons" (43), "because love grows by works of love, and man becomes better; but by pardons man does not grow better, only more free from penalty" (44), and such-like things as Luther says here, including his reminders that the gospel is the true treasure of the Church (62).

As Luther saw it, all this was a sign that the Church had drifted into Pelagianism, which he considered the perennial heresy. The emphasis on penance in the present life, and on the repayment of every remaining farthing in purgatory, so exalted justice over mercy as to make it impossible to rest in the latter.[6] There was no Divine Mercy Sunday in those days, nor (it seemed to Luther) any such message. The burden fell on the baptized to atone for his own post-baptismal sins, or to claim the help of the saints and of the Church in doing so, if he hoped to be saved. This amounted to salvation by works and raised the question as to how one could be certain that one's contrition was genuine and that one's works were sufficient.

That question was complicated by the regnant nominalism of Luther's day, which had grown from the seeds planted by the monk Roscellinus—seeds that Anselm had unsuccessfully tried to pluck out—into the stalk of Ockhamism, before flowering widely in the European universities. Nominalism was at the heart of the *via moderna*, which distinguished itself from the *via antiqua* of the realists. Realism, whether Platonist or Aristotelian or Christian, was committed to a mysterious, hierarchical, participatory universe arranged in ascending orders of beauty, truth, and goodness. Anselm had lately introduced into it a sophisticated doctrine of freedom and responsibility. Nominalists, however, were fascinated with divine transcendence and omnipotence, on the one hand, and with creaturely contingency, on the other, while lacking any obvious means of connecting the two. They were heavily preoccupied, anthropologically, with a nature/freedom dialectic that posed insoluble problems. The inscrutability of the divine will—in other words, the seeming arbitrariness of God and of the creaturely relation to God—was an unsettling source of *angst* in this still-religious milieu.

6. See, for example, the appendices to Aquinas's *Summa Theologiae* on purgatory: "For if the debt of punishment is not paid in full after the stain of sin has been washed away by contrition, nor again are venial sins always removed when mortal sins are remitted, and if justice demands that sin be set in order by due punishment, it follows that one who after contrition for his fault and after being absolved, dies before making due satisfaction, is punished after this life. Wherefore those who deny Purgatory speak against the justice of God" (App. 2, art. 1). It is one thing, of course, to deny purgatory and another to deny such an understanding of purgatory. Luther was beginning to rethink purgatory when he posted his ninety-five theses, but in his *Argument in Defense of All the Articles of Dr. Martin Luther Wrongly Condemned in the Roman Bull* (1521), with respect to art. 37, he confirmed his belief in its existence while questioning both the biblical warrant for the doctrine and of course the idea that the pope had authority over the souls in purgatory through indulgences. It was only in 1530 that Luther rejected the doctrine altogether (see Pelikan, *Christian Tradition*, 4:136f.). That was a difficult and decisive move, inasmuch as the doctrine's roots ran much deeper in the tradition than those of the doctrine of indulgences, which was still in its infancy. Of purgatory more will have to be said anon.

What comfort the *via moderna* could offer took the form of the maxim, "God will not deny his grace to anyone who does what lies within him." Unfortunately that maxim, which amounted to a kind of *pactum* or partnership—if we do our bit, God will surely do his[7]—only deepened the problem of the fearful or uneasy conscience. Its Pelagian logic was easy to spot. God endows us with natural gifts, and our stewardship of those gifts conditions his supernatural gifts. But that stewardship was the very thing in question. It was in question not only individually—am I really doing my best?—but collectively. What freedom of the will, what power to do good, is actually left to fallen man? Baptism removes the guilt of original sin but not its natural consequences.[8] It deals with original sin only as *reatus* not as *vitium*. How then can one so weakened and diminished by sin fulfill his part of the bargain? How can he become confident that he is in a position to receive saving grace, sacramentally or otherwise?

Luther was hardly alone in wrestling with such things, as modern scholarship has made increasingly clear.[9] But he himself had a particularly profound experience of the spiritual agony that results when a disturbed conscience confronts this burden of responsibility. It is fair to say that his was a personal crisis before it was a theological one. His own nominalism notwithstanding, Luther despised the arbitrary and wrathful God whose righteousness was the cold justice of an implacable and unyielding judge. And he despised his fellow churchmen who were turning the temple of God into a den of thieves. How, he famously demanded, can I get a gracious God?

7. In *Iustitia Dei* ([Cambridge: Cambridge University Press 1986], 83), Alistair McGrath notes Stephen Langton's paraphrase of *Facienti quod in se est Deus non denegat gratiam*, viz.: *Si homo facit, quod suum est, Deus debet facere, quod suum est.* McGrath traces the principle of the maxim back to Irenaeus at *Haer.* 4.39.2, though the context of that passage had long since faded from view. The permutations and reversals it underwent were numerous and sometimes radical, as he shows, now focusing on man's obligation, now on God's. Philip Hughes observes how in certain (crudely Ockhamite) circles God was "hailed as an arbitrary tyrant who must therefore, paradoxically, be merciful to man his victim." *A History of the Church: An Introductory Study*, 3 vols. (London: Sheed & Ward, 1935–47), 3:1274ff.

8. Cf. Aquinas *ST* 3.69.3, ad 3: "Original sin spread in this way, that at first the person infected the nature, and afterwards the nature infected the person. Whereas Christ in reverse order at first repairs what regards the person, and afterwards will simultaneously repair what pertains to the nature in all men. Consequently by Baptism He takes away from man forthwith the guilt of original sin and the punishment of being deprived of the heavenly vision. But the penalties of the present life, such as death, hunger, thirst, and the like, pertain to the nature, from the principles of which they arise, inasmuch as it is deprived of original justice. Therefore these defects will not be taken away until the ultimate restoration of nature through the glorious resurrection."

9. See, for example, Berndt Hamm, *The Early Luther: Stages in a Reformation Reorientation*, trans. Martin J. Lohrmann (Grand Rapids: Eerdmans, 2014). Luther's shifting allegiances and reactions remain a matter of debate, naturally. Cf. Denis Janz, *Luther and Late Medieval Thomism* (Waterloo, ON: Wilfred Laurier University Press, 2012).

As the religious thinkers of the sixteenth century struggled to reconcile a robust doctrine of sin and grace with an increasing emphasis on human autonomy and responsibility rather than on a more mechanical "religious extrinsicism," Anthony Levi observes, there appeared to be only two ways out of the dilemma: the way of the evangelical humanists, such as Erasmus, and the way of the Reformers. Each attempted to cut the Gordian knot: the former by means of a more robust Pelagianism, expressing a new confidence in human nature and in human perfectibility; the latter by returning to Augustine's emphasis on total depravity and on the sovereignty of divine grace—that is, by rejection of the *pactum* and its basic assumptions about human perfectibility.[10]

Luther would later credit Erasmus for recognizing "the grand hinge" on which everything turned, viz., the question of the freedom of the will, a subject on which Luther tacked far to starboard even of Augustine, while claiming the latter's support: "If we believe that original sin has so destroyed us that, even in the godly who are led by the Spirit, it causes the utmost molestation by striving against that which is good, it is manifest that there can be nothing left in a man devoid of the Spirit which can turn itself towards good, but which must turn towards evil. . . . Man, without grace, can do nothing but will evil!"[11] Adopting such a position, however, which lacked the nuances proper to the doctrine of total depravity, forced Luther to abandon significant features of Augustine's doctrine of grace even while he was recovering others. This kept the Reformer's ship moving away from the main fleet, so to say, as it was already from the fourth thesis of the 1517 *Disputation against Scholastic Theology*.[12] But it was the connection between this deviation and another that proved decisive, namely, Luther's embrace of the *sola fide*. Taking up that slogan— familiar to Gabriel Biel, a generation earlier, though rejected by him as "an error of carnal and idle men"[13]—was Luther's opening gambit, as we shall see.

10. See further A. H. T. Levi's introduction to Erasmus's *Praise of Folly* (London: Penguin, 1993), xxff. It is worth noting that one of the influences on Luther's choice was the *Theologica Germanica*, a work he much admired (in which see especially chap. 44).

11. See *De Servo Arbitrio* (1525), sec. 167f. (trans. Henry Cole; punctuation altered).

12. His concluding disclaimer notwithstanding, he was "in opposition to common opinion" (thesis 5) at a deeper level than he supposed. His radical view of the bondage of the will required him to take an equally radical view of grace. In order to emphasize that grace is the living presence of God in Christ by the Spirit (cf. theses 55 and 84), he found it necessary to throw overboard both patristic and scholastic distinctions between uncreated and created grace, operative and cooperative grace, actual and habitual grace, etc., all of which served, in his opinion, the religious extrinsicism and Pelagianism, not to say Aristotelianism—"virtually the entire *Ethics* of Aristotle is the worst enemy of grace" (thesis 41)—to which he objected.

13. Heiko Oberman, *The Harvest of Medieval Theology: Gabriel Biel and Late Medieval Nominalism* (Cambridge, MA: Harvard University Press, 1963), 183. (At n. 117 he supplies the Latin: "*Per hanc doctrinam tollitur error et presumptio quorundam carnalium et ociosorum hominum*

It remains to be said that Luther's discovery of a gracious God came, fittingly for an Augustinian, by way of a study of Romans. More precisely, it came by way of a fresh appropriation of Paul's assertion that "in the gospel a righteousness of God is revealed, through faith for faith" (Rom. 1:17). By the righteousness of God, opined Luther, we must not understand "the righteousness by which he is righteous in himself but [rather] that righteousness by which we are made righteous *by* God."[14] Now that may be a misreading of the passage, if not the epistle, for in Paul's thought there is no such disjunction. God demonstrates his *own* righteousness by acting in such a way as to establish ours.[15] The real question is—in what way? establishes how? But the passage nevertheless came to Luther as a great liberation. It invited a shift in focus from the terrible holiness or righteousness of God himself, in the light of which sinners can only stand condemned, to the holiness or righteousness that God freely shares with sinners—which meant no more useless striving to please God, no more anger against a God who demands from us what we are unable to give, and no more manipulation of the conscience by manipulative preachers. "This passage in Paul," he says, "became the very gate of Paradise for me."[16]

It is against this backdrop (rather hastily and crudely drawn) that we can pursue his argument in *The Freedom of the Christian*, or those parts of it that matter to us here, before attempting an engagement and critique. Luther modestly suggests to Leo that this little work "contains the whole of Christian life in a brief form, provided you grasp its meaning."[17]

An Outline of Luther's "Brief Outline"

Luther begins by describing man's twofold nature as intellectual and bodily, or inner and outer, in terms of the new man and the old man—that is, as

---

qui in sola fide salvari se putantes; allegant pro se illud Matt. 40 [Mark 16:16] '*Qui crediderit et baptizatus fuerit salvus erit.' Non attendentes quod fides sine operibus mortua est.* Hebr. 11 [6:1]. S I 19 C.") Oberman notes that Biel elsewhere associates the *sola gratia* slogan with the same error.

14. Martin Luther, *Lectures on Romans*, ed. and trans. Pauck Wilhelm, Library of Christian Classics 15 (London: SCM, 1961), 18, emphasis added.

15. Luther appeals to Augustine in support, but cf. N. T. Wright, *Paul and the Faithfulness of God*, Christian Origins and the Question of God 4 (Minneapolis: Fortress, 2013), 1456ff.

16. It became also the gateway for the German Reformation. Article 4 of the Augsburg Confession insists "that men cannot be justified before God by their own strength, merits or works, but are freely justified for Christ's sake through faith, when they believe that they are received into favour and that their sins are forgiven for Christ's sake, who, by his death, has made satisfaction for our sins. This faith God imputes for righteousness in his sight."

17. Permit me to recommend the longer, and differently focused, summary in chap. 4 of Michael Banner's *Christian Ethics: A Brief History* (Oxford: Wiley-Blackwell 2009), to which I shall advert later.

spiritual and carnal—and we should notice straightaway that he does not trouble himself to distinguish the different states of man in his twofold nature: man as created, lapsed, reconciled, and perfected.[18] In consequence, he associates the inner man with "righteousness or freedom" and the outer man with "unrighteousness or servitude," confusing constitutional categories with eschatological categories.[19] And from this he immediately infers the irrelevance of works—that is, "of any external thing"—to the production of righteousness or freedom. To things irrelevant he then adds the works of the soul itself, its contemplation or meditation.[20] What makes the soul righteous is the action *on* it of the Word of God, which takes the form of the gospel, and the faith *in* it that enables it to recognize and respond to the Word. "Faith alone is the saving and efficacious use of the Word of God, according to Romans 10"; and this faith, he insists, "cannot exist in connection with works," if the latter are understood to contribute to justification.[21] Justification is confined to faith alone, and faith is confined to the inner man alone.

A sort of panegyric to faith follows. "Faith, which is a small and perfect fulfillment of the law, will fill believers with so great a righteousness that they will need nothing more to become righteous."[22] It "makes the law and works unnecessary for any man's righteousness and salvation." Faith alone justifies, offering "a great treasure of benefits." It is like a wedding ring, joining the soul to Christ, as bride to bridegroom, in a nuptial exchange that renders the soul the beneficiary of everything that belongs to Christ.[23] Faith is "the source and substance of all our righteousness" and, in particular, the ground of our participation in the royal priesthood of Christ.[24]

Thus does Luther substantiate his thesis that the Christian "is lord of all things without exception," which he explicates, quite consistently, as an

18. Only in the third of these states does Luther's analysis hold, per 2 Cor. 4:16, to which he appeals (Lull, *Luther's Basic Theological Writings*, 596).

19. Thus also thesis 58 of the *Disputation on the Power and Efficacy of Indulgences*: "Nor are they the merits of Christ and the Saints, for even without the pope, these always work *grace for the inner man, and the cross, death, and hell for the outward man*" (emphasis added).

20. Lull, *Luther's Basic Theological Writings*, 597.

21. Ibid., 598f.

22. Ibid., 599f. In the union with Christ through faith, "all sin is swallowed up by the righteousness of Christ" (609).

23. Ibid., 600–604. Following up an insight of Johannes von Staupitz respecting this *admirabile commercium* (Hamm, *Early Luther*, 208), Luther speaks of a "royal marriage" between Christ and the soul. Unlike his mentor, however, "Luther described the event of the sinful soul's union with its heavenly bridegroom as a relationship between word and faith" (ibid., 211). Cf. Calvin, who at *Institutes* 4.17.2 locates this saving congress (there labeled *mirifica commutatio*) in the sacrament of baptism.

24. Lull, *Luther's Basic Theological Writings*, 605–8.

inner freedom. The kind of power it entails is not a controlling power but a liberating one. Nothing, no matter how grievous, "can do him any harm" who knows that he needs nothing for salvation except faith—that "he needs neither laws nor good works but, on the contrary, is injured by them if he believes that he is justified by them."[25] And this inner freedom also enables him to pray for and to teach others, adding a priestly dimension to the kingly power. By contrast, one who does not enjoy through faith this inner freedom from fear tries to exercise dominion for his own sake rather than for God's sake, thus unwittingly and unwilling becoming a slave to all things.[26]

Having dealt with the inner man and with the first thesis, the lordship thesis, Luther turns to the outer man and the servanthood thesis. His first concern is to address those who infer from the foregoing that good works are altogether irrelevant, rather than irrelevant only for the production of righteousness and freedom. Eschatology comes back into play. Their inference, he says, would be right, were we already perfected as "wholly inner and perfectly spiritual men." Yet we remain in the flesh, where we must "have dealings with men" and control our own bodies, disciplining it "by fastings, watchings, labours, and other reasonable discipline" to make it conform to the inner man. The need for good works arises with the need to rule one's own body, which "strives to serve the world and seeks its own advantage." These works of discipline, however, do not justify. Faith justifies the soul, and the justified soul, "out of spontaneous love in obedience to God," disciplines the body, which it recognizes as operating according to a contrary (self-seeking and self-justifying) principle.[27]

Here Luther does refer us to the prelapsarian state of man, whose soul is not in need of any justification but who tills the garden to provide for his body and to keep himself from idleness. He also introduces the eschatological distinctions we earlier accused him of neglecting. "Through his faith [the believer] has been restored to Paradise and created anew, [hence he] has no need of works that he may become or be righteous; but that he may not be idle and may provide for and keep his body, he must do such works freely only to please God." Since he is not yet wholly re-created, he must also allow his faith and love to become more perfect; yet "these are to be increased, not by external works . . . but of themselves"—a process on which he does not elaborate.[28]

Our attention is immediately arrested by what follows. Luther now puts forward his most innovative thesis, a double-edged thesis that strikes like a

25. Ibid., 610.
26. Ibid., 607.
27. Ibid., 610f.
28. Ibid., 612.

sword into the very heart of moral reason: "Good works do not make a good man, but a good man does good works; evil works to not make a wicked man, but a wicked man does evil works." A good tree, he reminds us, bears good fruit, and a bad tree, bad fruit. "As the man is, whether believer or unbeliever, so also is his work—good if it was done in faith, wicked if it was done in unbelief." Indeed, "a man must be righteous before he does a good work."[29]

This is his masterstroke, which bids fair to overcome any dualism and to restore the principle that "faith does good works" without prejudice to Luther's basic claim (which he believes to be Pauline) that good works justify no one. A good man is saved by faith; it is precisely faith that makes him good and enables him to do good. An evil man is damned by his unbelief and not by his evil works; it is unbelief that makes the person and his works evil, just as it is faith that makes them good. Works only show a man for what he is. Their value, in that respect, is merely declarative. What the man actually is, is determined by whether he has faith. The doctrine of works as a means of righteousness, he says, is a perverse and all-consuming leviathan that substitutes nature for grace and the glory of man for the glory of God.[30] Yet "penitence, confession, and satisfaction" have their place, and good works too, if they are understood to follow rather than to precede the grace that works through faith. The law has its place in pointing us to the gospel promises, while works have their place as an expression of faith in those promises. "Repentance proceeds from the law of God, but faith or grace from the promise of God," and faith "finds expression in works of the freest service, cheerfully and lovingly done, with which a man willingly serves another without hope of reward."[31]

Luther thus modifies his earlier claim that good works arise from the need to provide for and to discipline the outer man. For "a man does not live for himself alone in this mortal body to work for it alone, but he lives also for all men on earth; rather, he lives only for others and not for himself." It is to *that* end that he disciplines his body, in imitation of Christ. "Although the Christian is thus free from all works, he ought in this liberty to empty himself, take upon himself the form of a servant . . . and to serve, help, and in every way deal with his neighbour as he sees that God through Christ has dealt and still deals with him. This he should do freely, having regard for nothing but divine approval."[32]

---

29. Ibid., 613. Luther had already experimented with this in the *Disputation against Scholastic Theology*, which at thesis 40 proclaims: "We do not become righteous by doing righteous deeds but, having been made righteous, we do righteous deeds."

30. Lull, *Luther's Basic Theological Writings*, 614f.

31. Ibid., 617. The relation between repentance and faith does not get the attention it deserves. Is the former not a facet of the latter?

32. Ibid., 618. Strangely, it is not clear here whether this refers to the divine approval that is already his or to divine approval of his present course of action.

With this modification, Luther arrives at the QED. The paradox of his twin theses is resolved. The Christian is seen to be like Christ in lordship and like Christ in servanthood, and all this through faith alone, not through seeking "merits, rewards, and the things that are ours."[33] To the many Scriptures he has already piled up as stones of witness along the path of his argument, he now adds an appeal to the example of the Blessed Virgin, and of Paul and Timothy, which he contrasts bluntly to the "colleges, monasteries, altars, and offices of the Church." Among the latter he finds few that are "really Christian in our day." For their doctrine, in effect, encourages the Christian to live for and in himself, whereas a real Christian "lives not in himself, but in Christ and in his neighbour."[34] As for those who pervert the teaching of justification by faith by abolishing good works altogether, they overlook the fact that "our faith in Christ does not free us from works but from false opinions concerning works, that is, from the foolish presumption that justification is acquired by works."[35]

The true Christian leader must therefore "take a middle course" between two classes of men: the "unyielding, stubborn ceremonialists . . . who insist upon their ceremonies as means of justification," on the one hand, and the weak or simple-minded masses, the "timid multitude" that must not be led astray by a reactionary rejection of sacraments and ceremonies and good works, on the other hand. Of course it is the former rather than the latter who provide a real test of faith through their "pestilent, impious, soul-destroying traditions." They do not realize that their ceremonies are merely blueprints, which they have mistaken for the life of faith that is "the real and permanent structure" of Christianity. Here the less gentlemanly Luther reappears. In a final Romeward volley that belies the confidence expressed in his introductory letter, he attacks the religious and legal establishment led by "godless and blind popes and their flatterers," appealing instead to *theodidacti*—like himself, presumably—as the best hope for the future.[36]

Well, we are living that future and it is not quite the future Luther was looking for, but that is not our concern here. Our concern is with his argument and, in particular, with these two premises: (1) that the goodness of good works depends wholly on their being done in the freedom of faith, and (2) that they cannot be done in the freedom of faith if they are thought to

33. "Any work that is not done solely for the purpose of keeping the body under control or of serving one's neighbour . . . is not good or Christian" (ibid., 622).

34. Ibid., 623. Luther's realism about union with Christ (cf. p. 620) is touted by the Finnish school of Tuomo Mannermaa and company; see Carl Braaten and Robert Jenson, eds., *Union with Christ: The New Finnish Interpretation of Luther* (Grand Rapids: Eerdmans, 1998).

35. Lull, *Luther's Basic Theological Writings*, 624f.

36. Ibid., 625–28. Cf. the introduction to *De Servo Arbitrio*, where Luther speaks approvingly of "those who have imbibed the Spirit that holds sway in our books" (ibid., 175).

contribute anything to justification. Neither of these premises is sound, as we must now remark, yet by probing them it may be that we can make some progress in grasping the relation between justification and sanctification.

Agreements and Disagreements

Let us begin with a point of agreement. Luther asserts that through faith we have all that belongs to Christ and that we therefore have all the goodness there is. It is from that goodness that we ourselves are good and do good. Who will deny this? The Lord, the source of all goodness, is our righteousness. The question is not whether we have all the goodness there is but in what manner we have it and how we appropriate it. Certainly by faith, for "without faith it is impossible to please him," but also by faithfulness?[37]

Luther is sometimes ambiguous about that, and there is indeed a certain ambiguity in the biblical *locus classicus*: "For by grace are ye saved through faith; and that not of yourselves: it is the gift of God: Not by works, lest any man should boast. For we are his workmanship, created in Christ Jesus unto good works, which God hath before ordained that we should walk in them" (Eph. 2:8–10 KJV). These two Pauline statements require resolution, much like Luther's twin theses in *The Freedom of the Christian*. But is Luther's resolution—faith and justification precede, faithfulness and sanctification follow—the right one? Or is the relation between them more intimate, more mutual, more simultaneous?

We may set aside here the dispute with those who say that we have the goodness of Christ only by some juridical fiction; that is, with those who have taken the forensic turn in the doctrine of justification initiated already by Melanchthon.[38] For that turn, when completed, marginalizes sanctification altogether or else makes of it a purely human achievement. It tends, in the end, either to antinomianism or to moralism, both of which were anathema to Luther. His *simul iustus et peccator* notwithstanding, it is false to say that Luther taught an imputed righteousness without an imparted righteousness,

---

37. Heb. 11:6. The author here, like the Scriptures on which he draws, makes no distinction between faith and faithfulness.

38. In *Loci Communes* 8, Melanchthon argues that *fides* does not mean assent to Church teaching combined with a faithful life; rather, it means assent plus *fiducia* or trust (the former uniting us to the Church, the latter uniting us to Christ). The accompanying emphasis on imputed rather than imparted righteousness permitted Melanchthon to describe justification by faith as a "forensic" doctrine. Melanchthon's approach, however, of which Luther spoke approvingly, should not be confused with more radically forensic doctrines, which make the gift of righteousness into nothing more than a legal fiction (cf. McGrath, *Iustitia Dei*, 259).

or an "alien" righteousness without "our own proper righteousness."[39] He just wanted to be certain that our own proper righteousness, which we ourselves work, was itself understood as a participation in Christ and as a product of the alien righteousness that we do not work. Luther knew that faith has its works and that these works sanctify.[40]

Let us agree further that works, if truly good, are done in freedom. Here we are agreeing first of all with Paul and Irenaeus, for example, who argued that what differs for man under the new covenant is the ability granted him by the Holy Spirit to participate in the freedom of God himself, so that what he offers to God and neighbor is offered freely. (Irenaeus is particularly eloquent on the topic, as I have observed elsewhere, though it is hard to outdo Paul in 2 Corinthians.)[41] But should we say that the goodness of good works rests wholly in the freedom with which they are performed and in the faith that makes one free to perform them? Should we agree with Luther that "nothing makes a man good except faith, or evil except unbelief"?[42] If he means only that faith is a *conditio sine qua non* for goodness—since the goodness we are talking about is indeed a participation in Christ, whom we cannot enjoy apart from faith—then fine. He seems to say more than that, however, making goodness rest entirely on faith. And his argument for the absolute priority of justification over sanctification, such that the one is complete before the other even begins, depends upon that.

Luther thinks that good works, so long as they are thought not only to increase sanctification but also to increase justification, are *not* done in faith and, therefore, are not good after all. Faith tells us that we already have everything that we require for justification, vouchsafed to us in "the Lord our righteousness." From the gratitude accompanying this faith, we draw the motivation for the good works that enhance our own proper righteousness; that is, our sanctification. Justification precedes and empowers sanctification. We can't add to it. We can express it only in the way we live. To suppose that

39. Alien righteousness is the righteousness of Christ "imparted from without" in answer to original sin. Proper righteousness is what we work "with that first and alien righteousness" in disciplining the flesh, loving the neighbor, and fearing God. The second is the product of the first and "is set opposite our own actual sin" (Martin Luther, "Two Kinds of Righteousness," a sermon from 1519; see Lull, *Luther's Basic Theological Writings*, 157f.). The distinction is partly analogous to that between operative and cooperative grace, despite Luther's suspicion of such language. As for the *simul*, that was necessary to defend his view of concupiscence as a culpable fault even in the baptized.

40. See Lull, *Luther's Basic Theological Writings*, 613.

41. This indeed is the whole tradition through to Thomas Aquinas (see, e.g., *ST* 1–2.108 and 109). On Irenaeus, see my *Ascension Theology* (London: T&T Clark, 2011), 67f.

42. Lull, *Luther's Basic Theological Writings*, 614.

the way we live somehow constitutes or increases the thing itself is to deny the thing itself, which is neither faithful nor good.

Just here, of course, Luther is in sharp contradiction to Catholic teaching, as the Council of Trent made clear.[43] Again, we must not ignore or underestimate the extent of agreement. What is justification? To begin with, it is a pronouncement of belonging, a declaration of good standing with the covenant God and of being heir to the promises of that God. On what basis is the pronouncement made? Confession of faith. How is it made? Baptism. What does baptism signify? Union with Christ in his death and resurrection. What does it effect? Fellowship with God. Where does it lead? To eternal life. Arguably, all of this was and is held in common. But is justification, per Luther, something that is complete before the Christian life, as a process of sanctification, begins? Or, as the fathers of Trent insisted and the Catholic catechism still insists, is the whole process of sanctification a moment *internal* to justification?[44]

On the Catholic scheme justification precedes, accompanies, and follows sanctification.[45] It both grounds and includes it. Space is opened up by justification for sanctification to take place, as Luther asserts; but in taking place, sanctification contributes to justification, which Luther denies. It is not right, on the Catholic view, to say that our works cannot be done in freedom, and hence cannot be good works, if they are thought to contribute anything to justification.[46] Nor is it right, then, to say that good works do not make a good

43. Trent refused to limit justification to a declaration of good standing or (as Melanchthon has it in *Loci Communes* 8) to "the remission of sins, reconciliation, or the acceptance of a person unto eternal life." Justification "consists not only in the forgiveness of sins but also in the sanctification and renewal of the inward being by a willing acceptance of the grace and gifts whereby someone from being unjust becomes just" (session 6, Decree on Justification, chap. 7; *DEC* 2:671–81). "[W]e are said to be justified by faith because faith is the first stage of human salvation, the foundation and root of all justification" (chap. 8); but, "If anyone says that justifying faith is nothing else than confidence in the divine mercy that remits sin on account of Christ, or that it is this confidence alone which justifies us, let him be anathema" (canon 12; cf. canons 9–11).

44. This question can be answered by a consideration of the causes of justification (Decree on Justification, chap. 7): "Final cause, the glory of God and of Christ, and eternal life; efficient cause, the God of mercy . . . with the promised Holy Spirit . . . ; meritorious cause, his most beloved and only-begotten Son . . . who . . . made satisfaction to God the Father on our behalf; instrumental cause, the sacrament of baptism, which is the sacrament of faith. . . . Finally, the one formal cause is the justness of God [*iustitia dei*] . . . by which he makes us just . . . not merely to be considered just . . . , each one of us receiving individually his own justness."

45. This language is drawn from the Decree on Justification, chap. 16: "For Jesus Christ himself continually imparts strength to those justified . . . and this strength always precedes, accompanies and follows their good works, and without it they would be wholly unable to do anything meritorious and pleasing to God."

46. Cf. canons 24, 26, 31, and 32.

man, even if it is right to say that only a good man consistently does good works, and does them well. The freedom and the goodness come from God through Christ, in whom they are already complete; but in us they must grow, as we learn to walk in them. Justifying grace is the grace that not only counts the man worthy of his salvation but also makes him worthy. Sanctification is something achieved not after and alongside justification but in and with justification. Justification enables good works to be willed and done well, and good works willed and done well increase justification.[47]

But how, objects the Lutheran, can justification be increased if it is already ours in Christ, if the salvation it entails is "the gift of God—not because of works, lest any man should boast"? The Catholic response is that it can be increased through perfection of our union with Christ, which is a matter of faith, hope, and charity, not of faith alone.[48] Justification, says the catechism, "includes the remission of sins, sanctification, and the renewal of the inner man."[49] Its broad view of justification is stressed again in the next paragraph: "Justification has been merited for us by the Passion of Christ. It is granted us through Baptism. It conforms us to the righteousness of God, who justifies us. It has for its goal the glory of God and of Christ, and the gift of eternal life. It is the most excellent work of God's mercy."

Toward the end of his sermon on *Two Kinds of Righteousness*, a document contemporaneous with *The Freedom of a Christian*, Luther allows that "alien righteousness is not instilled all at once, but it begins, makes progress, and is finally perfected at the end through death."[50] This brings him quite close to the Church's position—or would do, if he were to acknowledge that this gradual instillation of Christ's righteousness incorporates our own proper

47. Those justified "grow and increase in that very justness they have received through the grace of Christ, by faith united to good works" (Decree on Justification, chap. 10). They are of course already *iustificati* even though they are still *viatores*. As McGrath points out, the Decree delineates three *status iustificationis*: becoming recipients of grace in baptism, cooperating with grace in a life of good works, and being restored to grace via penance (*Iustitia Dei*, 268; the final draft of the Decree does not actually deploy that terminology, however, and the transitions at chapters 10 and 14 are very fluid).

48. "In the process of justification, together with the forgiveness of sins a person receives, through Jesus Christ into whom he is grafted, all these infused at the same time: faith, hope and charity. For faith, unless hope is added to it and charity too, neither unites him perfectly with Christ nor makes him a living member of his body" (Decree on Justification, chap. 7).

49. CCC 2019. The same might be said for the outer man, Christ having been "raised for our justification" (Rom. 4:25).

50. Lull, *Luther's Basic Theological Writings*, 157. Cf. McGrath, *Iustitia Dei*, 36: "Augustine's discussion of *iustitia*, effected only through man's justification, demonstrates how the doctrine of justification encompasses the whole of Christian existence from the first moment of faith, through the increase of righteousness before God and man, to the final perfection of that righteousness in the eschatological city."

righteousness within it. If, that is, he were to allow that Augustine was right to say, "So while he made you without you, he doesn't justify you without you."[51] But Luther does not allow that, and in *De Servo Arbitrio* only hardens his stance against it.[52]

Justification: The Beginning or the End of Sanctification?

Luther wants to ground sanctification in justification, and that is right. Only it is not possible if justification is by faith alone. The doctrine of justification by faith alone can accommodate, and in its way encourage, gratitude as a motivation for sanctification. It can point to the freedom in which holiness really is Christlike and godlike. But it cannot supply as a basis for sanctification anything more than the virtue of faith; and the virtue of faith, isolated from the virtues of hope and charity, cannot provide a satisfactory form or guide for the ethics that ought to govern sanctification. Conversely, if hope and charity are also to provide that form, then sanctification is grounded in something other than justification. Or to put the matter another way: On the basis of justification *sola fide*, Luther sees in sanctification a descent from glory rather than an ascent from lower ends to higher. His approach to sanctification is all eschatology and no teleology. It lacks an account of how to pursue worthy ends worthily and offers no measurement for growth.[53]

Perhaps this is not surprising, given Luther's doctrine of the fall and his exaggerated view of the effects of original sin. The fall, as the Church understands it, though it affects the whole man—having corrupting and debilitating consequences for mind, will, affections, emotions, and body alike—does not make man anything other than man. And grace, overcoming those consequences, does not destroy but perfects man's nature. It belongs to our

51. This became axiomatic in mediaeval theology, but read in a semi-Pelagian way it helped give birth to the *pactum* or contract idea. There is no justification in Augustine for reading it in that way, of course, as an examination of its source (Sermon 169) shows. Appealing to Rom. 4:25, Augustine says that Christ rose for our justification in order to make us just. "You will be God's work, not only because you are human, but also because you are just. It is better after all to be just, than . . . just to be human." This is indeed God's doing, not ours, lest we be thought to have made something better than God had made. Yet (unlike our creation) it involves our consent, our willful sharing in Christ and in his sufferings; we have a part in it.

52. By some accounts, even his doctrine of creation is implicated in his teaching about the bondage of the will. See McGrath, *Iustitia Dei*, 204f.; cf. 315ff., contrasting Luther with Calvin and Newman.

53. "I will do nothing in this life except what I see is necessary, profitable, and salutary to my neighbour, since through faith I have an abundance of all good things in Christ" (Lull, *Luther's Basic Theological Writings*, 619). But the question is: What *is* necessary, profitable, and salutary?

humanity to pursue worthy ends worthily, which is just what sanctifying grace enables us to achieve. But Luther, who regards talk of a hierarchy of ends as an Aristotelian attack on grace, cannot see the good life as a striving upward. All that is bypassed by grace, done away with by grace, through justification by faith alone. Which inevitably obscures the relation between human nature and human ends, as between lower and higher ends, leaving the moral life without proper direction. It calls into question the role of reason in ethics, if not ethics as such. It also calls into question the role of godly fear, which (in his battle against ungodly fear) Luther's doctrine of faith tended to sublate.[54]

As far as I can tell, these are the main objections not only of modern readers of Luther such as Bonhoeffer[55] but also of the Council of Trent—objections that could be made only by confronting the Lutheran doctrine of justification. The council fathers observe that men "are born again unto a hope of glory, but not as yet unto glory."[56] They condemn those who hold to the *sola fide* "in such wise as to mean that nothing else is required to cooperate in order to the obtaining of the grace of justification" or who say that "the justice received is not preserved and also increased before God through good works" or who claim "that the good works of one that is justified are in such manner the gifts of God, as that they are not also the good merits of him that is justified."[57] In short, they insist that, while the grace of God frees one for good works, and indeed for good works freely done, good works freely done increase sanctification or holiness—that is, participation in Christ—which in turn increases the justification that is ours in Christ.[58]

54. See Decree on Justification, chap. 9 (cf. 16).
55. See Banner, *Christian Ethics*, 56ff.
56. Decree on Justification, chap. 13 (cf. 9, 11, and 15).
57. Canons 9, 24, and 32. McGrath thinks that Trent condemns "certain caricatures of Protestantism . . . rather than Protestantism itself" (*Iustitia Dei*, 272), but this seems over-optimistic, depending of course on what one supposes Protestantism itself to be. Canon 12, for example, would seem to condemn decisively Protestantism à la Luther, though Luther shared the Church's horror of that error which amounted to faith in faith.
58. It seems to me that "The Gift of Life," the controversial statement by Evangelicals and Catholics Together (*First Things* [January 1998]: 20–23) that preceded the Joint Declaration, skirts around this problem by talking about justification only in connection with the first of the three *status iustificationis*. Avery Dulles ("Two Languages of Salvation: The Lutheran-Catholic Joint Declaration," *First Things* [December 1999]: 25–30) makes much the same charge against the Declaration itself. On the other hand, it has been observed, especially by (still more skeptical) Lutheran and Reformed scholars, that what is attempted in these documents, including earlier prototypes such as the 1987 ARCIC statement, is much the same maneuver as was carried out at the Diet of Regensburg in 1541, four years before the opening of the Council of Trent. Melanchthon, Bucer, Eck, Gropper, Cardinal Contarini, et al. attempted a compromise based on their respective versions of a *duplex iustitia* doctrine. As R. Scott Clark puts it, "In his *Enchiridion* (1538) Gropper had taught that one is justified by an infusion of divine justice (*iustitia inhaerens*) which would lead to the addition of further

Luther, we should note, confessed something very like that in his forty-fourth thesis, when he said that "love grows by works of love, and man becomes better." What evangelical reason can there be for afterward refusing to admit that good works make a good man better and that evil works make an evil man worse? What rational options in ethics are left to us if we do not admit it? The advantage to the Catholic view (besides the fact that it is Catholic) is that it does not break the link between lower and higher ends, or between righteousness and reward, or between faith and reason, or between justification and sanctification. Union with Christ means freedom to be godlike, to act freely and not out of necessity, but to be godlike in an appropriately human way, as those who pursue worthy ends worthily and are rewarded by God for doing so, just as Jesus was.

One could wish that the Joint Declaration had given more attention to this. While it goes some way toward overcoming sixteenth-century differences by expressing agreement on the *solus Christus* foundation of justification and by asserting the integral unity of justification and sanctification, since both are found in Christ, it never really clarifies the nature of that unity or the bearing of the latter on the former. Hence it is rightly accused of begging the question.[59] Lest we ourselves beg the question, however, we must be reminded that the pivotal dispute is over whether justification is in some sense grounded in sanctification, not over whether sanctification is grounded in justification. The Catholic response is yes. Justification has precedence, in the order of grace, over sanctification, but it also has subsequence. If it is the beginning of sanctification, it is also the end.

Now, if we read *The Freedom of the Christian* making the most of its eschatology, we can see there a certain kind of subsequence. This appears if we map out the dichotomies in play in that document, attending to the

---

justice through sanctification (*iustitia acquisita*)" ("Regensburg and Regensburg II: Trying to Reconcile Irreconcilable Differences on Justification," *Modern Reformation* 7.5, 1998). On the Protestant side, Bucer had talked of a *iustificatio impii* through imputed righteousness and a *iustificatio pii* through imparted righteousness. Despite their many differences—What exactly was the former, and what was the faith by which it was received? And did the latter, the grace that transforms the believer and sanctifies his life, justify or did it not justify?—agreement on justification was proposed in the highly ambiguous fifth article. The result was rejected both by Luther and by Rome, and "the opinion that man is justified on the basis of *duplex iustitia*—that is, *iustitia imputata* and *iustitia inhaerens*" was not embraced at Trent (McGrath, *Iustitia Dei*, 262f.).

59. See, e.g., sections 25–27, which fail to address the *sola fide* problem. Section 38 remarks that the intention of the Catholic affirmation of the meritorious character of good works "is to emphasize the responsibility of persons for their actions, not to contest the character of those works as gifts, or far less to deny that justification always remains the unmerited gift of grace"—which may be so, but would hardly be enough to satisfy Trent.

different dynamics that inform them as Luther moves from anthropology to soteriology to ethics:

	A		B
1. ANTHROPOLOGY	outer/carnal old man	*contrasted with*	inner/spiritual new man
2. SOTERIOLOGY	commands (law) works (fear) reason self despair death ceremony	*overcome or superseded by*	promises (gospel) faith (love) revelation Christ hope life reality
3. ETHICS	discipline service	*eschatologically enabled by*	freedom lordship

These dynamics are seen to change as the argument unfolds, such that what appears at first as a simple opposition between A and B is reworked, first (soteriologically) as a supersession, then (ethically) as a retroactive relation of inclusion. Freedom enables discipline and lordship enables servanthood.

Seen in this light, Christian existence is an eschatological gift that breaks the chain of causality by which sin leads to despair and death—a gift that renders reason and law and works and ceremonies, and the self as participant in all this, free for God and hence for glory. This gift, which is attained by faith, enables its recipient to live gloriously, which here and now means living hopefully and charitably in Christ and in the neighbor. And this leads back to the glory whence it derives, faith having gone before so that hope and love may follow.

Problem solved? Not quite. Unless the eschatology is pried open to teleology, and the new man is seen to be the man who pursues worthy ends worthily, justification and sanctification remain unintegrated and the new man remains a mirage. At least two things are required to rectify the flaws in the arrangement and so to achieve integration.

One is anthropological. Unlike Luther, Paul correlates the inner/outer distinction to the old man / new man distinction only as an eschatological disparity in the present age: the soul is already being renewed, whereas the body (miracles of healing aside) is still subject to decay until the resurrection of the dead. As for the carnal/spiritual distinction, that is a matter internal to the soul, which insofar as it is being renewed is turning to God and relying on the Spirit of God (such is the spiritual man) rather than gratifying the flesh and relying on natural gifts (such is the carnal man). Luther conflates and confuses these distinctions. In order to keep them clear, we might rearrange the first section of our chart thus, after a fashion Luther elsewhere approves:[60]

	versus	
old/carnal		new/spiritual
(outer governing inner)		(inner governing outer)

Once we do this, however, the logic of the opening phase of Luther's argument is shown to lack the biblical warrant he claims for it. His identification of the new or spiritual man with the man of faith only, to the exclusion of works, is grounded dualistically in a body/soul opposition, though his subsequent move to eliminate the works even of the soul does not follow logically and lacks any grounding at all. Paul's doctrine of justification, on the other hand, is not based on the body/soul distinction but on the distinction between one who through the Spirit relies on God in Christ and one who, lacking the Spirit and relying instead on bodily and behavioral marks of the covenant, does not. This approach, unlike Luther's, does not rule out *ab initio* any internal relation of works to faith and of sanctification to justification. Otherwise put, it warrants the *sola gratia* but not the *sola fide*.

The other is at once soteriological and ethical. In the end, Luther restores the integral relation of faith and works, acknowledging with Paul that faith works through love.[61] But he does not restore the integral relation of justification and sanctification. Faith working by love has as its theological counterpoint—or rather it ought to have, but does not in Luther—justification working by sanctification.[62] We may understand the third or ethical section as recognizing that sanctification is enabled by justification, but we require also an indication of their true reciprocity, such that the latter precedes, accompanies, and follows the former, thus in turn being enabled by it:

justification	*working through*	sanctification
sanctification	*leading to*	justification

60. Cf. Lull, *Luther's Basic Theological Writings*, 206.

61. "This is a truly Christian life. Here faith is truly active through love, that is, it finds expression in works of the freest service, cheerfully and lovingly done, with which a man willingly serves another without hope of reward; and for himself he is satisfied with the fullness and wealth of his faith" (ibid., 617).

62. Which is why he still cannot see the unity between Paul and James, and continues to regard with suspicion the latter's epistle.

Here there is both subsequence and consequence. Sanctification is not only followed by justification but actually contributes to it, just as (for creatures) time is "followed" by and contributes to eternity. That is what Trent insists upon and what the Joint Declaration at least hints at, without reaching agreement about it.

The Primacy of Love

To reach agreement, it will be necessary to see that justification and sanctification recover their proper unity, but also that eschatology and teleology, grace and nature, gospel and law, revelation and reason, *res* and *sacramentum* overcome the internal opposition from which they have suffered in Protestantism.[63] But agreement cannot be reached without revisiting what is arguably Luther's most fundamental alteration of the tradition, namely, his reversal of the ordered relation between the coinhering virtues of faith, hope, and love. Whereas Augustine and the entire tradition followed Paul in choosing love as the best lens through which to view the Christian life, and indeed the Christian as such, Luther chose faith instead.[64] To this aspect of the problem we must now attend more directly.

It is not difficult to see how the doctrine of justification by faith alone generates—or rather dictates—a new approach to sanctification in which faith has priority over the other theological virtues. If the Christian *is* a Christian by faith alone, then he can only live out his new existence in a manner governed by faith. As Berndt Hamm puts it, "Love no longer forms faith; faith itself has become the form of a life guided by love."[65] Or as Luther himself puts

63. Was Aquinas not right to make the grace of the Holy Spirit the unifying factor, as, for example, at *ST* 1–2.106.2? "There is a twofold element in the Law of the Gospel. There is the chief element, viz. the grace of the Holy Spirit bestowed inwardly. And as to this, the New Law justifies. Hence Augustine says (*De Spir. et Lit.* xvii): 'There,' i.e., in the Old Testament, 'the Law was set forth in an outward fashion, that the ungodly might be afraid'; 'here,' i.e., in the New Testament, 'it is given in an inward manner, that they may be justified.' The other element of the Evangelical Law is secondary: namely, the teachings of faith, and those commandments which direct human affections and human actions. And as to this, the New Law does not justify. Hence the Apostle says, 'The letter killeth, but the spirit quickeneth'; and Augustine explains this by saying that the letter denotes any writing external to man, even that of the moral precepts such as are contained in the Gospel. Wherefore the letter, even of the Gospel would kill, unless there were the inward presence of the healing grace of faith." Luther may add his amen, but then his own sharp dichotomies must fall away.

64. Pelikan (*Christian Tradition*, 4:252; cf. McGrath, *Iustitia Dei*, 31, 204f.) notes how fiercely contested was the Reformers' claim to be following Augustine.

65. See Berndt Hamm, *The Reformation of Faith in the Context of Late Medieval Theology and Piety* (Leiden: Brill, 2004), 154ff.

it, works of love are performed "on the backside" of the Christian life.[66] But the doctrine of justification *sola fide* is itself the product of a change in the notion of faith that propels faith beyond hope and love into the chief place among the virtues. Hamm expounds this change at some length, arguing that Luther transformed faith into a concept that "attains its new dominance" by concentrating everything "in the question of relationship;" that is, in the question of standing with God—"how God judges me and how I judge myself before God"—rather than in the vexed qualitative questions about the penetration of divine goodness and truth into the sinner's life.[67] Hope and love are thus assimilated into faith from the very beginning, making faith a richer concept; whereas "the active and operative side of [hope and] love is quite different, with Luther distinguishing it as something that follows the justifying faith that leads to salvation."[68]

This justifying faith that already, in and of itself, affords salvation is what *The Freedom of the Christian* sets forth. It is a faith that casts out all fear. Or as Trent recognized, in usurping the place of love—for "there is no fear in love, but perfect love casts out fear"[69]—it casts out even godly fear, generating an ungodly confidence. Joseph Fletcher, who may be credited with the boldest effort to restore to Lutheranism the primacy of love, succeeds only at pressing this ungodly confidence still deeper into the heart of ethics. For the love in question is merely Luther's "faith" or faith-relationship writ large. Love, whether of God or neighbor, is an existential judgment about the standing of one before another. No doubt Luther himself would repudiate Fletcher as an antinomian, despite the latter's claim that his situation ethics

66. Hamm, *Early Luther*, 78n51. The expression *posteriora dorsi* is drawn from Ps. 67:14 Vulgate.

67. Hamm, *Reformation of Faith*, 167; cf. Hamm, *Early Luther*, 77ff. Hamm highlights the continuity with various strands of late-medieval thought, including a Christ- and Spirit-centered theology of mercy and grace, a growing emphasis on predestination, and explorations of the mystical union of Christ and the soul, in order to expose what was most innovative in Luther's own thought; viz., his notion that in the Word-faith relation the gift of righteousness is already fully given, here and now. (See esp. Hamm, *Early Luther*, 237f.)

68. Hamm, *Early Luther*, 78. "The new central role of faith depended on Luther's rejection of the medieval difference—indeed separation—between the objective teaching about the limits of human self-awareness and the subjectivity pursued in an affective spiritual way of life. Through his concept of faith, he combined the abstract language about the church's doctrinal truth with the subjective and existential language of prayer" (ibid., 79). But this new arrangement, with its personal appropriation—or should we say expropriation?—of assurance of salvation here and now, prior to and apart from the life to be lived in the here and now, was intolerable to the Church, as Hamm observes. How exactly it was new, and just why it was intolerable, are matters one might want to dispute.

69. First John 4:18 continues: "For fear has to do with punishment, and he who fears is not perfected in love."

splits the difference between legalism and antinomianism. What else can be said of one who claims that "all laws and rules and principle and ideals and norms, are only *contingent*, only valid *if they happen* to serve love in any situation"?[70] But Fletcher's ethical solipsism, in which everything, even and especially love, depends on the immediacy of revelation and of judgment in the present moment, owes a great deal to Luther's new concept of faith and to his dichotomy between faith and works.

Perhaps, however, there is another way to restore the primacy of love? Luther's genius, so to say, was to freeze-frame a crucial moment of evangelical truth that the theologians in his day, and even perhaps the magisterial referees, were in danger of missing—the moment in which sanctifying works appear in their true freedom. Of course this freeze-framing was also the danger of Luther. Think once more of the statement: "When a man is good or evil, this is effected not by the works, but by faith or unbelief."[71] To view all goodness or badness through the lens of faith or unbelief is a helpful and even a necessary exercise. But is it not equally helpful and necessary to view it through the lens of hope or despair, love or hatred, gratitude or ingratitude, obedience or disobedience? What the Catholic Church objects to, as we have seen, is not Luther's *solo Christo* or *sola gratia*, but his *sola fide*. It agrees with Luther that love is formed by faith (*caritas fidei formata*) but insists also that faith is shaped and nurtured by love (*fides caritate formata*). Otherwise put: To get the whole picture we must roll the film. We can allow Luther's experiment in *Freedom*, but only if we are prepared to repeat the exercise twice over, integrating the results according to the traditional ascending order of the theological virtues.[72]

So what happens if we repeat the exercise with hope as our lens, then love? That is, if we say that hope makes a good work good, and that only a *hopeful* man does good works in a good way, then come at last to love, making the analogous claim? It seems to me that the rehabilitation of Luther's thought, from a Catholic point of view, and the filling out of the relation between justification and sanctification in future ecumenical dialogue, can take place only through submission to such a process. And would that not facilitate (though it could hardly guarantee) the correction of certain flaws characteristic of Protestantism,

70. Joseph Fletcher, *Situation Ethics: The New Morality* (Philadelphia: Westminster, 1966), 30, emphasis original.

71. Lull, *Luther's Basic Theological Writings*, 614. Trent condemns this proposition if it means that "there is no mortal sin save unbelief" (Decree on Justification, canon 27); it doesn't condemn thinking about good and evil in terms of faith and unbelief.

72. Cf. Lawrence Feingold, *The Mystery of Israel and the Church*, vol. 3, *The Messianic Kingdom of Israel* (Louisville: Miriam, 2010), 194.

including that excessive subjectivity by which the *sola fide* produces an anti-ecclesial and antinomian individualism that serves not only Fletcher's purposes, for example, but serves also to isolate the secular sphere of politics and economics from exposure to the light of the gospel?[73] It would also facilitate the correction of those remaining strands within Catholicism (some of them quite broad) that tend to the kind of "works-righteousness" in which freedom is lacking and faith has not the liberating dimension Luther rightly emphasized.

I am not going to attempt this fuller exercise, which would require a book in itself. I want instead to come full circle to the subjects of penance and purgatory and indulgences, which were the goads that prompted Luther to pursue his innovative concept of faith and of justification by faith alone. That these subjects, and the practices around them, had been heavily Pelagianized and otherwise corrupted cannot be contested. That an evangelical understanding of them is possible, where sanctification is understood as a moment internal to justification, can be contended, though in the present book this can be done only briefly and in outline.

Penance, Purgatory, and Indulgences

On Luther's approach, since justification is complete prior to sanctification, sanctification (as we have seen) has the somewhat miraculous character of a descent from glory. Having been raised by faith and not by works to the heavenlies, we appropriate heavenly powers for earthly works. These works are not done for ourselves, but for Christ and the neighbor; for ourselves there is nothing that needs doing, other than the disciplining of the flesh. We await the day, however, when we shall be no longer *simul iustus et peccator*, when baptismal grace shall have prevailed over original sin as *vitium*, not merely as *reatum*, and over the actual sin that flows from this *vitium*. Of that hope we can and should see some evidence already in the present life, as the Church insists, but it is only in the life to come that the *simul* will cease. And that too, even more emphatically, will be a miracle, a miracle that does not require purgatory but only our liberation "from this body of death."[74] Meanwhile there is a place in this life for acts of contrition over sin and for reassurance that our true standing with God is already settled despite our sin, but there

---

73. Cf. Banner, *Christian Ethics*, 58, 67ff.; see also my *Desiring a Better Country: Forays in Political Theology* (Montreal: McGill-Queens University Press, 2015).

74. Rom. 7:24. It is this miraculous character that made it incomprehensible to Schleiermacher, for example, whose solution was to make all dogma—the *fides quae* along with the *fides qua*—an expression of Christian self-consciousness, pressing Luther's revision of the meaning of faith to its utmost extreme.

is no place for a penitential system that tries, as it were, to build from below a scaffolding of compensating works by which we can rise above sin and so attain glory—a glory that in fact is already ours. There is no place for indulgences either for the same reason.

How do things look from the side of the Catholic Church, which understands justification to include sanctification and to be complete only when sanctification itself is complete? Though the baptized person is indeed "hid with Christ in God" (Col. 3:3)—that is, for now, his justification—he does not yet, and cannot yet, take his stand in glory. He must take his stand where he is and come to glory only by way of a process of refinement, of advance in godliness, begun in this world and (except in rare cases) completed after death. Penance serves the process in the present life; purgatory *is* the process after death.[75] Penance keeps him fit for the Eucharist, and the Eucharist keeps him in touch with his true life in Christ, through whom he is "one-ed" with God.[76] Purgatory completes what penance and the Eucharist have begun. Purgatory is the eucharistic transition to glory as experienced by the soul (in so far as it still needs perfecting) on the other side of death. And whether on this side or that side, the soul may be aided in its progress toward glory from the treasury of merits, by the prayers of the saints and the good deeds of fellow travelers and the indulgences of the Church.

The magisterium, to be sure, has been quite reticent about purgatory, as is fitting, given that the doctrine is derived from sources (biblical, liturgical, and pastoral) that for the most part are quite cryptic.[77] Not that it has given an inch to those who, like the later Luther, deny purgatory, but it has recognized that much of what is said about purgatory is highly speculative and not always edifying. The fathers of Trent counsel their fellow bishops "to ensure that sound teaching on purgatory" is widely proclaimed while "the more difficult and subtle questions" are excluded from discourse with the unlearned. No more is positively asserted than "that purgatory exists, and that the souls detained there are helped by the prayers of the faithful and most of all by the acceptable sacrifice of the altar." Trent's reserve, taken together with its canons correcting the abuse of indulgences, etc., suggests that many of the Reformers' concerns were regarded as well grounded.[78]

75. Purgatory is better understood as a process than a place, though for us (even in the soul's separation from the body) every process has some kind of place as well as some kind of time; cf. Farrow, *Ascension Theology*, 134f.

76. And so also with our own true essence, as Julian says (see ibid., 122f.).

77. See Paul Griffiths, "Purgatory," in *The Oxford Handbook of Eschatology*, ed. J. Walls (New York: Oxford University Press, 2008), 427ff.

78. Session 25, Decree on Purgatory (*DEC* 2:774). Analogously, the fathers of Vatican II, while accepting "with great respect" and reiterating the teaching of earlier councils about Mary

It should be acknowledged, however, that what was said at Florence and Trent was shaped in part by a scholastic tradition that—though far from satisfactory—has persisted even into modern times, troubling the doctrine of purgatory and the practice of penance alike by obscuring their evangelical character. The basic premise of this tradition is "that temporal punishment is due to sin, even after the sin itself has been pardoned by God."[79] The effect is to give both penance and purgatory a flavor more punitive than remedial. Whatever may be said of penitential grace (and much is said), "purgatorial grace" is not a phrase that flows as freely as it ought from the tongue trained in this tradition. If progress is to be made in understanding the relation between justification and sanctification, or in the common evangelical concerns of the Catholic and Protestant traditions, this must be admitted and addressed. I would go so far as to say that the key that turns this particular lock might be the most important key in the bunch.

In the next chapter we shall attempt to find and use it. Meanwhile we should admit that some distinction between eternal and temporal punishment is right and necessary. We are fed with the bread of immortality, yet we still traverse a vale of tears. The murderer does not walk free from prison, or indeed the gallows, just because he repents and is baptized or (if already baptized) confesses and is absolved.[80] Of course he can still hope to go from the gallows to glory, if he does repent, just like every other sinner. But it is not so simple as that. In the tradition of which we are speaking, it is said that "God requires satisfaction, and will punish sin, and this doctrine involves as its necessary consequence a belief that the sinner failing to do penance in this life may be punished in another world, and so not be cast off eternally from God."[81] Suffering incarceration or even execution humbly may (or may not) be penance enough for murder, but the point is that each and every sin requires a temporal punishment, lest the divine justice be gainsaid and created order be overturned. Moreover, it matters to the Church, though not to the state, whether our murderer was or wasn't baptized before his crime, for

---

and the *communio sanctorum*, at the same time exhorts "in its pastoral solicitude . . . all whom it concerns to do their best to get rid of or to correct any abuses, excesses or deficiencies that have crept in here or there and to restore all to the fuller praise of Christ and of God" (*De Ecclesia* 8 at §52; *DEC* 2:891).

79. E. Hanna, "Purgatory," *The Catholic Encyclopedia* (New York: Robert Appleton, 1911), newadvent.org.

80. See, e.g., Aquinas, *ST* 3.69.2, ad 3. More generally: "Baptism has the power to take away the penalties of the present life yet it does not take them away during the present life, but by its power they will be taken away from the just in the resurrection when 'this mortal hath put on immortality'" (3.69.3).

81. Hanna, "Purgatory."

sin committed after baptism is graver, circumstantially, than sin committed before baptism. But let us leave that complication to one side for the moment and fix on the maxim that "God requires satisfaction, and will punish sin." At least four things need to be noted about this.

First, it conflates satisfaction (*satisfactio*) and punishment (*poena*). Lamentably, the careful distinction drawn by Anselm in *Cur deus homo* between offering satisfaction for sin and suffering punishment for sin was largely ignored by later schoolmen, including Aquinas, a point to which we will return shortly, though proper treatment of it must be reserved to the next chapter.

Second, it begs the question as to the determination of just punishment. It is one thing to speak of "punishments which satisfy the debt"[82] and another to know what they are. Is there a divine order that makes this particular sin worthy of precisely this temporal punishment? And, if so, is that order accessible to us so that we may do penance properly?

Third, it begs the question as to how temporal and eternal debts and punishments are related. Was Anselm mistaken when he famously pointed out to Boso that the latter had not yet considered the true weight of sin?[83] When he argued that any sin, no matter how slight, so offended against the true order of things as to render eternal happiness (which for us is the fulfillment of that order) impossible? If the pardon for sin and the restoration of true order is an achievement of Jesus Christ and of Jesus Christ alone, what exactly is the role of temporal punishment, whether in this life or in purgatory? What is the relation between what Christ does to satisfy divine justice and what we do? If there is an eternal debt that we cannot pay, which Christ pays for us, but also a temporal debt that we can and must pay before we can appropriate eternal salvation in Christ, is the one a debt to God and the other a debt to someone or something else? Or are they two distinct kinds of debt to God? Distinct how? And does Christ then do no more than open the door for us to work out our own salvation, or rather to work for it, as if our arrival at a just and justifiable condition, under which no further temporal debt is owed, rested on our self-sanctifying penitential labor? If there are two debts, an eternal and a temporal, one paid by Christ and the other by

---

82. Hanna, "Purgatory," once again: "This purgation, of course, is made by punishments, just as in this life their purgation would have been completed by punishments which satisfy the debt; otherwise, the negligent would be better off than the solicitous, if the punishment which they do not complete for their sins here need not be undergone in the future. Therefore, if the souls of the good have something capable of purgation in this world, they are held back from the achievement of their reward while they undergo cleansing punishments. And this is the reason we hold that there is a purgatory."

83. *CDH* 1.21.

the Christian, are there not two justifications rather than one justification that includes sanctification?[84]

Fourth, it fails to say how punishment and reform are related. Perhaps it cannot, since the operative concept of justice is largely retributive. To be frank, this does not even rise to the level of decent human parenthood, never mind to the fatherhood of God. It only invites the rebellion of a Luther, or of entire populations of Luthers. If we insist, as is more common today, that the aim of penitential and purgatorial justice is primarily remedial rather than retributive, the prudential question remains, of course. That is not a problem in principle, since every exercise of justice is prudential; and in purgatory, at least, the Prudence governing the process will be perfect!

Let us pause here a moment. The Council of Trent certainly incorporates the retributive in the remedial. It requires priests to assign appropriate penances, neither too heavy nor too light, and these are to be directed not only to the protection of the newly sanctified life, as a remedy against weakness, "but also at the punishment and correction of sins already committed."[85] This will deter the penitent from further sin, befitting both divine justice and divine clemency. The sacrament, however, is not "a forum of wrath or penalties," nor does it obscure "the value of the merit and satisfaction of our Lord." From which denials we may deduce that the satisfaction we offer, through penitential acts of our own, is not something supplementary to the satisfaction of Christ, as if the latter somehow fell short in balancing the scales of justice. It is rather a means of participating voluntarily in the self-offering of Christ that saves us, a participation essential to *iustitia acquisita*; that is, to justifying grace in its transforming and reforming work. "While by making satisfaction we suffer for our sins, we become like Christ Jesus who made satisfaction for our sins, and from whom is all our sufficiency, and we also have a most sure pledge thereby that, if we suffer with him, we shall also be glorified with him."[86]

---

84. And indeed, as Luther asked, if the temporal debt can be paid in part by others, drawing on the treasury of merits belonging to Christ and the saints, why can it not simply be paid in full by Christ himself or even by the vicar of Christ? His questions, and those of the other Protestant reformers, were not always fairly framed, but neither were they always fairly or fully answered. In any case, the charge that this was fertile soil for Pelagianism was indisputably true. (My use of the expression "two justifications," by the way, should not be confused with the Regensburg proposal discussed above in n. 58.)

85. Trans. mine: *sed etiam ad praeteritorum peccatorum vindictam et castigationem* (session 14, chap. 8; *DEC* 2:709).

86. Ibid. We may participate in three ways: by penances voluntarily undertaken to atone for sin (*pro vindicando peccato susceptis*); by penances imposed by the priest in the sacrament; "but also (and this is the greatest proof of love) by the temporal afflictions imposed by God and borne by us with patience" (chap. 9). "This satisfaction which we offer in payment for our sins is not so much ours that it is not also done through Christ Jesus; for we can do nothing

The council fathers, to be sure, are not as thorough on all points as one could wish. These were relatively early days, to say nothing of the serious circumstantial difficulties they faced. Moreover, they labored in the shadow of an approach to penance and to purgatory that was christologically deficient; the Reformers were not mistaken about that. Thinking about purgatory was determined by thinking about penance, and thinking about penance suffered from a certain diminished perspective on baptism itself, the sacrament of union with Christ in which both justification and sanctification are grounded. Let me explain.

The sacrament of penance exists to deal with the sin of the baptized. Fixing on the special problem of post-baptismal sin, however, may so isolate it from baptism as to deprive baptism of the fullness proper to it. Through baptism, the whole person—in his entire history—is united to Christ, is crucified, buried, and resurrected with him.[87] Baptism, in other words, is both protological and eschatological. It makes the person new, not merely for the sake of life in this world but for the sake of the world to come. Baptism, like the Eucharist, is the inbreaking of the world to come. It is immortality taking mortality captive, righteousness taking unrighteousness captive. The sacrament of penance is strictly derivative and supportive of this. It serves to strengthen the link between baptism and the Eucharist where that link is threatened. Unlike baptism, which is unrepeatable, and the Eucharist, which is constantly repeated, penance is repeated as necessary, so that the penitent (having subjected himself to the judgment of the Church) may stand anew in the justification that baptism entails and begin again in the company of the faithful to realize the sanctification without which no one shall see the Lord. It "is necessary for those who have fallen after baptism, just as baptism itself is for those not yet regenerated."[88]

There is a twofold danger to avoid here if we mean to keep penance in proper perspective as something derivative. We must neither make too much of baptism, rendering penance unnecessary, nor make too little of baptism, rendering penance a saving work independently and in its own right.[89] We

---

of ourselves as ourselves; with his cooperation we can do everything in him who strengths us. Thus we have nothing to boast; but all our boasting is in Christ, in whom we live, in whom we merit, in whom we make satisfaction and *yield fruits that will benefit repentance*, which have their worth from him, are offered by him to the Father, and through him are accepted by the Father" (chap. 8). "Such penances help to configure us to Christ, who alone expiated our sins once for all" (CCC 1460).

87. "For by baptism we put on Christ and become in him an entirely new creature, gaining full and complete remission of all sins" (session 14, chap. 2; DEC 2:704).

88. Session 14, chap. 2; DEC 2:704; cf. Heb. 12:11–14.

89. Following Gregory Nazianzen, the council fathers speak here of penance as "a laborious kind of baptism" (*laboriosus quidam baptismus*), but neither he nor they mean to make it out

may be tempted toward the latter if we assert carelessly that baptism covers only sins committed prior to it.[90] There is indeed a difference between sins committed before and sins committed after baptism; that is, between sins committed for want of the Spirit and sins that grieve the Spirit. But to say that baptism covers only sins prior to it (or in the case of an infant only original rather than actual sin) is at best a kind of shorthand that points us to the need for penance, which rests on and derives its power from baptism. There can be no question whatever of looking to the satisfaction made by Christ to cover pre-baptismal sin, while looking to the satisfaction *we* make to cover post-baptismal sin. It is the satisfaction made by Christ that covers both. That said, the self-contradictory aspect of post-baptismal sin requires for its full remedy a restoration of the self through voluntary acts of penance, precisely as participation in Christ. He who justifies us does not do so without us, as Aquinas reminds us,[91] and in this *modus iustificationis* our repentance is a reclaiming of what belongs to us in baptism by way of penance: "Those who fall away by sin from the grace of justification which they had received, can again be justified when at God's prompting they have made the effort through the sacrament of penance to recover, by the merit of Christ, the grace which was lost."[92]

---

as something equivalent to baptism. Gregory actually enumerates six baptisms, viz., those of Moses, John, and Jesus, and those of martyrial blood, penitential tears, and purgatorial fire. All of these belong in various ways to the perfect baptism of and in Jesus. That of blood is said to be "far more august than all the others, inasmuch as it cannot be defiled by after-stains" (Or. 39, NPNF[2], 7:358).

90. Twin errors are found, on the one hand, in the assertion that "solely by the remembrance of receiving baptism and of its faith, all sins committed after baptism are forgiven or become venial" (session 7, First Decree, Canons on Baptism, no. 10; *DEC* 2:686) and, on the other, in the postponement of baptism until death's door (canon 12), a practice already existent in the patristic period among those who anticipated or feared mortal sins yet to be committed.

91. *ST* 3.84.5: "'Sin, when it is completed, begetteth death.' Consequently it is necessary for the sinner's salvation that sin be taken away from him; which cannot be done without the sacrament of Penance, wherein the power of Christ's Passion operates through the priest's absolution and the acts of the penitent, who co-operates with grace unto the destruction of his sin. For as Augustine says, 'He Who created thee without thee, will not justify thee without thee.' (Tract. lxxii *In Joann.*) Therefore it is evident that after sin the sacrament of Penance is necessary for salvation, even as bodily medicine after man has contracted a dangerous disease."

92. "For this kind of justification is a restoration of the fallen, which the holy fathers suitably call a second plank for the grace shattered in a storm. It was for the sake of those who fall into sin after baptism that Jesus Christ instituted the sacrament of penance. . . . Hence it must be taught that the repentance of a Christian after a fall is very different from repentance at baptism: it includes not only ceasing from sins and detestation of them," but also confession, absolution and satisfaction "by fasting, almsgiving, prayers and other devout exercises of the spiritual life; these take the place, not indeed of eternal punishment which is remitted together with the guilt either by the sacrament or the desire of the sacrament, but of temporal punishment which . . . is not wholly discharged—as happens in baptism—by those who, lacking

Now this dialectic, though entirely fundamental, is readily obscured in the popular mind, perhaps even in some theological minds. And this leads to talk of making satisfaction through the suffering of temporal punishments as if that suffering could be set against sins committed after baptism, much as the sufferings of Christ are set against sins committed before baptism. Which is entirely false, as Luther knew. Trent, of course, pronounced an anathema against anyone who says "that once the grace of justification has been received, the fault [*culpam*] of any repentant sinner is forgiven and the debt of eternal punishment is wiped out, in such a way that no debt of temporal punishment [*reatus poenae temporalis*] remains to be discharged, either in this world or later on in purgatory, before entry to the kingdom of heaven can lie open."[93] But we must be guided both by the dialectic and by the context in interpreting this canon. The very legitimacy of the sacrament of penance and of the doctrine of purgatory was being challenged, and a basic antinomianism, touching on civil as well as ecclesial order, threatened to engulf the Church. There are indeed temporal debts, of one kind or another, that remain to be discharged, and this had to be reconfirmed. Whatever is owed after sin to the restoration of good order—in the soul, in the body, in the Church, in civil society, in the state—must be paid, and the restoration may entail a penal or retributive element. Yet absolution for sin, if granted, is granted on the basis of Christ and Christ alone.

There is a further problem, however, in the scholastic principle that "justice demands that sin be set in order by due punishment."[94] In its weightiest aspect, as offense against God deserving of eternal punishment, sin is borne by Christ and set right by the cross; in its less weighty aspect, as deviation from creaturely order, it nonetheless has consequences that must be borne by the sinner, and whatever debts of punishment are not paid in this life must be paid in purgatory, lest justice itself fail. That purgatory concerns only the soul, detached from the temporal and social conditions belonging to its proper unity with the body, is deemed not to matter. Punishment must be fully meted, one way or another; if not in the present life, then in time added. And this means that the sinner, from the moment he is baptized, pays for his own

---

gratitude for the grace of God which they have received, have grieved the holy Spirit and not feared to violate the temple of God" (Decree on Justification, chap. 14; *DEC* 2:676f.). The 1994 catechism supplies a brief history of the sacrament at §1447.

93. *DEC* 2:681.

94. *Summa Theologiae*, appendix 2. This is a variation on the maxim we found in Hanna ("Purgatory"), that God requires satisfaction and will punish sin. It sounds very like Anselm's statement that "God cannot remit sin without punishment" (*CDH* 1.19), that God's justice "allows nothing but punishment to be the return for sin" (1.24). Unfortunately it is no longer governed by the context in which Anselm places it (see n. 98 below).

sins. Christ ensures, and the sacrament of penance assures, that the penitent sinner is not disqualified from heaven, that he still has access to the grace of God in Christ. But purgatory ensures that no sin goes unrequited before he reaches heaven.

Is this what is meant by the Council of Florence when it says that *eoram animas penis purgatoriis post-mortem purgari*?[95] Whence arise these "cleansing pains" or penalties that purge the soul after death? From what are they purging it, and for what? Is their real purpose, as even Aquinas supposes, to fill up what is lacking in temporal punishment, to make sure that no one evades any due consequences of their fault? Surely not. The god whose justice, backed by infinite computational powers, squeezes every last punitive farthing from his purgatorial wards is not the God and Father of Jesus Christ.[96] We do well to interpret Florence and Trent in a manner more in keeping with recent teaching, and for that matter with the earlier teaching of Augustine and Anselm. For the scholastic approach does not do justice to the justice of God in Christ. It does not do justice to justification and therefore cannot do justice to sanctification. It was this error that led Luther into his own error; that is, to the abandonment of the doctrine of purgatory along with much else that belonged to the faith of the Church.[97]

---

95. DEC 1:527.

96. "In anger," says Jesus, "his lord delivered him to the jailers, till he should pay all his debt. So also my heavenly Father will do to every one of you, if you do not forgive your brother from your heart" (Matt. 18:21ff.). The warning is in earnest and is ignored at great peril; but it should not be overlooked that the anger in question stems from the servant's refusal to release his brother from a temporal debt just as he himself had been released from temporal debt. Nothing could be further from the truth than to suppose that God is bound to requite every sin with the temporal punishment due it.

97. I do not mean to saddle the schoolmen with Luther's own error. He was free to criticize the inauthentic features of the Christianity of his day, as we are of ours. But he was not free, nor are we, to reject Church doctrine or to rewrite the Church's liturgy (a subject we will take up in the next chapter) or to alter its canon or to defy its canon law. That sort of freedom is really a form of despair. Not the redemptive despair of the man who turns from the false object of trust to the true—that is, from himself to Christ—but the destructive despair of one who turns from the Church of Christ to himself or to some other supposed *theodidactos*. In his own manifesto, *Rationes Decem*, produced in 1581 shortly before his martyrdom from a clandestine loft at Stonor House, St. Edmund Campion pointed this out, albeit rather more pugnaciously than suits us in our more comfortable surroundings: "What induced that crime-laden apostate Luther to call the Epistle of James contentious, turgid, arid, a thing of straw, and unworthy of the Apostolic spirit? Despair. For by this writing the wretched man's argument of righteousness consisting in faith alone was stabbed through and rent asunder. What induced Luther's whelps to expunge off-hand from the genuine canon of Scripture, Tobias, Ecclesiasticus, Maccabees, and, for hatred of these, several other books involved in the same false charge? Despair. For by these Oracles they are most manifestly confuted whenever they argue about the patronage of Angels, about free will, about the faithful departed, about the intercession of Saints."

Purgatory is for our complete sanctification and, just so, for the fullness of our justification. Both are vouchsafed to us in Christ, who has indeed relieved us of the threat of punishment by offering satisfaction for sin. Just here Anselm's distinction between *satisfactio* and *poena* is particularly helpful. To make satisfaction for sin (*pro peccato satisfacere*) is not to undergo punishment but to make punishment unnecessary, and this is what Christ does on our behalf, since we are unable to do it for ourselves. On this approach, the treatment of the penitent sinner cannot be a matter of suitable punishments, for punishments belong to the impenitent who will not receive what Christ has done. It must rather be a matter of the suitable purification or restoration of the soul that has sinned, such that it is rendered fit—this too is a matter of divine justice, and in a still higher sense, for it is God doing justice to his own love and faithfulness—to receive eternal happiness with Christ.[98]

In this light, we see that the aim of purgatory is not punitive, at least not in the sense that prevails among the later schoolmen, who risk making the doctrine of purgatory a defense against any and every injury to divine justice, when that defense has already been made in Christ. Its aim, rather, is perfective, and any punitive element is governed by the confluence of *gratia sanans* and *gratia elevans* in sweeping the soul on to glory.[99] Purgatorial grace is the grace that completes what is lacking in our cooperation in the destruction of our tendency to sin, or in what makes us truly receptive of God and of glory. It is the grace that removes the remaining blight of sin that hinders the rendering of a free offering of ourselves to God through, with, and in Christ, so that we may properly enjoy with Christ the presence of God, partaking in the divine economy of giving and receiving that constitutes eternal life. Understood thus, it is an altogether evangelical doctrine.

If the chief aim of penance is reformation not retribution, the same is true a fortiori of purgatory.[100] Florence and Trent can and should be thus interpreted,

---

98. See again *CDH* 1.19 (*sine satisfactione, i.e., sine debiti solutione spontanea, nec Deus potest peccatum impunitum dimittere nec peccator ad beatitudinem . . . pervenire*) and 1.24. The debt of sin is paid either by satisfaction—meaning restitution, the restoration of what was wrongly taken—or by punishment, not by both. Restitution is essential to man's happiness; punishment is unhappiness. In the former there is both justice and mercy, wholly united; in the latter there is only justice. See further chap. 4, however, where the differences between Anselm and Aquinas will be probed and some mediation attempted.

99. Punishment can of course have "a medicinal purpose" (*CCC* 2266), but punishment in the secular sphere, or even in the ecclesiastical, should not be confused with the sacrament of penance or with the state of purgatory, neither of which are essentially punitive. *Reatus poenae temporalis* means one thing in the secular sphere and another in the ecclesial.

100. Obviously their proclamations on purgatory owe much to the scholastic heritage. Does that mean that we must ignore the fact that the scholastics erred in their thinking about purgatory, because they had erred already in their thinking about penance? Does it mean that we must

without injury to magisterial authority and without embarrassment about a debt to Luther and the other Protestant reformers. The catechism refers us to those councils, of course, yet it speaks of purgatory only very cautiously as the "purification of the elect, which is entirely different from the punishment of the damned"—thus clearly distinguishing between what Florence, in passing, lumps together by speaking *de penis purgatorii et inferni.*[101]

It is not quite so restrained in the matter of indulgences, however, and we must take this into account. First, the definition of Paul VI is repeated: "An indulgence is a remission before God of the temporal punishment due to sins whose guilt has already been forgiven, which the faithful Christian who is duly disposed gains under certain prescribed conditions through the action of the Church which, as the minister of redemption, dispenses and applies with authority the treasury of the satisfactions of Christ and the saints."[102] It is then pointed out "that sin has a double consequence," viz., depriving us of communion with God, if it is grave sin (this is eternal punishment), and attaching us in unhealthy ways to creatures (this is temporal punishment).[103] It is added that *both* consequences or punishments follow "from the very nature of sin" rather than being imposed "as a kind of vengeance inflicted by God from without," and that the latter remains when the former is remitted. The alleviation of the latter is ultimately by the fervent charity for God that overcomes our inordinate attachments. In short, the alleviation of the latter is by sanctification. But sanctification itself is the enjoyment of grace, and so it is that the power of binding and loosing that belongs to the Church extends to the aiding of the sinner's sanctification through the grace of indulgences. All of this precludes the understanding of indulgences in the manner to which Luther objected (as free passes, so to say) *and* the understanding of purgatory as essentially penal. The penalties or temporal punishments already exist. Purgatory is the remedy for, not the cause of, penalties, though as such it is indeed the cause of "cleansing pains."[104]

---

persist with the model still operative in Hanna ("Purgatory")? "This purgation, of course, is made by punishments, just as in this life their purgation would have been completed by punishments which satisfy the debt; otherwise, the negligent would be better off than the solicitous, if the punishment which they do not complete for their sins here need not be undergone in the future. Therefore, if the souls of the good have something capable of purgation in this world, they are held back from the achievement of their reward while they undergo cleansing punishments. And this is the reason we hold that there is a purgatory." I think not.

101. §1030; cf. *DEC* 1:557.

102. "An indulgence is partial or plenary according as it removes either part or all of the temporal punishment due to sin" (§1471; quoting *Indulgentiarum doctrina*, Norm 1).

103. §1472. More precisely, this is *one form* of temporal punishment, but it is altogether noteworthy that it is the form given, the form considered relevant.

104. See §1473. Origen is not far off the mark with this comment: "For if on the foundation of Christ you have built not only gold and silver and precious stones (1 Corinthians 3); but

It remains only to ask: If purgatory does not make good on missing temporal consequences, whether in tit-for-tat recompense of sin or in any other sense, and if indulgences do not have such a character or purpose as they were sometimes thought to have in Luther's day, what shall we say of the concern of the schoolmen with respect to the unevenness of just consequences for sin (that is, of those external to the soul itself, such as hangovers for heavy drinking, ostracism for hypocrisy, incarceration for crime, etc.)? Surely these are like those other temporal inequities that are the result of another's sin or of no particular sin at all, as poverty and disease and accident may be. We do not and cannot know the reason why one person is afflicted by them and another is not; nor can we say for certain that all will be brought into balance. What we can know is that this type of inequity will be swept away, in the remaking of the world, with every other imperfection.[105] What will not be swept away is the need for justice in the sons and daughters of God. Refusal to seek justice or any other virtue is incompatible with eternal life. Inadequate love of virtue or possession of virtue is what purgatory overcomes. God will indeed bring every deed into judgment in that sense, for every evil deed bears its own punishment within itself inasmuch as it leaves us further from glory and, absent appropriate forms of penance, places us more deeply in debt to purgatory. But purgatory, like penance, is no "forum for wrath and penalties" administered by avenging angels.[106] Benedict XVI remarks in *Spe salvi* that purgatory is "simply purification through fire in the encounter with the Lord," an encounter personal to each soul: "At the moment of judgement we experience and we absorb the overwhelming power of [Christ's] love over all the evil in the world and in ourselves. The pain of love becomes our salvation and our joy."[107]

---

also wood and hay and stubble, what do you expect when the soul shall be separated from the body? Would you enter into heaven with your wood and hay and stubble and thus defile the kingdom of God; or on account of these hindrances would you remain without and receive no reward for your gold and silver and precious stones? Neither is this just. It remains then that you be committed to the fire which will burn the light materials; for our God to those who can comprehend heavenly things is called a cleansing fire. But this fire consumes not the creature, but what the creature has himself built, wood and hay and stubble. It is manifest that the fire destroys the wood of our transgressions and then returns to us the reward of our great works" (*On Jeremiah*, Hom. 16 [*PG* 13, col. 445, 448]; quoted by Hanna, "Purgatory").

105. Inequities there will be, of course, and these entirely just; for some will be saved with their works, and be rewarded for them, while some will be saved "only as through fire" (1 Cor. 3:13–15).

106. Dante, whatever else we make of his *Purgatorio*, strikes the right note in the opening canto, in turning to "that second realm, which purifies man's spirit of its soilure . . . , where it becomes worthy of Paradise": glancing around as he emerges from hell, he observes that "the planet that promoteth Love was there, making all the East to laugh and be joyful" (trans. L. Binyon).

107. "It is clear," Benedict adds, "that we cannot calculate the 'duration' of this transforming burning in terms of the chronological measurements of this world. The transforming 'moment'

If nothing else, this passage shows that the Church is still pondering its doctrine of purgatory with a view to making it more thoroughly and more obviously evangelical. That is not so difficult a task if purgatory, the final stage of our sanctification, is kept firmly within the purview of the justifying and perfecting grace of God, which through the furnace of love completes what it began in the cold waters of baptism. For just as there is a water and a fire that destroy sin and sinners in holy judgment, indeed in vengeance, so that they no longer stand before God or interfere with the creatures of God, so there is a water and a fire that deliver sinners from sin in holy salvation, so that they may stand before God and the creatures of God in perpetual joy. Flood and conflagration are answered by font and purgatorial graces. Justification sanctifies, and the sanctified are justified. *Sola dei gloria*, as the Reformers were wont to say. Or, as the fathers of Trent said, "no Christian should ever either rely on or glory in himself and not in the Lord, whose goodness toward all is so great that he desires his own gifts to be their merits."[108]

---

of this encounter eludes earthly time-reckoning—it is the heart's time, it is the time of 'passage' to communion with God in the Body of Christ." (*Spe salvi* 47, or more briefly in §48: "in the communion of souls simple terrestrial time is superseded.")

108. Session 6, chap. 16; DEC 2:678.

4

Satisfaction and Punishment

Reckoning with Anselm

Some of the difficulties of the late-medieval era were connected, as we have seen, to confusion about the relation between satisfaction and punishment in atonement. Between Anselm and Aquinas a divergence already appeared on this very matter. The confusion was not resolved by the Protestant reformers, who were concerned only to say that Christ's atonement is entirely sufficient for the forgiveness of sins and, as such, incapable of being augmented by sacramental or penitential action. The Catholic reply, which did not deny that sufficiency but affirmed the need for sacramental participation in it, was difficult for Protestants to digest—not only because their *sola fide* and their nominalist commitment to univocity made it so, but because Catholics themselves were unclear about the role of punishment in satisfaction and hence unclear also about the nature of this participation. Penitential theory and praxis seemed to imply a topping-up of atonement through additional payments, as it were. We will deal with the nominalists later, in another connection; namely, the autonomy doctrine that develops in modernity as attention to sacramental solidarity recedes. What we need to do here is to probe more deeply into the theology of atonement, so as to clarify the relation in question and to capitalize on the contribution of Anselm. This, it may be hoped, will make more tenable the negotiation we were pursuing.

Satisfactio aut poena?

That sin cannot be winked at by a just God was never in doubt; that it cannot be overlooked by a merciful God, likewise. How would it be either just or merciful to excuse sin rather than to expiate it or to receive sinners qua sinners without relieving them of their sin? How could the holiness of God be maintained if sin were excused? How could the person come to perfection, or the creation attain to glory, if sin were passed over? But how is sin expiated? How is atonement for sin wrought? About this there was, and still is, dispute.

It is not difficult to find examples, then or now, of people who approach the atonement supposing it to consist in the carrying out of a fit punishment, borne by the savior rather than by the sinner—as if Jesus had said, "Punish me, not them," and the Father had replied, "My justice is satisfied so long as the punishment is meted out." On this view, divine justice lies in the dispensing of a condign punishment and divine mercy is the voluntary assumption of that punishment by the savior, who himself deserved no punishment.[1]

That is not how Anselm sees the matter, however. On his view, justice is restored either by satisfaction *or* by punishment. For the debt of sin is just that, a debt, which can be paid in the one way or in the other.[2] The sinner is a sinner because he abandons justice, because he is unwilling to preserve rectitude of will for its own sake. In this he has both defrauded God of the honor due him and defrauded the creation of its condign order, the order that conduces to happiness and perfection.[3] The essential nature of sin (though,

1. Luther goes still further in his 1535 commentary on Galatians at 3:13: "All the prophets of old said that Christ should be the greatest transgressor, murderer, adulterer, thief, blasphemer that ever was or ever could be on earth. When He took the sins of the whole world upon Himself, Christ was no longer an innocent person. He was a sinner burdened with the sins of a Paul who was a blasphemer; burdened with the sins of a Peter who denied Christ; burdened with the sins of a David who committed adultery and murder. . . . In short, Christ was charged with the sins of all men, that He should pay for them with His own blood. . . . He was not only in the company of sinners. He had gone so far as to invest Himself with the flesh and blood of sinners. So the Law judged and hanged Him for a sinner. . . . Being the unspotted Lamb of God, Christ was personally innocent. But because He took the sins of the world, His sinlessness was defiled with the sinfulness of the world. Whatever sins I, you, all of us have committed or shall commit, they are Christ's sins as if He had committed them Himself. Our sins have to be Christ's sins or we shall perish forever" (Martin Luther, *Commentary on the Epistle to the Galatians*, trans. Theodore Graebner [Grand Rapids: Zondervan, 1949]; *LW* 26:277–78).

2. If it is not paid for in either way, it is subject to no law (*CDH* 1.12), which is unfitting. See *CDH* 1.8 for an explicit repudiation of the view later espoused by Luther. (Cf. Karl Barth, *CD* 4.1:238, for an "in substance" endorsement of Luther.)

3. "The alternatives, voluntary recompense for wrongdoing, or the exaction of punishment from someone who does not give recompense, retain their own proper place in this same universal order and their own regulatory beauty. If the divine Wisdom did not impose these forms of recompense in cases where wrongdoing is endeavouring to upset the right order of

properly speaking, sin has no nature) is just this failure to render to God what is everywhere and always owed him, namely, gratitude and obedience; for the essential nature of the rational creature is to be a willing recipient of, and deliberate cooperator in, divine gifts.[4]

Now man is in no position to pay what he owes, even if he wants to. He is therefore subject to punishment; that is, to being deprived against his will of that which he has or hopes to have. He is altogether at odds with himself, as well as with God. If that situation is to be rectified, if what sin has made wrong is to be set right, the *eucharistia* and *obedientia* that was denied God must be offered after all.[5] Which is what only the God-man can do, and does, for he alone among men preserves justice in himself, doing the Father's will and rendering thanks freely. He gives to both God and man, "spontaneously and not as of debt."[6] As man, he offers what man ought to offer; for man, he offers still more, because he offers himself even unto death, when he is under no obligation or sentence of death. And this "still more" is of infinite worth, outweighing every actual or possible offense against God, because it is the offering not just of any man but of the God-man.[7]

---

things, there would be in the universe, which God ought to be regulating, a certain ugliness, resulting from the violation of the beauty of order, and God would appear to be failing in his governance. Since these two consequences are as impossible as they are unfitting, it is inevitable that recompense or punishment follows upon every sin" (*CDH* 1.15, trans. Janet Fairweather in *Anselm of Canterbury: The Major Works*, ed. Brian Davies and G. R. Evans [Oxford: Oxford University Press, 1998]; cf. 1.11).

4. Cf. *De casu diaboli*, which is governed by 1 Cor. 4:7, "What have you that you did not receive?" By extension, the person who is just and happy is a giver as well as a receiver of gifts. Failures of justice are indeed rooted, as Sarah Coakley suggests in "Sin and Desire in Analytic Theology: a Return to Genesis 3" (*Journal of Analytic Theology* 5 [forthcoming]), in disordered desire for good things; but, as Anselm has it, the original disorder, introduced by the devil, lies in distortion of the highest possible desire, the desire to be like God, when that is sought in a manner and at a time of one's own determining, rather than in union and communion with God. The fall, whether of the devil or of man, consists in a grasping after happiness that brooks no deferral; which is injustice, injustice to God, and this injustice places one outside the economy of gift in which alone justice and happiness are in fact possible.

5. "God needed not to save man in this way, but human nature had need that in this way it should satisfy to God" (Med. 11, "Of the Redemption of Mankind," in *St Anselm's Book of Meditations and Prayers*, trans. M. R. [London: Burns & Gates, 1872], 70). Otherwise neither would man be capable of happiness, nor would the good order essential to joy and happiness reign in creation.

6. Ibid., 71. Mary also preserves justice, but she has this capacity from him: "Keep joyful holiday, sweet Mother, joyful and unending in the peaceful vision of thy Jesus, the Author of thy immunity from sin" (Med. 13, "Of Christ," *Meditations and Prayers*, 85).

7. "He gave his life, so precious; no, his very self; he gave his person—think of it—in all its greatness, in an act of his own, supremely great, volition" (*CDH* 2.18). That he gave under no compulsion whatever is again made clear in the *Meditatio redemptionis humanae*: "Nor did human nature in [the] God-Man suffer aught by any kind of necessity, but only by free election.

On Anselm's view, then, punishment comes into play for those who do not avail themselves of the satisfaction Christ makes—those who refuse baptism and disdain the invitation, "Take, eat; this is my body, broken for you." It comes into play only for those who are not recipients of the inexhaustible reward he has merited for them. They will indeed be punished, and punished eternally, by being denied, with the fallen angels, any place among those who experience the presence of God and the goodness of creation. Their only contribution to that goodness will lie in the fact that they *are* properly punished, punished justly for the sin they unjustly committed.[8]

Anselm is not at all hesitant to talk about eternal punishment, especially in his analysis of the freedom of rational souls, who have the power to preserve what is originally given them (namely, rectitude of will) and are the cause of their own downfall.[9] Nor is he afraid to talk about penitence and temporal chastisements, since he is deeply interested in the reformation of the will among those who are being saved.[10] The emphasis, however, falls squarely on the satisfaction rendered by Christ and on the generosity of the divine mercy, which, without any injury to justice, makes a way of escape from eternal punishment:

Nor did it succumb unwillingly to any violence from without, but by spontaneous goodness, endured at once nobly and mercifully, for the honour of God and the benefit of mankind generally, the evils by wicked will inflicted on it; and that by no compulsion of obedience, but by the disposition of an almighty wisdom. For the Father did not impose death upon [the] God-Man by a compulsory imposition, but what He knew would be pleasing to His Father and profitable to mankind, that He voluntarily did" (*Meditations and Prayers*, 72).

8. Divine wisdom, in giving over to punishment the sinner who does not in Christ make satisfaction, changes "his wrong desire or action into the order and beauty of the universal scheme of things" simply by refusing to permit the violation of good order that unrequited sin would amount to (*CDH* 1.15). God does not otherwise make use of the sinner in depriving him against his will of what, by reason of his created vocation, belongs to him—viz., that he should be happy. (Here it is worth observing, *pace* Coakley ["Sin and Desire"], that Anselm is not at all concerned with theodicy; he is working rather at a theology of freedom, on which I will say more in chap. 7. Theodicy is always a mistake; from Anselm's perspective, a mistake in principle.)

9. Rational souls are also, in part, the causes of their own share in eternal life, for God wills that this be a feature, a godlike feature, of their eventual happiness. Speaking of good and bad angels, Anselm says: "For both received from God the possession [of justice] and the ability to keep it and the ability to forsake it. God gave this latter ability so that they would be able in some manner to give justice to themselves" (*DCD* 18; cf. *CDH* 2.10). Likewise with man, except that only Adam and Eve were analogously situated. Fallen man retains the power to preserve rectitude of will if he has it, but of course he doesn't have it unless he receives it back in Christ. Anselm, alas, does not address the situation of those to whom providence does not grant the opportunity to receive it back; indeed, he does not deal satisfactorily with the relation between infant salvation and the restoration of freedom.

10. Cf. Meditations 8 and 19. Both temporal chastisements and eternal punishment are imposed upon sinners contrary to their will; penitence, however, is an act of the will that makes good use of temporal chastisement.

Now the mercy of God which, when we were considering the justice of God and the sin of mankind, seemed to you to be dead, we have found to be so great, and so consonant with justice, that a greater and juster mercy cannot be imagined. What, indeed, can be conceived of more merciful than that God the Father should say to a sinner condemned to eternal torments and lacking any mean of redeeming himself, "Take my only-begotten Son and give him on your behalf," and that the Son himself should say, "Take me and redeem yourself." For it is something of this sort that they say when they call us and draw us towards the Christian faith. What also could be juster than that the one to whom is given a reward greater than any debt should absolve all debt, if it is presented with the feeling that is due?[11]

In sum, Anselm thinks that sin requires either payment or punishment and that payment averts punishment. The payment or satisfaction made by Jesus—his complete obedience of love, offered precisely where it need not be offered, viz., among sinners and under the sentence of death that hangs over sinners—is an offering of infinite worth that outweighs any and every sin by which man attempts to defraud God of the honor due him.[12] The reward he earns from God for the gratuitous donation of his life is more than sufficient to cover the entire human debt. This reward he shares freely by continuing to offer himself to those who will receive him. The circle of satisfaction or atonement is closed, so to say, by the embrace of the gospel and by humble reception of the sacraments. Punishment is therefore stayed.[13]

And what of Aquinas? How does he approach the matter? Aquinas doesn't draw the Anselmian distinction between satisfaction and punishment. His own distinction is between punishment, viewed simply (*poena simpliciter*)—that is, the punishment necessarily attached to particular sins by reason of their affront to just order, the punishment that is contrary to the will of the one committing the sin—and "satisfactory punishment" (*poena satisfactoria*), punishment that is freely received either for the purpose of conforming the

11. *CDH* 2.20 (trans. Fairweather, *Anselm of Canterbury*). *Si debito datur affectu*: that is, freely and gladly, in keeping with the economy of gift; thus also Irenaeus (*Haer.* 4.18.2; cf. 4.13.3), who is better at the pneumatology essential to any explanation of how souls are healed and restored in union with Christ.

12. See *CDH* 2.12; cf. Heb. 5:8–10. Jesus owes his whole life to God, like any other man; he does not, however, owe it to God to die. His death he adds superabundantly, as it were. This would not be so, of course, were death part of the original design for man, a view Anselm rejects in the previous chapter, though one might try to make the case that it was the *manner* of his death, rather than the death itself, that was a superabundant gift. (This, however, would weaken the argument. J. R. R. Tolkien does a fine job in *Athrabeth Finrod ah Andreth* of exploring and repudiating the view that death is natural to man.)

13. The word "punishment" all but disappears in book 2.

soul to God and restoring its lost powers or out of charity toward another who is not himself able to bear it.[14] Aquinas acknowledges that this second kind of punishment "loses something of the nature of punishment" (*diminuit aliquid de ratione poenae*) just because it is voluntarily received, but it remains punishment nonetheless.[15]

Jesus, of course, has no sin, original or actual, that could be punished. Yet in Aquinas's scheme (not unlike Luther's) God does inflict on him the punishment that belongs to the sins of others, which he patiently bears for our sake. This approach to atonement, which posits a vicarious suffering of the penalties due sin, requires Aquinas to argue that Jesus suffers both in body and in soul a suffering greater than any other man. Thus he adds to Anselm's account an emphasis on the extent and profundity of Jesus's suffering:

> He properly atones [*satisfacit*] for an offense who offers something which the offended one loves equally, or even more than he detested the offense. But by suffering out of love and obedience, Christ gave more to God than was required to compensate for the offense of the whole human race. First of all, because of the exceeding charity from which He suffered; secondly, on account of the dignity of His life which He laid down in atonement, for it was the life of one who was God and man; *thirdly, on account of the extent of the Passion, and the greatness of the grief endured*, as stated above. And therefore Christ's Passion was not only a sufficient but a superabundant atonement for the sins of the human race; according to 1 Jn. 2:2: "He is the propitiation for our sins: and not for ours only, but also for those of the whole world."[16]

14. With respect to the soul, see *ST* 1–2.87.6: "Now man is united to God by his will. Wherefore the stain of sin cannot be removed from man, unless his will accept the order of divine justice, that is to say, unless either of his own accord he take upon himself the punishment of his past sin, or bear patiently the punishment which God inflicts on him; and in both ways punishment avails for satisfaction." With respect to charitable substitution, see *ST* 1–2.87.7: "And since those who differ as to the debt of punishment may be one in will by the union of love, it happens that one who has not sinned bears willingly the punishment for another" (cf. *Supp.* 13.2).

15. *ST* 1–2.87.6. How punishment, voluntarily undertaken, otherwise differs in quality or quantity is not clear, except to say that it is governed by its medicinal purpose and desired outcomes. Ad 2 reads: "The virtuous man does not deserve punishment simply, but he may deserve it as satisfactory, because his very virtue demands that he should do satisfaction for his offenses against God or man." Ad 3 adds: "When the stain is removed, the wound of sin is healed as regards the will. But punishment is still requisite in order that the other powers of the soul be healed, since they were so disordered by the sin committed, so that, to wit, the disorder may be remedied by the contrary of that which caused it. Moreover punishment is requisite in order to restore the equality of justice, and to remove the scandal given to others, so that those who were scandalized at the sin many be edified by the punishment."

16. *ST* 3.48.2 (emphasis added). The passage referred to is at 3.46.6: "Fourthly, the magnitude of the pain of Christ's suffering can be reckoned by this, that the pain and sorrow were

Satisfaction and Punishment · 107

Anselm's teaching that Christ presents an offering that infinitely outweighs the dishonor done to God by the sin of would-be autonomous man, and that his reward is shared with all who by faith and the sacraments are joined to him, is not in dispute here; what is in dispute is whether Anselm is right in contrasting satisfaction to punishment—the *aut* in his s*atisfactio aut poena*. This *aut* Aquinas quietly elides.[17]

So: Is the punishment that attaches to sin removed because Jesus has already suffered it, as Aquinas thinks? Or is it removed because Jesus has offered a satisfaction that makes it unnecessary and unfitting, as Anselm thinks? Again, both agree that a debt is owed and that it is freely paid by the savior. One, however, calls the payment satisfaction; the other calls it satisfactory punishment. One does not have God punishing Jesus, but man; the other has God punishing Jesus through man. One thinks that sin requires payment and that payment averts punishment; the other thinks that payment is by way of bearing sin's punishment. One is focused on the honor that payment brings to God; the other on the benefit that punishment brings to man. These views are different, and the difference matters in particular to our penitential theology. Yet perhaps we can mediate between them by conceding to Aquinas that punishment does come upon Jesus *from* God, while conceding to Anselm that it is not directed at Jesus *by* God? If our mediation is successful, we will be in a better position to provide a solid point of reference to that theology.

The Punishment Jesus Does, and Does Not, Bear

With respect to the penalties or punishments attached to sin, we must distinguish between the temporal and the eternal. Temporal punishments are those that follow more or less directly and immediately from the sin itself.

---

accepted voluntarily, to the end of men's deliverance from sin; and consequently He embraced the amount of pain proportionate to the magnitude of the fruit which resulted therefrom."

17. At *ST* 1.47.3, Aquinas answers the charge that this would be unjust by appeal to Rom. 8:32: "God hath not spared His own Son, but delivered Him up for us all." He allows, of course, that "Christ suffered voluntarily out of obedience to the Father" but argues that the Father did deliver him up in three respects. "In the first way, because by His eternal will He preordained Christ's Passion for the deliverance of the human race, according to the words of Isaias" (here he appeals to Isa. 53:6, 10). "Secondly, inasmuch as, by the infusion of charity, He inspired Him with the will to suffer for us; hence we read in the same passage: 'He was offered because it was His own will.' Thirdly, by not shielding Him from the Passion, but abandoning Him to His persecutors." All this sounds very Anselmian, as does the elaboration in ad 1, until we read that God's goodness here "shines forth, since by no penalty endured could man pay Him enough satisfaction" (*cum homo sufficienter satisfacere non posset per aliquam poenam quam pateretur, ei satisfactorem dedit*). The elision is clear.

"In the day that you eat of it you shall die." Why? Because in departing from the path marked out by God man departs from God himself. He is put out of Eden and left to his own resources. These resources are still the good gifts God has given him in the natural order, but they are subject to corruption. Only communion with God can preserve them incorrupt (*ST* 1–2.109.2). Departing the path marked out by God is embarking on an entropic path, a cursed path, a path in which the intended consequences of human acts are realized, if they are realized at all, only with difficulty and at the cost of unintended consequences. Insofar as the act itself is sinful or tainted by sin, it will produce not order but disorder, not happiness but unhappiness, not security but insecurity. Those who take up the sword shall perish by the sword. Those who seek to save their lives shall lose it. And those who by copulation give new life shall not do so as the immortal gods of poetic fancy do; rather, they shall do so as those being gathered to their own fathers and mothers in the dust of the earth. "You are dust, and to dust you shall return."[18]

Eternal punishments are those that carry over into death and beyond death, effected by the judgment that leads to what the Apocalypse calls the second death. The first death, however difficult or easy, is itself a just penalty for sin, but not the whole of that penalty. For the disorder of sin is first and foremost a disordered relation to the Creator, not merely to the creature. It is therefore not addressed by the first death alone. It deprives man both of the happiness proper to this life and of the happiness proper to the world to come, the world to which the present world is but a prelude. "This is the sort of life that belongs to the human soul," says Anselm, "provided that it keeps to the purpose for which it exists: it will, at some time, live the happy life, the life truly immune from death and all distress."[19] Should it not keep to its purpose, however, it faces an endlessly unhappy life, shut out from the presence of its Maker, as Jesus himself taught. There it will suffer in perpetuity the penalties that correspond to its spiritual deformities, just as the righteous soul will enjoy the glories that correspond to its righteousness.

Of the first kind of punishment we ourselves are the primary agent or efficient cause, since it comes to us as a consequence of our own actions. As we try in vain to withdraw from the order proper to creatures, we deprive ourselves of the goodness of our own being and the goodness of others as well. We place ourselves, so to say, on the reverse side of divine providence and are thus banished from Eden. "God is not mocked, for whatever a man

18. Cf. Augustine, *De bono coniugali* 2.
19. *Monologion* 69 (trans. Simon Harrison, in Davies and Evans, *Anselm of Canterbury*); cf. *CDH* 2.2–4. By "soul" he means the whole person, mind and body.

sows, that he will also reap" (Gal. 6:7). On the other hand, we can sometimes say that God is the primary agent and efficient cause; for temporal punishment may come upon us as a targeted intervention, such as the fire that fell on Sodom or the plagues that fell on Egypt. Ordinarily, however, and often quite incommensurately, it comes to us at the hands of other sinners, or of cursed and mistreated nature, governed by general rather than special providence. It comes to us even by accident, as when a poorly built bridge collapses or the Tower of Siloam falls. As for eternal punishment, we must admit that, though we remain the architects of our own downfall, it is something into which we are cast by the direct order of Jesus Christ and by the determinate action of the holy angels, just as the armies of Pharaoh were cast into the Red Sea when the rod of Moses was thrust over it. Eternal punishment is an act of God that corresponds to a prior act of man, but God in his sovereignty (exercised through the incarnate Son) becomes the primary actor, as is only fitting in a universe that glorifies God.[20]

This distinction is important, because the very idea that justice is served only if Jesus bears the punishment due our sin requires us to say that he bears both the temporal and the eternal punishment—as if his Golgotha experience, for the purposes of justice, were equivalent to hell; whereas the satisfaction theory, which rules out his bearing of eternal punishment, does not rule out, but indeed requires, that he bear temporal punishment, though in what manner remains to be clarified. In filling out our account of that, we can remark also the difficulties with the *poena satisfactoria* approach.[21]

Now the life that Jesus lives, he lives among those already being punished, by and for their sins, with various temporal punishments. His prayerful decision in Gethsemane is to complete his occupation of this place, the place where man is handed over to suffering and death and the wiles of the devil, the place where he is left by God to his own resources—just as he asked to be when he demanded his own "proper" will, when he insisted on an autonomous will subject to no one, not even to God. Though Jesus has lived his entire life in this place, he is under no obligation to remain in it, since he himself has not pursued that kind of autonomy but has lived rather in faithfulness to

20. Matt. 24:48–25:46 and similar passages certainly warrant this claim; yet there is another side to it, as Dante noticed in leaving open the gate of hell; cf. Brian Horne, "The Cross and the Comedy," in *The Theology of Reconciliation*, ed. Colin Gunton (London: T&T Clark, 2003), 153.

21. Though Dante, as Horne ("The Cross and the Comedy") observes, owes much to Anselm in *Paradiso* c. 7, it seems that he follows Aquinas more closely in the present matter: "Sin alone is that / Which doth disfranchise him, and make unlike / To the chief good; for that its light in him / Is darken'd. And to dignity thus lost / Is no return; unless, where guilt makes void, He for ill pleasure pay with equal pain" (trans. Henry Cary).

his Father. It is by his own choice, then, that he becomes subject to suffering and death and the plans of the evil one: "For this reason the Father loves me, because I lay down my life, that I may take it again. No one takes it from me, but I lay it down of my own accord" (John 10:17–18). Without any other cause than love for God and for what belongs to God, he accepts the curse of the covenant breaker. He suffers Israel's fate at the hands of the Romans. He is crucified under Pontius Pilate.[22] That is the particular way that he also suffers every man's temporal fate, undergoing the sentence of death that falls on all who are born with original sin. That is the way he endures the punishment God had in mind when he said to Adam and Eve at the foot of the tree of the knowledge of good and evil, "In the day that you eat of it you shall die."

Is this God punishing Jesus? Not according to Anselm. Rather, it is what Aquinas would later call "a union of love"—though the love at this point is strictly unilateral—through which Jesus accompanies man to the bitter end, putting faithfulness in place of faithlessness every step of the way.[23] This, to be sure, means sharing the punishment that falls by general providence on sinful man and, by special providence, on those who have spurned the grace of the covenant; that is, on that man who has a second time abandoned the God by whom he was graciously partnered in spite of his sin. It also means (if we may borrow further from Aquinas) bearing a burden that the loved one has not and cannot bear. For Jesus suffers alone in a manner that no other does. Mary and John are there, at the foot of the cross, and a few others. But he is bereft of the comfort of his Father, the comfort that has preserved him in peace and sustained him throughout his life in the face of every other trial. He is bereft because he has willingly gone to the place that is outside the covenant promise and protection. He has gone all the way to the place man goes when he tries to go beyond God and to act without God.[24]

What kind of place is that? It is not a place where God is not, for in the present world there is no such place.[25] It *is* a place where God hides himself

22. Though neither Anselm nor Aquinas incorporates historical detail directly into the analysis in the way that Augustine does, say, or in the way a modern history-conscious theologian might, both are thinking historically. The difference is more one of genre than of substance.
23. Cf. 1 John 4:10. We are not wrong to detect something analogous to Irenaeus's recapitulation theory, though it is not as fully developed in Anselm. The flavor is that of the Epistle to the Hebrews. Jesus joins himself—freely and sovereignly—to man under discipline and sentence of death, tasting death with and for everyone, while referring all things back to God in high-priestly fashion (Heb. 2:9; cf. *Haer.* 2.22.4).
24. "Cursed be everyone who hangs on a tree" (Gal. 3:13; cf. Deut. 21:23 and Sir. 18:24).
25. Cf. Pss. 22 and 139. Neither at Golgotha nor at Birkenau is God altogether absent. As hellish as each is, hell itself (the everlasting "outer darkness" of Matt. 8:12, 22:13, and 25:30) is another place and another matter altogether. Though there, too, a form of presence—the presence of the one God, who is always and everywhere both justice and mercy—may be posited,

from man. It is a place where the human experience of God is an experience
only of absence, where there is only a "no" and not a "yes," and even the no
is not so much heard as deduced. *Eli, Eli, lama sabachthani!* Certainly the
turning away of the Father, who had always given him the assurance, "This
is my beloved Son, with whom I am well pleased," is the deepest depth of
this place, existentially, for it is the most severe consequence that attaches to
sin. "He was wounded for our transgressions, he was bruised for our iniquities." This wounding and bruising, as Aquinas argues, entails a suffering the
scale of which we cannot grasp—a suffering that seems, though it lasts but
a few hours, almost to break down the border between the temporal and the
eternal.[26] But when we ask who is causing this suffering, we must not say that
God is causing it, or that God is causing it with a view to punishing Jesus.
From Anselm's perspective, it would not be fitting for God to punish Jesus,
who has done nothing worthy of punishment.

On Anselm's satisfaction theory of atonement, what Jesus suffers, he suffers from man, not from God. Yes, he is punished, but he is punished by
man for being faithful to God, not by God for being faithful to man.[27] These
punishments come to him from God in the sense that they are the temporal
punishments proper to fallen man, but they do not come to him by God's
directive or punitive will but only by God's permissive will.

To put the matter in our own way: Jesus seeks out and situates himself at the
very place where man's wrath is directed toward God and where God's wrath
is consequently directed toward man—the place where God is not for man but
against him, because here he cannot be for him without being against him. And
what is this place, where man acts without God and quite decisively against God,
making himself at last the object of God's wrath? It is precisely the place—the
place in time, in the world as it now is—where God chooses to remain with
man after all, in the form of the God-man, thus subjecting himself to man's
otherwise futile, indeed impossible, attack on God. For it turns out that God is
present even where it seems, at least to the righteous, that he is not present; that
he is for us even where he is most against us; that his yes still resounds in his no.

Now nothing could be more plain than that Jesus suffers from man on
behalf of God. "The insults of those who insult thee have fallen on me."[28] But

---

even if that presence, by reason of creaturely perversity, is known only as the divine *No!* and
experienced as torment.

26. Aquinas tries in part to grasp it, on the temporal level, at *ST* 3.46.6: "Christ's sense of
touch, the sensitiveness of which is the reason for our feeling pain, was most acute. His soul
likewise, from its interior powers, apprehended most vehemently all the causes of sadness."

27. *CDH* 1.10; cf. Meditation 11.

28. Ps. 69:9, Rom. 15:3; cf. Roman Catechism I, 5, 11 (quoted in the 1994 *CCC* at §598).

may we not also assert that he suffers from God on behalf of man? In that he goes voluntarily to meet our fate—the fate that is at once the consequence of sin and the temporal punishment for sin, the fate that is decreed for us by God on what we called the reverse side of providence—yes. If we are following Anselm, however, we will not assert that God directly causes his suffering, that he is condemned by God, or that he is "punished by the just judgment of God" in place of sinful man.[29] This is a popular thesis in some quarters, but, as Karl Barth observes, it is not a thesis to be found in the New Testament.[30] Nor, we may add, is it taught in the Church's catechism. There it is said that "Jesus did not experience reprobation as if he himself had sinned, [b]ut in the redeeming love that always united him to the Father, he assumed us in the state of our waywardness of sin," giving himself up (and being given up by the Father) to the fate that follows sin, namely, death. It was thus that he made of himself a perfect offering and atonement and satisfaction for sin, though the logic of this "satisfaction" is not explained.[31]

The paradigmatic text, of course, to which all refer and with which all must reckon, is Isaiah 53. In that text there are two or three statements that lend support, prima facie, to the idea that Jesus is made the target of divine wrath:

> He was despised and rejected by men;
>   a man of sorrows, and acquainted with grief;
> and as one from whom men hide their faces
>   he was despised, and we esteemed him not.
>
> Surely he has borne our griefs
>   and carried our sorrows;
>   yet *we esteemed him stricken,*
>   *smitten by God, and afflicted.*
> But he was wounded for our transgressions,
>   he was bruised for our iniquities;

29. The quoted phrase is applied to man by Anselm at *CDH* 1.7; he is not there making the present point.

30. *CD* 59.2 (4.1:253). His subsection rubric, however, suggests that Barth is not following Anselm. That is already evident from 59.1 (4.1:175; cf. 165, 185, 203, and 215f.), where Barth has Jesus conceding "that the Father is right" in leading him to the cross, because he himself, having taken sinful flesh, "stands under the wrath and judgment of God." This construct, which at several points begs the question of the distinction between created and fallen humanity, Anselm could only regard as anathema.

31. At §602f. the *CCC* stresses the offering motif in a broadly Anselmian fashion. At §615 it says, "Jesus atoned for our faults and made satisfaction for our sins to the Father" (following Trent [*DS* 1529/*DZ* 799]: *sua sanctissima passione in ligno crucis nobis justificationem meruit, et pro nobis Deo Patri satisfecit*).

upon him was the chastisement that made us whole,
  and with his stripes we are healed.
All we like sheep have gone astray;
  we have turned every one to his own way;
and *the* LORD *has laid on him*
  the iniquity of us all.

He was oppressed, and he was afflicted,
  yet he opened not his mouth;
like a lamb that is led to the slaughter,
  and like a sheep that before its shearers is dumb,
  so he opened not his mouth.
By oppression and judgment he was taken away;
  and as for his generation, who considered
that he was cut off out of the land of the living,
  stricken for the transgression of my people?
And they made his grave with the wicked
  and with a rich man in his death,
although he had done no violence,
  and there was no deceit in his mouth.

Yet *it was the will of the* LORD *to bruise him*;
  he has put him to grief;
when he makes himself an offering for sin,
  he shall see his offspring, he shall prolong his days;
the will of the LORD shall prosper in his hand;
  he shall see the fruit of the travail of his soul and be satisfied;
by his knowledge shall the righteous one, my servant,
  make many to be accounted righteous;
  and he shall bear their iniquities.
Therefore I will divide him a portion with the great,
  and he shall divide the spoil with the strong;
because he poured out his soul to death,
  and was numbered with the transgressors;
yet he bore the sin of many,
  and made intercession for the transgressors.[32]

Of this text Anselm makes use only to insist that Christ's offering was "not under any compulsion but out of his own free will."[33] We may elaborate by

---

32. Isa. 53:3–12, emphasis added.

33. He is leaning on the Vulgate, but his point is that "absolute and true obedience is that which occurs when a rational being, not under compulsion but voluntarily, keeps to a desire which has been received from God" (*CDH* 1.10; cf. 2.17 and Meditation 11); it is in that sense, and only that sense, that Jesus is "commanded" to undergo his passion.

saying that, viewed from the side of man, it is punishment, administered by man in God's name. (Thus we "esteemed him stricken, smitten by God, and afflicted": not because God had struck him but because God had permitted him to be struck, blasphemously, by man.) Viewed from the side of God it is an acceptable offering, not required of Jesus but voluntarily made by him for our sake. In this offering Jesus becomes "the expiation for our sins, and not for ours only but also for the sins of the whole world" (1 John 2:2), because he makes himself a pure offering in the place where the fullness of iniquity occurs. Yet the italicized portions leave open the counterclaim that, if it is the will of God that he be bruised, if indeed it is God in his sovereignty and not merely man in his rebellion who puts him to grief, then we are justified in saying that God punishes Jesus in our stead and that this is what atones for sin.

Barth, for one, rejects or at least nuances this view, though he does not defend Anselm from the gross misreading by which he is made one of its authors. Barth's own approach appears quite concisely in *CD* 59.2 and is worth quoting at length, that we may properly appreciate and question it. The fine print paragraph (in the middle) is incorporated, since it is crucial:

> The very heart of the atonement is the overcoming of sin: sin in its character as the rebellion of man against God, and in its character as the ground of man's hopeless destiny in death. It was to fulfil this judgment on sin that the Son of God as man took our place as sinners. He fulfils it—as man in our place—by completing our work in the omnipotence of the divine Son, by treading the way of sinners to its bitter end in death, in destruction, in the limitless anguish of separation from God, by delivering up sinful man and sin in His own person to the non-being which is properly theirs, the non-being, the nothingness to which man has fallen victim as a sinner and towards which he relentlessly hastens. We can say indeed that He fulfils this judgment by suffering the punishment which we have all brought on ourselves.

> The concept of punishment has come into the answer given by Christian theology to this question from Isaiah 53. In the New Testament it does not occur in this connection. But it cannot be completely rejected or evaded on this account. My turning from God is followed by God's annihilating turning from me. When it is resisted his love works itself out as death-dealing wrath. If Jesus Christ has followed our way as sinners to the end to which it leads, in outer darkness, then we can say with that passage from the Old Testament that he has suffered this punishment of ours. But we must not make this a main concept as in some of the older presentations of the doctrine of the atonement (especially those which follow Anselm of Canterbury), either in the sense that by his suffering our punishment we are spared from suffering it ourselves or that in so doing he "satisfied" or offered satisfaction to the

wrath of God. The latter thought is quite foreign to the New Testament. And of the possible idea that we are spared punishment by what Jesus Christ has done for us we have to notice that the main drift of the New Testament statements concerning the passion and death of Jesus Christ is not at all or only indirectly in this direction.

The decisive thing is not that He has suffered what we ought to have suffered so that we do not have to suffer it, the destruction to which we have fallen victim by our guilt, and therefore the punishment which we deserve. This is true, of course. But it is true only as it derives from the decisive thing that in the suffering and death of Jesus Christ it has come to pass that in His own person He has made an end of us as sinners and therefore of sin itself by going to death as the One who took our place as sinners. In His person He has delivered up us sinners and sin itself to destruction. He has removed us sinners and sin, negated us, cancelled us out: ourselves, our sin, and the accusation, condemnation and perdition which had overtaken us. (CD 4.1:253f.)

Barth does not want to say either what Anselm is saying or what some mistakenly say Anselm is saying. He wants to allow for punishment by God as a component of the atonement, without allowing it to be the central feature. The central feature is that Jesus somehow gathers our fallen and damned humanity to himself and in himself disposes of it once and for all by freely submitting it to the judgment of God. He is, as the title of §59.2 states, "the Judge judged in our place." Short shrift is given to "the possible idea that we are spared punishment by what Jesus Christ has done for us."

The claim that Anselm's view is "not at all or only indirectly" present in the main stream of New Testament talk of atonement sounds a bit like the claim that Chalcedonian christology, say, is not to be found there directly. The exercise is after all, for both men, an exercise in *fides quaerens intellectum*.[34] The more serious difference between them is that Anselm thinks of Christ's action not as a "doing away" with sin and the sinner but rather as a merciful exercise in justice that does away with condemnation, and so with punishment, by putting faithfulness in place of faithlessness, humble submission in place of violent rebellion. In short, he thinks of it as the offering of something good rather than the annihilation of something evil.[35] And

---

34. Barth can perhaps claim support from a certain reading of Rom. 6. Anselm, I think, can claim a great deal of support from Hebrews and 1 Peter, for example. Barth, in any case, is not in a position to criticize others for deviating from the mainstream.

35. Barth can say the same: Jesus's suffering and dying "is only the negative form of the fulness of a positive divine righteousness" (CD 4.1:257). Jesus's obedience, his confirmation of the verdict of God, against man, is at the same time the very love of God that intervenes to rescue man by taking responsibility for him, turning man's false, self-justifying judgment into a true

this offering, on Anselm's view, merits an infinite reward to be freely shared with those who will receive it. In receiving it, of course, they must be united to Christ by faith and the sacraments and learn how to conform their own wills to God's. Being united with Christ means that justice is restored to the soul and that preserving rectitude of will, for its own sake, is again possible. On that path, and only on that path, can sin and the sinner be done away with and the threat of eternal punishment disappear, being replaced with true and eternal happiness.[36]

We ought not to overemphasize the difference between Barth and Anselm, but it is worth remarking that Barth's alternative is rather less capable of capturing Isaiah 53, with its central allusion to the pleasing aroma of the sin offering. It is quite capable, as is Anselm's, of capturing that dimension of the passage which shows the sovereignty of God working through the otherwise futile imaginings and actions of man. But it is not very able to capture the essential context of atonement theology in the sacrificial system of Israel. "Behold, the Lamb of God, who takes away the sin of the world!"—this is not about annihilation, pure and simple, but about propitiation.[37] It is likewise worth remarking that Barth's annihilationist approach leads to, or rather is already situated in, a Protestant distaste for the sacramental and suspicion of shared merits. This suspicion exacerbates a tendency to view the self-sacrifice of Jesus as bringing an end to all sacrifice, rather than bringing all sacrifice to its proper end, a subject we will pursue in later chapters.

Now propitiation does involve putting the Son to grief, a grief than which there is none greater; but Barth and Anselm are more or less on the same page in saying that it does not involve the Father working out his wrath against Jesus. The propitiation of God, and the removal of guilt before God, is not through punishment but through satisfaction, even if it takes place only by way of punishment. And just here we must observe that punishment itself is not annihilated, whether it be temporal or eternal punishment. Man, even Christian man, still dies, and may die violently; moreover, and despite Barth's misgivings on the subject, hell still awaits those who in death are found outside of Christ. What propitiation has changed is that the temporal punishment that is death no longer need be the anteroom to hell but can instead be the gateway to heaven, just because Jesus Christ has made an offering in

and godly judgment. Jesus's self-offering is free and glorious in its freedom. But it is telling that the priestly function is here almost totally absorbed into the judicial (275ff. notwithstanding).

36. Again, see *CDH* 1.10.

37. Barth might have let his Grünewald altarpiece reproduction, which he kept in his study, teach him more about that.

and through death, our common temporal punishment, that averts eternal punishment. He has harrowed Hades to deliver us from hell.

Further Dangers in Regarding the Cross as *Poena Satisfactoria*

Thus far we have been accommodating Aquinas by allowing for the incontrovertible fact that Jesus undergoes the common punishment of fallen man that is suffering and death, while maintaining with Anselm that it is not this punishment that satisfies divine justice but rather the pure offering of Jesus, and that the punishment Jesus undergoes he undergoes by reason of the permissive will of God rather than the punitive will of God, the latter being operative only indirectly through the autonomous will of fallen man. It seems right now to fortify this position by observing two great mistakes that are often made by those who put punishment in the central place, even if Aquinas himself does not make them, or at least does not make the second of them.

The first, which was mentioned at the outset, is to suppose that the place of punishment occupied by Jesus is, in its own way, hell. As awful as it is, it is not hell, but only the anteroom to hell. It cannot be hell, because God, in turning away from man (such is the formal cause of hell and the efficient cause for entering hell) is still, in the person of Jesus, turned toward him. It cannot be hell, because in the person of Jesus man himself is not turned away (such is the material cause of hell, or the precondition for being consigned to hell) but rather remains steadfastly turned toward God. In other words, it is a place of punishment, but it is not *that* place of punishment.[38] And if we want to say with Aquinas that the punishment in question is somehow reparative, that it is *poena satisfactoria*, we must certainly qualify that by saying with Anselm that, while the satisfaction rendered (by virtue of who is rendering it) outstrips sin's entire desert, it does so not by exhausting the suffering or penalties that sin under judgment brings but rather by meriting a *stay* of judgment and deliverance from sin's deserts.

This bears further elaboration, before we mention the second mistake. Jesus does not suffer damnation. Though he goes to the place of punishment that leads to damnation—taking Golgotha, the place of the skull, the place of godforsakenness, as that place—he does not go there in the manner that

---

38. The harrowing of hell (*infernus*, the underworld, Hades), which afterward takes place, does not imply that hell itself—that "lower hell," prepared for the devil and his angels, to which Clement VI refers in challenging Armenian doubts regarding the claim, *quod Christus non destruxit descendendo ad inferos inferiorem infernum* (*DS* 1077; *DZ* 574a)—has been entered or experienced by Jesus. On all of this see the *CCC* 606–35, which provides much evidence that Anselm is indeed "mainstream."

others do or experience it as they experience it. He goes trustingly and obedi-
ently. He goes to their fated punishment in such a way as to render it moot.
That is the whole point. The blow is struck, to be sure, though it is man who
strikes it, not God. It falls on him only because he wills to be present where
it is struck. In his own metaphor, by remaining faithful to his mission he
drinks the cup his Father has handed him. Or, in the Mosaic metaphor, he
climbs Mount Moriah, laden with our sins like so many fagots for the fire,
that he may make offering to God for and among sinners. Like Isaac, he is
himself innocent. Unlike Isaac, he does not emerge unscathed. He is broken
and yields up his spirit. His body is laid in a tomb. His soul treads the paths
of the dead. Yet he himself is the offerer, and the offering he makes satisfies
all justice, making eternal punishment unnecessary and unfitting. Even this
temporal punishment—death in deprivation of the covenant promises—is
overturned on appeal by the resurrection.

Was his death a sacrifice for sins? Certainly. Was it a propitiation of divine
wrath that restored divine favor? Yes. Was it necessary for the forgiveness of
sins? Assuredly. "He himself bore our sins in his body on the tree. . . . Christ
also died for sins once for all, the righteous for the unrighteous, that he might
bring us to God"—even if he must come to the realm of the dead to find us
(1 Pet. 2:18–3:22). But we must not suppose that in any of this *God* was tor-
menting Jesus, as if extracting from him a just payment in human pain for
or from each and every fagot he bore. We must not suppose that atonement
was effected because the divine wrath was spent and exhausted on him, as if
God were acting in a frenzy of passion or, alternatively, coldly and implacably
requiting sin blow for blow. That notion is so far unworthy of God as to be
blasphemous. Nor is it a coherent notion.

God's wrath against sin is real. His back is turned against this place of
the skull. There is darkness in the heavens from the sixth to the ninth hour.
It is as dark for Jesus as for anyone else—indeed, far darker. Heaven is no
longer open. The beatific vision is obscured. The Father's comforting voice
is no longer heard. The Spirit is not giving him the water of life to drink. His
suffering surpasses anything either Caiaphas or Pilate can inflict. But in all
of this he loves the Father with a perfect love. And who would dare say that
the Father loves less well than Jesus? Who would dare imply that Jesus, even
momentarily, is *not* the object of his love? Were Jesus, at any point, not to be
loved by the Father, either the incarnation would cease to be or God himself
would cease to be.

Is God, then, punishing Jesus only with the remedial punishments of love,
with the rod of temporal discipline, for the sake of our eternal health and
salvation? That, on a hasty and one-sided reading, might seem to be Thomas's

view, but it is not. Moreover, it has insurmountable difficulties. Jesus has no need of such punishments and cannot benefit from them. Nor is the benefit he brings us, as our faithful high priest, contingent upon his suffering all the temporal punishments due our sin (which in fact he cannot, for many of them are particular to the sins in question) or a punishment equivalent to all the punishments due our sin. (What would be remedial about that, apart from reinforcement of the connection between sin and punishment?)[39] Besides, it leaves untouched the matter of the eternal punishment due our sin, which can only be accounted for either by falling back into the false position just mentioned or by accepting Anselm's alternative.

It will immediately be objected that this is a false dilemma. Can we not speak of God's implacable administration of punishment, for the sake of divine justice, to one whom God does in fact continue to love dearly even in the midst of this administration? Can we not set aside the blasphemous anthropomorphisms while retaining the idea that Jesus suffers what is somehow the equivalent of eternal punishment? Shall we not posit this equivalency without prejudice to a temporal or remedial punishment that serves, at the very least, illustrative purposes? And would this not make sense of the traditional emphasis on baptism as covering, all at once and in its entirety, original and actual sin up to the point of baptism while requiring a further dispensing of temporal punishments for sins committed after baptism? Can we not thus side with Aquinas after all, allowing Anselm's point about the infinite merit of Christ's offering without denying that what Christ undergoes is, in the fullest sense, divine wrath against sin, a vicarious punishment inflicted by God and, ultimately, by God alone?

This is what ordinarily is meant by substitutionary atonement, a construct more Thomist than Anselmian. But it is not tenable. What, after all, is the punishment inflicted by divine wrath? What is the divine wrath itself? Divine wrath is the loving God actively refusing our demand that he be other than he in fact is and that we be other than we in fact can be. That is a fearful business; indeed, there is nothing more fearful. To demand that God not be God and that the creature be as God without being like God or in God is to demand hell. Jesus, however, makes no such demand. If he tastes the divine wrath, he does not do so as one whose face is set against God. So he cannot experience, vicariously or otherwise, a punishment reserved for those destined to depart with the devil and his angels into the eternal fire, those who themselves are the material cause of their own punishment. What he experiences in and with

39. This reinforcement, when considered with respect to post-baptismal sins, leads straight to the dilemma with which Luther wrestled.

the unjust and inhuman punishment meted out by man is the forlornness of remaining in the place on which the Father has turned his back. Yet even then and there he follows his Father with a pure and devoted will. "Into thy hands I commit my spirit!"[40]

No such experience was ever had by man or angel, nor will be. His cry of dereliction is a cry of faith from the depths of what otherwise would be, or become, hell. But he does not suffer the eternal punishment *of* sinners, though he does suffer temporal punishment with and for sinners. He suffers it in such a fashion as to fulfill the obligation to God of faith and gratitude and honor that our sins prevent us from fulfilling. He offers himself to God on our behalf, as our representative, where no offering we could make would be worthy or acceptable. He offers himself even in and from the place where our situation is hopeless, the place of God's turning away. And his offering is received, so that no man ever need be in such a place again. That is propitiation. That is atonement, or the key moment in atonement.

So much for the first mistake. The second mistake is to suppose all this to be, if not a human hell, then a *divine* one—an eternally painful and sorrowful diremption in God. This is the more serious mistake, because it tries to save the unity between Jesus and God at the expense of the unity of God himself. It dispenses with the divine perfection of impassibility, to which both Anselm and Aquinas were firmly committed.[41] *Au contraire*, it is the God-man who, precisely as a man, suffers whatever he suffers of both the human and the divine wraths, which are so utterly different in character.[42] It is not the holy Trinity, God qua God, who suffers either. About this we must be perfectly clear, where so much modern theology is either not clear or simply mistaken, falsely imagining some eternal paroxysm of divine suffering.[43] And we can be clear, if we confess that it is not, properly speaking, Jesus from whom the Father turns; he turns rather from us as we ourselves turn against God

40. In Jesus, man is indeed "the friend of God and not his enemy" (Barth, *CD* 4.1:251). When he stands in for us, and so in effect stands up for us—our representative as well as our substitute—he does this as God's friend and our friend. But does he do it, as Barth thinks, by "delivering up sinful man and sin" to "the limitless anguish of separation from God" (253), or does he do it by delivering up himself *to* God, as Anselm thinks? If Barth makes no distinction here, it is because, unlike Anselm, he supposes Jesus to have assumed fallen humanity (258f.). All this bears significantly on his inability to think properly with the Church about the relation between atonement, priesthood, and offerings (see 275ff.; cf. my "Ascension and Atonement," in *The Theology of Reconciliation*, ed. Colin E. Gunton [Edinburgh: T&T Clark, 2003], 67ff.).

41. "For we affirm that the divine nature is undoubtedly incapable of suffering" (*CDH* 1.8).

42. One is holy, the other unholy; one is righteous, the other unrighteous; one is simple and pure, the other complex and conflicted; one is glorious, the other altogether inglorious.

43. See Thomas Weinandy, *Does God Suffer?* (South Bend, IN: University of Notre Dame Press, 2000), for a review and refutation of this latter-day heresy.

in Jesus. Jesus alone knows and experiences this in all its profundity. For in him God has chosen—both as God and as the only truly free man, a point Anselm, like Maximus, rightly belabors—to side with man even in deciding against him. In him God has chosen to be among us after all, to be with us and for us just where we are most determined to be against him and without him. It is in that choice, and because of it, that the wrath of man is given the divine object it sought, and the wrath of God is applied to man redemptively rather than destructively.

There is here no diremption in God, no ontological breach between Father and Son to be overcome by the Spirit in some Hegelian—that is, in some frankly idolatrous—fashion. There is only the breach between God and man, the hamartiological or volitional breach that is overcome by the God-man, who in perfect unity of will with the Father betakes himself to the place where God otherwise cannot and will not be and just there presents himself to the Father on our behalf to shrive us of our rebellion and sin. There is no atonement that takes place in the secret recesses of the divine eternity, as if the doctrine of the Trinity *were* the doctrine of atonement. There is only the atonement that takes place in and through the God-man, acting as a man. For the Son did not make an offering of God to God, but of man to God; and this is sufficient, just as Anselm says it is. He made an offering of infinite worth when he offered, not merely in life but in death, the humanity that was and is his own humanity.[44] Where that offering is rejected there remains no offering. God is not secretly present in hell, and hell is not secretly present in God.

The Value of Not Conflating Satisfaction and Punishment

What has become of our attempt to mediate between Anselm and Aquinas? Both men see Jesus as suffering the judgment, as experiencing the doom of man, and eminently so. Neither would contest the claim that God uses the evil of man both as the instrument of doom and as the means of rendering that doom salvific. God punishes man by man, and himself becomes the man who is thus punished, so that in receiving the punishment with charity, he may offer it back to God as satisfaction. Both know that God reserves everlasting wrath for those who are not found in Christ as the beneficiaries of his satisfaction. This commonality, however, should not obscure the crucial difference between

44. Anselm even speaks of an offering of his humanity to his divinity (*CDH* 2.18). Those who try to address the problem of atonement by making it a problem in God, requiring a resolution in God, rather than recognizing it as a problem in man that requires resolution by the God-man, fall at last into the same unfathomable folly that ruined the gnostic theologians.

them, which we may restate thus: Anselm, unlike Aquinas, does not attempt to measure the punishment that Christ endures by the sins man has committed, but rather he measures the salvation Christ procures by the worthiness of Christ himself, who made his offering on behalf of man and in gruesome solidarity with man. Aquinas, for his part, tends to conflate the punishment meted out by man with that meted out by God, measuring this punishment against the sins and finding it sufficient. While he certainly considers the worthiness of the one who undergoes the punishment, he attempts to factor in also a symmetry between sin and punishment, so that he may speak not merely of *satisfactio* (a glorious, superabundant *satisfactio*) but of *poena satisfactoria*.

Our mediation favors Anselm but does not rest entirely content with him. Anselm knows how to say that Jesus is a sin offering and has rendered satisfaction for sin; it is not clear that he knows quite as well how to say that God has laid on him the iniquity of us all. Aquinas knows how to say that Jesus bears our iniquities, that he is stricken for our sins and experiences our punishment; it is not clear that he knows as well how to say that this freely assumed punishment is not directed by God at Jesus, or that Jesus does not bear something that approximates eternal wrath. He therefore shifts the focus, if only accidentally, from sufficient offering to sufficient punishment, and this carries over into his doctrine of penance and of purgatory and into his understanding of what it means to realign the soul with God. It lends a penal flavor to his sacramental and spiritual theology and thus also to his ecclesiology.[45] Or perhaps we should say that this was already happening and that Aquinas reflects and to a certain extent entrenches it. On the other hand, Anselm has left himself open to the kind of misinterpretation to which he was subjected in the Protestant Reformation and is still subjected to in some antinomian and sub-ecclesial forms of evangelicalism.[46]

We usually think of Anselm as the one whose theology is at risk of being over-determined by an aesthetic sense, a sense of *convenientia*, that requires

---

45. As at *ST* 3.49.3, ad 2. Cf. *Supp.* 12.2 and 12.3, where satisfaction is said to be "the act of justice inflicting punishment" in suitable measure. (Anselm is here misused in support: "The definition of Anselm amounts to the same, for he says that 'satisfaction consists in giving God due honor'; where duty is considered in respect of the sin committed." Things get worse at 13.1, where in ad 3 Anselm's logic is abandoned altogether.) For penitential theology the implications are fairly straightforward. A work needs, if it is to be satisfactory, both "to be good, that it may conduce to God's honor, and . . . penal, so that something may be taken away from the sinner thereby" (15.1). The voluntary suffering of penal "scourges" is what renders them satisfactory as well as remedial. On this voluntary suffering, the whole system comes to rest.

46. I am thinking, for example, of J. Denny Weaver's *The Nonviolent Atonement* (Grand Rapids: Eerdmans, 2001); see my review in the *International Journal of Systematic Theology* 6.1 (2004): 93–96.

speculative details not attested by Scripture and tradition. But here it seems to be Aquinas who is more at risk of that. Not that such a procedure is necessarily false or its results inevitably faulty; far from it. These are two extraordinary speculative theologians, whose speculation is habitually presented at the bar of Scripture and tradition. The risk that Aquinas takes here, however, is the risk of making God himself the true author of Jesus's suffering and of making punishment the only cure for sin—as if justice demands punishment and cannot be satisfied without it, as if punishment and satisfaction are always one and the same thing.[47] He does not deny directly Anselm's contention that justice is achieved by the quality or worth of the free self-offering of the God-man, but he does reject Anselm's *satisfactio aut poena*.

Much hangs on this rejection, as we saw in the previous chapter. Does created order, and with it divine justice, demand a detailed audit of sin and punishment or only an assurance that sin is fully atoned for? What are the implications for human justice? What are the implications for penitential theology and the doctrine of sanctification? What are the ecumenical implications? Some distinction between satisfaction and punishment is necessary in order to prevent penitential theology from becoming the legalistic beast it is quite capable of becoming and those reactionary responses that threaten to evacuate the sacrament of penance either of sacramentality or of penance itself.[48]

If sin deserves eternal as well as temporal punishment, and if Jesus did not suffer eternal punishment, this Anselmian distinction is strictly necessary and Aquinas erred in rejecting it.[49] Its primary pastoral application is to reinforce the point that the proper cure for sin lies in satisfaction, not in punishment. Christ alone having achieved this cure, of course, the only pastoral question—and, ecclesially, the only really divisive one—is the question of appropriation. How do we benefit from the cure? This is what penitential theology must tell us.

In his third meditation, *Deploratio virginitatis male amissae*, Anselm leaves little to other contenders in the matter of penitential lament. The soul betrothed to Christ, having fallen into sin, comes to know itself all over again

---

47. That may be true, circumstantially, for fallen man (*CDH* 1.24), but it is not true in and of itself; nor is it true that the unity of justice and mercy in God is maintained by a transfer of divine punishment from us to Jesus.

48. The Catholic Church is currently struggling with the latter reaction, as I have remarked in "To Hell with Accompaniment," *First Things* (March 2017): 39–43.

49. Conversely, if "in its weightiest aspect, as offence against God deserving of eternal punishment, sin is borne by Christ and set right by the cross," while temporal punishments are something altogether different and must be borne by us, then the cross must be equivalent to hell. Cf. Aquinas, *ST* 3.1.2, ad 2.

as a creature sliding toward the abyss, doubly faulted by reason of its betrayal of baptism through undisciplined passions. "Whence, then, O God, am I to draw for myself the corrective of such deep depravity? Whence for Thee, O God, satisfaction for so black a sin?" But once again the answer lies in the mercy of Christ's own satisfaction. "True it is that my conscience and sense of guilt deserves damnation, and that my penance is not enough for satisfaction; but yet it is certain that Thy mercy out strips all Thy resentment."[50] In the eleventh meditation, the *Meditatio redemptionis humanae* which recapitulates *Cur deus homo*, he is reassured that he who "returns to God with worthy repentance" is received by reason of the payment already effected by Christ. "Those, then, who choose to approach with worthy disposition to this grace are saved; whilst those who despise it, since they pay not what is due from them, are justly damned." And he adds: "Lo, then, Christian soul, here is the strength of thy salvation; here is the cause of thy freedom; here is the price of thy redemption. . . . Make this in this present life thy daily bread, thy nourishment, thy support in pilgrimage; for by means of this, this and nothing else, shalt thou remain in Christ and Christ in thee, and in the life to come thy joy shall be full."[51]

When we allow Gethsemane to interpret Golgotha, the freedom of Christ to govern the offering of Christ, rather than imposing on the whole a punitive frame of reference, then penitential theology can be oriented to the realignment of the will rather than to the making up of a deficit of punishment. This is the key we were seeking in our previous chapter. To the satisfaction already made by Christ nothing need be added by us; indeed nothing can be added by us, whether at baptism or after it. What is always required—here Luther was quite right—is that we should learn to cast ourselves upon Christ, and Christ alone, as the means of entering and, as oft as necessary, reentering the love of God. It is the work of the Holy Spirit to realign our own wills with his, and so also with the Father's. Penitential theology should have no higher aim than to clarify the grace of the triune God that restores us to that love and to the will to justice without which the will to happiness is forever frustrated. "All that I am is Thine by creation; make it all Thine by love," prays Anselm. "Behold, O Lord, my heart lies open before Thee; it tries, but of itself it cannot; what self cannot, do Thou!"[52]

In this work there remains a need to distinguish between greater and lesser goods and between sins according to their gravity, which may involve the

---

50. *Meditations and Prayers*, 30–31.
51. Ibid., 72.
52. Ibid., 74.

pedagogy of punishment; but there is no need, if we reckon with Anselm, for knowledge of any alleged order that makes this particular sin worthy of precisely this temporal punishment.[53] There remains a need for penance, but no room for ordering penance to retributive rather than remedial justice.[54] There remains a need to pursue sanctification as an essential feature of justification; but there is no possibility of misunderstanding justification as something that is achieved partly by the free grace of baptismal forgiveness, based on the payment made by Christ, and partly on subsequent penalties paid by the baptized for subsequent sins.[55]

Moreover, once we see that that the satisfaction we render for our own (post-baptismal) sins, through the imposition of *poenae* that deter and good works that reform, is not in addition to Christ's satisfaction, as if to make up some deficiency thereof, but rather by way of willing participation in it, there remain no serious grounds for objecting to Trent's claim that the penance entails satisfaction and not simply reform. Priests should indeed "bear in mind that the satisfaction they impose should not only be aimed at protecting the new life and at being a remedy against weakness," but be aimed also *ad praeteritorum peccatorum vindictam et castigationem*; that is, for binding as well as loosing.[56] Why? Because what Christ has died to offer satisfaction *for* must needs be identified, both by the Church and by the offending member, as that which can have no proper place in the Christian life. "While by [thus] making satisfaction we suffer for our sins, we become like Christ Jesus who made satisfaction for our sins, and from whom is all our sufficiency, and we also have a most sure pledge thereby that, if we suffer with him, we shall also

53. That approach is already rejected by Ps. 51. In any event, it entails a penitential calculus more difficult than the eudaemonic calculus of the consequentialists; which is to say, it is quite impossible.

54. That is, in the fashion dictated by the scholastic principles that "justice demands that sin be set in order by due punishment" and that "temporal punishment is due to sin, even after the sin itself has been pardoned by God" (see chap. 3, n. 6). St. Philip Neri seemed instinctively to grasp the alternative we are seeking. He knew how to make penance very particular to the penitent, just because he knew how to orient it to the reform of the soul rather than to the punishment of sin.

55. When Anselm says, "supposing it should come about after this pardon that they should sin again, and provided that they should then be willing to give satisfaction in a suitable way and receive correction, they would receive pardon again through the effective power of this same agreement" (*CDH* 54), does he not make clear that it is the payment made by Christ that undergirds the pardon?

56. Session 14, chap. 8; *DEC* 2:709. If, say, a fast is imposed, it is not the fast that forgives the sin but rather the grace of God in Christ; the purpose of the fast is both to judge and condemn the sin and to guard against it. This is a form of satisfaction, to be sure; but only by participation, through *imitatio* or emulation, in the one and only satisfaction offered by Christ. It is not payment for sin but accompaniment on the *via crucis*.

be glorified with him."[57] Just so, there are no grounds for falling into the cheap, antinomian grace that Bonhoeffer lamented in the Protestant sphere and the fathers of Trent in the Catholic.

57. Trent wants to hold together penance as penalty deterring from sin and as remedy for the weakness that leads to sin. It is in the wise combination of these that it finds our *satisfactio* a participation in Christ's *satisfactio*. For my part, I have no wish to be found among those "innovators" who "so emphasize that a new life is the best penance as to take away the whole force and practice of satisfaction" (ibid.).

5

Whose Offering?

Doxological Pelagianism as an Ecumenical Problem

Man, though today in the West he is taking systematic steps to forget it, is defined naturally by a vocation to worship God and supernaturally by a vocation to commune with God. As that model pastoral theologian, James B. Torrance, writes in one of his unpublished but widely distributed papers on public worship:

> In our Christian doctrine of creation, we believe that God has made all creatures for his glory. The lilies of the field, the sparrow on the housetop, the universe in its vastness and remoteness, all glorify God, but they do not know it. But God has made man to be the priest of creation, to express on behalf of all creatures the praises of God, so that through the lips of man the heavens might declare the glory of God, that in our worship we might gather up the worship of all creation.[1]

This human priesthood is not, however, ours to make of whatever we will. It has not been left to us to dispose of as we please. That is because it is grounded in the high priesthood of Jesus, "the One True Worshipper." To construe it in deliberate abstraction from Jesus Christ is for the Christian an act of doxological Pelagianism. Indeed, it is a Cain-like act.

1. James B. Torrance, "Worship in the Reformed Church: The Purpose and Principles of Public Worship" (lecture, DMin seminar, Fuller Theological Seminary, Pasadena, CA, n.d.), 1.

Torrance appeals to Hebrews 8:2, which "describes our Lord as the *Leitourgos*, 'the Minister of the sanctuary, the One True Worshipper, the Leader of our worship, who has gone ahead to lead us in our prayers and intercessions.' As such the *leitourgia* (worship) of Jesus is contrasted with the *leitourgia* of men. This is the Worship and Offering which God has provided for men and which alone is acceptable to God." A little later on he remarks that "the mystery, the wonder, the glory of the Gospel is that He who is God the Creator of all things, and worthy of the worship and praises of all creation, should become man and as a man worship God, and as a man lead us in our worship of God, that we might become the sons of God we were meant to be."[2]

The anti-Pelagian refrain of Torrance's doxology is that Christ's worship is our worship in the communion of the Holy Spirit. Leaning on Calvin's powerful exposition of baptism, Torrance emphasizes the *mirifica commutatio*: "His worship is our worship, through a wonderful exchange." That exchange lies at "the heart of the theology of the sacraments, particularly of the Lord's Supper," he says, "which so enshrines the *mirifica commutatio*." In the Supper, Christ takes what is ours that he might give us what is his. This is the foundation and the *conditio sine qua non* of authentic worship. The wonderful exchange, of course, is effected in the Son's assumption of our humanity and in his offering on the cross. But it does not cease there; it is not confined to that short tract of history in which time is opened to eternity. It continues still, the ascended Christ working through the Spirit to give us back our humanity, already renewed in himself, saying "Take, eat: this is my body, which is broken for you" (1 Cor. 11:24 KJV).

Letting Scripture interpret Scripture, Torrance points us to the principle articulated in Galatians 2:20, "it is no longer I who live, but Christ who lives in me." Of this principle he makes eucharistic application. "Worship," he insists again, "is our participation through the Spirit in the worship of Christ." It is human action—our human action—yet "in such a way that He is the One who acts in us and through us, so that our worship becomes real worship." In a sister paper, "Two Views of Worship in Scotland Today," Torrance further contrasts this authentic worship with the Cain-like worship that rests not on our high priest but on whatever offering we fancy ourselves able or compelled to bring out of our own inadequate resources.[3] "Man is

2. Ibid., 2–3.
3. James B. Torrance, "Two Views of Worship in Scotland Today" (lecture, DMin seminar, Fuller Theological Seminary, Pasadena, CA, n.d.). See further his *Worship, Community and the Triune God of Grace* (Downers Grove, IL: InterVarsity, 1996); and "The Place of Jesus Christ in Worship," in *Theological Foundations for Ministry: Selected Readings for a Theology of*

never more truly man than when he worships God" in Spirit and in truth, as the priest of creation. Moreover, "the Church is the Church" precisely in her worship. But it must never be supposed that genuine worship can be offered by man out of his own resources.

Professor Torrance is not concerned here with the relation between the eucharistic heart of Christian worship and Christian life broadly considered, or with the relation between Christian worship and other attempts to exercise the human vocation to worship. He is concerned with Christianity's sacramental integrity. He notes for his Reformed brethren both the right intention and the problematic outcome of Catholic eucharistic practice:

> "We offer . . . and yet it is not our offering. It is Christ." This is what (in intention at least) Rome seeks to say in the Mass. "It is bread . . . and yet suddenly we know that it is not bread. It is Christ!" There is an evangelical intention. But from our Reformed point of view she says it in the wrong way. She makes the moment of *conversio* what takes place in the elements, in the act of consecration—no doubt as the act of God in the action of the priest. But this obscures, in too Pelagian a fashion, the heart of the Gospel of grace that the real *conversio* of our humanity took place in the substitutionary self-consecration of Jesus, in His life, death and resurrection, in the once-for-all action of our One High Priest, in whose life and action we participate through the Spirit, who now renews us in the image of God. Calvin and Robert Bruce could speak of a "conversion" in the use of the elements, in their being set apart from all common use to this holy use and mystery, but not in the sense of a change in the elements themselves.[4]

But Torrance also observes a pitfall of which Protestants must beware. The latter may so stress the coming of God to meet us, perhaps in particular the coming of the Spirit to instruct and command us through the Word of God or (it may be) to perform some mighty work, that they forget the Spirit's mediatorial role in "lifting us up to Christ" that Christ may in turn "present us with himself to the Father." What happens, he asks, when we thus lose sight of "the priestly ministry" of the Spirit? Is it not just the same as when we overlook "the continuing Priesthood of Christ in representing man to God"? Is it not indeed a cause of that overlooking? "We can then so obtrude our own response to the Word in Pelagian fashion, that we obscure or forget the God-given Response made for us by Jesus Christ. It is possible so to obtrude

---

Church in Ministry, ed. R. S. Anderson (Grand Rapids: Eerdmans, 1979), 348–69. Cf. also T. F. Torrance, *Theology in Reconciliation* (London: Geoffrey Chapman, 1975), 131ff.

4. Torrance, "Worship in the Reformed Church," 9–11.

our own offering of praise, that we lose sight of the One true Offering of praise made for us."[5]

There is plenty of doxological Pelagianism to go around, in other words. That fact was driven home for me when, speaking on the topic not long ago in a Protestant context, I was challenged by one gentleman who asked, "What difference does it make how we worship? If we believe in Jesus we can worship as we please." I tried to point out to him that he had just made the case better than I had. His remark was proof of the Pelagianism in question. It was not evidence of our liberty *in* Christ but of our tendency to try to live, and even to worship, apart from Christ and in our own way.

But whence arises this form of Pelagianism? Is it possible that doxological Pelagianism of this kind arises in and with Protestantism itself? Or, to be more precise, in and with Protestant views of the Lord's Supper or Eucharist? I think it does, in fact, and I want now to elaborate on that a little by thinking further about the Eucharist, drawing (by way of contrast) on Irenaeus and on Martin Luther. In due course we will return to Professor Torrance, which means also to Calvin.

The Eucharistic Economy

The first serious treatment of the Eucharist is an application of the *lex orandi, lex credendi* principle by Saint Irenaeus. In book IV of *Adversus haereses* he appeals to the Church's central doxological rite in refutation of the gnostics. How, he asks, can those who are persuaded that the material creation is the work of a defective deity offer up with the Church that same material creation to God? Either they must abandon their contention that the God who made the earth is not the one true God, or they must abandon the Eucharist itself.

> How can they say that the flesh, which is nourished with the body of the Lord and with His blood, goes to corruption, and does not partake of life? Let them, therefore, either alter their opinion, or cease from offering the things just mentioned. But our opinion is in accordance with the Eucharist, and the Eucharist in turn establishes our opinion. For we offer to Him His own, announcing consistently the fellowship and union of the flesh and Spirit. For as the bread, which is produced from the earth, when it receives the invocation of God, is no longer common bread, but the Eucharist, consisting of two realities, earthly

---

5. Ibid., 9. One wonders how much of this criticism is quietly aimed at Barthian as well as fundamentalist one-sidedness. The Torrance brothers distinguished themselves from fellow Barthians by concerning themselves much more deeply with doxological issues.

and heavenly; so also our bodies, when they receive the Eucharist, are no longer corruptible, having the hope of the resurrection to eternity.

Now we make offering to Him, not as though He stood in need of it, but rendering thanks for His gift, and thus sanctifying what has been created. For even as God does not need our possessions, so do we need to offer something to God.[6]

Irenaeus is not content, of course, merely to observe the inconsistency of the gnostics. He has much more to say about the Eucharist as he expounds the continuity between creation and redemption, between the old and new covenant, between Israel and the Church. No one should suppose that sacrifices and oblations have no place in the latter. On the contrary, it is never fitting that man should appear in God's presence empty-handed.[7] What has changed under the new covenant is the offerer, not the need for an offering; just as what has changed is our relation to the law, not our need for the law. The new covenant offering is more truly offered, and the evangelical law more truly obeyed, because the Church is much more deeply embedded in the divine economy of giving and receiving that grounds and governs the human relation to God. God certainly does not need our offerings, for God needs nothing at all. But we need to offer, so that we can be like God and so participate in the divine economy. We need to offer *freely*, for that is how God (who needs nothing at all) himself offers. He does not barter; he simply gives and gives freely. The only offering worthy of God is one that in the offering partakes of the freedom of God.

And how is such an offering possible for us? We take bread and wine, products of human hands derived from the gifts of nature—material nature—and we invoke over them the Word of God; which gifts, in receipt of that Word, become the body and blood of Christ, a heavenly and not merely an earthly reality. This, by divine grace and power, is both God's offering to us and our offering to God. It is freely given by God and received by us; in the very act of receiving it is freely returned to God and received by him, for he always receives his own Son. When we ourselves are in receipt of this divine gift, when

---

6. *Haer.* 4.18.5–6, ANF 1:486.

7. Sir. 35:3–12: "Do not appear before the Lord empty-handed, for all these things are to be done because of the commandment. The offering of a righteous man anoints the altar, and its pleasing odor rises before the Most High. The sacrifice of a righteous man is acceptable, and the memory of it will not be forgotten. Glorify the Lord generously, and do not stint the first fruits of your hands. With every gift show a cheerful face, and dedicate your tithe with gladness. Give to the Most High as he has given, and as generously as your hand has found. For the Lord is the one who repays, and he will repay you sevenfold. Do not offer him a bribe, for he will not accept it; and do not trust to an unrighteous sacrifice; for the Lord is the judge, and with him is no partiality."

we have thus communicated with God in Christ, body and soul, it becomes in us the seed of immortality. We too become, mutatis mutandis, earthly and heavenly. For we who had nothing of our own to give to God in pure freedom have had something of God's placed in our hands and in our mouths.

This something is indeed a free gift, an acceptable gift, a gift God can reward by still further giving. He lends to us that we may lend back to him, that he in turn may pay with interest, "counting out the increase." Now we are engaged in the economy of God, the economy that for us is an ever-expanding economy, a eucharistic economy in which we are never forced back into our own finite resources alone, in which we never fall back exhausted into ourselves but live forever in God.

> Just as a cutting from the vine planted in the ground fructifies in its season, or as a corn of wheat falling into the earth and becoming decomposed, rises with manifold increase by the Spirit of God, who contains all things, and then, through the wisdom of God, serves for the use of men, and having received the Word of God, becomes the Eucharist, which is the body and blood of Christ; so also our bodies, being nourished by it, and deposited in the earth, and suffering decomposition there, shall rise at their appointed time, the Word of God granting them resurrection to the glory of God, even the Father, who freely gives to this mortal immortality, and to this corruptible incorruption.[8]

Now subsequent tradition developed eucharistic theology in a variety of ways, some more and some less helpful. Not all of these insights flourished; some certainly faded from view. But any move (witting or unwitting) to undermine this economy at its core by moving it off of its gold standard, so to say—that is, by denying that the eucharistic elements, the bread and the wine, were actually changed into the body and blood of Christ by the free power of the Word of God invoked over them—met with a stern rebuff. For Christ himself is the currency of this economy, and participation in Christ, body and soul and divinity, is the ground of any truly free exchange with God.

To make impossibly short a very long story, the gold standard was eventually secured theologically by way of the word transubstantiation.[9] Irenaeus,

8. *Haer.* 5.2.3, ANF 1:528.
9. Hildebert de Lavardin, archbishop of Tours, supplies the first known use of the word in this context, in the eleventh century. It quickly came into general use. Lateran IV affirmed that Christ's "body and blood are truly contained in the sacrament of the altar under the forms of bread and wine, the bread and wine having been transubstantiated, by God's power, into his body and blood." It should be noted that the term precedes widespread adoption of an Aristotelian frame of reference and outlasts it as well. (Trent itself deploys the word *substance* but not the word *accidents*.) The idea captured by the term is to be found already among the fathers. See, for example, Ambrose, *On the Mysteries*, 50–52, NPNF² 10:324: "For that sacrament

to be sure, would have thought that word a peculiar linguistic tool, just as he would have thought the *homoousion* a peculiar linguistic tool. But I have little doubt that he would have accepted both words, for both refuse to allow any other mediator of this exchange than Christ himself. Not so the Protestant reformers, for whom *transsubstantiatio* was not a fitting word for whatever it is that takes place in the eucharistic consecration and celebration. Indeed, they began to think of that word—together with the whole sacrament of the Eucharist and the wider sacramental system of the Church—in connection with a quite different controversy, namely, the Pelagian one. How did that happen, and to what effect?

Disrupting the Economy

We may focus here on Luther, who (when expressing one of his several minds on the subject) objected that *transsubstantiatio* was "a monstrous word and a monstrous idea." The monstrous idea was not merely the conversion of one thing (bread or wine) into another (body and blood), which he thought on a par with alchemy, but the support this lent to the notion of the Mass as a sacrifice and a good work. Recall that the first "Babylonian captivity" of the sacrament was the refusal to provide the cup to the laity. The second, more serious captivity (though the laity generally did not bother with it) was the doctrine of transubstantiation, which he thought must fall to Ockham's razor and be replaced with something on analogy with Chalcedon. The body of Christ (in the literal rather than the ecclesial sense) should be understood to coexist with the bread as the divinity of Christ coexists with his humanity.[10] The third and most serious, indeed "wicked," captivity was the widespread and firm belief "that the Mass is a good work and a sacrifice."[11]

It should be remarked that everyone agrees that a valid point is contained in Luther's objection to the first "captivity," and in the clericalization of the Church implicated there. It should be further remarked that Irenaeus's own wording in the famous passage quoted above, "consisting of two realities," leaves room for consideration of Luther's second objection. There can be no doubt about the fact that tradition had evolved on this point, and Luther was convinced that it had evolved wrongly. He could insist vigorously on the

---

which you receive is made what it is by the word of Christ. But if the word of Elijah had such power as to bring down fire from heaven, shall not the word of Christ have power to change the nature of the elements?"

10. Or, for that matter, with the closed womb or shut door when passing through.

11. *The Babylonian Captivity of the Church*, part 1 (*LW* 36:11–57), in Timothy Lull, ed., *Martin Luther's Basic Theological Writings* (Minneapolis: Fortress, 1989), 291; see 283ff.

hoc est, without conceding a *conversio* understood as *transsubstantiatio*. But it was the third captivity that most concerned him and (here) most concerns us.

Luther did not bother himself too much in the early going, at least, with the charge from the Reformed side that transubstantiation, or for that matter his own view, amounted to bringing Christ down out of heaven. He regarded that as a misunderstanding, and so it is, though not for the reasons Luther gives. As a critique of his own view it has some cogency, as I have argued elsewhere.[12] As a critique of the doctrine of transubstantiation it fails to grasp either the understanding of substance in question (which is not spatial) or the real problem (which is temporal, or rather eschatological). It fails in fact to reckon with the mysteriousness of the sacrament.[13] What Luther did consistently bother himself with was the commerce in spiritual goods that the notion of the Mass as a good work and a sacrifice seemed to encourage, the same "most impious traffic" that also flourished around indulgences.

He was on solid ground here, respecting this wicked commerce, if we may judge the matter by the Tridentine reforms. He was wrong, however, in his theological response, as in his self-appointed role as arbiter and judge. He was right to insist that the Mass is a word of promise with a sacramental guarantee and that the right posture toward it is faith and gratitude: "What godless audacity is it, therefore, when we who are to receive the testament of God come as those who would perform a good work for him!"[14] But he was wrong to say that the Mass "is nothing but promise." Wrong (for reasons semiotic as well as theological) to say that "there is greater power in the word than in the sign . . . in the testament than in the sacrament." Wrong to cut off "the prayers which we offer at the same time" from the sacrament itself. Wrong as well to attack the *opus operatum* as a "fraudulent disguise" for idolatry.[15] Wrong above all to deny that, in the Mass, Christ himself is

---

12. *Ascension and Ecclesia* (Grand Rapids: Eerdmans, 1999), 173ff.; "Between the Rock and a Hard Place: In Support of (Something Like) a Reformed View of the Eucharist," *International Journal of Systematic Theology* 3.2 (2001): 167–86. Cf. Luther's "The Sacrament of the Body and Blood of Christ—against the Fanatics" (Lull, *Luther's Basic Theological Writings*, 314ff.).

13. Luther himself would presumably be happy with §1333 of the new catechism, which says quite simply: "The signs of bread and wine become, in a way surpassing understanding, the Body and Blood of Christ; they continue also to signify the goodness of creation." The catechism stands by Trent, however, and indeed by Thomas, affirming transubstantiation (§1376).

14. Lull, *Luther's Basic Theological Writings*, 304.

15. It is not quite accurate to say with Lull (ibid., 293n85) that the *ex opere operato* principle is held "without any reference to faith or lack of faith" on the part of the recipient, since it is understood that "the fruits of the sacrament also depend on the disposition of the one who receives them" (CCC 1128). It should be observed, in any case, that Luther himself allowed an *opus operatum* as regards the word and the sign, though not of offerings such as prayers, which were ineffective if those praying were unrighteousness.

offered up "to God the Father as an all-sufficient sacrifice."[16] Or so says the Catholic Church.

Luther knew that we are not to appear in God's presence empty-handed. The witness of Scripture makes that plain. Yet he regarded "the common belief that the Mass is a sacrifice, which is offered to God," as "the most dangerous" of stumbling blocks. He acknowledged that the canon of the Mass and the whole tradition stood behind this. Nevertheless (for such, frankly, was Luther's audacity) he determined that all must give way to his own rendering of the "simple" words of Christ, on pain of losing the gospel itself. The only sacrifice was that which comprised the offerings of the people: their money, their prayers, their devotions. The bread and wine to be consecrated belonged to these offerings, but once consecrated they were no longer offered. The sacrament itself was received but not offered. The Church, qua Church, made no offering.

Now these were indeed "corrupt and perilous times." There was good reason to be concerned, very deeply concerned, with the state of the Church. Hence the Council of Trent, which spent much more effort reforming Church practices and clarifying Church teaching than condemning the excesses of the Protestant reformers. These excesses were multiplying, naturally, and Luther himself became concerned about those who were taking his own thinking in a direction he did not wish it to go; viz., toward antinomianism and toward pure sacramental nominalism, in which communion with Christ lost all ecclesial concreteness and became ideational rather than actual, or actual only as ideational. He now worried about the "fanatics," who rejected the real presence altogether, and wrote against Radical Reformation tendencies, appealing (as he did against the Reformed) to his fateful doctrine of ubiquity. The chief danger on that side was that the egg should be sucked dry, to use his words; that the body and blood should be removed altogether from the bread and the wine; that the presider should say, "Take, eat, this is my body," with no more meaning than if he were to say, "Take and eat; here sits Hans in a red jacket."[17] Luther's response was pastoral as much as hermeneutical and doctrinal. The sacrament, he began to emphasize, was real assurance to the individual person that God was making good on his promise for him or her, that Christ could be laid hold of precisely here as one's very own. "For although the same thing is present in the sermon as in the sacrament," there is something more in the latter, something particularly given to each communicant. The true body and blood of Christ "is there given to them and is

---

16. See Lull, *Luther's Basic Theological Writings*, 298–307.

17. "Against the Fanatics" (*LW* 36:335–61), in Lull, *Luther's Basic Theological Writings*, at 325; cf. 315.

their own." Christ has not given himself to us merely "*ut signum*, that is, as mere sign," but effectively and with real benefit, in love and for love.[18]

Luther might have pointed out here that apart from this economy of love, rooted in Christ himself and in the receiving of Christ, the danger of Pelagianism lurked; the danger, that is, that our own works of love would be understood as ours alone rather than as works of Christ in us. But he did not seem to recognize or to worry sufficiently about the very same danger that was hidden in his own approach. He wanted a real union with Christ, an ontic participation in and with Christ, and was not prepared to set aside the body and blood dimension of this union and participation. His ubiquity doctrine, however, seemed to critics on both sides to undercut his argument, both theoretically and pastorally. History declares them right, as far as I can tell. It proved very difficult to maintain the *hoc est* in the sense of "here and not there." The gates were opened to the desacralization of the Church itself and to the resacralization of the world in (eventually) a neopagan fashion to which Luther would certainly have objected in his usual boisterous manner.

This swelled, rather than quelled, the rising tide of Pelagianism that he detested in the humanists and the traditionalists alike, and that he suspected in the fanatics as well. But, I am beginning to think, it was especially deadly in combination with his insistence that the Mass was not an offering, though it contained offerings in the form of prayers, gifts, and piety. What was this but a detachment of our offering from Christ's, which, as Professor Torrance observes, is at the very heart of doxological Pelagianism? In Luther—not first in Luther or only in Luther but crucially in Luther, given his pride of place in the Protestant Reformation—the eucharistic basis for viewing the Church as an economy of gift, of receiving and offering, mediated by Christ in both directions, is called into question. The canon of the Mass, apart from the words of institution, is excised from the liturgy like a cancerous growth by this self-appointed surgeon.[19] Just as the bread and wine stand alongside the

---

18. Ibid., 327ff.

19. One can look at this quite differently, of course, stressing instead Luther's caution about breaking with tradition (cf. Vernon P. Kleinig, "Lutheran Liturgies from Martin Luther to Wilhelm Löhe," *Concordia Theological Quarterly* 62.2 [1998]: 127f.). Yet the break was decisive. "We must dare something in the name of Christ!" But to take a red pen to the canon of the Mass? One wonders, by the way, if Lutherans today have pondered the Pelagian implications of putting an admonition to the people in place of the canonical prayer: "I exhort you in Christ that you give attention to the Testament of Christ in true faith, and above all to take to heart the words with which Christ presents His body and blood to us in forgiveness; that you take note of and give thanks for the boundless love that He showed us when He saved us from the wrath of God, sin, death, and hell by His blood; and that you then externally receive the bread and wine, that is, His body and blood, as a guarantee and pledge. Let us then in His name, according to His command, and with His own words administer and receive the testament" (Divine Service III).

body and blood rather than being converted into the body and blood, the offerings of men now stand alongside the offering of Christ rather than being taken up in, with, and through the One who himself *is* our offering.

The ripple effects of this kind of thinking, and of this course of action, are not difficult to observe. In due course the Church visible becomes simply a human construct, what like-minded individuals do when they band together, agreeing with this or that person who supposes that he knows what the "simple words" of Jesus mean, or just how the Scriptures should be read and applied, or how the liturgy should go. Pelagianism and fissiparousness go hand in hand, as Luther knew or should have known; and ecumenism, no matter how much effort is expended on it, is incapable of overcoming either. The shards of Christendom continue to fester in the open wounds of our post-Reformation civilization.

Recovering the Economy

James Torrance recognizes even among the Reformed a tendency to separate the Christian's offering from that of Christ's. The later Lutheran tendency to conflate the two, producing a kind of hyper-Pelagianism, may be less prevalent there, apart from very liberal circles. But nevertheless the problematic tendency exists. So what are we to make of Torrance's solution? With Calvin, Torrance wants to keep the active, "ongoing" priesthood of Christ clearly in view and to keep the work of the Spirit equally in view. He even presses the latter to the extent of speaking of the "priestly" mediation of the Spirit, lest on the one hand worship be reduced to what we ourselves do, or on the other hand we be left out of the one true worship altogether.

Torrance worries, as we saw, that Protestant worship too often obtrudes "our own offering of praise." Of course he also thinks that the Catholic Church, in making the *conversio* something that happens to the bread in the act of consecration, obscures "in too Pelagian a fashion" the fact "that the real *conversio* of our humanity took place in the substitutionary self-consecration of Jesus . . . , in the once-for-all action of our One High Priest." The alternative he proposes to the latter is to speak instead "of a 'conversion' in the *use* of the elements"—in short, of a transignification rather than a transubstantiation. The alternative he proposes to the former involves closer attention to liturgical and homiletical language, some adjustments to Reformed liturgies, and especially more frequent communion through the reattaching of the Lord's Supper to the Lord's Day.

Several questions present themselves, however, from a Catholic perspective. First, on what grounds—and to stand against the whole doxological tradition of the Church up to the Reformation they must be very serious grounds indeed; more serious, I venture to say, than Luther's or even Calvin's—are we to declare that it does not belong to the heavenly ministry and mediation of Christ to give himself to us in the fashion the Church believes and says he does? Otherwise put, on what grounds do we deny that the *mirifica commutatio* is anchored in the *conversio* that the Church (in the words of Trent) "has fittingly and properly called transubstantiation"?[20] Why indeed should participation in Christ not involve just that *conversio* of the elements of which the Church speaks: a *conversio* that is more, profoundly more, than a transignification; and a *communicatio* that is more, much more—though never less—than an *anamnesis* empowered by the Spirit? Why should the *anamnesis* suffer loss, as Torrance seems to think, by means of the *conversio* and of a real *communicatio* in the body and blood, truly present because truly given, and truly received when received in the grace of the Spirit?

Second, what are the implications of the recommended alternative? I have put a label on it that Torrance did not, but that others (even some ecumenically minded Catholics) have; viz., transignification. If the consecration is no more than transignification, it is undeniably the case that the *conversio* in question is something *we* do, not something that God in Christ does, even if Christ was the first to do it. It is a *conversio* sans *commutatio*, a *conversio* that requires no action of God or of Christ or even of the Spirit. It may be that the gathering of the community, as Barth would say, and its "work of memory" or *anamnesis*, is, when and where authentic, an inspired reflection on earth of Christ's own "memorial" in heaven. And in the darkness of this fallen world we may call that wonderful, even *mirifica*. But does this consecration that is no more than a special "use" of bread and wine not ground the whole business precisely on what we do, rather than on what our great high priest does?

Third, is it not the case that Calvin's construct, with which Professor Torrance is working, requires him to transfer to the Spirit both the language and the office of priestly mediation in order to prevent as far as possible a lapse back into the Pelagianism that he sees and rightly rejects in the Reformed tradition and (a fortiori) in Protestantism and evangelicalism more generally? Or, if not to transfer, then to reduplicate? The Father indeed has two

20. "Because Christ our Redeemer said that it was truly his body that he was offering under the species of bread, it has always been the conviction of the Church of God, and this holy Council now declares again, that by the consecration of the bread and wine there takes place a change of the whole substance of the bread into the substance of the body of Christ our Lord and of the whole substance of the wine into the substance of his blood. This change the holy Catholic Church has fittingly and properly called transubstantiation" (session 13, chap. 4; cf. *DEC* 2:695).

hands, as Irenaeus loved to say, and these two hands are distinct.[21] It is to Calvin's credit that he tried to reinvigorate sacramental *pneumatology* and to the Torrances' credit that they tried to reinvigorate, against Barthians and Zwinglians, *sacramental* pneumatology. But it is telling that pneumatological language here becomes priestly language—that a priestly office, analogous to Christ's, is bestowed on the Spirit. Is it possible that Protestantism must do this, or attempt to do it, just because it will not allow that the once-for-all *conversio* that takes place in and through the incarnate Son is participatable, body and soul, through the eucharistic act of this same Son, our great high priest—and, yes, through the instrumental consecration performed by the ministerial priesthood, acting *in persona Christi* in the exercise of their sacramental character?

But what then becomes of priesthood? If the priesthood of Christ, of the Word made flesh, operates only *in remoto*—that is, in the distant past of earthly history and in the distant space of heaven—if what is needed, then, is not merely the mediation of the Spirit but a new priesthood of the Spirit, what will distinguish Reformed Christianity from its Joachimite predecessor? What will distinguish it from the radical occasionalism of the later Barth, for that matter, or of its charismatic brethren? What will preserve it from the dissipation of the so-called Emerging Church? What indeed will prevent it from suffering the same fate that Lutheranism has suffered by reason of its ubiquity doctrine?[22]

Would it not be better, accepting with St. Irenaeus the constant teaching of Scripture and the constant witness of the Church's *lex orandi*, to say that we must not appear in God's presence empty-handed and that in "the Eucharist of the body and blood of Christ" an oblation or sacrifice is rendered to God in freedom? That just there is a real participation by divine grace in Christ who "loved us and gave himself up for us, a fragrant offering and sacrifice to God"? Approached in this way, as I remark in *Ascension Theology*,

> It is difficult to see how the eucharist could ever be reduced to a mere act of remembrance or of inner enjoyment, as it has in many Protestant communities and among poorly taught Catholics. Such a reduction can lead nowhere but to the very Pelagianism that the reformers feared and hoped to eradicate.

21. Distinct, and perfectly coordinated; cf. *Haer.* 5.1f., 5.6, 5.20.

22. Lutherans attempted to solve the problem that way, rather than by a new and deeper appeal to the work of the Spirit. But in speaking of the Spirit's ministry in a fashion too closely analogous to that of Christ, the Reformed can also produce in the end a conflation of the two. Those who sense the danger here may then be found pounding on the same sacramental "nail" that T. F. Torrance (*Space, Time and Incarnation* [London: Oxford University Press, 1969], 34) heard Luther pounding on, to no avail.

Where there is a refusal to allow that a real offering of Christ is made by the church in, with and through Christ, it is allowed instead (implicitly or explicitly) that some other offering should take place. Where it is not Christ himself who both offers and is offered, something else must be offered and someone else must do the offering. Where there is not a real communion in his body and blood, where our offering is not conjoined to his and mediated by his through that communion, we ourselves become the primary offerers and offering. That is a theological, moral and material mistake of the utmost consequence. Without adequate recognition of the real absence of Christ, the church itself has no real absence; knowledge of his presence renders it prone to self-glorying and to illusions of worldly power, to making martyrs of others rather than walking the path of martyrdom itself. Without the real presence of Christ, on the other hand, the church has no real presence either. It is not sufficiently potent in or against the world; it falls prey first to sectarianism, then to Erastianism.[23]

One reviewer of that book, who shares the Torrances' and Calvin's love of Hebrews, praised it for the connection it makes between ascension, communion, and new creation. By way of critique he proposed only that we leave transubstantiation out of the equation: "For Farrow, Christ must be *physically* available at the table or else the connection between eucharist and new creation is sundered. But the eucharist can certainly be a *celebration* of Christ's ongoing bodily existence without also being a *participation* in that existence."[24] He does not mention my charge, which is also (and first) Torrance's charge, that to say so is Pelagian. Nor does he seem to grasp the nature of the claim that is being made. If Jesus is our offering, and if that offering is indeed our offering, such that we are included in and with him, then we ourselves must be recipients of him, body, soul, and divinity. If we are not, either he offers and we do not, or he offers one thing and we another.[25]

23. *Ascension Theology* (London: T&T Clark, 2011), 69; cf. Eph. 5:2.
24. Mike Kibbe, italics original (https://wheatonblog.wordpress.com/2013/08/05/2091/). A colleague in Evangelicals and Catholics Together has suggested that my attempt to place the doctrine of transubstantiation in a more eschatological light is a kind of cheating, since tradition hasn't always done that. To which I reply that Catholics have always believed in the ability of the Church to bring forth from its treasure house things old and new. The same critic also thinks that my discussion of the *conversio* effected in those who communicate ought, logically, to be precisely the same *conversio* involved in transubstantiation itself. Certainly not. If one holds with Aquinas that "Christ's actual body and blood" and his "mystical body" are respectively "the first thing and the ultimate thing of which the Eucharist is the [effective] sign," one has already made a distinction here (*ST* 3.73.1; see chap. 6 below).
25. In his review, "At the Right Hand" (*First Things*, Aug./Sept. 2011: 62–63), Hans Boersma acknowledges my rejection of "the Pelagianism inherent in memorialist views of the Eucharist," my Calvin-like focus on our heavenly high priest, and my eschatological rather than Aristotelian

Neither alternative is acceptable. The question is not whether we offer or what we offer; we offer glory and honor to the Father, in the unity of the Holy Spirit, "through him, with him, and in him," as the canon of the Mass says. The only question is whether there is a *conversio* of the bread and wine in its time and place and purpose, as that which we consume together and by which we are nurtured together, such that we have not bread and wine and the limited goods belonging to bread and wine but rather the body and blood of our Lord and the unlimited benefits they bring. The Church has always said, from the moment the question arose, that there is indeed such a *conversio*, a change of substance, though it has certainly not pegged this to an Aristotelian physics or metaphysics. It has said so because Jesus said so: *hoc est corpus meum*. And it has said so in defiance of the proposal, put forward from time to time, that the bond between Jesus and ourselves is merely intellectual and volitional, or alternatively that it is effected only in heaven and not also on earth. For in neither case would any seed of heaven, of immortality, actually be planted within us, except in some gnostic sense; nor would any truly inclusive offering be made.

It is the great merit of Torrance's approach that it does not seek celebration without participation. For if there is only celebration without participation, that celebration is strictly our own and there is no worship that can escape the charge that it is merely what we do. But what if participation is posited, yet posited as something strictly "spiritual"? What if there is no communicable gift of the one Jesus Christ, body and soul and divinity? Are matters really any different? Torrance has it right: Christ's worship is our worship. But how do we participate in that worship unless Christ offers himself to us, and so offers us with himself to God? How do we participate unless he gives us himself *to* offer and takes us to himself that we *may* offer? Surely it is only thus that we appear before God neither empty-handed nor with a false offering. As the *oratio super oblata* for the fifth day of the Nativity puts it:

---

frame of reference. But he too confesses his puzzlement as to "why Farrow still insists on using the unhelpful language of transubstantiation." Now one can agree, as Boersma does in *Heavenly Participation: The Weaving of a Sacramental Tapestry* (Grand Rapids: Eerdmans, 2011), 158f., that there are periods of ossification in the discussion of any dogma, which lead to the detaching of one thing from another in an unraveling of the tapestry of theological thought, and that this happens with the notion of transubstantiation. One can agree that there are periods of recovery, and that the *communio* ecclesiology of Vatican II represents such a recovery. Moreover, one can agree that "just as the Catholic Church has begun to focus more strongly on the fellowship of the church community, so . . . is it time for evangelicals to celebrate much more unambiguously the real presence of Christ in the Eucharist" (ibid., 119). But this does not answer the question as to the nature of the real presence or of the Mass itself; nor does it address what tradition has consistently said on the subject.

Receive our oblation, O Lord,
by which is brought about a glorious exchange,
that, by offering what you have given,
we may merit to receive your very self.
Through Christ our Lord.[26]

Now in the Catholic liturgy the faithful are invited by the priest to join in this offering: "Pray, brethren, that my sacrifice and yours may be acceptable to God, the almighty Father." They reply, "May the Lord accept the sacrifice at your hands, for our good and the good of all his holy Church." This "at your hands" (*de manibus tuis*) distinguishes the role of the priest, who acts *in persona Christi*, from that of the people, making evident again that what is transpiring in the Mass is nothing if not the work of Christ himself. It does not really arise from the people but is provided for them, in the *conversio* of the gifts they bring. It is by grace—marvelous and miraculous grace—that both priest and people are able to engage in the *commercia gloriosa* that constitute the eucharistic economy.[27] And engage they do, for body and soul they are made partakers of Christ, who is both offerer and offering.

In the Reformed tradition, even in places where Torrance's corrective is taken to heart, things appear to be otherwise. For in that tradition the Spirit, who unites the faithful to Christ "substantially," does so only by drawing the soul upward into heavenly places.[28] On earth, tokens of Christ are set forth only as tokens. Nothing is exchanged but words and assurances. The sacrament itself is just a visible word. It is not through the hands of the priest that one joins in the self-offering of Jesus to God. It is not by the mouth that one receives Jesus. One does not receive him bodily at all, except by extension through the communion of souls. Jesus is said to offer himself continually before God in heaven, and one is joined to him there by the mystical union that the Spirit creates between our souls and his. This union is not to be construed as purely passive. According to Torrance it is right to say, "We offer, and yet it is not our offering. It is Christ." It is right to say, "We worship, in such a way that He is the One who acts in us and through us, so that our

---

26. Prayer over the Offerings, Fifth Day within the Octave of the Nativity of the Lord. *Suscipe, Domine, munera nostra, quibus exercentur commercia gloriosa, ut, offerentes quae dedisti, teipsum mereamur accipere* (*Missale Romanum*, Editio Typica Tertia, 2002). An early version of this prayer is found in the sixth-century Verona Sacramentary (cf. Daniel McCarthy, "Glorious Exchanges," *The Tablet*, 16 August 2008, 15).

27. Cf. my *Ascension and Ecclesia*, 175ff.

28. The Vatican II liturgical reforms, which were meant to make plainer the participation of the people, have been a source of tension in part because they have sometimes had the effect of obscuring this point.

worship becomes real worship." But is Christ actually offered for us and by us here and now? Do we actually receive Christ here and now, both body and soul? Apparently not, for there is no *conversio* of the gifts, only of their use. Viewed from below, at least, our worship is strictly semiotic, albeit imbued (ideally) with evangelical intention and with faith that the Holy Spirit will render it heavenly or substantial. The Church is wrong to say, as the Roman Canon does in Eucharistic Prayer I:

> Therefore, O Lord, as we celebrate the memorial of the blessed Passion, the Resurrection from the dead, and the glorious Ascension into heaven of Christ, your Son, our Lord, we, your servants and your holy people, offer to your glorious majesty from the gifts that you have given us, this pure victim, this holy victim, this spotless victim, the holy Bread of eternal life and the Chalice of everlasting salvation.

So the question remains: Who or what exactly is offered on earth, and how? Who does the offering, and on what basis? Or is there no offering after all, but only, as Zwingli insisted, the recollection of an offering?[29] None of this is clear where the *conversio* is denied.

There is no way out of this dilemma by conceding the real presence of Christ pneumatologically while refusing to concede the conversion of bread and wine, by the Spirit, into the very body and blood of Christ. Christ's spiritual presence is promised whenever two or three are gathered in his name to pray or bear witness or serve. But to speak of that kind of presence, as wonderful as it is, only begs the question of the Eucharist as the Church's unique and definitive act of *leitourgia*, *martyria*, and *diakonia*—as the one act that grounds in Christ all its other acts and secures its being *as* the Church.[30]

---

29. In her book *Calvin's Ladder: A Spiritual Theology of Ascent and Ascension* (Grand Rapids: Eerdmans, 2010), Julie Canlis develops a Calvinist theology of participation into which she wants to inject a healthy dose of Irenaean thinking. She seeks common ground between the two by stressing that, for Calvin, participation in the Spirit gives substance to the sacramental sign; by the Spirit there is somehow a true eating and drinking of Christ. But she admits that it is not clear in Calvin, as it is in Irenaeus, that the physical participates fully in the spiritual (166f.). Hence it is not clear either whether the eating and drinking is anything but a pious activity of the soul. As for the eucharistic economy, construed in Calvinist terms, we offer ourselves to be fed and, having been fed, offer the sacrifice of praise and gratitude. Canlis rightly worries that, where this is understood "as our response to Christ rather than our place with Christ in his self-offering to the Father" (169), the sacrament is reduced from *communio* to *imitatio*. Unfortunately she does not press this ecclesiologically by addressing the fact that, absent the *conversio*, "our place with Christ in his self-offering" remains merely an intellectual or pedagogical affair—a matter of mental formation.

30. Otherwise put, it begs the question of the relation between baptism and the Eucharist, or between the individual and the Church. We might also say that it begs the question of the relation between John 6 and 14.

Neither is there a way out by positing some kind of consubstantiation or impanation, as the Lutheran tradition does, for the putative coexistence of bread and body is posited precisely to avoid the notion of sacrifice and offering, or at all events to hold apart the offering of Christ and the offerings of the faithful. In both cases a miracle of private faith is placed where the miracle of transubstantiation ought to be, and the eucharistic economy is undone. There may be full allowance for the fact that Christ has made his great offering on earth, once for all, that he presents it still in heaven on behalf of the baptized, that the faithful are assured some part in that and in the reward it merits. Yet the only offering to be made here and now, by us, is our own private offering, or no offering at all.

Whose offering? In the Latin sphere this is not merely *an* ecumenical problem; arguably it is *the* ecumenical problem. It is intimately linked, of course, to the question of justification and sanctification and to the matter of doctrinal and pastoral discipline; that is, to the question of the keys. Denial that the Church joins in Christ's own offering to God secures the divorce between justification (based on his past offering) and sanctification (based on our present offerings). It also establishes the indeterminacy of the Church, as no certain offerer of no certain offering, just a voluntary association of more or less right-minded and right-living individuals, celebrating when and as they please, offering to God their evangelical intentions or something else substantively their own. But justification cannot be divorced from sanctification, as we have already seen. And the Church is not indeterminate. It is what it is because through Christ it offers Christ, and itself only in and with Christ. Which means that ecumenism, if a kind of substitute for Catholicism, is no solution either to Pelagianism or to the aforementioned fissiparousness. Neither is the "open table" that Torrance championed, so long as there is an unresolved dispute as to what is on that table.

6

Transubstantiation

Sic transit mundus ad gloriam

The Protestant Reformation's attempted repudiation of Pelagianism by extraction from the eucharistic economy of grace—that is, by rejection of the
sacrifice of the Mass and thus of the Church's own proper participation in
the one self-offering of Jesus Christ—was its greatest error. It did not and
could not accomplish, except by way of the Tridentine response it helped
provoke, what needed to be accomplished, namely, the removal of the Pelagian
elements and other abuses encumbering that economy. In the churches of the
Reformation it is not the *mirifica commutatio* or *commercium gloriosum* that
has come into focus under the *sola gratia* banner; what has appeared there
instead, in far too many cases, is the Cain-like offering of the man who worships as he pleases and relies on his own resources.[1]

The Mass, properly approached, is in every way evangelical. Bread and
wine are presented at the altar for the sake of an exchange, a wonderful
exchange that rests on the conversion of those elements, by the power and
grace of God, into the life-giving body and blood of Christ. This *conversio*,
fittingly called transubstantiation, belongs to the *esse* of the Church militant;
without it there would be, here and now, no Church, only individual disciples

---

1. See further my remarks in *Canadian Converts: The Path to Rome* (Ottawa: Justin Press,
2009), 82, about today's self-referential Pelagianism "with its much-diminished element of the
asceticism Pelagius himself advocated," a Pelagianism produced by the triumph of the *sola
fide* over the *sola gratia*.

in their chosen communities. Its facticity is *de fide*, as Trent declares;[2] yet it is also a grand mystery, containing an eternal surprise, that cannot be fully described or explained.

That is not to say, however, that it has been explained as well as may be or that there is no more work to be done in the attempt to understand what can be understood about it. On the contrary, there are many puzzling features that still invite attention, with the hope of theological progress and a clearer presentation of the mystery. Some of these features appear in Thomas Aquinas's treatment of the subject or are noticeable by their absence there. His treatment remains a touchstone, not only because of its influence on Trent but also because it already raises (and addresses) most of the objections that later appeared among the Protestant reformers. It is with Thomas, then, that we shall begin, asking with him what sort of conversion we are talking about and what really happens to the bread and wine. In the end we will answer somewhat differently, having explored eschatological territory he left unexplored.[3]

Thomas on Conversion

Now, ordinarily, a conversion involves some sort of transformation. Expressed in scholastic terms, one thing is converted into another only if they have matter in common, which is given a new form, or if they exist within

---

2. "In the first place, the holy council teaches and openly and without qualification professes that, after the consecration of the bread and wine, our lord Jesus Christ, true God and true man, is truly, really and substantially contained in the propitious sacrament of the holy eucharist under the appearance of those things which are perceptible to the senses" (session 13, chap. 1; *DEC* 2:693).

3. It may be conceded that Thomas's view was not paradigmatic. It may also be conceded, as James McCue argues in "The Doctrine of Transubstantiation from Berengar through Trent: The Point at Issue" (*Harvard Theological Review* 61.3 [1968]: 385–430), that transubstantiation was far from a fixed concept and that one of Luther's main objections to it was that the Church was in no position to regard it as *de fide*. McCue is mistaken, however, in suggesting that it had (and has) no great necessity or importance. That "the anti-Albigensian confession of faith of Lateran IV was not interpreted as a dogmatic exclusion of all theories of the real presence other than transubstantiation until eighty-five years after that council" (424), and that transubstantiation's triumph came about in a rather haphazard fashion, leads him to inquire whether the Catholic Church might yet reconsider. But, quite apart from issues around "the nature and function of dogma" (430), McCue's inquiry fails if the other two contenders, viz., annihilation and consubstantiation, prove false. While demonstrating their falsity is not our concern here, it must be observed that neither is capable of being given the kind of eschatological interpretation we are seeking for transubstantiation—not without falling into heresy—which already seems a good reason for regarding them as false. That we *are* seeking such an interpretation already sets us apart from Thomas, however, for whom "the eucharistic conversion is a miraculous this-worldly change, not an eschatological event" (Matthew Levering, *Sacrifice and Community: Jewish Offering and Christian Eucharist* [Oxford: Blackwell, 2005], 133).

an underlying subject greater than both, which brings about the change of one substance (with its matter and form) into another. Otherwise we are not talking about a conversion at all, though we might perhaps be talking about the removal of one thing in order to substitute another. Either way, we are talking about a temporal process. But transubstantiation is not a temporal process. According to Thomas, it is not a transformation at all. Here there is no matter in common nor any underlying subject in which both exist. God himself does not make of bread the body of Jesus, which he made already from the Virgin; neither does the body of Jesus come to earth to convert bread into itself.[4] Yet transubstantiation is a conversion. The body does not exist in or alongside the bread. Nor does God annihilate the bread. It would not be fitting that he should destroy the natural gifts that are brought before him, which are both his own handiwork and that of his grateful worshipers.[5] Annihilation, moreover, would again mean that the body of Christ would have to move from heaven in order to take the place of the bread.[6]

So what exactly is this strange conversion that has been labeled transubstantiation? Thomas contends that it is an instantaneous change from the whole substance (*tota substantia*) of bread to the whole substance of Christ's body. Since divine action "extends to the whole nature of being," God is capable of bringing it about that "the whole substance of one thing be changed into the whole substance of another."[7] This language, as used by Aquinas (things may be otherwise with the Tridentine fathers who adopted it), rules out any mere mutation or transformation. There is no alteration in the bread itself, as if matter were to receive a new form, or form new matter; or as if one form-and-matter reality, however quickly, were to become another within

4. As Stephen Brock observes in "St. Thomas Aquinas and the Eucharistic Conversion," *The Thomist* 65 (2001): 558, Thomas at *ST* 3.75.8 flatly "denies that the bread can properly be said to 'become' the body of Christ." Brock is responding to Germain Grisez, "An Alternative Theology of Jesus' Substantial Presence in the Eucharist" (*Irish Theological Quarterly* 65.2 [2000]: 111–31), who is troubled by this denial.

5. God is the creator; he gives being and goodness to creatures. He is not a destroyer, and "non-being is not from him," though "when God's creative and preserving causality is removed, the thing reverts to the non-being it had of itself before it was created" (Anselm, *DCD* 1; cf. Aquinas, *ST* 3.75.3).

6. The arguments Thomas deploys (*ST* 3.75.2) against coexistence of bread and body are these: the body would have to leave heaven and travel simultaneously to several earthly places; *hoc est corpus meum* would have bread as a referent; adoration of the sacrament would entail idolatry; and the rule against taking the eucharist along with ordinary food would be incoherent. The first of these four—were it persuasive—would also tell against annihilationism.

7. *ST* 3.75.4. Levering (*Sacrifice and Community*, 144) sometimes renders *tota substantia* as "entire being."

a common subject greater than both. There is instead the substitution of one substance for another—a succession of substances, so to say, yet without any successiveness or transitional relation between the two. This succession must nevertheless be understood, in this one unique instance, "to consist in a conversion of one into the other" rather than in the removal or annihilation of the one for the sake of the other.[8]

In sum, the miracle of transubstantiation involves a sui generis succession that is not a transformation but is a conversion. It is hardly satisfactory to leave it at that, however, as Thomas himself intuits. Interestingly, he speaks of this miracle as entailing a sublation or withdrawal of the distinction between the two substances:

> Form cannot be changed into form, nor matter into matter by the power of any finite agent. Such a change, however, can be made by the power of an infinite agent, which has control over all being, because the nature of being [natura entis] is common to both forms and to both matters; and whatever there is of being [entitatis] in the one, the author of being can change into whatever there is of being in the other, withdrawing [sublato] that whereby it was distinguished from the other.[9]

While this remark remains somewhat cryptic, perhaps we can elaborate it thus: The same God who establishes and upholds all such distinctions in the natural world chooses to suspend the relevant distinction here, so that his divine act of giving and sustaining the being and substance of bread becomes instead the act of giving and sustaining the being and substance of the body of Christ. The being-there of bread becomes, without any temporal process

8. Thus Brock, "Eucharistic Conversion," 537ff. Brock freely deploys the expression "succession of substances," but this must not be confused with the successiveness that Aquinas rejects. There is "a certain order of substances" (ST 3.75.4, ad 1; cf. 3.75.7) but no temporal transition from the one to the other and no dependence of the latter on any change in the former, even though there is a conversio. Cf. McCue ("Point at Issue," 394), who mentions that "Roland Bandinelli, in whose writings we first find the word 'transsubstantiatio,' favored succession rather than what we have been calling transubstantiation."

9. ST 3.75.4: Ad tertium dicendum quod virtute agentis finiti non potest forma in formam mutari, nec materia in materiam. Sed virtute agentis infiniti, quod habet actionem in totum ens, potest talis conversio fieri, quia utrique formae et utrique materiae est communis natura entis; et id quod entitatis est in una, potest auctor entis convertere ad id quod est entitatis in altera, sublato eo per quod ab illa distinguebatur. Brock ("Eucharistic Conversion," 548) translates: "By the power of a finite agent, form cannot be changed into form, nor matter into matter. But by the power of an infinite agent, which has action bearing on all being, such a conversion can come about, because there is a nature of being common to the two forms and to the two matters; and the author of being can convert what there is of entity in one to what there is of entity in the other, with the elimination of that by which the one was distinguished from the other."

effecting the change, the being-there (non-dimensively) of body.[10] Yet even if we think we can make sense of such a claim, the word *conversio* does not seem altogether apt. There is one thing and then, by the grace of God, there is another. That which nourishes our bodies only for mortal existence gives way to that which nourishes us for immortal existence. On Thomas's account, it still seems truer to say that the latter is substituted for the former than that the former becomes the latter through conversion. In other words, he is not altogether convincing in positing a conversion that is not in any sense a transformation.[11]

Noticing this, and recalling that *conversio* is the Church's own word for this miracle, Germain Grisez argues against Thomas that the bread does become body, by a complete conversion of the former into the latter. Stephen Brock notes that Durand of Saint Pourçain, writing not long after Aquinas, proposed something similar, suggesting that the sacramental conversion resembles the conversion of food into that which is fed. The matter of the bread loses the nature or form of bread and shares instead in the nature of the body of Christ.[12] But if this is conversion, it is conversion as transformation—however sudden and however miraculous—and Brock thinks that Trent, by adopting Thomas's language about the conversion of the whole substance of bread into the whole substance of body, effectively excludes that.[13] In response to Grisez, Brock insists with Aquinas that the bread does not become body in any transformationist sense, while also rejecting the annihilationist alternative by maintaining that "the bread passes away, not into nothing, but into the body of Christ," albeit without itself becoming that body.[14] He observes that

10. No nominalist flavor is intended. God does not arbitrarily change the order of things, but generously exchanges one gift for another for the sake of communion in the sacrifice of Christ (on which see further Levering, *Sacrifice and Community*, 135ff.).

11. Is there really, as Gilles Emery claims, a close association in Aquinas between the conversion of substance and "our own conversion in Christ who is the end [*finis*] of this conversion" (Levering, ibid., 162f., per Gilles Emery), if the former conversion lacks any transformative aspect?

12. Brock, "Eucharistic Conversion," 535. Cf. Timothy Thibodeau, "The Doctrine of Transubstantiation in Durand's 'Rationale,'" *Traditio* 51 (1996): 308–17.

13. Brock is correct that Trent's use of "whole substance" cannot be taken in a merely quantitative sense.

14. "On the annihilation account," explains Brock (ibid., 544f.), "the change in the contents of the sacramental species would only be a result. Underlying it would be two changes, simultaneous but distinct: a change in the bread—its ceasing to exist—and some change in the body of Christ through which it begins to exist there where the bread was. By contrast, on the conversion account, there is only one change, the change in the bread. The body of Christ would be the term of that very change. As Thomas puts it, this succession can be called a conversion because it agrees with natural change not only in the fact that something one and the same remains, but also in the fact that one term 'passes away into the other' (*transit in alterum*). The

in Thomas the sacramental species or appearances, which remain through-out, serve as a kind of subject for the conversion, though admittedly in an exceptional manner, since they are not greater than either bread or body and are not even proper to the latter.

Here Brock adds a touch of his own, suggesting that the sacramental action itself exists *sicut in subiectio*, the two substances (bread and body) serving as "a sort of subject for it," albeit only logically and not actually, since bread and body never exist simultaneously.[15] But this seems rather to avoid the *conversio* question than to answer it. Would it not be better to say that God himself, in his *opera ad extra* as creator and redeemer, provides the subject? That is, to speak of a *conversio* that takes place in God's providential care for his people and in his determination to provide sustenance for them? Where he gave only bread he now gives, according to their need—not more bread, as by the Sea of Galilee, but—living bread, the bread of life, the body of Christ. Of course, that is not what the Church has intended to signify by using the word *conversio*, which does not in the first instance reference the action of God (or its liturgical mediation) but rather the substance of the bread, which God converts into body. And it must be admitted, I think, that Thomas's account is easier to understand as a succession or substitution—as an exchange of one thing for another—than as a conversion of one thing into another. While Brock believes that "the analogy between 'the substance under the accidents' and the subject of a transformation saves the language of conversion,"[16] it seems to me *only* to save the language. More generously, it allows for a conversion from one reality (the presence of bread under its accidents) to another (the presence of body under those same accidents) but not of one substance into another.[17]

The fathers of Trent, who seem at times to lean heavily on Thomas, do not incorporate this feature of his work into their conciliar declarations. Their language, though near to his, is more traditional:

> But since Christ our redeemer said that was truly his own body which he was offering under the form of bread, therefore there has always been complete conviction in the church of God—and so this holy council now declares it once

---

bread passes away, not into nothing, but into the body of Christ. The coming to be of Christ's body in the host starts from the bread." The something one and the same that remains is the bread's accidents.

15. See ibid., 537ff.

16. Ibid., 564.

17. To defend that adjustment, Brock has to bring in, or to suggest that Aquinas brings in, a sacramental order of grace between the natural and the supernatural, an order based on "a human utterance of the Word incarnate" (ibid., 565). More will be said about that in a moment.

again—that, by the consecration of the bread and wine, there takes place the change of the whole substance of the bread into the substance of the body of Christ our Lord, and of the whole substance of the wine into the substance of his blood. And the holy catholic church has suitably and properly called this change transubstantiation.[18]

Here we have conversion of the whole substance of the bread, without qualification by reference to *id quod entitatis est*, to what there is of entity or being. We have something closer to the simplicity of Ambrose than to the subtlety of Aquinas. We do not have a mere transformation of bread, but we do have a real conversion: *ex pane fit corpus Christi.*[19] Bread does not cease to be so that body can be. The bread becomes body at the invocation of the Word and the Spirit, who exercise the same power that is exercised in creating and again, if somewhat differently, in renewing the creation: "It was not the body of Christ before consecration," says Ambrose, "but after consecration, I tell thee, it is now the body of Christ. He spake, and it was made: he commanded, and it was created." Then comes the eschatological, the baptismal, contextualization: "Thou thyself didst formerly exist, but thou wast an old creature; after thou wast consecrated, thou didst begin to be a new creature. Wilt thou know how thou art a new creature? Everyone, it says, in Christ is a new creature."[20]

Near the beginning of the Church's reflection on this, Irenaeus had spoken of the consecrated host in terms of "two realities, an earthly and a heavenly."[21] Tradition has developed this not by speaking of the simultaneity of these realities or by making them successive but rather by holding the one to be convertible into the other without any corresponding change to the other. As the Tridentine catechism puts it: "This conversion, then, is so effected that the whole substance of the bread is changed by the power of God into the whole substance of the body of Christ, and the whole substance of the wine into the whole substance of His blood, and this, without any change in our Lord Himself. He is neither begotten, nor changed, not increased, but

---

18. . . . *per consecrationem panis et vini conversionem fieri totius substantiae panis in substantiam corporis Christi domini nostri . . . quae conversio convenienter et proprie a sancta catholica ecclesia transsubstantiatio est appellata* (session 13, chap. 4; DEC 2:695).

19. Ambrose, *De sacramentis* 4.4 (§19).

20. Ambrose, *De sacramentis* 4.4 (§16); cf. 4.5 (§23) and *De mysteriis* 52: "But if the word of Elijah was powerful enough to bring down fire from heaven, will not the word of Christ be powerful enough to change the characters of the elements [*ut species mutet elementorum*]?" (trans. T. Thompson [London: SPCK, 1919]).

21. *Haer.* 4.18.5; cf. Ambrose, *De sacramentis* 4.4 (§15), 5.4 (§24); and John of Damascus, *De fide orthodoxa* 4.13. (Aquinas at *ST* 3.75.2 deploys Ambrose against John, or a certain reading of John.)

remains entire in His substance." And, though the elaboration offered sounds at many points as if it were taken straight from Thomas, the catechism states that the body of our Lord is "rendered present by the change of the bread into it."[22] Perhaps it is necessary, then, not only to question Aquinas but to search for an alternative account, one more attuned than medieval and Counter-Reformation theologians were to the eschatological note struck by the early fathers.

The Inadequacy of Substance/Accidents Analysis

This alternative will be easier to discover if we do not over-invest in the categories of substance and accidents. The old catechism, to be sure, speaks of "the third great and wondrous effect of this sacrament, namely, the existence of the species of bread and wine without a subject." On this effect it has but little to say, and it appends a warning that all these doctrines "should be explained with great caution, according to the capacity of the hearers and the necessities of the times." But what does it say? "Since we have already proved that the body and blood of our Lord are really and truly contained in the Sacrament, to the entire exclusion of the substance of the bread and wine, and since the accidents of bread and wine cannot inhere in the body and blood of Christ, it remains that, contrary to physical laws, they must subsist of themselves, inhering in no subject." We should not be hasty in clarifying this deduction.[23] The explanatory apparatus in vogue in the sixteenth century is not itself part of the universal ordinary or extraordinary magisterium,

22. So also the new catechism (§1375, referencing Ambrose): "It is by the conversion of the bread and wine into Christ's body and blood that Christ becomes present in this sacrament."

23. *Catechism of the Council of Trent*, part 2, "The Sacraments: The Eucharist" (trans. J. A. McHugh and C. J. Callan [1923; repr., Charlotte, NC: TAN Books, 1982], 140ff.): "The Catholic Church firmly believes and professes that in this Sacrament the words of consecration accomplish three wondrous and admirable effects. The first is that the true body of Christ the Lord, the same that was born of the Virgin, and is now seated at the right hand of the Father in heaven, is contained in this Sacrament. The second, however repugnant it may appear to the senses, is that none of the substance of the elements remains in the Sacrament. The third, which may be deduced from the two preceding, although the words of consecration themselves clearly express it, is that the accidents which present themselves to the eyes or other senses exist in a wonderful and ineffable manner without a subject." This third, which is deduced, insofar as it concerns something not only admirable but ineffable, which has been explained in different ways in different times and was not defined in precisely these terms by the council itself, may or may not be construed (as here) in terms of substance and accidents. That the catechism says that "this has been at all times the uniform doctrine of the Catholic Church" only shows that it is not the substance/accidents distinction but the substance/appearances distinction that is in view.

nor does it reappear in the new catechism.[24] Hence it is not forbidden to seek an improved apparatus for saying the same thing that the council and the catechism—both catechisms—are concerned to say, though any account of the miracle of transubstantiation must reckon with the fact that the *species* or *accidentia* belonging to bread and wine in some fashion remain with us when body and blood are being given in place of bread and wine.[25]

Let us begin with basics. If *substantia* refers to the concrete reality (in the union of form and matter) that makes something what it actually is, standing firm beneath the accidents that inhere in it (features such as quantity, quality, location, etc., that change according to entelechic development or through external forces), then *transsubstantiatio* refers to the fact that the concrete reality of the body and blood of Jesus is made present by conversion of the concrete reality of bread and of wine. Yet in this presence the former lacks the spatial extension and other accidental features that naturally belong to it. Or rather, it is present for us, not apart from these accidents, which are present by concomitance, but in distinction from them; so that, by offering and receiving the body and blood of Christ under the accidents proper to bread and wine, we may share in Christ's own offering in a fashion suited to us. The giving and receiving of the body and blood is our means of participation in the entire, indivisible person and work of Christ, who is for us a just offering and sacrifice.

This is a humble and reverent, rather than a rationalistic, claim. It is not a product of speculative reason, operating by extension of its own first principles, but rather an attempt to say what must be said in defense of the Church's faith that the dominical *hoc est corpus meum* is no mere figure of speech.

24. When Antoine Arnauld, anticipating objections to Descartes's view of transubstantiation, states that "it is an article of our faith that the substance of the bread passes out of the bread of the Eucharist, and that only its accidents remain" (quoted in Richard A. Watson, "Transubstantiation among the Cartesians," in *Problems of Cartesianism*, ed. Thomas M. Lennon, John M. Nicholas, and John W. Davis [Montreal: McGill-Queen's University Press, 1982], 132), he makes *de fide* an explanatory apparatus that is not *de fide*, or so Descartes says in his letter to Mersenne of March 1642. One need have no sympathy with Descartes's theory of superficies to agree, or to join in questioning whether the miracle of transubstantiation really entails, as Arnauld suggests, a "sundering" of substance and accidents, such that "flesh lies trembling under accidents unnatural to it" (Watson, "Transubstantiation among the Cartesians," 133, paraphrasing Fr. Mesland). Indeed, one need have no sympathy with Descartes at all, whose half-serious proposal to Mesland that transubstantiation does not even require that bread become body, only that it somehow be conjoined to the mind or soul of Christ (ibid. 135f.), shows where he himself was headed. In the next chapter we will discover that our whole culture, to its great peril, seems to have followed him.

25. *Species* here in the older sense, not as referencing forms or kinds, and *accidentia* also in the non-technical sense in which it serves as a partial synonym for *species* (cf., e.g., the *sed contra* and *respondeo* at *ST* 3.77.1).

It is nonetheless problematic, or can become so, when it begins to speak of accidents that inhere in no substance. Which is to say: when it gets distracted by the idea of free-floating accidents, a notion that on the Thomistic scheme seems necessary[26] but generates more problems than it solves.

Substance/accidents analysis, though a sort of common sense indispensable in ordinary thought, suffers philosophically from the fact that it depends on a distinction between primary and secondary matter that is no longer tenable, and from the fact that it cannot readily accommodate modern ideas of space and time. When the substance of Christ's body is said to be non-dimensively present simultaneously at multiple locations, is it not falsely assumed that time is an undifferentiated constant, an absolute, and that space is a firm and fixed container? This is not tenable either, now that we know space and time and matter and energy to be mutually implicated in a continuum that cannot so neatly be unpicked. But quite apart from such modern difficulties, which add new layers of concern, substance/accidents analysis, when faced with the miracle of transubstantiation, *already* seems to lose its common-sense character and merely to complexify, rather than to clarify, sacramental description.

Consider: If the substances of bread and wine are not simply eliminated but, as the Church teaches, changed—yet changed in a way that leaves their accidents unchanged—what are we to make of these accidents? Do they aspire, as it were, to their newfound independence from the substance of which they are the accidents, or does the miracle of transubstantiation deprive them somehow of their nature *as* accidents? Neither option seems at all satisfactory, the order of grace being a higher form of order rather than a venture into disorder. And how are we even to distinguish accidents from substance if the accidents, in being deprived of the substance, are deprived of nothing that belongs to it, including what it is for and what it does? Otherwise put: If the communicant (or for that matter, the mouse that breaks into the tabernacle)[27] is nourished by the consecrated host in the same way as by the non-consecrated host, if everything we would expect of bread qua substance is still provided by the accidents alone, does "substance" even matter? Does the distinction hold? Does the statement that this is not bread have any meaning?

---

26. As Brock observes, the lingering accidents "are needed in order to make it possible to speak of any genuine sort of change in the succession from the bread to the body of Christ, for they are the only thing that remains intact throughout the succession" ("Eucharistic Conversion," 541, per *ST* 1.45.2, ad 2).

27. *Quid sumit mus* was a common medieval question, raised already in principle by Hippolytus's caution about reverent care for consecrated hosts. Aquinas answers it by saying that an irrational animal "eats Christ's body 'accidentally,' and not sacramentally, just as if anyone not knowing a host to be consecrated were to consume it" (*ST* 3.80.3, ad 3). Cf. n. 50 below.

The Reformers were not wrong to raise this sort of objection; they were just hasty in drawing their conclusions.

Much more fundamental than substance/accidents analysis is the sacramental distinction between *signum* and *res*. Thus, in treating baptism, Aquinas says that "three things may be considered: namely, that which is sacrament only [*sacramentum tantum*]; that which is reality and sacrament [*res et sacramentum*]; and that which is reality only [*res tantum*]. That which is sacrament only, is something visible and outward; the sign [*signum*], namely, of the inward effect: for such is the very nature of a sacrament." This *signum* is water and its use.[28] That which is sacrament and reality is the baptismal character, and that which is reality only is inward justification. In the case of the Eucharist, that which is sacrament only is the bread and wine; that which is sacrament and reality is *corpus Christi verum*, Christ's true body; and that which is reality only is "the effect of this sacrament."[29] Here there is a crucial difference, of course, for we are indeed dealing with a sacrifice or offering. Here bread and wine become what they signify (viz., the body and blood of Christ), whereas in baptism the water, though sanctified, does not become anything. It is this difference that we are trying to understand, and we are positing that substance/accidents analysis is not the best way to approach it.[30]

In point of fact, Trent itself does not speak of accidents but rather of *species* or appearances, of which one must speak in order to articulate the fact that what is seen, felt, and tasted belongs not to the *res* (that is, to the substance of body) but to the *signum* (that is, to the substance of bread),

---

28. That is, "the washing . . . 'done together with the prescribed form of words'" (*ST* 3.66.1, quoting Lombard).

29. *ST* 3.73.6. This seems somewhat cryptic. Might we say, by analogy with baptism: bread and wine and their use; communion with Christ, in the ecclesial body of Christ, by virtue of sharing the *corpus Christi verum*; the salvation and transformation effected by participation in the self-offering of Christ? That, at all events, would be a more dynamic account.

30. Levering (*Sacrifice and Community*, 146) argues that "once the issue is clearly seen as having to do with bodily presence in this world, then metaphysical reflection upon bodily presence is necessary in order to proclaim the mystery, precisely as a mystery of bodily presence." Unfortunately, "in this world" is not subjected to critical scrutiny; it is taken as a self-evident starting point that controls the metaphysical reflection. Useful distinctions are drawn between Aquinas and Bulgakov, for example, whose "spiritualizing" eschatology and anthropology certainly won't do (cf. my *Ascension Theology* [London: T&T Clark, 2011], 144f.). But since the whole analysis is attempted in abstraction from temporal questions, as if heaven were a distinct place but not a distinct time, Levering is forced with Thomas to try to think the presence of Jesus non-eschatologically. "Substance," by his own admission, "remains elusive as describing a bodily but not sensible reality" (165). Still, he says, if we conceive of substance "as present 'as a whole is in a part,'" we can apprehend the truth affirmed in faith that Christ does not move from the right hand of the Father and yet is fully present in every consecrated host." Well, maybe—but does this come to anything more than defining substance by presence and presence by substance?

while asserting that the *res* and not the *signum* is what is being offered by Christ to the faithful and, just so, with and for the faithful to God. Merely distinguishing substance from appearances does not take us very far, however, in addressing the difficulty posed by the perdurance, after the consecration, of the appearances proper to the *signum*, since through the consecration *signum* is converted to *res*; and putting "accidents" for "appearances" carries us no further at all, unless it carries us into trouble.

We create a problem for ourselves when we try to make sense of what comes "after" or in consequence of the consecration while remaining strictly within our own spatio-temporal framework. Recall the context of the consecration within the wider eucharistic exchanges: We offer bread to God in thanksgiving. God returns it (via the consecration) as body so that we can have a share in the offering of Christ, which is not bread but body. The offering we make in and with Christ is not bread but body, just because God has returned bread as body. That is the very point made by the doctrine of transubstantiation, is it not? When the priest speaks the words of consecration *in persona Christi*, he speaks (as Brock observes) in a fashion partly analogous to the creative fiat.[31] He speaks and God effects something new, something he himself cannot

---

31. The analogy is incomplete, for the creative fiat is an imperative, not an indicative. Nevertheless, "the consecration makes the host to be the body of Christ through signifying it to be the body of Christ." Normally, explains Brock ("Eucharistic Conversion," 561ff.), "the truth of a declarative sentence in the present tense depends upon the reality of what it is about. But with the truth of the Word of God, it is the other way around. Whatever the eternal Word of God says to be the case is the case, just because he says so. . . . In the sacraments, human enunciations share in this power of the Word of God." He appeals to Aquinas: "The power to convert that exists in the formulae of these sacraments follows upon their signification" (*ST* 3.78.4, ad 3). This means that transubstantiation "belongs to an order which is in some way between the order proper to the nature of created causes and the order proper to the uncreated first cause." It belongs to "a created supernatural order, the order of grace," in which it is possible to say *Hoc est corpus meum* with the effect that the substance of the body of Christ, instantaneously and non-dimensively, becomes present in place of the substance of bread, under the accidents of bread. There are two problems here, however. First, none of this helps answer the question about the subject of the change, a question Thomas's view makes all but unanswerable. Before there was the substance of bread; now there is the substance of body. If the bread and the body are only "a sort of subject," a subject logically but not actually, then the true subject might appear to be the sacramental action itself. Would that not pose a great danger? Christ's risen body fully obeys his rational soul. He can will to be present, in body as in spirit, as and where and when he pleases. He can will to be present by the sacramental means that we know pleases him, according to the promise he made. But should the liturgical action be seen as the real subject of the change from bread to body, would that not imply that the act of consecration is greater than the body itself? Would it not entail an identification of the Church with its Lord that precedes its being in receipt of his body and blood? And has the Church ever suggested such a thing? Perhaps Brock does not mean to suggest it either, but as we shall see—this is the second problem—his analysis of Thomas reveals the sacramental fiat to be the foundation of a distinct order of grace *within* creation, rather than something in service to the transformation *of* creation. This greatly multiplies the peril.

effect. This something new is not effected *ex nihilo*, however, but *ex vetere*. Bread from the old creation is returned as body from the new creation, linking the two. How God effects this is not open to human examination, of course, any more than how God creates in the first place is open to human examination. And neither is *the effect itself*—at least not for now, not in its entirely. For the old cannot contain the new but must be transformatively contained by it. Thus Irenaeus rightly remarks that flesh and blood cannot inherit the kingdom of heaven but can however be taken *for* an inheritance by it.[32] Likewise when the bread and wine are taken, for the sake of the gift of body and blood, the effects of that gift on our bodies and souls and on the spatio-temporal framework in which we exist liturgically and sacramentally can be grasped only from the other side, from the end to which we are thus conducted, from the kingdom itself. We do well always to bear this in mind and not try to force the new into the old intellectually when in fact the old is being cracked open and taken up into the new. Jesus Christ is with us not as one subject to our time but as one bringing our time (and space and matter) into subjection to his time, the time of the new creation.

Consider, in this light, the differences between Aquinas and Calvin. Aquinas contends that after the consecration, where bread appears, we have body and not bread; whereas Calvin insists that we have bread only—bread being given on earth and body being given in heaven, to which by a special grace of the Holy Spirit the human spirit is lifted up. Both men might reasonably appeal to Irenaeus, perhaps, for support. But Irenaeus does not say, with Aquinas, body only; nor does he say, with Calvin, bread only. Calvin's model might seem to make sense of Irenaeus's assertion that the bread, when consecrated, is no longer common bread but *eucharistia*—something that now conjoins two realities, one springing up from the earth and the other springing down from heaven[33]—but it does not actually do so, because for Calvin there is no conjoining that is not purely intellectual. Bread remains on earth, while body remains in heaven. "By the corporeal things which are produced in the sacrament," he says, "we are by a kind of analogy conducted to spiritual things." When bread and wine are given us, we are to *think* analogously, so that by means of these symbols we may recognize "this mystery of the secret union of Christ with believers [that is] incomprehensible by nature."[34]

---

32. Irenaeus, *Haer.* 5.9; cf. my *Ascension and Ecclesia* (Grand Rapids: Eerdmans, 1999), 63f.

33. That is, the Word of God (Irenaeus, *Haer.* 4.18.5; *PG* 7.1, col. 1029). In Greek: ἐκ δύο πραγμάτων συνεστηκεῖα, ἐπιγείου τε καὶ οὐρανίου. In Latin: *ex duabus rebus constans, terrena et coelesti.*

34. Calvin, *Institutes of the Christian Religion* 4.17.1. This may bring to mind Flannery O'Connor's remark, "Well, if it's a symbol, to hell with it" (*Collected Works* [New York: Library of America, 1988], 977); but Calvin does not say that it is *just* a symbol.

Calvin thus departs from the tradition, leaving the bread as bread while failing to take into account the bodies of the faithful, which participate only in *signum* and not in *res*. It is otherwise with Irenaeus, who acknowledges a coincidence, in the consecrated host, of an earthly and a heavenly reality and immediately adds that "our bodies, when they receive the Eucharist, are no longer corruptible, having the hope of the resurrection to eternity." For Irenaeus, "spiritual" sustenance is not a food of which the spirit alone partakes. It is for the body as well—a food provided by the creative act of God in conjoining the whole person, even in his mortality, to the whole Christ in his immortality. To stop short of that is to stop short of the faith of the Church.

But in the Irenaean analysis there is a qualification, in the form of a "just as" that cuts two ways, upsetting Aquinas as well as Calvin: just as the bread is both bread and no longer bread, our bodies are both corruptible and no longer corruptible. This early formulation seems to leave open what substance/accidents analysis closes off; namely, an eschatological interpretation of the conversion of bread into body, an interpretation that does not require us to choose between Aquinas and Calvin but rather to say something different from what either is saying. For both, in their own way, are still attempting to fit the new into the old rather than the old into the new, and this is done at a steep price. The price for Calvin is a bifurcation between the Church visible and the Church invisible as well as a bifurcation of body and soul. The price for Thomas Aquinas is the positing of a sacramental order of grace *parallel* to, rather than transformative of, the natural order. Brock is right that, on Thomas's view, "what lies between the natural order and the strictly divine order is a created supernatural order, the order of grace."[35] But this sets up the priesthood and the Church itself as that order, when in fact there is no such order. That is the greatest danger of Thomas's approach; indeed, of any approach that regards the eucharistic conversion as "a miraculous this-worldly change, not an eschatological event."[36] It makes the Church, especially the Church *qua* clerical institution, a sort of natural supernatural. It domesticates the grace that redeems and ultimately perfects nature, the grace that transforms the old creation into the new, by making it out to be a second *gratia creans* rather than the instrument of *gratia sanans et elevans*.[37]

35. "Eucharistic Conversion," 565.
36. See again n. 3 above.
37. This has deleterious institutional and political consequences, leading, for example, to false ideas of Christ's social kingship; cf. chap. 5 of my *Desiring a Better Country: Forays in Political Theology* (Montreal: McGill-Queens University Press, 2015).

From the Old Creation to the New: "May He Make of Us an Eternal Offering"

Transubstantiation, not as a metaphysical system but as a fitting name for a real change from bread to body and wine to blood, is dogma. *In sanctissima Eucharistia sub speciebus panis et vini ipsemet Christus Dominus continetur, offertur, sumitur.*[38] Thomas's interpretation is certainly not dogma, nor is the substance/accidents analysis he employs, though Trent's substance/appearances dichotomy is. Whatever the merits of Thomas's approach, and whatever the need to preserve a philosophically robust notion of substance (which the old catechism does by taking up Thomas's substance/accidents distinction), we need something more eschatologically dynamic, as I have argued in *Ascension Theology*.[39] We need something that takes into account, as far as possible, what we have learned both about nature and about grace, which perfects nature. We need something entirely in tune with Scripture, liturgy, and dogma, which teach us to approach the whole matter by reflecting on gifts and offerings made in the old creation for the sake of the new.

The bread and wine, which are presented as gifts, are first of all gifts of God to us, so that we, in returning them to God, may share in the divine economy of giving. This economy is mediated by Christ, who through the eucharistic *conversio*, by the agency of the Holy Spirit, supplies his own body and blood in place of bread and wine, the very body and blood that he presents to the Father in heaven.[40] This, becoming also our offering, enables us to participate sacramentally in heavenly life as such: "Look, we pray, upon the oblation of your Church and, recognizing the sacrificial Victim by whose death you willed to reconcile us to yourself, grant that we, who are nourished by the Body and Blood of your Son and filled with his Holy Spirit, may become one body,

---

38. CIC (1917), canon 801. The French translation reads rather differently: *Dans la très sainte eucharistie, sous les espèces du pain et du vin, le Christ lui-même est une présence, une offrande, une nourriture.*

39. See 71ff. In "Substance Made Manifest: Metaphysical and Semantic Implications of the Doctrine of Transubstantiation," *St. Anselm Journal* 9.2 (2014): 1–21, Joshua Hochschild insists that "the fact that the language community of the Church insists on the notion of 'transubstantiation' (not merely 'real presence') is itself significant, and by it the Church is committed to some meaning of 'substance,' whether technically Aristotelian or not" (14). This can be conceded, so long as Trent's "fittingly" is borne in mind, and Hochschild's "whether . . . or not."

40. "There is indeed this which is common to the most holy eucharist along with the other sacraments: it is a sign of sacred reality and the visible form of invisible grace. But in it there is found the excelling and unique quality that, whereas the other sacraments first have the force of sanctifying at the moment when one uses them, in the eucharist the author of holiness himself is present before their use" (Trent, session 13, chap. 3; *DEC* 2:694).

one spirit in Christ. May he make of us an eternal offering to you."[41] And this participation changes us too, opening us to glory, as the eastern fathers and liturgies have emphasized. Communion with Christ in the reception or use of the gifts—presenting ourselves for the great Present—completes the sacramental participation, planting within us the seed of immortality. The entire exchange is finished only when "the mortal puts on immortality" (1 Cor. 15:53) and stands before God in the new creation.

When we regard things thus, thinking in terms of the liturgical dynamic that characterizes both the old and the new covenant, the movement from old creation to new is held before us. The very matter of the old creation is already caught up in this movement through the descent and ascent of Jesus, converted not in substance but in glory through his priestly work. It is caught up in this movement also, by extension, through the sacraments, and especially in the eucharistic *conversio* by which bread and wine become the body and blood of Christ. This latter mystery, which is entirely in the service of the former, is the means by which we remain in touch—quite literally in touch—with our ascended Lord and high priest while we await his reappearance from the holy of holies, at which we ourselves shall be made to live and serve in the fullness of the divine presence. It is the means by which we too are made, not of or by ourselves, but "through him, with him, and in him," offerers and offerings.

"Ascribe to the LORD," says the psalmist, "the glory due his name; bring an offering, and come into his courts!" (Ps. 96:8). This is just what is done in the holy Mass, as Prayer I testifies.

> To you, therefore, most merciful Father,
> we make humble prayer and petition
> through Jesus Christ, your Son, our Lord:
> that you accept and bless these gifts,
> these offerings,
> these holy and unblemished sacrifices,
> which we offer you firstly for your holy catholic Church.

And where is the true altar at which the offering is made? It is in heaven, as Irenaeus says, for that is where our Lord presides.

> In humble prayer we ask you, almighty God:
> command that these gifts be borne

41. Roman Missal, Eucharistic Prayer III. Albert the Great, in his work *On the Body of the Lord* (trans. Sr. Albert Marie Surmanski, Fathers of the Church Mediaeval Continuation 17 [Washington, DC: Catholic University of America Press, 2017]), brings together all these motifs, beginning with that of trinitarian gift. His analysis of eucharistic change is Aristotelian, however.

by the hands of your holy Angel
to your altar on high
in the sight of your divine majesty,
so that all of us, who through this participation at the altar
receive the most holy Body and Blood of your Son,
may be filled with every grace and heavenly blessing.

In the consecration, the bread is made body. One substance is converted into another, another to which it is naturally ordered; not, however, by natural but by supernatural conversion, and not to natural but to supernatural effect. The outcome of this conversion—body being offered rather than bread—remains unseen by us. That is not because of a separation of substance from accidents but because of a positional or situational separation. We who present bread but share in the offering of body, and actually receive body, do so from the beginning rather than the end of our transformation into those who are fit for the courts of the Lord. We do so as those who are not able to see what goes on there or even what is happening here. We do so from the beginning, not from the end, of the *conversio* of the sacramental signs. The end is given us, even here at the beginning, but that it is given us we cannot see except with the eyes of faith.[42] The seeing and tasting requires our complete transformation; that is, it requires our own arrival in the new creation.

What has passed our lips as food, O Lord,
may we possess in purity of heart,
that what has been given to us in time
may be our healing for eternity.

That the bread is made body, and the wine blood, our senses cannot tell us; only faith can tell us. This faith expresses itself in the adoration offered in this time and place, to this consecrated host that "contains" Christ. But the containing is an opening rather than an enclosing, if we may put it that way, an opening in which our here and now is relativized to his there and then. It is a mistake, surely, to try to think this the other way around, forcing heaven into earth rather than granting to earth its access to heaven.

It is not so difficult as it first appears to square this approach with that of Trent—and square it we must if we are to maintain its merits—for the fathers of Trent were merely defending the Eucharist at the point of attack, not attempting a full account of it. "In the first place," they write, "the holy council teaches and openly and without qualification professes that, after the consecration of the

42. Not ordinarily, at any rate, though legend has it that Thomas was once permitted to see.

bread and wine, our lord Jesus Christ, true God and true man, is truly, really and substantially contained in the propitious sacrament of the holy eucharist under the appearance of those things which are perceptible to the senses."[43] Though we find here the language of containment that (in its misuse) we are questioning, we also find this qualification: "Nor are the two assertions incompatible, that our Saviour is ever seated in heaven at the right hand of the Father in his natural mode of existing, and that he is nevertheless sacramentally present to us by his substance in many other places in a mode of existing which, though we can hardly express it in words, we can grasp with minds enlightened by faith as possible to God." This not only establishes heaven (which must be construed not naively as simply another and higher place but rather as the beginning of the new creation) as the proper point of reference but also leaves open the exact manner in which the heavenly Lord makes himself truly and substantially present for us under the appearances of perceptible things. After all, we are not talking about his submission, all over again, to our place and time, as in his earthly trials. No, we are talking about his embrace of us in the midst of our own time of trial so as to lift us into union and communion with himself.[44]

Later magisterial documents, conscious of the patristic orientation, have taken care to develop an eschatological frame of reference for thinking about these things: "Having passed from this world to the Father, Christ gives us in the Eucharist the pledge of glory with him."[45] "In the earthly liturgy we take part in a foretaste of that heavenly liturgy which is celebrated in the holy city of Jerusalem toward which we journey as pilgrims, where Christ is sitting at the right hand of God, a minister of the holies and of the true tabernacle."[46] "Truly this is the *mysterium fidei* which is accomplished in the Eucharist: the world which came forth from the hands of God the Creator now returns to him redeemed by Christ."[47] This prayer from the third Sunday of Lent nicely contextualizes the *sacramentaliter praesens* by pointing to its ultimate purpose and effect:

43. "*Principio docet sancta synodus et aperte ac simpliciter profitetur in almo sanctae eucharistiae sacramento post panis et vini consecrationem dominum nostrum Iesum Christum, verum Deum atque hominem, vere, realiter ac substantialiter sub specie illarum rerum sensibilium contineri*" (session 13, chap. 1; DEC 2:693).

44. Seen in context, the *continentur* is a dynamic rather that a static concept, concerned not with a particular spatio-temporal modality but with a real flesh and blood *communio*. Its source is chapter 1 of Lateran IV (*DS* 802), which against the Albigensian heresy made a very Irenaean point about union and communion: *in qua idem [ecclesia] ipse sacerdos est sacrificium, Iesus Christus, cuius corpus et sanguis in sacramento altaris sub speciebus panis et vini veraciter continentur, transsubstantiatis pane in corpus, et vino in sanguinem, potestate divina: ut ad perficiendum mysterium unitatis accipiamus ipsi de suo, quod accepit ipse de nostro.*

45. CCC 1419; cf. 1405 (which leans on St. Ignatius).

46. *Sacrosanctum concilium* 8.

47. John Paul II, *Ecclesia de Eucharistia* 8; cf. Benedict XVI, *Sacramentum caritatis* 11.

> As we receive the pledge of things yet hidden in heaven
> and are nourished while still on earth
> with the bread that comes from on high,
> we humbly entreat you, O Lord,
> that what is being brought about in us in mystery
> may come to true completion.

It may also be mentioned that the eastern *epiklesis*, which sounds a clear eschatological note, has found again its proper place in Eucharistic Prayers II–IV.

We should not assume, then, that Trent's *contineri* militates against eschatology; nor should we overlook the fact that the fathers stopped short of formally embracing or dogmatically defining the Thomistic analysis. The substance is one thing, while what is seen and touched and tasted appears to be another—they say no more and no less than that. No more, because they offer no formal philosophical account; arguably, they do not even allow for one. No less, because they refuse not only the sacramental nominalism of the Swiss Reformation and especially of the Radical Reformation, but even the two-substance or coexistence model adopted by the Lutherans. The whole substance of the bread is converted into the whole substance of the body. Only in and through that conversion is our participation in the heavenly offering guaranteed. Only because of it can it really be said, as later documents (making the eschatology more overt) have gone on to say, that "in this gift Jesus Christ entrusted to his Church the perennial making present of the paschal mystery" and "brought about a mysterious 'oneness in time' between that Triduum and the passage of the centuries."[48]

Trent, particularly when read in the larger context of tradition, both earlier and later, does not require us to believe that the species or appearances of bread and wine are suspended accidents, detached for a time from their

---

48. *Ecclesia de Eucharistia* 5; cf. §18 (emphasis original): "The acclamation of the assembly following the consecration appropriately ends by expressing the eschatological thrust which marks the celebration of the Eucharist. . . . The Eucharist is a straining towards the goal, a foretaste of the fullness of joy promised by Christ . . . ; it is in some way the anticipation of heaven, the 'pledge of future glory.' In the Eucharist, everything speaks of confident waiting 'in joyful hope for the coming of our Saviour, Jesus Christ.' Those who feed on Christ in the Eucharist need not wait until the hereafter to receive eternal life: *they already possess it on earth*, as the first-fruits of a future fullness which will embrace man in his totality. For in the Eucharist we also receive the pledge of our bodily resurrection at the end of the world: 'He who eats my flesh and drinks my blood has eternal life, and I will raise him up at the last day' (Jn 6:54). This pledge of the future resurrection comes from the fact that the flesh of the Son of Man, given as food, is his body in its glorious state after the resurrection. With the Eucharist we digest, as it were, the 'secret' of the resurrection. For this reason Saint Ignatius of Antioch rightly defined the Eucharistic Bread as 'a medicine of immortality, an antidote to death.'"

proper substances. Does it not permit us to propose instead that the proffered gifts of bread and wine, despite being truly converted into body and blood, are nonetheless seen and experienced just as before, for the simple reason that we ourselves—though we benefit eternally from that conversion through which we receive him, whole and entire, who is the ground of our salvation and transformation—are not yet so transformed as to enable us to perceive the change in question? In short, because we walk by faith and not by sight?

To partake of Christ sacramentally in the Eucharist means to partake of him here and now in the same mystical communion of body and soul by which we will be animated in the kingdom of God, only in a fashion that will not be necessary in the kingdom, a fashion mediated by the conversion of bread and wine. This conversion is usually said to result in a heavenly substance (the body or blood of Christ) existing in a new and secret way under foreign, earthly accidents (those belonging to bread and wine). Might it not be said instead that an earthly substance, together with its accidents, is converted into a foreign, heavenly substance, albeit in such a manner that we cannot at all track the change except by the faculty of faith?[49] That we cannot follow the change with our senses need not be put down to a separation of substances from accidents but attributed rather to the fact that we who witness it still belong bodily to the spatio-temporal frame of the present world even though we are receiving, instead of bread, the holy body that belongs to heaven and the new creation. While that gift enables us to participate in heaven, it does not as yet enable our senses to discern what our faith discerns—the heavenly reality itself, which does not exist within or alongside bread or under the appearances of bread but exists as that which graciously bids the bread, as offered, to become the body, as given.[50]

49. Jacques Rohault, in defense of Cartesianism, tried to explain the continued appearances of bread and wine as an act of God on us; that is, as an intervention in the process of perception (Watson, "Transubstantiation," 138). The situation, I propose, is rather the reverse. God does not compel or enable us to see anything, and without that enablement it is impossible that we should see. We see only what we saw before, because we are not able to track the change in question. Perhaps I should add, in my own defense, that I am aware that the Council of Constance condemns the proposition that "the accidents of the bread do not remain without a subject" (DS 1152; cf. Watson, "Transubstantiation," 142). This is targeted against Wycliffe and tells also against Rohault; it has no purchase, however, on my proposal. For in Wycliffe that proposition is allied to the more fundamental claim (condemned at DS 1151 and again by Trent's second canon) that the material substance of bread and wine remain, and I make no such claim. I do interpret "the species of bread and wine only remaining" (DS 1652) as a reference to what we see or experience pro tem; that is, until we see clearly and experience rightly what is actually happening.

50. On this approach, there is no both/and such as Trent's second canon rejects; that is, no bread and wine coexisting with body and blood. It might be said, however, that the celebrating community and communicants coexist with themselves in that eschatological differentiation

Either way, we are insisting that the bread, when consecrated, is not merely a means of communion in Christ's body but actually becomes his body, given for us and to us. But in the latter case, we are thinking in terms of the passing of the old creation to the new rather than being content to think exclusively of the entry of the new into the old. The gift of bread becomes the gift of body, and the substance of bread the substance of body, in this fashion: Through consecration, the bread is united to Christ in his self-presentation to God as the firstfruits of creation. At his command, it passes with him to glory, in anticipation of the regeneration of all things. It therefore participates with him in the beginning of that regeneration. It does not do so, however, by remaining bread. It does so as body. For in this passing it is made to become body, body as shared. And thus it causes us, too, to begin our passage to glory, though we do not see or taste or feel that glory as yet, and cannot fathom the regeneration that is already taking place in this sacramental form, preparing us to be, with him, an eternal offering to God.

Body as Shared

To become body, body as shared. What do I mean by that? Not quite what Anscar Vonier and Matthew Levering mean, when they speak of Christ's body as taking on "an entirely new mode of being, the sacramental mode."[51] Not

---

or dynamic to which Paul alludes in Col. 3:1–4. Hence it appears to them that bread and wine coexist with the body and blood, when in fact they don't. The communicants cannot go by these appearances; that is precisely the point. And the mouse? The mouse can go by them, for the mouse does not exist in that tension, or even for the sake of it. The answer to the *quid sumit mus* is that the mouse eats bread, because the mouse (except in the sense indicated in 2 Pet. 3:10) is not party to the "after" that the consecration effects. The mouse, unlike the human person (faithful or unfaithful), is not communicating but merely eating. And it is eating what was there before the consecration, not what is there after it. For the mouse exists only in the "was" and not in the "is." Now, for greater certainty, I do not mean this subjectively, but objectively. It has nothing to do with the consciousness of the mouse, though it has something to do with the nature of the mouse. What the consecration effects is a real change from bread in the old creation to shared body in the new, which means also a real change from the here and now of the old to the there and then of the new. And though the mouse inhabits the very same world in and from which this change is effected—the new being made *ex vetere*—when it encounters the consecrated host it encounters it strictly from the before and not from the after, from the here and now and not from the there and then. In Thomas's language, it encounters it only accidentally, not substantially. All I am trying to do is transpose the language of the accidental versus the substantial into its proper eschatological key, leaving behind false problems about free-floating accidents by thinking the dynamic of substantial change through the prism of the cross and resurrection, the ascension and the parousia.

51. Dom Anscar Vonier, *A Key to the Doctrine of the Eucharist* (Eugene, OR: Wipf & Stock, 2002), 218; quoted in Levering, *Sacrifice and Community*, 163. Cf. Charles Journet, "Transubstantiation," *The Thomist*, 38 (1974): 740: "What is it then that takes place at the

quite what Aquinas means when he says that "Christ's body is substantially the same in this sacrament, as in its proper species, but not after the same fashion; because in its proper species it comes in contact with surrounding bodies by its own dimensions: but it does not do so as it is in this sacrament."[52] For they remain focused on one side of the dynamic only (presence in the old creation) and moreover are indicating a mode that is entirely sacramental, whereas I am trying to indicate a mode that belongs to Jesus in his ascension and will belong to him eternally—a mode of existing ecclesially as well as individually, a mode of existing perichoretically in the Spirit such that he can share himself with us substantially, whether sacramentally in the passing of the old creation or non-sacramentally in the arrival of the new.

We are not in a position, in this life, to say much about this mode, other than that, in the time of Christ's absence, it is fitting that it be mediated in this fashion, through the use of these most fitting signs, bread and wine. It is worth noting that Aquinas can posit this mediation even in the presence of Christ; for he is working on the assumption that at the Last Supper, before our Lord's sacrifice had been fully rendered on the cross, there was a real giving and receiving of his present mortal body, that "the same body of Christ which was then seen by the disciples in its own species was received by them under the sacramental species" (ST 3.81.3). This would seem to indicate a kind of perichoresis, would it not? It is also worth noting, however, that while the fathers of Trent shared this assumption, it is not strictly required by their declarations. What they contend could be maintained just as well on the quite different supposition that the dominical institution of the sacrament is not already the sacrament itself but only the provision for it; that there is as yet

---

moment of consecration? The *empirical activities*, the externals, or the sensible appearances of bread are not touched. The *inmost being* of the bread—of this mixture which is bread—is detached from it by the effect of divine omnipotence, so as not to be annihilated but 'changed,' 'converted' into the body of the Lord, who, according to the manner of existence that is proper and natural to him, dwells unchanged in heaven, but who, by this fact, is moreover made present under the borrowed appearances of bread. There are not two Christs, but *two modes of presence of the one Christ:* one 'natural,' in the glory of heaven, the other 'sacramental,' under the veil of the externals or empirical activities of bread. This, which WAS bread, IS now the body of the Lord. And what enveloped the bread, now envelops the body of the Lord. *Only the veil of the appearances separates us from the radiance of his glory."* This analysis treats time as a constant rather than as something subject to the effects of the *conversio*.

52. ST 3.81.4. "And therefore, all that belongs to Christ, as He is in Himself, can be attributed to Him both in His proper species [*in propria specie*] and as He exists in the sacrament; such as to live, to die, to grieve, to be animate or inanimate, and the like; while all that belongs to Him in relation to outward bodies, can be attributed to Him as He exists in His proper species [mode of existence], but not as He is in this sacrament; such as to be mocked, to be spat upon, to be crucified, to be scourged, and the rest. Hence some have composed this verse: 'Our Lord can grieve beneath the sacramental veils, but cannot feel the piercing of the thorns and nails.'"

no complete sacrament where there is no completed offering—where there is no cross, no resurrection and ascension, no absence, and no "mantle" of the Spirit left to the Church in that absence. Care ought to be taken, in any case, that the institution of the sacrament at the Last Supper is not treated in a fashion that tends to de-eschatologize the sacrament and so to confuse it with ecclesial existence as such.[53]

Ecclesial existence as such, and what John Zizioulas calls the ecclesial hypostasis, is a mode of being that, without compromise to the particularity of body or soul, is shared. Again, it is difficult for us to say much about this, other than to observe that in the resurrection the body will be fully obedient to the soul, and the soul fully obedient to God, and in our spiritual union with

---

53. "Our Redeemer at the last supper instituted this so admirable sacrament when he bore witness in express and unambiguous words that, after the blessing of the bread and wine, he was offering to them his own body and his own blood" (session 13, chap. 1, *DEC* 2:694). Cf. chap. 3, and the Tridentine catechism: "As a divine and admirable pledge of this love, knowing that the hour had now come that He should pass from the world to the Father, that He might not ever at any period be absent from His own, He accomplished with inexplicable wisdom that which surpasses all the order and condition of nature. For having kept the supper of the Paschal lamb with His disciples, that the figure might yield to the reality, the shadow to the substance, He took bread, and giving thanks unto God, He blessed, and brake, and gave to the disciples, and said: 'Take ye and eat, this is my body which shall be delivered for you; this do for a commemoration of me.'" All of this invites the question as to how we should distinguish between the institution, at the Last Supper, of the new covenant meal and the sacrament of the Eucharist as such, which comes into effect when our Lord has entered the holy of holies with the offering of his own body and blood and the Spirit has been poured out on the Church. It is not uncommon to make no distinction (cf., e.g., Anselm, *Letters on the Sacraments*, 1.3). Thomas makes only a very modest distinction when he indicates that the disciples received the same body that they beheld speaking to them: the body "ready for the passion" (*ST* 3.81.3). But surely we must understand some difference in the gift or in the mode of giving, since Christ had not yet suffered and been glorified and could still be clung to by his disciples. In some qualified sense, we may grant that his consecrating words at the Last Supper had a proleptic character fulfilled only in the Church's sacrament. At all events, we must be clear that the Eucharist does not exist to perpetuate the Last Supper, but the Last Supper to inaugurate the Eucharist. We must also be clear that the miracle involved transcends our temporal categories, just as it transcends our spatial and material categories. Plainly we cannot, by focusing on the Last Supper alone, get at the true nature of transubstantiation in its service to that mystery by which "the sacrifice of the cross . . . once carried out on Calvary is re-enacted in wonderful fashion" and applied to us for the forgiveness of sins (*Mysterium fidei* 27). We must keep the whole picture in view. And we need not worry that this line of thought somehow encourages the error of transignification or transfinalization, rejected by Paul VI in *Mysterium fidei*; that it permits a denial that "what now lies beneath the aforementioned species is not what was there before" but has been transformed into something completely different (46f.; cf. §11). For the Last Supper finds its terminus in the Eucharist, in which the body and blood of Christ are made *vere, realiter ac substantialiter* present by *conversio*. When we keep this in mind, however—when we do not try to make sense of transubstantiation strictly from within the narrative of the Last Supper—we are less likely to mishandle the spatial metaphor "beneath" through abstraction from the dynamic of salvation history.

God both soul and body will be possessed in such a way as to be fully open not only to God but also, mutatis mutandis, to fellow members of the ecclesial body of Christ, to fellow citizens of the heavenly city who enjoy God and one another in communion with God. That is one reason why the spousal union that hints at this openness will be surpassed and superfluous. Sacramental presence is a provisional form of participation in that ecclesial communion of body and soul, made possible by the instrumentality of bread and wine, transubstantiated into the body and blood of Christ willingly shared with us even here and now. Hence, despite what has already been said about transubstantiation, it is not inappropriate—though, from an eschatological perspective, it is insufficient—to refer to the consecrated host as containing or comprising the substance of the body of Christ, on whose mediation ecclesial existence entirely depends. The form of this world is passing away, as Paul says. Yet it is in this world that the gifts of bread and wine are presented and consecrated. When consecrated, they are made to belong to the heavenly world, the world where Christ is seated at the right hand of God, which is also the foundation of the world to come. Not only do they belong to that world; for us they contain it sacramentally. To put it the other way around, by *conversio* they open upon it in such a way as to become Christ in his self-communication.[54] Nothing is added to him thereby except communion with us; but to us is added both communion with him—body, soul, and divinity—and, in that communion, the beginning of our own transformation. For in the conversion of these gifts is the end of our world and the presentation to us of the world to come. In

54. As Jean Corbon puts it in *The Wellspring of Worship* (1980, ET 1988; 2nd ed., San Francisco: Ignatius Press, 2005), 39: "The coming of the eternal mystery shakes our death-marked time and causes it to gape open." I confess coming only after the fact to knowledge of Fr. Corbon's fascinating, if at times frustratingly elusive, work. Obviously I find myself much in sympathy with a great deal of it, including what is most relevant here; viz., that the resurrection and ascension make possible a new pentecostal mode of being as communion, entailing "the end of a relationship to Jesus that is still wholly external" (60). The new relationship is realized through space- and time-transforming inclusion in the liturgy of love that is now embodied in our heavenly high priest, a liturgy "that 'causes' the present world 'to pass' into the glory of the Father in an ever more efficacious great Pasch" (63). With Fr. Corbon's construction of all this, compare the diagram at p. 158 of my *Ascension Theology*. I worry, however, that his attention to everything but the *conversio* that is fittingly called transubstantiation begs the question about the bread and the wine with which the Western Church has always found it necessary to wrestle. I also worry that time as "the measure of movement" (Corbon, *Wellspring*, 59n4; cf. 56) is conflated with time as decadent and death dealing, and about the potentially Teilhardian implications of claiming that the Spirit is busy converting everything into Christ's glorious body (see 101, 107, 262, e.g.; but cf. 180ff.). Yet there is full agreement that Christ's "heavenly liturgy is the gestation of the new creation" (68) and that the eucharistic celebration is an eschatological participation in the same, involving a transformation of time. Here is a Dominican whose Middle Eastern roots have enabled him to pioneer a post-Thomist approach to the Eucharist, which can also be brought to bear on the problem of transubstantiation.

the conversion of these gifts, the stuff of our world goes, graciously, to its appointed end, and we with it. To communicate worthily is to begin to pass into the kingdom of God and of his Christ. It is to welcome the seed of immortality, which is Christ himself, the hope of glory.[55]

That these things are so we can "grasp with minds enlightened by faith as something possible to God," but we cannot grasp them very well by separating substance and accidents. That late-medieval approach has a certain heuristic value, especially in the support it lends to the doxology of the here and now, of Christ with us and for us, of his true and real presence, of the adorable bodily presence of our Savior and his saving offering. There is a danger, however, in its tendency—which is certainly not the tendency of the liturgy itself—to present this to our minds in some dimensionless and de-eschatologized fashion, where our space but not our time, and hence not the whole σχῆμα τοῦ κόσμου τούτου, is made relative to that of the risen and ascended Lord.[56]

What is gained by taking the view I have been proposing? Not simply that the problematic substance/accidents analysis becomes unnecessary but that the sacrament is rendered less susceptible to certain abuses, particularly to those that domesticate the divine grace operative in it by way of a theology of pure presence or, for that matter, of pure absence or some merely "spiritual" presence. Positively, it becomes easier to say that bread actually becomes body rather than being displaced by body. It becomes body as shared, body as given, body as the joint possession of Jesus Christ, whose body it is, and of the members of his bride, the Church. What *that* means it is not possible to say at present in any very satisfying way, but this is no cause for embarrassment. For as bread becomes his body "given for us" right here and right now, it does so in such a way as to commence the transformation of our own mortal

---

55. To the question whether the eucharistic economy has any effect on Christ himself, we must not hesitate to give a positive answer. For the self-offering of Christ—one and the same Christ who suffered in Jerusalem, with his one and only perfected human body and soul, in the one and only heaven of heavens to which he has gained access—is in each and every Eucharist rendered or disposed, through the power of the Holy Spirit there invoked, for *these* worshipers and *this* local ecclesia, such that they are redemptively included in his life with the Father. The eucharistic relations are real relations, just as every baptism is a real relation, and in different ways they affect all who are party to them. They affect us and our bodies. They affect the ecclesial body of Christ, making it properly present on earth and adding to its wealth in heaven. Thus they affect Jesus himself, though he remains who he is and where he is and as he is.

56. Christ's body is not in this sacrament as if in a place (*ST* 3.76.5), but for Aquinas it is in this sacrament as if in a time. Why is that? Can that be right? The flip side of this coin appears if we consider *ST* 3.1.1, ad 4, regarding the incarnation: "God is great not in mass but in might; hence the greatness of his might feels no straits in narrow surroundings." But these narrow surroundings cannot be thought spatially only; they much also be thought temporally. We saw already in chap. 2 Aquinas's difficulty in doing so and the impact on his eschatology. Here in sacramental theology, where the eschatology is needed, it is lacking. *Figura transit mundi huius!*

bodies into an immortality we cannot yet grasp either. By faith we know that his body is present with us substantially, but certainly not statically—that it is present transformatively, and that only on the other end of the transformation will we properly experience and comprehend what is being given. By faith we know that, through a miracle of divine grace, we who are fed on the bread-become-body are beginning to pass with him into glory, that "the world which came forth from the hands of God the Creator now returns to him redeemed by Christ."[57] And, in all of this, doxological Pelagianism is ruled out, whether as a Catholic temptation or a Protestant. The communion in which we believe is pure gift, and the glory of the giving and receiving of the gift is a glory that redounds to God alone and to his Christ, and only thus to his holy Church and the members thereof.

---

57. *Ecclesia de Eucharistia* 8; cf. *Dies Domini* 47f. and *Mysterium fidei* 24f., in which spirit the argument of this chapter, subject as it is to subsequent magisterial clarification, is presented for consideration.

7

Autonomy

Sic transit anima ad infernum

Shortly before the turn of the twelfth century, while still at Bec, St. Anselm encountered the teachings of Roscellinus Compendiensis. Roscelin, who is sometimes referred to as the father of nominalism,[1] was among those who had begun to question the existence of natures or universal substances. He held concepts such as genus and species to be mere intellectual conveniences backed by nothing real. Even the word "God" seemed to him thus. Gregory Nazianzen had famously remarked, "When I say 'God' I mean Father, Son and Holy Spirit,"[2] indicating that the divine *ousia* cannot be abstracted from the divine persons; the three persons *are* God, and God *is* the three persons. But Roscelin pressed this truth in a false direction, a tritheistic direction. There are three divine persons whom we, for convenience, *call* God. Reviving a dispute long since resolved, he claimed that the only alternative to this view was patripassionism. Roscelin recanted, under pressure, at the Synod of Soissons in 1092. Nevertheless, he and his party persisted in this heresy afterward, drawing an uncharacteristically heated rebuke from Anselm.

1. Nominalism, as I have said elsewhere, shifted the focus "from kinds of things (*genera*) to individual things, from being *qua* analogical participation to being *qua* mere facticity, from a concern with ends (*teloi*) to a concern with immediacy" (*Desiring a Better Country: Forays in Political Theology* [Montreal: McGill-Queen's University Press, 2015], 48, cf. 142f.).

2. "For Godhead is neither diffused beyond these, so as to bring in a mob of gods; nor yet is it bounded by a smaller compass than these, so as to condemn us to a poverty-stricken conception of Deity" (Gregory Nanzianzen, *Oration* 38.8; NPNF², 7:347).

In addition to a few short letters on the subject, Anselm wrote against Roscelin in *De incarnatione*, published from the See of Canterbury, to which he was elevated in 1093. His language is scathing:

> Therefore, those modern dialecticians—nay, heretics of dialectic—who consider universal substances to be merely sounds [*flatus vocis*] . . . should be completely blown off [*exsufflandi*] in debates about spiritual questions. . . . For how can those who do not yet understand how several men are in species one man understand in that most secret and highest nature how several persons, each of whom is perfect God, are one God? . . . [Moreover] those who cannot understand anything to be man except an individual will in no way understand "man" except as a human person; for every individual man is a person. How then will they understand man . . . to be assumed by the Word—that is, that another *nature*, not another person, is assumed?³

Anselm, in other words, repudiated Roscelin's nominalism on the grounds that it was incapable of properly grasping either the doctrine of the Trinity or the doctrine of the incarnation, the basic facts on which human salvation rests. Indeed, he repudiated it on the basis that it was unwilling to submit itself to the truth that had been disclosed to Christian faith over the centuries or to ecclesial methods of reasoning. "Before I examine this question," wrote Anselm,

> I will say something to curb the presumption of those who, with blasphemous rashness and on the ground that they cannot understand it, dare to argue against something which the Christian faith confesses—those who judge with foolish pride that what they are not able to understand is not at all possible, rather than acknowledging with humble wisdom that many things are possible which they are not able to comprehend. Indeed, no Christian ought to question the truth of what the Catholic Church believes in its heart and confesses with its mouth. Rather, by holding constantly and unhesitatingly to this faith, by loving it and living according to it, he ought humbly, and as best he is able, to seek to discover the reason why it is true. If he is able to understand, then let him give thanks to God. But if he cannot understand, let him not toss his horns in strife but let him bow his head in reverence. For self-confident human wisdom can, by thrusting, uproot its horns more quickly than it can, by pushing, roll this stone.⁴

3. Anselm, *De incarnatione* 1 (St. Anselm, *Opera Omni: Electronic Edition*, 2:9f. / *PL* 158, col. 0265 [cap. 2]; trans. mine). The final sentences read: *Denique qui non potest intelligere aliquid esse hominem nisi individuum, nullatenus intelliget hominem nisi humanam personam. Omnis enim individuus homo est persona. Quomodo ergo iste intelliget hominem assumptum esse a verbo, non personam, id est naturam aliam, non aliam personam assumptam esse?*
4. Ibid. (trans. Jasper Hopkins and Herbert Richardson, *Complete Philosophical and Theological Treatises of Anselm of Canterbury* [Minneapolis: Arthur J. Banning], 2000).

This was a contest of great moment for our civilization. Alas, it was a contest that began to shift in favor of Roscelin. Self-confident human wisdom continued its thrustings, and nominalism was soon advancing throughout Europe, triumphing in the Reformation and then more thoroughly in the Enlightenment, until at last, in our own time, its horns have come almost entirely off, as Anselm said they would. Or so it appears, if we attend to the concept of autonomy that has emerged from the nominalist tradition—a concept we will later call on Anselm to help us criticize, for it is a concept to which he had given much thought prior to his encounter with Roscelin, and his blazing rhetoric can be explained, perhaps, by his intuition as to where the whole business must lead.

Inventing Autonomy

In general, nominalism did not follow Roscelin in a tritheistic direction. It veered back toward Sabellianism, while falling christologically (as Anselm predicted) into adoptionism. The movement began to come into its own in the fourteenth century, while the universities were still in turmoil over the role of Aristotle and the relation between pagan and Christian learning, and the Church in turmoil over the mendicant orders and the Franciscan dispute with the papacy. William of Ockham—vastly more able than Roscelin but also to be numbered among the *dialecticae haeretici*—deserves first mention here, for he it was who brought nominalism to the fore and began the process of dismantling the scholastic project.[5] It was Duns Scotus, however, a true trinitarian and a defender of realism, who provided the opening through which his fellow Franciscan would pass.[6] In contrast to Thomas, who subordinated the will to the intellect in a manner that left some doubts about the will's freedom, and about its role in the life of the world to come, Scotus gave primacy to the

5. In *Inventing the Individual: The Origins of Western Liberalism* (Cambridge, MA: Harvard University Press, 2014) Larry Siedentop rightly directs our attention to William of Ockham as a pivotal figure in the emergence of modern liberalism, the foundations of which were already laid by the fifteenth century. Siedentop sees this liberalism as threatened by the recent forgetfulness of its origins in Christian moral thought. But Ockham himself is surely responsible for the path of forgetfulness, as critics such as Étienne Gilson and Richard Weaver have insisted.

6. Charles Peirce lauds both men, while siding (metaphysically, not theologically) with Scotus: "William Ockham or Oakum, an Englishman, is beyond question the greatest nominalist that ever lived; while Duns Scotus, another British name, it is equally certain is the subtilest advocate of the opposite opinion. These two men Duns Scotus and William Ockham are decidedly the greatest speculative minds of the middle ages, as well as two of the profoundest metaphysicians that ever lived" ("Lecture I: Early Nominalism and Realism" [MS 158: Nov.–Dec. 1869], available at www.iupui.edu/~peirce/writings/v2/w2/w2_31/v2_31x.htm).

will. The will, being the faculty from which charity springs, is nobler than the intellect, the faculty from which knowledge springs, though of course God, the ultimate object of both, is at once the Good and the True, to be known and loved in the unity of his Being.[7] For his part, Ockham treated the will as if it had not merely primacy but actual priority, as if it preceded the intellect and were somehow independent of it.[8] Moreover, he was far more skeptical than Scotus about the ability of the intellect to achieve meaningful knowledge of God or the mind of God, though he still allowed that something of the divine decisions and directives could be known through special revelation.

This isolated faith from reason and left the latter to interpret the creaturely world pretty much on its own, without reference to God. Where God did come into view, the focus was on the sheer power of his will—a power both absolute and, from man's perspective, inscrutable if not arbitrary.[9] Anthropology naturally followed suit. The emphasis began to fall on the raw power of choice rather than on what is chosen and why it is chosen. The freedom of the will lay in its supposed indifference, in its lack either of inherent dispositions

7. Cf. Robert Prentice, "The Voluntarism of Duns Scotus, as Seen in His Comparison of the Intellect and the Will," *Franciscan Studies* 28 (1968): 63–103; and John C. Médaille, "Heaven as the Home of the Free: The Primacy of the Will in Duns Scotus" (unpublished manuscript, 26 November 2011, available at www.academia.edu).

8. Servais Pinckaers, *The Sources of Christian Ethics*, trans. M. T. Noble, 3rd ed. (Edinburgh: T&T Clark, 1995), 332. According to Pinckaers, from Peter Lombard's definition of free will as "that faculty of reason and will whereby one chooses the good with the help of grace, or evil without that help" (II *Sent.*, dist. 24 c. 3), Thomas went on to describe freedom "as a faculty proceeding from reason and will, which unite to make the act of choice." For Thomas, the one who both thinks and wills acts freely, whereas for Ockham "free will *preceded* reason and will in such a way as to move them to their acts." The former's "entire moral doctrine was based on the natural disposition toward beatitude and the perfection of the good, as to an ultimate end," while the latter generated a nature-freedom dichotomy in which "the natural inclinations . . . were rejected from the essential core of freedom." To that dichotomy several others were attached: freedom *or* law, freedom *or* reason, freedom *or* grace, etc. (see Pinckaers, *Sources*, 330ff.).

9. T. F. Torrance (*Theological Science* [Oxford: Oxford University Press, 1969], 62ff.) denies the arbitrariness. Given the above dichotomies, however, and the downplaying of the *potentia ordinata* in favor of the *potentia absoluta*, it is odd to find Torrance suggesting that Ockham was more or less on the right track—that he just couldn't quite find his way because he still worked within a medieval framework that lacked the "unitary" mode of thought which had characterized the patristic period. On the other hand, it is not odd that Torrance should praise him for helping to open up a more empirical mode of thought, for Ockham certainly found new ways to stress what Scotus had called *haeccitas*. Yet we must not forget that the birth of experimental science belongs to the Lateran IV generation, to the likes of Robert Grosseteste (a Franciscan of Augustinian and neoplatonist persuasion) and Albertus Magnus (a Dominican with Aristotelian interests) and Roger Bacon. These men already understood that, since God had created the world freely, human knowledge of it must follow an empirical path. That understanding (*pace* Michael Gillespie, *The Theological Origins of Modernity* [Chicago: University of Chicago Press, 2008], 190) was hardly a "nominalistic" one; it stemmed rather from the newly dogmatized *creatio ex nihilo*.

or of external compulsions, in its capacity to do evil as well as its capacity to do good. This was the idea of freedom that Anselm had already rejected in *De libertate arbitrii*, an idea that dislocated personhood from its trinitarian and sacramental context—that is, from its rootedness in communion—and pushed it in the direction of self-possession or self-determination.[10]

An old problem now became much more acute. Is human freedom really compatible with divine freedom? Anselm had tried to address this also, especially in *De concordia*, correcting the trajectory of the Augustinian tradition while dealing with popular confusion about the matter. But nominalism revived the fortunes of incompatibilism, favoring either radically Pelagian or predestinarian solutions. These errors on the left and on the right found their respective homes among the humanists and the Reformers, and eventually among the secular champions of free will and their determinist counterparts, where (under the influence of German idealism) they would synthesize in support of the modern autonomy project.[11] More vital to that project, however, at least in the early going, was Ockham's successful attack on the realism that had prevailed as far as Scotus.

This attack, as Joshua Hochschild helpfully explains, was an attack not on universals as such but on the notion that natures and forms are real. Everyone understood universals to be mental constructs; the question was how they could be justified and how they should be employed. Put differently, no one involved thought that there were universal substances such as "man" that existed independently both of actual men and of the mind itself.[12] The question was whether "man" is merely a semantic convenience, contrived by the mind, for referring all at once to a lot of individual men or whether it signifies a nature by virtue of which each of those individuals *is* a man. Anselm, Aquinas, Scotus, and the rest believed (though their accounts of this were not identical) that natures were intuited by the mind, which was a fit instrument both for recognizing and for conceptually abstracting or

---

10. Like Roscelin, Ockham found the orthodox doctrine of the Trinity incomprehensible, supposing it to be a simple contradiction that asserted threeness and oneness of the same thing in the same way, and to be a prime example of why philosophy and theology should not be confused.

11. "Compatibilism" is a contemporary term that is normally used to refer to determinism and free will rather than, as here, to divine will and human will; see, for example, Alfred R. Mele, *Autonomous Agents: From Self-Control to Autonomy* (Oxford: Oxford University Press, 2001), part II. Compatibilism in that sense is necessary for determinists who wish to support the modern autonomy project, whether they connect it to some grand Enlightenment or idealist vision of universal progress or are merely libertarian.

12. See Joshua P. Hochschild, "What's Wrong with Ockham? Reassessing the Role of Nominalism in the Dissolution of the West," *Anamnesis Journal* (December 2014).

universalizing them, so that human knowledge could be properly ordered to reality. They were "realists" because they believed that the individual things that make up creation are designed by God according to distinct natures or kinds and have from God the appropriate form that makes them what they are. Now a form is the instantiating principle whereby a nature actually exists in an individual, which is the only way it can exist, and whereby the individual as such exists in its unity and integrity. (Forms are multiple, then, in two senses. First, quantitatively: This man is not that man, though both have the form of a man. Second, qualitatively: Each of these men, to be a man, has more than one nature by reason of his form. He has the nature of an animal, for example, but as a rational animal he has also an intellectual nature. He is a man only if both of these natures are simultaneously instantiated in him; the instantiating and unifying principle is the form or soul.)[13] Thus the concept in the mind, which has the character of universality, corresponds to the actual facts of creation. The mind can know William of Ockham, say, both as a man and as this particular man, because the mind is inherently suited to grasping and abstracting forms and to recognizing combinations of natures in forms.

Ockham himself, however, didn't agree and applied his razor to much of this. Talk of natures and forms causes us to see double, to posit and wrestle with realities within or behind the things that actually present themselves to us. This we need not and should not try to do. In Hochschild's words, "Ockham did not do away with objective reality, but in doing away with one part of objective reality—forms—he did away with a fundamental principle of explanation for objective reality"; that is, "he did away with formal causality." Unfortunately, since formal causality "secures teleology," guaranteeing that "the ends or purposes of things follow from what they are and what is in accord with or capable of fulfilling their natures," teleology was also a casualty. One could no longer understand things in terms of their ends, in terms of what they are for.[14] This made a great deal of difference in trying to explain men to themselves. It made it difficult to explain, for example, what

13. Soul in just that sense, not in the synecdochal sense that refers to the man specifically in his consciousness, mind, or will. The soul is the "subsistent form" that makes him a man. See William Carroll, "Souls Matter" (*Public Discourse*, 11 March 2015).

14. Hochschild ("What's Wrong with Ockham?," 5f.) explains: "It is commonly said that modern science neglects formal causes but attends to efficient and material causes; but classically understood, efficient and material causes cannot function or even be conceived without formal causes, for it is form which informs matter, giving concrete objects their power to act on other objects. The loss of formal causality is thus in a sense the loss of efficient and material causality as well—an implication that is not quite fully realized until we see it brilliantly explored in the philosophy of David Hume."

virtue is and why it is important. Above all, it made it difficult to explain to men that that they are *for God*. And that inability is at the very root of the modern autonomy project.

The loss of teleology, as many have noted, was both liberating and debilitating for science; for politics and ethics and theology it was only debilitating. It was debilitating for thought itself, which no longer knew how to stratify and organize itself. Indeed, the situation was worse than that. Hochschild points out that the excising of natures and forms—or rather, the vain attempt to do so—raised immediately the specter of radical doubt. "This was noticed not only by the first generation of Ockham's critics, but even by Ockham himself, who proposed thought experiments about God manipulating our minds to make us think things that are not true."[15] It was only later, however, after the self-discrediting of religion in the sixteenth and early seventeenth centuries, that someone appeared who was ready to make doubt itself into a new beginning for man.

That someone was Descartes, who became the anti-Anselm of a new nominalist era. Anselm began with faith in order to let reason do its proper work of unfolding the relation between God and man that is realized and revealed in Christ. Descartes sought to press from systematic doubt—doubt about both God and man, without consideration of Christ or of anything at all that presents itself to the senses—complete certainty about the self and ultimately, on that foundation, a *mathesis universalis* governing all knowledge.[16] If this was a rejection both of nominalist skepticism and of rationalist presumption, it was also a highly Promethean project.[17] As J. B. Schneewind points out,

15. Ibid., 6. We cannot concern ourselves here with the wider influence of Ockham or with his many other departures from Scotus, including the different relation to Aristotle, on the one hand, and to Anselm on the other, in which he stood. Nor can we take an interest in his war with the Oxford Thomists, his quarrel with the pope, and his permanent alienation from the Church. Suffice it to say that he became increasingly critical, not only of Aristotle and the scholastic tradition but also of the authority of the Church and of tradition generally. As the nominalist movement advanced toward the Reformation and the Enlightenment, it would manifest the same tendency, with the same result.

16. For Descartes, "all the treasures of science and of wisdom" are hid in "contemplation of the true God" (Meditation 4.1; cf. Col. 2:2f.), but the path to finding these treasures is the path of disengagement "from all matter" rather than disengagement merely from "weighty cares and wearisome toils" (Anselm, *Pros.* 1). His Meditations are, so to say, a rewriting of the Monologion without the Proslogion and indeed without the Creed on which the Anselmian texts rest. Gillespie (*Theological Origins*, 175ff.) is quite right to highlight the Hermetic and Rosicrucian features of Descartes's enterprise, which he also describes as rooted in Eckhart's "mystical identification of the cosmos with the divine" (339n42).

17. Descartes sounds very much like Anselm when he says to Mersenne: "Generally we assume ourselves that God can do everything we are capable of understanding but not that He cannot do what we are incapable of understanding, for it would be presumptuous to think

Descartes proposes "a thoroughgoing ethic of self-governance" in which no appeal can be made either to the revealed mind of God or to supposed final causes.[18] His universal science is an exclusively human construct, wherein God becomes impotent because the field of knowledge is completely controlled by man.[19] It is Descartes who represents the transition from late-medieval to modern nominalism, which distinguishes itself by aiming at "a powerfully free human will,"[20] beholden to no religious dogma, and at complete mastery over nature. It is Descartes who treats doubt and certainty as a far more fundamental axis than doubt and faith. It is Descartes who also begins, as Michael Gillespie observes, to collapse thinking into willing, through his performative (not syllogistic) assertion, *cogito ergo sum*—who thus makes the principle of his new science the "individual autonomy that arises out of the self-assertion and self-positing of the human will."[21]

---

that our imagination has as much magnitude as His power" (see Gillespie, *Theological Origins*, 195). Like Ockham, however, Descartes puts this assumption to work by arguing that even the law of non-contradiction, or indeed the law of love, is not grounded in God himself and could be overturned by the will of God. See e.g., *Writings* III, 235, in *The Philosophical Writings of Descartes*, 3 vols., trans. John Cottingham, Dugald Murdoch, Robert Stoothof, and Anthony Kenny (Cambridge: Cambridge University Press, 1984–91).

18. "Descartes is no atheist, but he does not think that we can use rational knowledge of God to solve problems either in theory or in practice. His God is at least as inscrutable as the God of Luther and his predecessors, perhaps more so. . . . Descartes offers an a priori proof of God's existence, and an a priori proof to show that he is not a deceiver; he thinks of God as the creator and the indispensable continuing ground of the existence of the world; but his voluntarist insistence on keeping God untrammeled entails that although God's existence and power explain everything in general, they can never be used to explain anything in particular. What is true of physics and biology is equally true of morality." J. B. Schneewind, *The Invention of Autonomy: A History of Modern Moral Philosophy* (Cambridge: Cambridge University Press, 1998), 185.

19. Thus Gillespie, *Theological Origins*, 40f.: "Man . . . becomes master and possessor of nature by dispossessing its current owner. . . . This is possible because man in some sense already is God, or at least is the same infinite will that constitutes God." (Gillespie develops this thesis in chapter 6; see esp. 200ff.)

20. "The claim to a powerfully free human will was something new in Descartes's time" (Timothy J. Reiss, "Descartes, the Palatinate, and the Thirty Years War: Political Theory and Political Practice," *Yale French Studies*, 80 [1991]: 128). Descartes sang its glories to Queen Christina: "Besides that free will is in itself the noblest thing in us, insofar as it makes us somehow like God and seems to exempt us from being subject to him, so that its good use is thus our greatest benefit, it is also the one [thing] most properly ours and most important to us. It follows that it alone can beget our greatest satisfactions" (quoted in Reiss, "Descartes," 127; see *Writings* III, 326). On the other hand, Descartes sounds almost Thomist in claiming that the will "consists simply in the fact that when the intellect puts something forward for affirmation or denial or for pursuit or avoidance, our inclinations are such that we do not feel we are determined by any external force" (Meditation 4.8; cf. 4.12).

21. *Theological Origins*, 200; cf. 196ff. The "rethinking of thinking as willing" can be viewed the other way around, however (cf. Schneewind, *Invention of Autonomy*, 187f., per Descartes, *Writings* III, 56 and 97). Moreover, Descartes complains about the confounding of the functions

Descartes's inversion of Anselm deserves some elaboration, which we will later give it. For the moment, it suffices to notice that the nature/freedom dilemma was exacerbated by the fact that divine attributes were being distributed both to nature and to man himself. In the absence of teleology, it was not at all obvious how man, who belongs to the general nexus of cause and effect that he aspires to understand scientifically rather than theologically, can also rise above it, so that he may exercise control over it and over himself. That question was of urgent political interest after the trauma of the Thirty Years War, and with the appearance of Newtonian science it gained in philosophical urgency as well. Kant was among those who made a concerted effort to address it by removing what was left of the old metaphysics and re-investing all its grandeur in the thinking and willing individual, who himself is the very font of scientific and moral order. Kant's attempt got bogged down, however, in what Garth Green aptly calls the aporia of inner sense; that is, in Kant's failure to explain how the thinking self retains the capacity to cognize natural phenomena given his account of its *in*capacity when it comes to cognizing itself.[22] Kant thought it necessary to restrict the soul's self-knowledge in order to insulate rational thought from theology and thus from the perils of religious strife. The modern edifice required such insulation, while requiring also (non-theological) principles of government that would accord men their proper dignity as something more than machines.[23] Just how to achieve the latter was a puzzle he bequeathed to modernity, without the requisite picture on the box.

Meanwhile, another project (in Gillespie's terms, a more Petrarchian one) was gathering steam. It was intensely focused on cognition of the self, or at least on the self's volitional and affective dimensions. "I am devoting my last days to studying myself," said Rousseau in the first walk of his *Reveries*, and to considering "the successive variations of my soul."[24] Men, after all,

---

of intellect and will (*Writings* III, 195). The *res cogitans* is a sensing, imagining, understanding and willing *res*. Willing is the active, and understanding the passive, aspect of the soul or mind, which is one and simple (ibid., 182).

22. Or conversely, as Green points out to me, how the soul is incapable of cognizing itself given Kant's account of its cognition of natural phenomena. See Garth W. Green, *The Aporia of Inner Sense: The Self-Knowledge of Reason and the Critique of Metaphysics in Kant*, Critical Studies in German Idealism 3 (Leiden: Brill, 2010), 5–10, 223ff., esp. n. 234.

23. Cf. Gillespie, *Theological Origins*, 258ff. On the exclusion of theology Kant is categorical: "I maintain that *all attempts* to make a speculative use of reason in regard to theology are entirely fruitless and are, by their intrinsic character, null and void, and that the principles of reason's natural use lead *to no theology whatever*" (A636, B664, emphasis original). See further Garth W. Green, "Kant and Henry: An Inheritance of Idealism and a 'Turn' for Phenomenology," *Analecta Hermeneutica* 4 (2012).

24. J.-J. Rousseau, *Reveries of the Solitary Walker*, trans. Peter France (London: Penguin, 2004), 32ff.

are not content to leave altogether unread either their own souls, much less those of their neighbors, and there is much mischief in the attempt to read the latter. Rousseau did not at all like the readings volunteered by those who once were close to him. He would render an account of himself to himself, a kind of last judgment, as it were, carried out *coram se*. Who, after all, God aside—and Rousseau, like Kant, was happy to leave God aside—could match his uniquely privileged reading of himself? If Descartes elevated the human will to something in principle divine, while Kant allowed man a godlike capacity to order the phenomenal world in his own mind, Rousseau granted him a godlike capacity to measure himself. In that respect, Rousseau fancied himself a latter-day Augustine, though William Blake, for one, was not buying it—the Frenchman's confessions and reveries, he proclaimed, were nothing but self-justifying dissimulations.[25]

Dissimulating or no, Rousseau turned the older Renaissance quest for self-understanding in the direction of what we think of today as personal authenticity, though it may be more accurate to call it self-absorption.[26] He and Kant thus produced quite distinct, even contradictory, notions of autonomy. For Kant, autonomy still consisted in self-rule according to the dictates of reason. Not so for Rousseau, or for the Romantics, whose quest for autonomy was more aesthetic than rational.[27] By the time this latter stream had passed down as far as J. S. Mill and the nominalists of the nineteenth century, autonomy specified rather the power of self-discovery, or indeed of self-authorship, through the spontaneous exercise of the will, to which even reason must be subordinate. The enemy here was still society, or the disapproving other, but that other was more abstractly (and theologically) construed as a product of the "Calvinistic" theory according to which "the one great offence of man is self-will." The right response to such intellectual despotism was the doctrine that "it is only the cultivation of individuality which produces, or can produce, well-developed human

25. "Rousseau thought Men Good by Nature; he found them Evil & found no friend. Friendship cannot exist without Forgiveness of Sins continually. The Book written by Rousseau and called his Confessions is an apology & cloke for his sin & not a confession." William Blake, "To the Deists," in *The Complete Poetry and Prose of William Blake*, ed. David V. Erdman, rev. ed. (New York: Doubleday, 1988), 200.

26. Where "authenticity conditions" are understood to "include the capacity to reflect upon and endorse (or identify with) one's desires, values, and so on" (John Christman, "Autonomy in Moral and Political Philosophy," *The Stanford Encyclopedia of Philosophy*, revised 9 January 2015), are not self-absorption and dysphoria predictable outcomes?

27. Andrew Henscheid's dissertation, "Love's Authority: Kierkegaard and the Question of Autonomy" (PhD diss., Fordham University, 2011), draws attention to Kierkegaard's resistance to the autonomy/heteronomy binary and contrasts his approach to autonomy with both the rational and the "aesthetic" option.

beings."[28] Liberty to be oneself—that was the first thing to be prized: a liberty grounded in "the inner domain of consciousness," with "absolute freedom of opinion and sentiments on all subjects," a liberty expressed in "tastes and pursuits" and by "framing the plan of our life to suit our own character"; in short, "of doing as we like," however foolish or perverse we might seem in the eyes of others.[29]

Notwithstanding the enormous upheavals and calculated, systemic violence of the twentieth century—a century far bloodier in its wars and enterprises of irreligion than the seventeenth, a century that lends little support to Millian optimism and much to Calvinist pessimism—this project and this way of thinking permeates our political and legal discourse today. A cure is still being sought, with almost quixotic determination, for our excessive Calvinism; that is, for the frustration of spontaneous self-development by social and religious norms. Salvation from that frustration is to come from autonomy, and autonomy alone. The only real question is whether and how far autonomy can or should be imposed on individuals and on the communities to which they belong.

Sola Autonomia

Ben Coburn offers a straightforward definition of autonomy, so conceived: "Autonomy is an ideal of individuals deciding for themselves what is a valuable life and living their lives in accordance with that decision."[30] He is leaning here on Joseph Raz, who has done much to extend Mill's project and to correct its inconsistencies.[31] We will pause awhile with Raz as an influential proponent of an autonomy-based society.

In chapter 14 of *The Morality of Freedom*, Raz tells us that the goal of autonomy is self-authorship, which is achievable by agents who possess the requisite mental capacities, are exposed to an adequate range of options, and are

---

28. J. S. Mill, *On Liberty* (London: Dent & Dutton, 1972), chap. 3, 119ff. We leave aside the question of what "well-developed" can mean in a nominalist milieu, observing only that the idea that humans can and should be well-developed was not abandoned in the nominalist revolution, as one might expect.

29. Ibid., chap. 1, 75.

30. Ben Coburn, *Autonomy and Liberalism*, Routledge Studies in Contemporary Philosophy 19 (New York: Routledge, 2010), 19.

31. The differences between Raz and Mill are significant. If Mill taught us that Freedom + Diversity = Spontaneous Development, or Individual and Social Progress (cf. my *Desiring a Better Country*, 49), Raz wants to teach us that Autonomy + Pluralism = Political Freedom. If Mill was the messiah of utilitarianism, Raz is a powerful critic thereof, and so forth. What they have in common will nonetheless prove of greater concern.

relatively free from coercion or manipulation.[32] This capacity for "conscious self-creation," we must observe, controls the idea of freedom rather than being controlled by it.[33] In Raz, even more than in Mill, it is bound up with moral pluralism and legal positivism; that is, with the rejection of morality-based law. It deploys the principle of diversity to generate what Mill calls "a variety of situations" and Raz "an adequate range of valuable options,"[34] backs it up by a harm principle that is really a permission principle—do what you please, so long as you allow others to do likewise—and, just so, erases traditional moral and religious constraints, altering quite fundamentally the cultural landscape. It reshapes the idea of personhood itself, which becomes project based. Personhood is reduced to agency, and the rights attached to persons are made contingent upon their mental and/or affective capacities, even upon their willingness to use those capacities in furtherance of diversity.[35]

This kind of thinking has placed the unborn and the infirm, the not yet capacitated and the incapacitated, outside the sphere of rights-holders and has put in doubt their basic value—even their very lives. It has also taken on that Rousseauvian flavor of forcing those inside to be free. For one who lives in "an autonomy-enhancing culture" *must* be autonomous; autonomy itself is not a choice, though self-realization is a choice.[36] At the same time it has brought teleology back into play, since one's well-being depends on one's goals.[37] But now teleology is something purely private, even when projects are shared. For where personal autonomy is the starting point, and moral pluralism based on

32. See Joseph Raz, *The Morality of Freedom* (Oxford: Clarendon, 1986), 369: "The ruling idea behind the ideal of personal autonomy is that people should make their own lives . . . control-ling, to some degree, their own destiny, fashioning it through successive decisions throughout their lives" in our rapidly changing world. The autonomy discourse thus appears as a discourse of hope, albeit one oblivious to the deep vein of skepticism and despair that plagues the modern West.

33. Ibid., 390. Its relation to morality and to moral autonomy is more obscure. Raz distin-guishes personal from moral autonomy by asserting, negatively, that the latter (particularly in its Kantian form) reduces authorship "to a vanishing point" and, positively, that the former "is no more than one specific moral ideal which, if valid, is one element in a moral doctrine" (370n2). Cf. Gerald Dworkin, *The Theory and Practice of Autonomy* (Cambridge: Cambridge University Press, 1988), 34ff.; see also John Rawls, *Political Liberalism*, exp. ed., Columbia Classics in Philosophy (New York: Columbia University Press, 2005), 455f., who provides a different taxonomy.

34. Raz, *Morality of Freedom*, 408.

35. "The capacity to be free, to decide freely the course of their own lives, is what makes a person. Respecting people as people consists in giving due weight to their interest in having and exercising that capacity. On this view, respect for people consists in respecting their interest to enjoy personal autonomy" (ibid., 190; cf. 408f., however, where it seems that positive freedom, or the capacity to control and create one's own life, derives *its* value from the actual living of an autonomous life).

36. Ibid., 375f.

37. Ibid., 391.

the incommensurability of values is affirmed, there can be nothing properly public, much less anything upwardly open to some transcendent unity.

Nothing properly public? That may seem a very odd thing to say of Raz, a liberal perfectionist who insists that values and projects are embedded in social and legal forms and who finds rights-based morality inadequate.[38] Raz rejects moral individualism (that is, he believes in collective goods that have intrinsic rather than merely instrumental value) and commits himself to a moral world in which individual agency is one pole and a common culture the other."[39] He even maintains that "autonomy is valuable only if exercised in pursuit of the good."[40]

That the good provides a bridge between private and public flourishing, between individual options and collective policy, may be taken as read in any defense of perfectionist liberalism. How otherwise could one posit, as Raz does, a state prepared to take strong measures in support of autonomy, to discourage pursuit of baser goods, to enforce assimilationist policies, to liberate people from communities that inhibit their autonomy, even perchance to liberate them from vices or bad habits?[41] Yet it is not at all clear that this bridge is passable. For Raz, like Mill, is a worshiper of the Unknown Good.[42] He is committed to "the humanistic principle which claims that the explanation and justification of the goodness or badness of anything derives ultimately from its contribution, actual or possible, to human life and its quality."[43] He believes autonomy to be an ultimate value for living a quality life. He thinks art, for example, to have ultimate value insofar as it helps to explain the

38. His label is "right-based moralities," a right being "the ground for a duty of another" (ibid., 208). For present purposes, however, we may singularize the noun and pluralize the adjective, since Raz does not mean to contrast "right" and "rights."

39. Ibid., 193; cf. 198, 426. The adjective "moral," we are told, will ordinarily be used roughly in the sense of "evaluative" (136). Intrinsically valuable things are of three types: those valuable in themselves, constituent goods, and "ultimate goods or values" (200). The last of these serve as transcendentals; that is, they require no justification but can be used to justify others.

40. Ibid., 381.

41. An autonomy-based morality requires "a perfectionist doctrine which holds the state to be duty-bound to promote the good life" (ibid., 426). It is ready to embrace "paternalistic measures" (422) and indeed to go "beyond means-related paternalism . . . in sanctioning measures which encourage the adoption of valuable ends and discourage the pursuit of base ones" (423). Perfectionist principles "suggest that people are justified in taking action to assimilate the minority group, at the cost of letting its culture die or at least be considerably changed by absorption," though gradual transformation is preferable to "precipitate disintegration" (424).

42. The good, for Mill at least, is still happiness itself, as it was for Augustine and Aquinas, only Mill cannot quite say what happiness is; "an existence as rich as possible in enjoyments" is as close as he comes (*On Liberty*, chap. 3; cf. Augustine, *Mor.* 18; *Trin.* 13.6–12).

43. Raz, *Morality of Freedom*, 194. This principle "sets a necessary condition for the acceptability of moral theories." Being quality-based, it does not absolutize, but relativizes, human life.

meaning of life. But he does not know, or is not prepared to say, what the meaning of life might be or how ultimate values exist independently of those that we generate for ourselves. The good life is simply the successful life, the life of personal well-being as measured by "the successful pursuit of valuable goals" freely adopted.[44]

No doubt it is beyond the humanist remit to say more. But this means that Raz is still trying to do the impossible, indeed, to do something of which he himself is critical in anti-perfectionist liberalism; namely, to produce a theory of the morally and politically right without committing to any particular conception of the good, other than the good of personal autonomy—and even that is an ideal he thinks he can describe "without commitment to the substance of the valuable forms of life with which it is bound up."[45]

Such is the nominalist doom. One who does not acknowledge natures and forms cannot acknowledge any definite hierarchy of ends.[46] And because he cannot acknowledge any definite hierarchy of ends, he must either take the utilitarian route, with Mill, or seek refuge, as Raz does, in incommensurability. He can never really say what the good is, or how goods cohere. Is personal autonomy "a constituent element of the good life"? Does it in fact concern "the complete art of the good life"?[47] How can we be sure of that if we can-

44. Ibid., 318; cf. 289. Raz defends the idea of collective goods with intrinsic value against moral individualism, but his discussion of these goods boils down to the notion that man is a social animal and that some of the things he typically considers worthwhile cannot exist as purely private goods (ibid., 206); it does not carry us much beyond that.

45. Ibid., 395. See 136f., where Raz observes the failure of both neutralist and exclusionary anti-perfectionism to make clear their distinction between good and right or to recognize that good and right stem from a common source. But what *is* that source? On this crucial question he is far from clear. Later on he tells us that there is "but one source for morality and for personal well-being," viz., the "communal pool of values" (318f.). So how does that pool gather, and how are we to make our judgments as to whether it has become polluted? What distinguishes a social form as moral or wicked? All this remains unspecified. When Raz asks who the morally good person is, he answers, "he whose prosperity is so intertwined with the pursuit of goals which advance intrinsic values and the well-being of others that it is impossible to separate his personal well-being from his moral concerns" (320). That sounds almost Augustinian, but for the fact that he will not move from the abstract to the concrete.

46. To dispense with hierarchy altogether is not possible, of course. As Raz says, human goals "are commonly nested within hierarchical structures," and one measures the importance of an action "by its contribution to the highest goals it serves" (ibid., 292f.). But the nominalist's denial of real relations (a denial already in place in Roscelin), combined with the later denial of true knowledge of God or of the divine will, renders recogntion of a univeral moral hierarchy impossible. From which it seems to follow that: "A choice is not good because of the goodness of the action chosen. On the contrary, an action is good because it is chosen" (Francis Canavan, "From Ockham to Blackmun: The Philosophical Roots of Liberal Jurisprudence," in *Jerusalem, Athens, and Rome: Essays in Honour of James V. Schall, S.J.*, ed. Mark D. Guerra [South Bend, IN: St. Augustine's Press, 2015], 67).

47. Raz, *Morality of Freedom*, 397; cf. 408.

not say with any authority what the good life is? A person, we are told, lives autonomously "only if he pursues the good as he sees it." But what is the force of "as he sees it"? Aquinas would say that everyone acts under the aspect of the good, even when doing evil. Is that what Raz means?[48] (If so, he is not far from the kingdom after all.) Or does he mean, as he appears to mean, "only if he pursues the particular goods that he chooses"? That again begs the question as to what is good and how it is known to be good.

A similar question arises when we learn that "the ideal of autonomy requires only the availability of morally acceptable options."[49] Morally acceptable to whom? To the individual himself, or to the community, or to some authority higher than the community? Who decides what is morally acceptable, and how? If the individual alone, then personal autonomy becomes indistinguishable from moral individualism and indeed moral relativism, which Raz disavows. If the community, then what happens to autonomy? If something higher than the community—the state or its gods—then we must say something about how the state chooses its gods or determines its collective moral commitments. It won't do to say that the morality of the state is or ought to be built on autonomy alone, for that is both highly reductionist and by no means self-evidently true. In practice, it has never been attempted and could never be achieved.

One reason for that is its failure (presumably for fear of "Calvinism") to take sufficient account of the corruption of the will and the public effects thereof. Raz claims only to be idealizing the role of the will in practical reason, in "the interplay of independent value and the self-creation of value," but can he be sure that he is not idealizing something already corrupt?[50] That the will itself can be corrupt he readily acknowledges. The paradigmatic case appears to be the refusal to live autonomously, to seek self-realization, even when there is the possibility of doing so. But is this the original corruption, the font of corruption, or should we look elsewhere for that? And what exactly does it mean to realize oneself, if not to incline to, and arrive at, the good that is proper to one's nature, in a fashion unique to one's own person and situation?[51]

48. Ibid., 412; cf. Aquinas, *ST* 1–2.94.2.

49. Raz, *Morality of Freedom*, 381; cf. 205.

50. Ibid., 389. In Rousseauvian fashion, Raz seems happy enough to shift the burden of moral corruption onto society: "the main source of deviation between morality and a person's concern for his own well-being arises where the social forms available to him in his society are morally wicked" (319f.).

51. Such is the realist view, which in its Christian form rests on a consideration both of nature and of person. It is still reflected, to some degree, in Raz's own approach; that is, in his "ideal of free and conscious self-creation" and in his claim that "a person's life is autonomous if it is to a considerable extent his own creation" (ibid., 408). But what we find here is that the

If one is building not merely a psychology but a moral and a political theory—in short, an entire anthropology—around the idea of autonomy, one must face such questions. Unfortunately, it is a genetic trait of the nominalist always to stop short of an entire anthropology; for if that were achieved, it would amount to a refutation of nominalism itself. The brake Raz likes to apply is his incommensurability thesis. One cannot weigh or judge between values, between projects, between virtues, between courses of action in those many spheres of life where the will is necessarily un- or under-determined by reason, where there is no comparative moral or evaluative function for reason to perform.[52] This thesis nicely buffers every sphere to which it is applied from queries about natures or cross-examination about putative goods.

Now it is true that the person, being finite, must express his nature finitely, choosing between goods. It is true that choices between goods may, without fault and to our benefit, be under-determined by reason. It is also true that different projects or pursuits may be well served by different virtues. But it does not follow that the virtues themselves are competitive or mutually exclusive.[53] Nor does it follow from the fact that the person is situated in an imperfect world that some choices entail moral conflicts of the kind Raz imagines—conflicts built into the nature of things, as it were, or situations in which one can only do wrong.[54] Why not say rather, as the realist would say, that different pursuits require for their perfection distinct applications of the various virtues, which are neither altogether discrete nor conflictual, and that if the choice generates real moral conflicts there is likely something wrong with one or more of the pursuits in question?[55] But in that case one cannot move, as Raz does, from value pluralism (or the claim that there is more than one "optimal" form of life) to moral pluralism (entailing "real conflicts between

---

nature/person dialectic, having morphed under the influence of nominalism into a nature/free-dom dialectic, has become oppositional, with all the emphasis placed on the second element.

52. See ibid., 388f. and chap. 13. Incommensurability is simply incomparability: "A and B are incommensurate if it is neither true that one is better than the other nor true that they are of equal value" (322). Perhaps the prominence of this topic and the use that is made of it can be traced back to the mistaken notion that behind the will that chooses rationally there is a will that simply chooses—the "free" will, or the will in equipoise.

53. See ibid., 396f.; cf., for example, Augustine, *Mor.* 25.

54. See Raz, *Morality of Freedom*, 357ff. Conflicts in the nature of things are necessary for those who deny that things have natures.

55. Almost everything at issue could be approached through this one question: Is there really such a thing as an irresolvable moral dilemma? Christianity has a long tradition of rejecting the "dirty hands" view of life and of defending the maxim that it is never licit to do evil that good may come. Raz, however, does not regard Christianity as a qualified participant in the kind of public reason he wishes to promote. One of the most remarkable features of *The Morality of Freedom* is that it is written as if nothing noteworthy was thought or said on the subjects it treats until the last century or so. In that sense it is a tour de force of the self-indulgent practical reason.

independent moral considerations") and so to legal positivism (law based not on morality but only on itself, or more precisely, on the determination to support exercises in autonomy).[56]

If one tries to do so, nothing can prevent the perfectionist "mission creep" that only a more robust anthropology could possibly justify. That mission creep is especially evident in Raz's deployment of Mill's harm principle. Raz wants to minimize state coercion, yet he leaves the exception clause wide open to abuse because he specifies harm only by reference to autonomy. The state may coerce in order to protect autonomy and in order to enhance autonomy. It may coerce to guarantee toleration, which on Raz's view entails a refusal even to offend the neighbor through negative moral judgments, lest that offense somehow inhibit him from pursuing his projects.[57] It may develop assimilationist policies that don't count as coercion, even if they "liberate" citizens from their natural communities. An autonomy-based doctrine of political freedom can contemplate all of this. It is not afraid, within certain limits, to call for the enforcement of morality.[58]

Now Raz is quite right to say that those who work on some other basis than the autonomy principle must make the harm principle, if they want to retain it, intelligible on that basis. So absorbed is he in his autonomy foundationalism, however, that he doesn't pause to consider the alternatives that have been put forward. Augustine, for example, suggested long ago that doing harm to no one should be combined with doing good to whomever one can. In other words, the relation to the neighbor was defined positively as well

---

56. Raz (ibid., 404) may be a legal positivist, but he knows that the law has *some* connection to morality. What connection, exactly, is more difficult to say. When one looks, for example, to chap. 6 of his *Between Authority and Interpretation: On the Theory of Law and Practical Reason* (Oxford: Oxford University Press, 2009), one finds only a heavily qualified positivism. "*The law's task, put abstractly, is to secure a situation whereby moral goals which, given the current social situation in the country whose law it is, would be unlikely to be achieved without it, and whose achievement by the law is not counter-productive, are realized*" (178, italics original).

57. "Toleration implies the suppression or containment of an inclination or desire to persecute, harass, harm or react in an unwelcome way to a person" and is a virtue particularly where the said inclinations or desires "are thought by the tolerant person to be in themselves desirable" (Raz, *Morality of Freedom*, 401). Against a failure of toleration that involves merely the giving of offense, however, state coercion should not be used except in extreme cases (421). Our courts today seem rather confused, alas, about what constitutes an extreme case.

58. See ibid., 422ff. The logic is simple: "Autonomy means that a good life is a life which is a free creation. Value-pluralism means that there will be a multiplicity of valuable options to choose from, and favourable conditions of choice. The resulting doctrine of freedom provides and protects those options and conditions" (412). In doing so, it can justify placing restrictions on one person for the sake of another or even for his own sake. It can justify coercion to protect autonomy, if only to protect autonomy (419).

as negatively. He also argued that doing good to the neighbor means doing good to the soul as well as to the body, and that doing good to the soul means helping it toward God, its highest good. This, of course, was an exposition of the two great commandments—of loving God and loving the neighbor as oneself.[59] On Raz's scheme, however, as on Mill's, the first commandment is to pursue "our own good in our own way," and the second is like unto it: "do not attempt to deprive others of theirs, or impede their efforts to obtain it."[60] This is negative and not positive, despite Raz's sporadic efforts to incorporate something like a neighbor principle. It therefore falls to the *state* to provide the positive element, and that positive element includes (safeguards notwithstanding) an expansive approach to coercion, as liberal perfectionism always does.

We have tarried with Raz to illustrate the character of the contemporary Millian project; indeed, of any project that does not know how to order things to their proper ends, which can hardly be done without acknowledging those ends. Talk of "different fundamental concerns" and incommensurable options, or of the "incompatible virtues" required to pursue them, is not so much an appreciation of diversity as an attempt to describe a world lacking hierarchy and wholeness, just as the autonomy principle is an attempt to supply what moral reason is missing in that world, viz., a meaningful point of reference. One price paid for this point of reference is that the only truly public thing *is* the commitment to autonomy and to moral pluralism. Otherwise put: what is public is precisely what is not shared, what rebuffs every attempt to share. The autonomy principle acts like an acid to dissolve what remains of the moral and cultural fabric of Christian civilization.[61]

Radical Autonomy

Here we must mention an altogether different figure, whom we passed by when we left Rousseau for Mill and Raz—Nietzsche, that great champion, as Barth rightly remarked, of man without his fellow man.[62] Nietzsche's *über*-autonomous individual already knows how to create and re-create himself, and does not dissemble about his motive for doing so. He too acknowledges an interplay between independently existing values and self-generated values; but the purpose of the latter is to *overcome* the former, which exist only as

---

59. See Augustine, *Civ.* 19.14 and *Mor.* 46–56.
60. Mill, *On Liberty*, chap. 3. Because there is no God principle here, there is no true neighbor principle either.
61. Its next challenge is Islam. It is highly doubtful, however, that it has the resources to resist Islam. Certainly it does not have the demographic trajectory to do so.
62. See Karl Barth, *CD* 3.2, 231ff.

limiting, largely decadent, social constructs. The master project of Nietzsche's autonomous person is the pursuit of power, the will to power, and "all that enhances the feeling of power," for which it is necessary to combine the discipline of self-rule with the spontaneity of self-authorship.[63] We must mention Nietzsche because it is where the Rousseauvian, the Millian, and the Nietzschean streams converge, and the social constructionist critique comes into full Foucaultian flow, that we have the conditions for the radicalization of the autonomy doctrine that is taking place today.

Now, social constructionism is a many-headed hydra that we will also pass by quickly, noting only that what began as a series of sensible debates about the objective and subjective dimensions of knowledge, the relation between nature and nurture in the acquiring of knowledge, and the mediating role of social institutions managed in relatively short order to become a very foolish, hyper-nominalistic debate about whether there *is* any such thing as "nature" or objective reality and whether social institutions are ever anything but arbitrary instruments of oppression manufactured by the powerful.[64] This could not have happened quite the way it did without Foucault's deployment of Nietzsche, nor could it have taken quite so potent a political form without the legacy of Marx and Engels and Gramsci, though that is another matter. All that really concerns us here is that we have become locked into a dirty war of counter-cultural ideologies, which like most wars (especially those of European origin) involve shifting tactical alliances between parties of very different views and vested interests.[65]

From our vantage point the alliances between social constructionist forces and the modern autonomy movement are the most significant. These have certainly been crucial in effecting the rapid alterations to the public sphere recently witnessed. They have led both to a radicalization of the very idea of autonomy and to an escalation of efforts to shift what is left of the common culture ever further from its "Calvinism" (not to mention its capitalism). *Autonomy and dignity!* is the battle cry of these combined forces,[66] and a

63. Friedrich Nietzsche, *The Anti-Christ* (Costa Mesa, CA: Noontide, 1988), second aphorism; cf. Nietzsche, *The Genealogy of Morals* III §7. The first principle of *his* humanism, as he says, is rather different!

64. Critics such as Ian Hacking and Paul Boghossian are right to find here, at least at the fringes, an almost Berkeleyan form of doubt about the existence of external reality.

65. Some of these coalitions, naturally, are focused on sex and the cultural institutions built up around it, which make for obvious targets. See, for example, E. Michael Jones, *Libido Dominandi: Sexual Liberation and Political Control* (South Bend, IN: St Augustine's Press, 2005), though curiously Jones makes no mention of Foucault.

66. Dignity is added to autonomy, forming a hendiadys that better serves identity or group rights while permitting broader appeal to traditional (largely Christian) respect for persons and communities.

look at some of the targets already captured shows us just how far we have traveled on the nominalist trajectory from Descartes's *cogito ergo sum*. We have traveled all the way to *I am the sole author, owner, and disposer of my own existence*; and even to *I am who or what I say I am, and I have the right to be perceived and treated as such*.[67] It is to the service of these claims that autonomy is now pledged in the public sphere.

As regards ownership, take for example the success of assisted-suicide legislation in various Western jurisdictions. The preamble to the Canadian version, Bill C-14, opens with the words: "Whereas the Parliament of Canada recognizes the autonomy of persons who have a grievous and irremediable medical condition that causes them enduring and intolerable suffering."[68] What follows renders a right to dispose of one's life at the time of one's choosing, and to state assistance in doing so. On what grounds? Autonomy and dignity. (The Supreme Court decision behind C-14 deploys that hendiadys at least half a dozen times.)[69] The operating assumptions of the legislation are that dignity resides in autonomy, that autonomy means self-ownership, and that self-ownership entails the right to self-disposal, even under conditions making the exercise of that right difficult or impossible.[70] Suicide is made both morally legitimate and, where the state is concerned, morally compelling. It is an act that no longer has to be exercised in defiance of the state, or even with the state's indifference, but may now command the

67. Or in the simpler expression of Andrej[a] Pejič, "to be perceived as what you say you are is a basic human right" (cited in Noah Michelson, "Super Model Andreja Pejic Comes Out as Transgender," *Huffington Post*, 24 July 2014). The Rousseauvian element is quite pronounced here. As Louis Dupré points out (*The Enlightenment and the Intellectual Foundations of Modern Culture* [New Haven: Yale University Press, 200], 66): "If feelings constitute the core of selfhood, as Rousseau thinks, the self never *is*, but continuously *becomes* and redefines itself." How then can the self be recognized, except on the Pejič principle? That principle may also be seen as an extension of the Fichtean self-positing "I," albeit with the loss of all nuance. Cf. Reinhard Hütter, *Bound to Be Free: Evangelical Catholic Engagements in Ecclesiology, Ethics, and Ecumenism* (Grand Rapids: Eerdmans, 2004), 119–24.

68. Bill C-14 (First Session, Forty-second Parliament, 64–65 Elizabeth II, 2015–2016).

69. *Carter v. Canada*, 2015 SCC 5 (1 S.C.R. 331) §59, for example, speaks of "personal autonomy and fundamental notions of self-determination and dignity." For a fuller analysis of *Carter*, see my "The Acid of Autonomy" (*Convivium*, 1 June 2016). On the interplay between radical autonomy (or what he calls "foundational autonomy") and the relation of the citizen to the state, see David Novak's highly prescient piece, "Suicide Is Not a Private Choice" (*First Things*, Aug./Sept. 1997).

70. Not, of course, under *any* conditions; there must be "grievous and irremediable" suffering. The central focus of the ongoing debate in Canada is about who gets to judge that, and whether the judgment can be made without reference to the proximity of natural death. In the jurisdictions that Canada has emulated, the general tendency is to say that the individual himself will judge it and that, since it is a matter of self-ownership and self-determination, it need not be tied to particular illnesses or stages of illness.

resources of the state.[71] Many have pointed out that this provision may well be motivated on the part of the state by a cost-benefit analysis over against palliative care. Some have noted, with justified alarm, that it confirms not merely the individual's but the state's freedom to act independently of any heteronomous moral code. Whatever benefits accrue to the state, however, the fact is that the aiding and abetting of suicide has suddenly become a public institution—almost a signature public institution, we might say—just because it so nicely captures the dialectic of personal autonomy and state provision of "an adequate range of acceptable options."

As regards authorship, take the equally dramatic advance of same-sex marriage, to which the social constructionist forces have made a much greater contribution. At the heart of the US Supreme Court's decision in *Obergefell v. Hodges* we find analogous logic, assumptions, and language, viz., that of autonomy and dignity: "A first premise of the Court's relevant precedents," we are told, "is that the right to personal choice regarding marriage is inherent in the concept of individual autonomy." Or again: "The fundamental liberties protected by the Fourteenth Amendment's Due Process Clause extend to certain personal choices central to individual dignity and autonomy, including intimate choices defining personal identity . . ." Or yet again: "There is dignity in the bond between two men or two women who seek to marry and in their autonomy to make such profound choices."[72] Autonomy and dignity demand that the oldest of all public institutions, the institution of marriage, be redefined. And why? Because it must now bear witness to autonomy as self-authorship. It must become a better vehicle for self-definition.

Almost identical language and reasoning govern the transgender legislation that is cropping up in sundry jurisdictions, entitling biological males to the rights and privileges belonging to biological females and vice versa. How

71. Or perhaps we should turn this around and say that it no longer *can* be exercised in defiance of the state. The existentialists of the last century, who wondered whether the decision to die by one's own hand might not be the truest exercise of autonomy, requiring the greatest possible concentration of inwardness in defiance of every heteronomous force, seem quite remote to us now.

72. Thus Justice Anthony Kennedy, for the majority in *Obergefell v. Hodges* 135 S. Ct. 2584 (2015). To make good on this, of course, the Court had to pretend, as Justice Samuel Alito noticed, that families are constructs of the will alone and not natural outcomes at all. Moreover, as Justice Clarence Thomas observed, it had to reject the idea "that human dignity is innate and suggest instead that it comes from the Government." That is the price exacted by the myth of autonomy as it operates here. If marriage is not really about the foundations of a family but about autonomy and dignity, and if human dignity rests on what one thinks of oneself, which rests in turn on what others think of one, it must come to rest at last on the support and goodwill of the state. (Cf. my *Nation of Bastards: Essays on the End of Marriage* [Toronto: BPS, 2007], written after Canada made the same move in 2005.)

could it be otherwise, on the principle that autonomy entails self-authorship and self-definition? If sex (actual bodily difference) is no longer relevant in marriage, why should it be relevant anywhere else? Let autonomous persons exercise their self-authorship as they please, particularly where their own bodies are concerned. For public purposes we will simply replace the concept of sex, that biological binary, with the infinitely more malleable concept of gender, which is socially and individually constructed. After all, you are what you say you are and you should be treated as such.

Here we do indeed see the horns of human wisdom coming off. The Canadian court finds in the right to life, liberty, and security of the person a right to assisted suicide. The American court finds in due process the right of a man, not to marry—for that right he already has—but to "marry" a man.[73] In both countries, courts and legislatures increasingly hold that respect for autonomy and dignity requires recognition of a man as a woman and a woman as a man, simply on the say-so of the person in question. Which is absurd. And for the sake of that absurdity, the law is busy evacuating itself of the body and of identity based upon the body. As it does so, identity becomes a legal fiction, and law becomes lawless, beholden to no objective reality. For there can be no real law, and no real justice, where the subjects of law and justice are entirely self-determining—where they are the lawgivers and high priests of their own existence, and able, as it were, to transubstantiate themselves by the mere declaration, *haec est persona mea*.

Now we must not too quickly try to pin all this on nominalism, whose long war on both nature and tradition we have been reviewing, or on those particular forms of nominalism that appear among the social constructionists. There are other, more immediate factors to consider, not the least of which is the determination (for the sake of more frequent sexual pleasure) to evacuate the body of its reproductive powers and, *in extremis* or even quite ordinarily, to evacuate the womb of the so-called product of conception,

---

73. Both countries have begun fulfilling Raz's prophecy—or was it a prescription?—in *Morality of Freedom*: "More recent changes," he wrote, "are uncertain and incomplete. Some tendencies, e.g., to communal families, or open marriages, may wither away. Others, e.g., homosexual families, may be here to stay. It is too early to have a clear view of the consequences of these developments. But one thing can be said with certainty. They will not be confined to adding new options to the familiar heterosexual monogamous family. They will change the character of that family. If these changes take root in our culture then the familiar marriage relations will disappear. They will not disappear suddenly. Rather they will be transformed into a somewhat different social form, which responds to the fact that it is one of several forms of bonding, and that bonding itself is much more easily and commonly dissoluble. All these factors are already working their way into the constitutive conventions which determine what is appropriate and expected within a conventional marriage and transforming its significance" (393).

whose personhood is arbitrarily and unjustly denied. Recent attempts to detach legal from biological identity certainly display the character imprinted at that particular font of iniquity.[74] However, the radical autonomy claim that *I am whoever I say I am*, whatever else it is, is the ripened fruit of nominalism and voluntarism. For nominalism, which began by insisting that a nature is something sovereignly attributed to some particular thing by the mind, has inevitably worked its way around to denying individuals any nature at all other than that which they choose for themselves. And voluntarism, which began by subtly dividing the divine will from the divine intellect—thus generating the conditions under which the human will could seek its own triumph over the intellect, which it falsely credited with the power to create rather than to recognize natures[75]—has naturally come around to denying the possibility of any real knowledge of either God or man. Cartesian and Kantian attempts to overcome skepticism have failed, and the subjectivists have increasingly prevailed. One result is this bizarre thesis that parodies, and so blasphemes, the divine Name—which is no longer uttered in polite society, not out of reverence for God but rather out of reverence for God's emancipated creatures.

Among the most striking ironies here is the fact that, having at first laid all the stress on the empirical, on what is known by the senses and by bodily experience, nominalism should wind up warring against the body itself.[76] But the autonomous will really has no choice but to attack the body as well as the mind. For the body is the most obvious locus of the given, the most stubborn impediment to the power claimed by the will.[77] Over the first five centuries of the nominalist era, the attack was focused on the ecclesial body; that is, on the authority of the Church, which Anselm astutely made a point of defending

74. See Daniel Moody, *The Flesh Made Word: A New Reason to Be against Abortion* (Atascadero, CA: Createspace Independent Publishing, 2016). Moody analyzes the fact that *gender*, a purely mental construct, is replacing *sex*, a bodily reality, linking this development to the legalization of abortion.

75. Readers must forgive the economy. I mean, obviously, that the will moved the intellect to falsely credit itself. As David Hart puts it, referring to the voluntarist aspect of fourteenth- and fifteenth-century nominalism: "Here explicitly, for the first time in Western thought, freedom was defined not as the unobstructed realization of a nature but as the absolute power of the will to determine even what that nature might be" (*Atheist Delusions: The Christian Revolution and Its Fashionable Enemies* [New Haven: Yale University Press, 2009], 225).

76. Thomas and Scotus, both realists, albeit in quite different fashion, laid great stress on the senses also but without tending toward any such error. In the hands of the nominalists, however, the body itself has fallen victim to the instability of the will that is free before and apart from the work of the intellect, before and apart even from the twin orientations to happiness and justice.

77. Hütter (*Bound to Be Free*, 118f.) remarks on the "tragic" nature of the body, as the locus of heteronomy, even in Kant.

prior to addressing Roscelin's errors. As the attack intensified, the body of Christ in its primary sense became the target. The real presence of that body in the Mass no longer made sense to nominalists, whether Catholic or Protestant, except perhaps as a prop to the dubious authority of the Church. Today's resurgent gnosticism, with its open assault on the human body as such, required another five centuries, for it necessitated the complete undoing of Christendom and the generation of those very different moral and political and legal conditions under which it might hope for success. It had indeed to await the advent of technological conditions to which it might appeal for an alternative to the life limited and constrained by the body, and with those conditions the final dissipation of the spiritual sensitivities and disciplines that shaped our civilization.[78]

That nominalism's autonomy doctrine, in whatever theater of operation, always seems to end with an attack on the body should not surprise us. As John Paul II put it in *Veritatis splendor*, "a freedom which claims to be absolute ends up treating the human body as a raw datum, devoid of any meaning and moral values until freedom has shaped it in accordance with its design."[79] That it always seems to begin with an attack on the Church should not surprise us either. For the refusal to learn the goodness of the body through the incarnation of the Son, the refusal to receive the dignity of personhood through the

78. Technology has opened a new front in the battle against the body, known as transhumanism. As Martin[e] Rothblatt puts it, we are moving toward a new species, which Rothblatt dubs *persona creatus*, a self-created species independent of its present biological substrate ("Mind Is Deeper Than Matter: Transgenderism, Transhumanism, and the Freedom of Form," in *The Transhumanist Reader: Classical and Contemporary Essays on the Science, Technology, and Philosophy of the Human Future*, ed. Max More and Natasha Vita-More [Oxford: John Wiley & Sons, 2013], 317–26). Perhaps Rothblatt means *persona (re)creata*, or perhaps the gender-confused inflection is a deliberate reflection of his own change of "gender." At all events, he explicitly links the transgender agenda with the transhumanist, and invests heavily in both. Those who doubt the seriousness of the transhumanist movement and its determination to overcome the body would do well to read Steve Fuller's *Humanity 2.0: What It Means to Be Human, Past, Present and Future* (New York: Palgrave Macmillan, 2011), noting in particular the ethics of coercion laid out in its final chapter.

79. "Consequently, human nature and the body appear as presuppositions or preambles, materially necessary for freedom to make its choice, yet extrinsic to the person, the subject and the human act. Their functions would not be able to constitute reference points for moral decisions, because the finalities of these inclinations would be merely 'physical' goods, called by some 'pre-moral.' To refer to them, in order to find in them rational indications with regard to the order of morality, would be to expose oneself to the accusation of physicalism or biologism. In this way of thinking, the tension between freedom and a nature conceived of in a reductive way is resolved by a division within man himself. This moral theory does not correspond to the truth about man and his freedom. It contradicts the Church's teachings on the unity of the human person, whose rational soul is *per se et essentialiter* the form of his body" (John Paul II, *Veritatis splendor* 48).

Son—which is to say, non-autonomously, in communion, as gift rather than achievement—means that the ecclesial body and, more fundamentally, the eucharistic body is *the* body that cannot be tolerated. That is why we cannot simply return to Kant, say, who tried to tether autonomy to reason. For that would not take us back behind the will's war against reason, prosecuted by way of nominalism's proposal to think reality without kinds and voluntarism's proposal to think it without ends.[80] No, we need to go back much further than Kant if we wish to correct that. We need to return to Anselm and try to understand both freedom and autonomy quite differently.

Non mea voluntus sed tua fiat: Freedom and Autonomy Reconstituted

We have been mapping, very hastily, a watershed in Western intellectual history. Cascading down Roscelin's side is the nominalism from which has emerged, like a rainbow over a treacherous, rock-strewn pool, the myth of autonomy. That myth knows neither the divine nature nor human nature. It knows only the spontaneously self-creating individual and the increasingly Leviathan-like state that mediates between individuals according to no law but its own. This state, we must now observe theologically, is busy ensconcing in law the precise notion of autonomy that Anselm identified as characterizing the primal fall. Which means also that it is becoming both manipulative and coercive, for the solitary individual always stands naked before the state, having lost the clothing of a culture thick with mediating institutions.[81]

In chapter 4 of *De casu diaboli*, written just before the controversy with Roscelin broke out, Anselm says of the devil that he fell by insisting on his own autonomous will, thus making himself equal to God. "Even if he did not will to be wholly equal to God," remarks Anselm, "but something less than God against the will of God, by that very fact he inordinately willed to be like God, because he willed something by his own will, as subject to no one" (*propria voluntate, quæ nulli subdita fuit*). "It is for God alone thus to will something by his own will, such that he follows no higher will." And Anselm adds: "Not only did he will to be equal to God in presuming to have his own

---

80. To borrow the succinct phrasing of Oliver O'Donovan, *Resurrection and Moral Order: An Outline for Evangelical Ethics* (Grand Rapids: Eerdmans 1986), 49: "The proposal to think reality without ends, 'voluntarism,' must be viewed in the same light as the proposal to think it without kinds, 'nominalism.' It is an artifice of thought."

81. This is the legacy of Hobbes, whom we also passed by. Hobbes it was who passed on the nominalist heritage in its most politically germane form. Cf. Canavan, "From Ockham to Blackmun," 63ff.

will, but he even willed to be *greater* by willing what God did not want him to will, because he put his own will above God's."[82]

Now, even were we to suppose that the devil willed to be like God in some fashion that God himself willed him, in due course, to be like God—a reasonable supposition congruent with Genesis 3—the autonomous character of this willing doomed the devil, as it dooms man, to the path of self-destruction. But autonomous willing of just this sort is what the myth of autonomy is all about. Indeed, it is what the modern notion of liberty is all about. Recall the notorious passage from *Planned Parenthood v. Casey*: "At the heart of liberty is the right to define one's own concept of existence, of meaning, of the universe, and of the mystery of human life."[83] This contention is not merely foolish, but diabolically foolish, assigning to man what belongs to God.

The right response, however, is not to repudiate the very idea of autonomy but to get autonomy right by rediscovering the nature of freedom.[84] This can be done only by appeal to the faith of the Church and to the tradition that flows down the side of the mountain on which Anselm stands. For in that tradition, truth makes for freedom, and freedom for autonomy. Both the *ordo essendi* and the *ordo cognoscendi* are different: One must know the truth in order to be free. Moreover, the truth that sets free is not found either in mental abstractions or in actually existing universals, forms, natures, etc., but rather in the active expression of the divine nature through the incarnation. The truth that sets free is the Truth in person, constituting in and with himself a communion of persons.[85]

Somewhere near the apostolic headwaters of this tradition stands St. Irenaeus, who liked to refer to man, or at least to Christian man, as *homo gratus*—the man who renders thanks for what is given, the man who is caught

---

82. *Quia præsumpsit habere propriam voluntatem . . . quoniam voluntatem suam supra dei voluntatem posuit* (PL 158, col. 0333).

83. *Planned Parenthood v. Casey* 112 S. Ct. 2791 (1992).

84. We must reverse Raz, in other words, understanding autonomy by way of freedom. Cf. *Veritatis splendor*, 40: "At the heart of the moral life we thus find the principle of a 'rightful autonomy' [*iustae autonomiae, Gaudium et spes* 41] of man, the personal subject of his actions. . . . The rightful autonomy of the practical reason means that man possesses in himself his own law, received from the Creator. Nevertheless, the autonomy of reason cannot mean that reason itself creates values and moral norms. Were this autonomy to imply a denial of the participation of the practical reason in the wisdom of the divine Creator and Lawgiver, or were it to suggest a freedom which creates moral norms, on the basis of historical contingencies or the diversity of societies and cultures, this sort of alleged autonomy would contradict the Church's teaching on the truth about man. It would be the death of true freedom: 'But of the tree of the knowledge of good and evil you shall not eat, for in the day that you eat of it you shall die' (Gen. 2:17)."

85. Cf. John 1:9, 17; 8:12ff.; 14:1–17:26.

up in an economy of giving that is, so to say, eucharistically financed by God.[86] It is *homo gratus* who, in receiving the truth gladly, discovers what it really means to be like God and so to be free. Irenaeus was familiar, in its fledgling gnostic form, with the autonomous man who despises his creatureliness and hopes to reinvent himself as God. He was familiar with rejections of the body. But he also knew that those who reject the body find the whole man lapsing into unreality, not advancing in liberty. To advance in liberty, it is necessary to advance in self-rule, the self-rule that is a holding fast to the good.[87] It is only thus that the faculties of the soul become disciplined "in the practice of things pertaining to God" and that the soul itself eventually receives "a faculty of the Uncreated, through the gratuitous bestowal of eternal existence." As for those who "go beyond the law of the human race, and even before they become men wish to be like God their creator, they are more destitute of reason than dumb animals," he says.[88] "For how shall he be a god, who has not as yet been made a man?" Only by "preserving the framework" of God's own workmanship can man "ascend to that which is perfect." The test of his seriousness about freedom lies just there.[89] Those who fail the test subject themselves instead to "the aim of him who envies our life"—that evil one, the devil, who seeks to render us disbelievers in our own salvation and blasphemous against our creator.[90]

Now it is difficult to say how much Irenaeus Anselm knew, but the similarity of his own arguments in *De libertate arbitrii* and *De casu diaboli* is striking. The latter work begins with the question "What do you have that you have not received?" and tries to show that the whole process of creation and perfection is a participation in the divine economy of gift (which is how he understands theology itself). It is in the short-circuiting of that economy that the fall occurs. Anselm is on the same page with Irenaeus: Human dignity and human destiny lie in the very thing the devil falsely claims God does not want for man; namely, that he should be like God and enjoy something

---

86. *Haer.* 4.11 (*ANF* 1:474f.).

87. "For it is in man's power to disobey God and to forfeit what is good; but that brings no small amount of injury and mischief. . . . Because man is possessed of free will from the beginning, and God (in whose likeness man was created) is possessed of free will, advice is always given him to keep fast the good, which is done by means of obedience to God" (*Haer.* 4.37.4).

88. *Haer.* 4.38 (see *ANF* 1:518ff.).

89. See *Haer.* 4.39.3 (*ANF* 1:523): "Those persons, therefore, who have apostasized from the light given by the Father, and transgressed the law of liberty, have done so through their own fault, since they have been created free agents, and possessed of power over themselves."

90. "For whatsoever all the heretics may have advanced with the utmost solemnity, they come at last to this, that they blaspheme the Creator, and disallow the salvation of God's workmanship, which the flesh truly is" (ibid., preface to book 4; *ANF* 1:463).

like the divine freedom. And how does that come about? Not by opposing himself to God but by freely aligning himself with God. But here we need a fuller account of Anselm's own understanding of freedom, which we may draw from his later work, *De concordia praescientiae et praedestinationis et gratiae dei cum libero arbitrio*.[91]

In *De concordia* Anselm describes the will and the reason as powers or instruments of the soul, each of which is dependent upon the other for its proper functioning. The will has two instruments of its own, which he calls *affectiones* or dispositions: the disposition *ad volendum commoditatem* (to will what is to one's advantage, viz., what tends to health and happiness) and the disposition *ad volendum rectitudinem* (to will what is right and just).[92] The will-to-advantage, which is also the will-to-happiness, does not itself make one happy, of course, while the will-to-justice already makes one just, so long as one has it. No one is just who lacks it,[93] and unlike the former it can be lost. The will itself, as given by God to man, is created in and with these two dispositions and is free insofar as it has them both. Had it but one of the two it would not be free, for it would will necessarily.[94]

It is in the latter, however, that freedom appears, for the latter takes the human creature outside itself in a way that the former does not. The will-to-justice disposes man to that which is not simply for his own benefit but is somehow greater than that.[95] So he has been made with a will-to-justice as well as a will-to-advantage. The groundwork has already been laid, in the very structuring of his agency—as both rational and volitional, and as having these twin *affectiones* of the will—for him to be both just and happy, living in such a manner as to come to enjoy God. He has been made in freedom and for freedom. Otherwise put: he has the habit of going outside himself already

---

91. A work in which he signs off by reinforcing the economy of gift: "I wanted as a gift to impart to those who ask for it that which I have received as a gift" (*DC* 3.14). Scotus, by the way, shows more familiarity with this work than does Aquinas, whose preoccupation with Aristotle arguably led him to a somewhat less satisfactory account.

92. *Affectio huius instrumenti est, qua sic afficitur ipsum instrumentum ad volendum aliquid. . . . Ita instrumentum volendi duas habet aptitudines, quas voco, affectiones'. Quarum una est ad volendum commoditatem, altera ad volendum rectitudinem* (*DC* 3.11; *PL* 158, col. 0534).

93. Nor are the actual uses of their will, though these be outwardly in conformity with justice, for they are not ordered to justice for the sake of that justice itself, but only for the sake of what is perceived to be to one's advantage.

94. See further Anselm, *DCD* 13–14.

95. In a certain sense, man *need* not go outside himself, if we may thus paraphrase, though he *ought* to, because he is made to know and love God (*ad intelligendum et amandum se creavit*, *DC* 3.13; *PL* 158, col. 0538) and so to enjoy God. In another sense, he must go outside himself, and for this very purpose, or he cannot be happy; his inalienable disposition to seek his own advantage will in the end be frustrated.

within himself as he comes from the hand of God, and he has also the power to keep doing so. That is his freedom as he first experiences it.

He can be neither just nor happy, however, without actually willing to be so.[96] And this means that he must decide whether to preserve justice, the justice he has been given; that is, whether to preserve rectitude of will for its own sake. Now, he has the power to preserve it and that power is inalienable; but the will-to-justice itself is not inalienable, like the will-to-advantage.[97] That it is not inalienable means that he may make it truly his own, if he desires, such that it becomes both grace *and* merit, both gift *and* possession. In that way he himself becomes its coauthor, which is just what God wants for him. In preserving rectitude of will for its own sake he confirms himself in his freedom, and confirms that freedom as his very own. Conversely, in not preserving it he renders himself un-free, and the other, inalienable *affectio* becomes a form of bondage. So his freedom is tested, and this testing happens precisely at the point (every point) where he must go outside himself by willing to preserve justice for its own sake, which is to say, at the point where he must choose to will what God wills him to will, to be autonomous in a godly rather than a diabolical way.

In sum: Man's creaturely freedom entails from the beginning his power to preserve the will-to-justice. This he ought to do, and this he knows how to do, but this he is not compelled to do. When he becomes, by his own choice, unjust, refusing to do it, his freedom remains only in the sense that he is still the kind of creature who could preserve that will, that *affectio ad volendum rectitudinem*, if he had it. He remains the kind of creature (a rational soul) who can still direct himself this way or that. What he does not remain is someone who actually has the second *affectio* and who can therefore hope to attain the goal of the first: the full and proper human happiness that comes from knowing, loving, and enjoying God. For the first *affectio* is (as we said) an inalienable gift, whereas the second is not.[98] The knowledge that the first somehow depends on the second remains, as does the rational capacity to discern many of its features, but the power to restore the lost *affectio* was never given, nor is it self-generating. That power belongs to God alone, and

---

96. *Intentio namque dei fuit, ut iustam faceret atque beatam naturam rationalem ad fruendum se. Sed neque iusta neque beata esse potuit sine voluntate iustitiae et beatitudinis* (DC 3.13).

97. He cannot help seeking his own advantage, though he must learn how best to do that. And perhaps this is the place to observe that Kant's failure lay not in stressing the will's duty to reason—which is his version of the will to justice—but rather in overlooking the ultimate advantage of happiness, which his late-nominalist skepticism about God, and even about Aristotle, made an unreliable if not incomprehensible goal.

98. If it were, there would be no testing and therefore no confirmation from the side of man, and therefore no true freedom.

only the God-man can produce it, renewing the will-to-justice through his own submission to the Father.[99]

Freedom thus lies in the faithful reception, preservation, and use of the two *affectiones*. Pursuant to that reception and preservation and use, creaturely freedom becomes godlike and both *affectiones* become inalienable. For true freedom does not lie in the *capax peccati*. It lies in cooperation with God, who is Freedom itself, just as he is Truth itself and Happiness itself.[100] God is *non capax peccati* and creaturely freedom, insists Anselm, consists neither in the capacity to sin nor in a separation from God that would make further sin impossible. (That would be hell.) It consists rather in the kind of participation in God that makes sin unthinkable, the kind of participation that renders the second *affectio* just as inalienable as the first. For the will is most free when it not only maintains its rectitude but is no longer in danger of losing it; that is, when its simultaneous dispositions to justice and happiness are unassailable, when what is given by God in a provisional form has been received in that form by the creature and preserved in such a way as to merit being given again in a permanent form through a new and higher participation in God.

In this new and higher participation, happiness is completely given because the *visio dei* is given. There is no longer any tension, then, between justice and happiness, or rather between justice and the pursuit of happiness, such as characterizes the provisional form of freedom. When given the superabundant perfecting grace, man, like God, is happy in justice and just in happiness. He is *non posse peccare*. He is free for justice and just in his freedom. He is free for happiness and happy in his freedom. He is whole and complete, enjoying the fullness of being, in the unity of being and goodness that belongs to God himself and to all things made by God.[101] And he is, in the proper sense,

---

99. How does the man who has become un-free receive freedom? In *De liberate arbitrii* 10 this is identified as a great miracle, greater even than the resurrection of the body. The miracle is based (per *De incarnatione* 10, *CDH* 1.9, 2.10, 2.18) on the achievement of Jesus Christ, who freely subjects himself to the Father and wins for man this reward. The effectual application of the reward is presumably a function of the life-giving Spirit, who enables a willing-with-Jesus, who wills with and for the Father. (Anselm is less clear than Irenaeus about the pneumatological aspect, though he attempts in *De concordia* to show the synergy between this enabling grace and our enabled freedom.)

100. "God is not able [to do] anything opposed to Himself or anything evil, since He is so powerful in happiness and justice—or better, since He is so all-powerful in simplicity of goodness (for happiness and justice are one good in Him and not different goods)—that nothing is able [to cause] any harm to the Supreme Good" (*DCD* 12; trans. Hopkins and Richardson). Creaturely freedom means that sin is at first possible, but the possibility of sinning is not what constitutes freedom; if it did, God himself would not be free, nor would the creature ever arrive at a godlike freedom. The capacity to sin has its good in the fact that not sinning enables one to give justice to oneself (*DCD* 18) and so to become the coauthor of one's freedom (see *CDH* 2.10).

101. Cf. *DCD* 1.

autonomous. He is autonomous with the same autonomy by which Jesus said to the Father, "Not my will, but thine, be done" (Luke 22:42), and to his disciples: "No one takes my life from me, but I lay it down of my own accord. I have power to lay it down, and I have power to take it again; this charge I have received from my Father" (John 10:18).[102] This kind of autonomy is not incompatible, but fully consonant, with heteronomy. It is autonomy that willingly acknowledges heteronomy, rather than repudiating it, and finds true freedom and true power in doing so. It is autonomy conjoined with heteronomy through a communion of persons. In short, it is the autonomy of love, in which self-rule is for the sake of obedience and self-authorship is a glad coauthorship with God.[103]

Here we do well to recall, lest we make the mistake of conceding that we are now engaged in some purely private discourse lacking any public bearing, that nominalism forces us to ask whether we can speak meaningfully of *man* or only of men. That is a question that goes to the heart of human culture, as Charles Peirce astutely observes in his Berkeley review:

> The question whether the genus *homo* has any existence except as individuals, is the question whether there is anything of any more dignity, worth, and importance than individual happiness, individual aspirations, and individual life. Whether men really have anything in common, so that the community is to be considered as an end in itself, and if so, what the relative value of the two factors is, is the most fundamental practical question in regard to every institution the constitution of which we have it in our power to influence.[104]

102. If it is power you love, observes Anselm, consider this: Those who are united to God "will be all-powerful with regard to their wills, as God is with His. For just as God will be able to do what He wills through Himself, so through Him they will be able to do what they will; because, just as they will not will anything save what He wills, so He will will whatever they will, and what He intends to will cannot not be" (*Pros.* 25, trans. M. J. Charlesworth).

103. As Anselm puts it in *Meditatio redemptionis humanae* 51: "Thus, then, He exhibited a free obedience to the Father, inasmuch as He spontaneously willed to do what He knew would be pleasing to the Father. And hence, since this utter goodness of will was the Father's gift to Him, He is not improperly said to have received it as a precept of His Father's. In this way, therefore, it is that He was obedient to the Father even unto death; and that, as the Father gave Him commandment, so He did; and that He drank the chalice which His Father gave Him. For the obedience of Human Nature is exhibited at once in full perfection and in uttermost freedom, when it voluntarily surrenders its own free will to the will of God, and when, with a freedom all its own, it perfects the good will which was therefore accepted because unexacted." (*St Anselm's Book of Meditations and Prayers*, trans. M. R. [London: Burns and Gates, 1872], 144f.) John Paul II indicates that we may think of this "genuine moral autonomy," in which freedom and law unite, as "participated theonomy," because here "human reason and human will participate in God's wisdom and providence" (*Veritatis splendor* 40f.).

104. Charles S. Peirce, *The Essential Writings*, ed. Edward Moore (Amherst, NY: Prometheus Books, 1998), 63.

It is the realist rather than the nominalist who can give each its due: man and men, the community and the individual, heteronomy and autonomy, justice and happiness. But not, perhaps, just any realist. Anselm could, because his realism was informed by the doctrines of the Trinity and the incarnation.[105] Like Irenaeus and Augustine before him, he was ready to defend, with weapons his opponents lacked, the good life as a truly *social* life and, just so, to struggle in the earthly city—not just in theory but in practice—for something that would reflect at least a little of the light of the heavenly city, that "supremely cooperative, supremely ordered association of those who enjoy God and one another in God."[106]

So long have we been travelling on Roscelin's road, however, that today we hardly know what to do with the likes of Anselm. We cannot conceive of an autonomy that is not opposed to heteronomy. We think of freedom simply as whatever enhances the power to live an autonomous life. What is public (the work of God in human history) we call private, and what is private (one's sexual psychology, for example) we call public. And in consequence we have a culture that is rapidly disintegrating into conflicting autonomy claims and coercive public institutions, not to mention one increasingly alienated from the body.

Roscelin's road is the way of nominalism, which has led to the perversion of autonomy and freedom, depriving us of both private and public goods. But how foolish we would be if we supposed that we have traveled this road only by philosophical mistake, by a misreading of the conceptual or linguistic or metaphysical map! Anselm already knew that the problem ran much deeper than that, as he made clear in his own critique of Roscelin. We ourselves can penetrate to the heart of the matter by returning briefly in conclusion to Descartes, whom we identified earlier as the anti-Anselm of our modern era.

The Heart of the Matter

Let us lay out their differences: For Anselm, the will is twofold, and sin arises in not preserving the will to justice for its own sake. For Descartes, the will is

---

105. The nominalist, denying the existence of forms or natures, finds himself in consequence unable to consider communities and institutions as anything more than instruments for the advancement of individuality—meaning always, in the last analysis, his own individuality.

106. Thus Augustine, *Civ.* 19.13; cf. 22.30. Anselm, for whom "fittingness" and beauty are basic categories (see David S. Hogg, *Anselm of Canterbury: The Beauty of Theology* [London: Ashgate, 2004], 1ff.) would not entirely disagree with Nietzsche's claim that "only as an aesthetic phenomenon is the universe eternally justified"—something implicit in his doctrine that the number of redeemed humans will be equal to the number of the fallen angels. The aesthetics in play, however, is an aesthetics for which the happiness of each and every one in that number is indispensable.

simple, and sin arises in extending its use to matters not clearly understood by the mind, where "it easily turns aside from what is true and good," which is to say, it is the combination of will and intellect, not of different *dispositiones* of the will, that makes room for sin or error.[107] For Anselm, the human will and the human intellect are both analogically related to the divine, and symmetrically so. For Descartes, the human will, like the divine, is in principle infinite, while the human mind, unlike the divine, is constrained by finitude and ignorance, though it does have the divine capacity to intuit simple truths all at once and comprehensively.[108] For Anselm, rectitude of will entails a posture of faith, gratitude, and obedience, such that one freely wills what God wills. For Descartes, rectitude of will is a refusal to form judgments about what the mind cannot clearly conceptualize and present to itself as indubitable. For Anselm, freedom is first of all the power to preserve rectitude of will for its own sake (that is, to maintain justice) and then, in due course, an inalienable participation in the justice and happiness of God. For Descartes, freedom is either the free will itself in its ability to assent or refuse to assent—hence "whatever is voluntary" may be called free—or the condition of one who is not abusing the will by affirming what the mind cannot present as indubitable.[109] For Anselm, autonomy is self-rule under and for God, beginning

107. Descartes, Meditation 4.9 (*Writings* II, 40f.; cf. *Writings* III, 97, where he says that "error or vice" exist "only in the intellect," meaning, we may suppose, internally to the soul as the locus of both reason and will). Like the Greeks, Descartes seems to equate sin with ignorance and error—*omnis peccans est ignorans*, as he observes to Fr. Mesland—if we understand the error in question as that of the will straying beyond the mind's proper clarity in the judgments it effects and the pursuits or avoidances upon which it determines. It is worth remarking that the virtue of being resolute—of being "decisive in one's actions even when one [is] undecided in one's judgements" (*Writings* III, 97)—stands in considerable tension with this, a tension not alleviated, but only obscured, by speaking later of "a firm and constant resolution to carry out whatever reason *recommends*" (*Writings*, III, 257, emphasis added).

108. "My being deceived," says Descartes, "arises from the circumstance that the power which God has given me of discerning truth from error is not infinite" (Meditation 3.4). See further Schneewind, *Invention of Autonomy*, 188f., who observes the distinction between divine freedom, in which the will is indifferent by virtue of its omnipotence, and human freedom, in which the will must seek reasons for its action. In the same letter to Mesland, Descartes makes clear that he does not suppose *human* freedom to consist in indifference, for that would be incompatible with the doctrine of grace and with the unity of will and intellect, both in God and in man (*Writings* III, 233f.; cf. 179, 244ff., 342, and Meditation 4.8). Had Descartes been guided fully by these latter ideas, however, his philosophy would have turned out very differently.

109. Letter to Mesland (*Writings* III, 234). Here, preserving rectitude of the will for its own sake means following the Method, exercising the will to doubt, determining "never to judge where the truth is not clearly known" (Meditation 4.16). The will to doubt perfects man by allowing him to overcome error, thus making him as far as possible like God in the mind also. Or rather, that and the master-virtue of fortitude—of being resolute in one's determination to act decisively on what reason recommends—make him like God, since God himself is resolute.

with the exercise of the power to preserve justice. For Descartes, autonomy is the capacity to will and to reason much as God wills and reasons, and the deliberate exercise of that capacity.[110]

Now the sign, if not the sum, of these differences appears in their respective ontological arguments. Anselm's is an articulation of the self-evidence of God in the dependence *on* God of creaturely reason about God. As with all his arguments (even those that operate in hypothetical mode *remoto Christo*), it moves from disclosure to faith, from faith to understanding, from understanding to demonstration, and from demonstration to delight and adoration.[111] Here, one and the same God who discloses his being by naming himself to and for man, as YHWH and Father, also discloses his being by allowing human reason to identify him (prayerfully, *post factum*) as "that than which nothing greater can be thought" and hence as that which truly is, that which cannot coherently be thought not to be. For that than which nothing greater can be thought is, whatever else it is, the ground of all being and all thinking, and it makes no sense at all to try to think of it as not being. This is not an

110. Some wonder whether talk of God thus collapses into talk of autonomy (cf. Peter A. Schouls, "Descartes and the Autonomy of Reason," *Journal of the History of Philosophy* 10.3 [1972]: 320ff.). No doubt it does, in due course, though not perhaps for Descartes himself. The problem for Descartes himself is his determination to do philosophy without reference to theology. "Why didn't I discuss the freedom that we have to follow good or evil? Simply because I wanted to stay within the limits of natural philosophy, avoiding theological controversies as much as I could." What this means in practice is that philosophy moves outward from the self and extends as far as the addition of "our idea of God," but no further. And once "God" is fully in the grasp of the philosopher and his ideas, the collapse in question may very well take place. (See again the May 1644 letter to Mesland, from which the above quotation is drawn, noting the problem with transubstantiation that appears already as a portent of that collapse.)

111. The argument is a gift. It is an a posteriori recognition of the highest being and the highest good, of that which exists for its own sake and not for the sake of something else, made possible by the restoration of *iustus* to the rational soul, which "was created to the end that it should love and choose, above all, the highest good, and that it should do this, not because of something else, but because of the highest good itself" (Anselm, *CDH* 2.1). Hence: "I acknowledge, Lord, and I give thanks that You have created Your image in me, so that I may remember You, think of You, love You. . . . I do desire to understand Your truth a little, that truth that my heart believes and loves. For I do not seek to understand so that I may believe; but I believe so that I may understand" (*Pros.* 1). To be sure, Descartes also says, with respect to the gift of intellect, "I have every reason to render thanks to God" (Meditation 4.12), and of will, "I have to thank the goodness of him who bestowed it on me" (4.14). Yet he has learned this from himself, not from God. There is a great deal in the fourth Meditation that echoes Anselm, but it often rings hollow. The latter would never say, as the former does—though no one is more of a stickler about error than Anselm—that "it is in being superior to error that the highest and chief perfection of man consists" (4.17). For Anselm, the highest and chief perfection of man is to know, love, and enjoy God and to know him not merely as the guarantor of freedom from error but as the holy Trinity, the author of life and happiness.

exercise in hyper-realist enthusiasm. It is not a simple category mistake that confuses internal thought with external reality. It is not merely the recognition that human reason requires parameters, that it requires limits to give it its specificity, nor an attempt to deify its upper limit, thus deifying reason itself. It is an attempt to make reason reasonable by permitting it to say, in its own way, what revelation has already said: "whoever would draw near to God must believe that he exists and that he rewards those who seek him" (Heb. 11:6). In other words, Anselm's ontological argument does not move from thought to being, or from definition to reality, except by way of a prior movement from being to thought and from reality to definition. It does not establish the being of God by the thinking of man but rather establishes the thinking of man by the being of God. It is—as its genre declares it to be—the mind's grasp of a grace already bestowed. It is a confession, an *ac*knowledgment, of the unity in God of being and truth. "No creature has anything of itself."[112]

Descartes's argument, on the other hand, is an articulation of the self-evidence of the self to itself, to which is appended a claim about God. Like Rousseau's later reveries, it is conducted *coram se*, not *coram deo*. It begins, to be sure, with a question about God, but the question is not a prayerful response to God. Indeed, if it is a response at all, it is a response to the devil. For the question with which it begins is a question about the veracity or reliability of God, a variant of the question posed long ago to Eve. Descartes's argument proceeds by granting, hypothetically, that God might choose to deceive him through his own faculties. Which is to say, it begins and proceeds by doubt. He who would come to God must first *doubt*, if not whether God is, then whether God is always truthful.[113] This doubt, of course, is put by Descartes to good use, guaranteeing that everything else, everything provided by his faculties, must receive the same treatment. In the end, only the doubter himself is left as that which cannot or, at all events, will not be doubted, and in this end is a new beginning, a new foundation: certainty about the self, from which all other certainties will be derived. As for God, he is still that than which nothing greater can be conceived, but he *is* that for no other reason than that the self-positing self requires it. For the self that is fully buffered by systematic doubt from all possibility of deception finds that in positing itself it must also posit God and Nothing along with itself, as the limits that center or situate it. Otherwise it has no situation at all and its self-certainty disappears. But God, being the opposite of Nothing, cannot be defective

112. Anselm, *DCD* 1. See further Karl Barth, *Anselm: Fides Quaerens Intellectum* (London: SCM, 1960).
113. An impossible distinction, as Anselm would quickly point out.

either in truth or in being, and will not systematically deceive us through our faculties.[114] So the devil is defeated by Descartes, and doubt, which has the first word, does not have the last word.

Here we have two contrasting ontological arguments, one resting on God, the other resting on the self. Each purports to provide certainty of that of which it speaks, but both are also (and at the same time) acts of faith. Anselm's is an act of faith in God, Descartes's an act of faith in himself. God, to be sure, appears in both, yet the God of the one is not the God of the other. Descartes's God is an accessory, if not a function, of the self. (It was a small step for others to propose that "God" was indeed merely a function of the self, even if Descartes did not think so.) Neither his being nor his truth are the being or truth of the God of Anselm, for it is only a question about God, and not God himself, that Descartes admits as his starting point. Which means, from Anselm's point of view, that the devil is not defeated at all, at least not by Descartes.

Once again it should be evident, as it was in Anselm's response to Roscelin, that nominalism itself is not the heart of the matter. Nominalism is as much symptom as cause. The heart of the matter, the fundamental problem according to *De incarnatione*, is the diabolical determination of the will, which is deployed as if it were strictly one's own and subject to no one, not even God. It was to confront exactly *that* that the Son was sent into the world:

> The one who was to assume manhood [*hominem*] was to go to war against the devil and, as I have said, to intercede for man. Both of these, namely, the devil and man, by robbery willed to make themselves like God, willing as if their will were strictly their own . . . Now the will of an angel or a man is strictly his own when contrary to the will of God; for when someone wills what God forbids him to will, he has no author of his will except himself . . . But it belongs only to God to have a will strictly his own; that is, a will subject to no one. Whoever therefore uses his will autonomously strives by robbery to be like God and is guilty of attempting, as far as he is able, to deprive God of the dignity that is proper to him alone, and of his unique excellence.[115]

114. Just as Nothing is that than which nothing lesser can be conceived, God is that than which nothing greater can be conceived. Situated between these poles (the completely empty and the perfectly full) I cannot, without contradiction, suppose the latter to be the cause of error, which springs from lack or defect. Or again, God, who is only known to be in the same act that I will myself to be, cannot without contradiction be thought to be a deceiver; he is rather the guarantor of all my clear and distinct ideas. The uncertain God of the nominalists and the Reformers is therefore banished along with the skepticism of the skeptics: "Since it is impossible that he should will to deceive me, it is likewise certain that he has not given me a faculty that will ever lead me into error, provided I use it aright" (Descartes, Meditation 4.2).

115. *De incarnatione* 10 (*PL* 158, col. 0277 [cap. 5]; trans. mine), with which compare again Luke 22:40–43: "And when he came to the place he said to them, 'Pray that you may not enter

Anselm saw evidence of that guilt in Roscelin's stubborn heterodoxy as regards the Trinity. There can be no doubt that he would have seen evidence of it also in Descartes's will-to-doubt. What is that will-to-doubt, if not a refusal to allow even the mind its proper dependence on God? And where does it lead, if not to the myth of autonomy, which has as its political shadow the myth of neutrality—the state also reasoning and behaving as if God were not? And how could it all turn out, if not by uprooting the horns of self-confident human wisdom, which cannot by any means roll the stone of faith when it is founded squarely upon Christ? The soul, or the civilization, that even attempts to roll that stone, whether by nominalism or any other device, has already planted at least one foot in hell. Its only hope is genuine repentance—to bend the knee, willingly and gladly, to him who truly has vanquished the devil, who also intercedes for man with the Father in heaven.

---

into temptation.' And he withdrew from them about a stone's throw, and knelt down and prayed, 'Father, if thou art willing, remove this cup from me; nevertheless not my will, but thine, be done.' And there appeared to him an angel from heaven, strengthening him."

8

For the Jew First

Reaffirming the Pax Paulinica

Jerusalem will be trodden down by the Gentiles, until the times of the Gentiles are fulfilled.

Luke 21:24

A hardening has come upon part of Israel, until the full number of the Gentiles come in, and so all Israel will be saved.

Romans 11:25–26

It is no surprise that these sayings, by Jesus and Paul respectively, are the focus of much attention today. The surprise—the sudden and startling surprise—was the return of Israel to the land and of Jerusalem to Jewish habitation and control. This is seen by many Christians as a sign that the times of the Gentiles have begun to run out, and not only in Jerusalem. Indeed, it is difficult to know how else to see it, for there are no mere accidents of history, not on this scale, where the city of the Great King is concerned. The gradual unmooring of Western civilization from Christianity, together with the moral chaos lately caused by that great apostasy, both inside and outside the Church, is also rightly seen as such a sign. So too, in my judgment, is the resurgent gnosticism of our day, which is on display in a growing disdain for, even hatred of, the human body in its vulnerability and frailty and in our increasingly grim determination to dominate it from birth to death, disposing of it as and when we please. The demographic suicide of Europe may be peculiarly Western—the only proper way to be "post-Christian"—but many other nations and cultures are being drawn into the death spiral it has created, as abortion and contraception and homosexuality are systematically pushed upon them by what remains of Western wealth and power, concentrated now in the hands of a few. Then of course (and this is not unrelated, for human despair is an amalgam of self-hatred, hatred of the other, and hatred of God) there is the virulent anti-Semitism and anti-Zionism that is still being stirred up on all sides, whether secularist or Islamist: that, and the unprecedented persecution of "those who keep the commandments of God and bear testimony to Jesus."[1]

While the advance of the gospel, especially where there is persecution, will produce in those places, as it always does, a renaissance of hope and a recovery of sanity, must we not expect with this not only a prolonging but also a deepening of the mystery of lawlessness that advances parasitically alongside the gospel and precisely because of it?[2] In this era of globalization, the struggle between law and lawlessness, between Christ and Antichrist, is also being globalized. The globe is finite. Terrestrial history is finite. Time is not greater than space.[3] We have, therefore, every reason to believe that the times of the Gentiles are running out, though we have no reason to be anxious about that or even to regard it as something with unavoidably negative implications for life in the present or for investment in the future. Neither, on the other hand, should we view or plan the future without reference to it. The pre-Christian era was very long indeed, and the pre-Jewish era far longer yet. But a post-Christian era cannot be long, because a post-Christian era is not a time of ignorance such as God once overlooked but rather (by definition) a time of rebellion that can and must lead to the day of judgment, to the great

---

1. Rev. 12:17. Erik Peterson remarks that "whoever regards the relationship of the Church to the synagogue simply as a historical and not a theological problem inevitably ends up repeating the gnostic gambit by trying to eliminate the Old Testament and the Messiah 'after the flesh'" (*Theological Tractates*, ed. and trans. Michael Hollerich, Cultural Memory in the Present [Stanford, CA: Stanford University Press, 2011], 201n22).

2. I have explained this in chap. 6 of my *Ascension Theology* (London: T&T Clark, 2011).

3. *Pace* Pope Francis, the four "Hegelian-tinged" principles he developed as a young man in Argentina and pursued in his unfinished doctoral thesis on Guardini, the first of which he also incorporated (along with the others) into *Lumen fidei* 57, *Evangelium gaudii* 221ff., *Laudato si'* 178, *Amoris laetitia* 3 and 261, artificially oppose time to space and falsely elevate process over substance, becoming over being, etc.; see my "The Francis Reformation," *Catholic World Report*, 28 February 2018.

and terrible day of the Lord, and to the dramatic salvation of all who call on his name, all who are "waiting for and hastening the coming of the day of God" (2 Pet. 3:12).

Which brings us back to the Jews, whom we know today as a gathered and not merely a scattered people. Are we not now confronted with the need, with the urgent need, to reckon with something that for some centuries it has been convenient to ignore, or to regard simply as a brief and transitory moment in the history of the Church, when in fact it is a principle of that which calls the Church into being: namely, that the gospel of God concerning his Son, and the power of salvation at work in that gospel, is "to the Jew first and also to the Greek" (Rom. 1:16)? Are we not confronted by a question about the conversion of the Jews, about the lifting of that "hardening in part" of which Paul spoke, about the flourishing again of the natural branches of the cultivated tree, the tree into which we ourselves were grafted from the wild trees of the Gentiles? Must we not reckon with the fact that only thus will "all Israel" be saved?[4] But how are we to reckon with it? Even among those who are well aware that we must reckon with it, there is much disagreement.

Waiting for Elijah or Pursuing the *Postulatum*?

The major disagreement is between those who call for a concerted mission to the Jews and those who urge cooperation without mission—or a mission, we might say, that consists only in cooperation.

The former approach harks back to the nineteenth century, where it appears most notably in the *Postulatum pro Hebraeis* that was positively received, though not officially promulgated, by the hastily concluded First Vatican Council:

> The undersigned Fathers of the Council, humbly yet urgently, beseechingly pray that the Holy Ecumenical Council of the Vatican deign to come to the aid of the unfortunate nation of Israel with an entirely paternal invitation; that

---

4. The wild trees of the Gentiles are to be uprooted and burned with fire, along with branches broken off from the cultivated tree, as both Paul and Peter, like the prophets before them and Jesus himself, foretell. Only the Edenic tree, sprung again to life in Christ, watered, cooled, and protected from the fire by the mists of the Spirit (cf. Irenaeus, *Haer.* 3.17), will be saved—though a great and wonderful tree that is, with its native branches and its branches grafted from every nation! "All Israel" therefore means, whatever else it means, all Jews who then remain *and* all Jews and Gentiles who are organically attached to this tree. There is no need of, and no merit in, playing off these meanings one against the other. Cf. N. T. Wright, *Paul and the Faithfulness of God*, Christian Origins and the Question of God 4 (Minneapolis: Fortress, 2013), 1231–57, noting his discussion of Paul's reworked rabbinical polemic around the identification of "all Israel."

is, that it express the wish that, finally exhausted by a wait no less futile than long, the Israelites hasten to recognize the Messiah, our Savior Jesus Christ, truly promised to Abraham and announced by Moses; thus completing and crowning, not changing, the Mosaic religion.[5]

It is significant that this document, signed by a majority of the bishops, presents the goal of the mission as a "completing and crowning, not changing, [of] the Mosaic religion" through Jewish embrace of Jesus as the Messiah. It thus acknowledges that the gospel belongs to the Jewish people first of all, as the primary recipients of the promises of God, though it does not pass over the fact that they have, of their own accord, endured a wait "no less futile than long."[6]

The latter hails to the twentieth century, having its roots, on the Catholic side, in a certain approach to *Nostra Aetate* and, on the Protestant side, in the so-called new perspective on Paul that is traced to the work of Krister Stendahl, E. P. Sanders, and James Dunn. Here, in no small part because of the Holocaust, the stress falls more on the "not changing" than on the "completing and crowning." Some even posit a further delay of the Jewish embrace of Jesus until the parousia. Of the time of the end, the time following the times of the Gentiles, St. Augustine says:

> The last judgment is that which he shall settle on earth; coming to effect it out of heaven. . . . And this judgment shall consist of these circumstances, partly precedent and partly adjacent:

> Elijah shall come,
> the Jews shall believe,
> Antichrist shall persecute,
> Christ shall judge,
> the dead shall arise,
> the good and bad shall sever,
> the world shall burn and be renewed.

5. Cf. Michael Forrest and David Palm, "On the Relationship between the Jewish People and God" (*Catholic Register*, 27 October 2010). Pius IX is said to have remarked to the Lémann brothers, who presented the *postulatum*: "*Vos estis filii Abrahae, et ego.*"

6. Roy Schoeman, *Salvation Is from the Jews* (San Francisco: Ignatius, 2003), 35f.; trans. from the text provided by Joseph and Augustin Lémann in *La Cause des Restes d'Israël: Introduite au Concile Oecuménique du Vatican sous la bénédiction de S.S. le Pape Pie IX* (Lyon: Emmanuel Vitte, 1912), 79–81. On whether a concerted mission to the Jews amounts to hastening the end of history, see *La Cause des Restes d'Israël*, 121ff. On its possible effects, see also Lawrence Feingold, *The Mystery of Israel and the Church*, vol. 3, *The Messianic Kingdom of Israel* (Louisville: Miriam, 2010), 228f.

All this we must believe shall be, but how and in what order, our full experience then shall exceed our imperfect intelligence as yet.[7]

On the present approach, waiting for Elijah is just the ticket. After all that has happened during the times of the Gentiles, surely only God can present Jesus again to the Jews. Among the Jews (who find this approach less threatening) it is emphasized that our eschatological intelligence is indeed highly imperfect. Even the question of messianic identity cannot be answered now, though Christians mistakenly suppose themselves to know the answer.[8] On the Christian side, of course, it is the messianic agnosticism of Jews that is mistaken, but it is not the business of Christians to insist that they be set right on the matter. The business at hand is simply to facilitate a proper respect for the Jewish people.

For new perspective scholarship, which began by trying to read Paul first, and then the New Testament as a whole, without the distorting spectacles of Reformation law/gospel dualism,[9] this is not the key issue or question. Among the many dividends of rediscovering the essential Jewishness of Paul and the early Church, however, is that Torah observance, past or present, is no longer seen as a sort of Jewish Pelagianism. Nor is the New Testament detached from the Old in quasi-Marcionite fashion. Jews and Judaism are regarded as worthy partners in biblical studies, as in political theology and culture criticism, etc. Even Roman Catholicism begins to look somewhat less objectionable than once it did, though it continues to be regarded with suspicion as a peculiar mixture of law and gospel. Yet there remains (and that suspicion already hints at it) a certain ambivalence in the new perspective. The law/gospel dualism seems rather to be reduplicated than to be resolved. For either Torah is good for the Jew but not for the Christian, or it is good for the Jewish but not the Gentile Christian.

7. *Civ.* 20.30 (trans. J. H., 1610). Augustine's own "imperfect intelligence" led him to believe, mistakenly, that Israel would never return to the land. See Paula Fredriksen, "*Secundum Carnem*: History and Israel in the Theology of St. Augustine," in *The Limits of Ancient Christianity: Essays on Late Antique Thought and Culture in Honor of R. A. Markus*, ed. W. Klingshirn and M. Vessey (Ann Arbor: University of Michigan Press, 1999), 40f.

8. Cf. Tikva Frymer-Kensky, David Novak, Peter Ochs, and Michael Signer, "*Dabru Emet*: A Jewish Statement on Christians and Christianity" (National Jewish Scholars Project, 10 September 2000): "The humanly irreconcilable difference between Jews and Christians will not be settled until God redeems the entire world as promised in Scripture. Christians know and serve God through Jesus Christ and the Christian tradition. Jews know and serve God through Torah and the Jewish tradition. That difference will not be settled by one community insisting that it has interpreted Scripture more accurately than the other; nor by exercising political power over the other."

9. Cf. N. T. Wright, *Paul and the Faithfulness of God*, 1413. For some, naturally, it worked the other way around.

Here all may speak of the gospel of Moses, and of Torah as translating that gospel into praxis in such a way as to establish boundary markers for the people to whom it has been vouchsafed, the people of the Mosaic covenant. All may acknowledge that the gospel of Jesus establishes a new covenant or a new form of the covenant, with new boundary markers, especially the rite of baptism, and with this new covenant a new, dominical form of the law. So far, so good. But there is a volatile fault line over the relation between the gospel and law of Moses and the gospel and law of Jesus. For at least one prominent new perspective scholar, N. T. Wright, and those in his camp, the latter supersedes the former in a fashion that applies to Jews as well as Gentiles. For many others, however, the latter does not supersede but exists alongside the former, which retains its validity and force for Jews, even Christian Jews. As for Catholicism, among its shortcomings are these twin failures: its disinclination to acknowledge the binding nature of the Mosaic covenant for Jews and its tendency to produce false analogues to Judaism with which to oppress Gentiles.[10] From the vantage point of this camp, both the camp opposite and the Catholics sit too lightly to the Mosaic law, though the Catholics compound their error by introducing a law of their own; the great mistake both make is their refusal to repent of the sin of supersessionism.

To complicate matters further, some Catholics who are zealous for *Nostra Aetate* have joined the anti-supersessionist camp, whereas on my view they ought to have joined forces cautiously, in a very loose coalition, with the camp opposite. But to make good on this contention I must address what I regard (with Wright) as a largely misguided argument over supersessionism.

Hyper-Protestant Post-Supersessionism

I want to begin by disposing straightaway of the kind of anti-supersessionism we find on display, for example, in a recent article by Joel Willitts.[11] Willitts

10. Those of Wright's persuasion accuse it only of the second failure, viz., the tendency to produce sacerdotal and halakhic analogues.

11. "Jewish Fish (ΙΧΘΥΣ) in Post-Supersessionist Water: Messianic Judaism within a Post-Supersessionistic Paradigm," *HTS Teologiese Studies/Theological Studies* 72.4 (2016): a3331 (https://doi.org/10.4102/hts.v72i4.3331). This brief, poorly edited piece is no landmark in the literature but does provide a convenient account of an increasingly common point of view that began to appear some time ago as an attack on "fulfillment theology" and was afflicted from the outset with Ruetherite exaggeration (see Rosemary Reuther, *Faith and Fratricide: The Theological Roots of Anti-Semitism* [New York: Seabury, 1974]). Indeed, its early impetus seems to have come from Protestant Catholics such as Reuther and my late colleague, Gregory Baum. For a balanced view, cf. Gavin D'Costa, "What Does the Catholic Church Teach about Mission to the Jewish People?," *Theological Studies* 73 (2012): 590–613.

wants to read the New Testament in a way that "takes the Jewish nature of the apostolic documents seriously, and has as its goal the correction of the sin of supersessionism." The old, sinful exegete is the man or woman or ecclesiastical or scholarly body that has colluded in "the continued exclusion of Jewish ethnic identity in the church." This sinner has been exposed as such through a "growing recognition of multiculturalism and contextualisation on the one hand, and the recent presence of a movement within the body of Messiah of Jewish believers in Jesus on the other." In this light, it is now possible to say that "the church's established approach to reading Scripture that leads to the elimination of ethnic identity must be repudiated." It is time, he tells us, to respect the New Testament for what it is: "an ethnic document" that, received as such, "will promote the church's cultivation of real embodied ethnic particularity." This will "correct a *deep-seated sin* within the Christian tradition."[12] It will lead, as it were, to a new and improved catholicism, to "a universal ecclesiology that celebrates diversity, fights cultural hegemony and supports diverse ethnic expressions of faith in Jesus." Perhaps, though this remains unsaid, it will even help somehow to atone for the Holocaust.

From a Catholic perspective—let us not mince words—the hubris that characterizes heresy and heretics from Marcion onward still characterizes those who are trying desperately to disown the Marcionite element in their Protestant heritage, which element they have projected backward onto the entire history of Christianity and which they insist on seeing in it today. While "most denominations in the last half century have thoroughly denounced the supersessionism that has shaped the interpretation of every aspect of the NT" since the second century, suggests Willitts, it remains the case that teaching and preaching is governed by the law/gospel dialectic that Luther found in Scripture. That Luther found that dialectic *missing* between the second and sixteenth centuries is a point Willitts passes over, or rather a point he here contradicts. The real Reformation is taking place only now, in the new perspective discovery that the Scriptures were falsified by just such a dialectic from the early fathers right through to the Reformers and down to the present time. Hence repentance of supersessionism is still half-hearted or, at all events, confused.

In most cases today, both scholars and Christians alike choose one of two perspectives on the Mosaic Law. With the arrival of the Messiah, either (1) the Mosaic Torah has been superseded and annulled, or (2) it has been superseded but has become an indifferent issue of preference. The latter position refers to

12. Willitts, "Jewish Fish," 2 (emphasis his, hyphenation mine); in my use of this short document I will for the most part dispense with pagination and correct typos where necessary.

the continuing practice of Jewish law as a matter of *adiaphora*, meaning "things indifferent." So for interpreters of the NT, the ritual requirements of the Torah have been *either* annulled *or* rendered irrelevant and ultimately unnecessary. So to do them is either to put one's eternal destiny at risk or, if not spiritually disastrous, undesirable nevertheless, since such external things are no longer required for salvation.[13]

It is as if the Reformation only exacerbated an existing Catholic problem (law/gospel dualism, supersessionism) of which it must now be cured by a combination of multiculturalism or diversity theory and a penitentially post-supersessionist hermeneutic; that is, by reading the New Testament in a way that "*constructs* social space for Jewish ethnic identity within the *ekklēsia* of the Messiah Yeshua."[14]

Wright, who in these circles is much vilified, rightly remarks on the curious hybrid to be found here, a hybrid Willitts describes as "an approach, not a method." According to Wright, the genesis of this approach lies in the Enlightenment-inspired substitution of "sociological/religious categories for eschatological ones."[15] Reckoning with Jesus requires us to think rather in eschatological terms, a point to which we will return. Wright also finds it odd that anti-supersessionist zealots, as he regards them, should so readily take up with postmodernism, which is itself deeply supersessionist. Whether it is odd or quite predictable may be debated, but from a Catholic perspective, something more must be said. This whole approach is sub- and even anti-ecclesial. It tries to use Marcion to undo Marcion, Luther to undo Luther; that is, it tries to reconcile Scripture to Scripture either by eliding Scripture or by setting Scripture against tradition. It is also rather Pelagian, for it understands the Church and its spaces to be something we construct and may freely reconstruct. Moreover, it is viciously circular. It assumes what it is trying to prove, namely, that unless Jews participate in the Church without alteration of the manner of life determined by the Mosaic covenant, they are not really participating *as* Jews. At the same time—as Jewish critics such as David Novak have noticed—it takes away from non-Christian Jews the right to say what Jewishness is and even what Judaism is.

While I sympathize with these Jewish critics, I do not share their assumption that a Jew cannot, in any meaningful religious sense, be a Christian.

13. Ibid.
14. The emphasis again is his, and the postmodern (not to say Pelagian) social constructionism likewise.
15. Wright, *Paul and the Faithfulness of God*, 1413.

I do agree with them, however, that any Jew who practices Christianity is ipso facto altering radically the Mosaic manner of life and must necessarily dispense with certain key features of it, features essential to Judaism as it has evolved since the failure of the Bar Kokhba revolt. Willitts wants to read the New Testament as positing a Church that is one-part Jew and one-part Gentile, each living in a recognizably Jewish or Gentile way yet somehow doing so together. His question is how we can read it that way to good effect, such that what is posited (or taken as posited) actually becomes a reality. But we ought rather to ask whether the gospel of Jesus Christ embodied in the New Testament does indeed imply such a thing and what it did or would look like.[16]

Now, despite our incompatible ecclesiologies and hermeneutical commitments, we may agree that the gospel implies "the abiding presence of both circumcised and uncircumcised in the *ekklēsia*," in the sense that it was and remains a gospel for the Jew first and also for the Greek. That is the *pax Paulinica*. But what exactly is their relationship under the gospel, and how are they one new man in Christ? In Christ, what does it mean to be among the circumcised, and what does it matter? Elsewhere, Willitts sets out four key assumptions:

1. God's covenant relationship with the Jewish people (Israel) is present and future.
2. Israel has a distinctive role and priority in God's redemptive activity through Messiah Jesus.
3. By God's design and calling, there is a continuing distinction between Jew and Gentile in the church today.
4. For Jews, distinction takes shape fundamentally through Torah observance as an expression of covenant faithfulness to the God of Israel and the Messiah Jesus.[17]

16. Those of us who do not read the New Testament as Willitts ("Jewish Fish") insists we read it are fostering yet again "the erasure of Jewish ethnic presence within the church." This loaded objection rests on his purely circular argument. To his key question—"*How do we read the New Testament, so that the ekklēsia of* Yeshua, *the Messiah, remains a community of the circumcised and uncircumcised?*"—I answer that he has put the wrong question, which ought to be a nonutilitarian question about the gospel itself: a *what* question, not a *how* question. To his own answer—"a post-supersessionist framework is *necessary* if we are to recapture and sustain the 'truth of the Gospel'"—I respond that his question presupposes his answer, that it is not really a question at all but simply an assertion, and that the assertion is false.

17. Willitts, "Jewish Fish," 4; cited from Joel Willitts and David J. Rudolph, eds, *Introduction to Messianic Judaism: Its Ecclesial Context and Biblical Foundations* (Grand Rapids: Zondervan, 2013), 317, where Willitts is describing "an emerging post-supersessionist approach to the New Testament."

The first three are uncontroversial. The fourth, however, must be contested, together with Willitts's idiosyncratic, functionalist definitions of supersessionism and post-supersessionism. Supersessionism, he says, "refers to any interpretation of the NT that, intentionally or unintentionally, would lead to the eventual disappearance of the Jewish ethnos from within the church of Jesus the Messiah." Post-supersessionism, on the other hand, "is a unified 'sensibility,' an 'intuition' if you like, about the kind of conclusions that are satisfactorily valid historically, exegetically and theologically in the light of the historical circumstances and intentions of the NT canonical documents." This sensibility about "satisfactorily valid" conclusions involves a conviction that for almost two millennia the Church has failed to fulfill its divine mandate.[18] It has failed to be a proper "community of difference." Which is also to say: it has failed to proclaim and to live the gospel. And just there is the quite impossible hubris of which I spoke.

The Catholic, to be sure, will generally be sympathetic to the new perspective—understood as a Protestant enterprise, for the Catholic Church never approved of the old perspective. He will be quite unwilling, however, to look for some lost truth that long ago was replaced by a lie. A Catholic cannot accompany those who are on some putative quest for the historical Jesus, the historical Paul, or the historic early Church, much less for a freshly imagined "multicultural" Church, in which the trick is to find a special but not altogether exceptional place for Jews, alongside Palestinians and other identity groups. Catholics know (witness Raphael's misnamed *La Disputa*) that they coexist eucharistically with Jesus of Nazareth, with the apostles and prophets, and with the whole communion of saints, including Abraham, Moses, and David. Not to put too fine a point on it, they reject or ought to reject every attempt to reinvent the Church or its gospel. They do not believe in salvation by hermeneutics. Nor do they believe in salvation by escape to a remote past or to a more ideal future. And the reconciliation they seek is always a reconciliation in Jesus Christ, which permits of, but is never beholden to, any lesser kind of reconciliation. *Nostra Aetate* makes this clear. "The Church believes that by His cross Christ, Our Peace, reconciled Jews and Gentiles, making both one in Himself."

So a Catholic cannot abide this impenitent penitence, this hubristic hyper-Protestant post-supersessionism. But what is to be said of supersessionism itself? Mainly that it has, quite unnecessarily, become a bogeyman, from which a dispassionate review of the range of alternatives respecting the *berit hadasha*

18. See Willitts, "Jewish Fish," 3f.; a "satisfactorily" valid conclusion is, apparently, one that confirms one's intuitions.

will already rescue us. After that review—and after the selection of a perfectly reasonable and evangelically necessary form of supersessionism—we
will try to ask and answer questions about the proper expression of covenant
faithfulness for Jews within the Church of Jesus Christ. We will try, that is,
to say what the gospel does and does not require of them. This will be done
by thinking in eschatological terms.

Supersessionism: A Taxonomy

If anyone objects that there are already too many labels for supersessionism
and too many taxonomies, I will not disagree. Still, we need before us some
taxonomy, so here is mine. Like every other, it works both with covenants
and with covenant peoples, but it is governed by the former, not by the latter. It is a taxonomy of positions with respect to the *berit hadasha* before it
is a taxonomy of positions with respect to the people of God. The debate
about supersessionism is bedeviled by an unfortunate reversal of the proper
order here. If supersessionism is taken "to denote the belief that the church
has taken the place of the Jews as the elect people of God" and that the Jews
are therefore (qua Jews) no longer elect, the whole conversation gets off on
the wrong foot;[19] or rather, it doesn't really get off at all. For this of course
contradicts the fact that the gifts and calling of God are irrevocable, hence
it must be rejected. What makes a Jew a Jew? Being a physical descendent of
Abraham, called to walk according to Torah so as to inherit the promises made
to Abraham, Moses, and David. It follows that Jews, Christian or otherwise,
are called to walk according to Torah. Case closed. We will have, somehow,
to fit the gospel of the new or renewed covenant into that.

   But this is wrong. It is the covenant itself, and the gospel in its covenantal
dimensions, that must come first. Only then can we answer questions about
the people or peoples of God. And there is indeed not only a succession but
a supersession of covenant forms wherever there is a supersession of covenant representatives or mediators. The Abrahamic covenant comes to include

19. The quotation is from Bruce D. Marshall's "Christ and the Cultures: The Jewish People
and Christian Theology," in *The Cambridge Companion to Christian Doctrine*, ed. Colin Gunton
(Cambridge: Cambridge University Press, 1997), 82. Marshall, on my view, does get off on the
wrong foot, his faulty definition forcing him to seek a solution in a voluntary embrace of the
law as a kind of boundary marker distinguishing Jewish Christians as Jewish, while denying
the law's soteriological function. We will touch later on what he has to say in "Christ and Israel:
An Unresolved Problem in Catholic Theology," in *The Call of Abraham: Essays on the Election
of Israel in Honor of Jon D. Levenson*, ed. Gary Anderson and Joel Kaminsky, Christianity
and Judaism in Antiquity 19 (South Bend, IN: University of Notre Dame Press, 2013), 330–50.

within itself the Mosaic and the Davidic and, eventually, the eschatological *berit hadasha*, mediated by none other than the Messiah and effected by the direct action of the Holy Spirit. The latter is most certainly a supersession, for Jesus (as he himself pointed out) is greater than David and Solomon, greater than Moses and Aaron, greater than Abraham and even Melchizedek. Seen in this light, the attack on the very word "supersessionism" is in danger of becoming an attack not on anti-Semitism but on the gospel itself. According to the gospel—witness especially the wonderful Epistle to the Hebrews—the Messiah has come, Jesus has superseded all his forerunners and even the mediating angels through whom the covenant and its terms were communicated to his forerunners and, for that matter, to his mother. In these last days God has spoken to us through his own Son. Nothing, therefore, remains just as it was.

One starts there, surely, or one starts nowhere Christian. The task is to work out the implications, to distinguish between what follows and what does not follow from the gospel. The taxonomy offered below, its rather pedestrian labeling notwithstanding, will help us make that distinction. We will content ourselves with speaking of hard supersessionism, soft supersession, and anti-supersession. Only the middle category affords viable alternatives, and it is to the middle category that we shall have to attend afterward, though there is one increasingly popular version of anti-supersession that we will also have to consider more closely before we are done.

A. Hard Supersessionism

Here the old covenant, in all its forms, is regarded as abrogated by the new, as if all previous agreements were null and void. The consequences for the people of Israel can be viewed in at least two ways:

1. The abrogation or cancellation of the old covenant entirely disinherits them. They become like every other people in their ethnic and/or national form. That is, they are subject to divine providence but of no further relevance to human salvation. Their past belongs to salvation history, but their present and future do not. Even their past survives only as a kind of dividend that is re-invested in the Church.[20]

---

20. There is a place here for what Kendall Soulen calls "economic" supersessionism, if what goes under that label is the view that the people of Israel, as a covenant people, belong strictly to a transient stage in the history of redemption; not by reason of being sinful but because their proper role "is to prepare for salvation in its spiritual and universal form" (*The God of Israel and Christian Theology* [Minneapolis: Fortress, 1996], 29). Perhaps the classic modern expression of that transiency can be found in Schleiermacher's Fifth Speech; cf. *The Christian Faith*, §12. There is however a fundamental difference between Schleiermacher's neo-Marcionite supersessionism

2. The abrogation does not merely disinherit the people of Israel but leaves them to a fate of perpetual suffering as a sign of human reprobation. In this form, hard or "punitive" supersessionism regards the people of the old covenant as always worthy of both divine and human disapprobation because of their rejection of the Messiah and their stubborn refusal to recognize or participate in the new covenant.

Nota bene: In neither version has this ever been authentic Church teaching.[21] It has, however, crept into the thinking of influential Christians, whose errors have been used to sanction violence against Jews. Moreover, in its harsher, punitive form it has secular analogues in key modern figures such as Lessing

---

and the anti-Marcionite supersessionism of Irenaeus, which Soulen treats at length in describing the origin of the economic approach. What Irenaeus says about God as a wise architect (*Haer.* 4.14.2), Schleiermacher can also say in his way. But whereas the latter strips away all reference to political and priestly Israel like the husk from the kernel, Irenaeus is constantly thinking about the value of everything God does in and with Israel in divine preparation for the Church (which he regards as a "reciprocal rejoicing" between the saints of the old and new covenants, *Haer.* 4.7.1) and in the Church in preparation for the world to come. What Soulen calls "a flaw in the heart of the crystal"—"a vision of carnal Israel's obsolescence after Christ" and hence also, however ironically, the relative unimportance of the old covenant Scriptures—is rather a flaw in Soulen's reading of Irenaeus. Nothing could be further from the truth than that "the Israelite dimension of Christian faith" and the Scriptures that bear witness to it are "rendered largely irrelevant for shaping conclusions about how God's consummating and redemptive purposes engage creation in universal and enduring ways" (Soulen, *God of Israel*, 48). On the contrary, *everything* is relevant, as one of the key passages Soulen points to, *Haer.* 4.21, demonstrates. Its contrast between "Jacob" and "Esau" is a contrast not primarily between Israel and the Church but between the believing and the unbelieving, between those in every age who inherit and those who do not inherit: "Various coloured sheep were allotted to this Jacob as his wages; and the wages of Christ are human beings, who from various and diverse nations come together into one cohort of faith" (4.21.3). Note that at *Haer.* 5.35, he speaks (connecting Gal. 4:26 with Isa. 49:16) of "the Jerusalem that is from above," the Jerusalem that is "the mother of us all," as the very same Jerusalem that has been delineated by nails on the hands of God in the crucified Christ. Irenaeus actually belongs, in the present taxonomy, at B.1. See further my *Ascension and Ecclesia* (Grand Rapids: Eerdmans, 1999), 43–85.

21. *Intret, intret in patriarcharum familiam gentium plenitudo* . . . "May the fullness of the gentiles enter into the family of the patriarchs, and may the sons of the promise receive the blessing in the seed of Abraham which his sons by the flesh renounce" (Leo I, Sermon 32). Even as Anselm would later argue that redeemed humans more than make up for the loss of fallen angels, so Leo suggests here that the redeemed from the nations more than compensate for the loss of unbelieving Jews. Erik Peterson (*Theological Tractates*, 201n21; *quod vide* for both texts) adds this prayer from the Gelasian Sacramentary: "Grant that the fullness of the whole world may cross over to the sons of Abraham and to the dignity of Israel." But of course the Mass already repudiates the calumny that the Catholic Church teaches a "replacement" theology that amounts to the substitution of one people for another. See, for example, the prayers after the second, third, and fourth readings of the Easter Vigil. "Almighty ever-living God, surpass, for the honor of your name, what you pledged to the Patriarchs by reason of their faith, and through sacred adoption increase the children of your promise."

and Kant and Hegel, whose subordination of the particular to the universal provided philosophical justification for attacks on the unassimilatable Jew, fanning the flames that would eventually produce the Aryan idolatry that led to the Holocaust. Hard supersessionism must indeed be rejected as incompatible with Scripture and tradition and as inimical to all that is right and just.

B. Soft Supersessionism

Soft supersessionism regards the new covenant (ברית חדשה) as a continuation of the old, if in thoroughgoing transformation.[22] The old is understood first of all as the Abrahamic covenant, which for a time took on the Mosaic form but has now been fulfilled messianically. Here too the consequences can be viewed in at least two ways:

1. Because this fulfillment and transformation is eschatological, inaugurating but not yet fully delivering the kingdom of God, the Mosaic form, though superseded, does not disappear from history completely, but continues (sans temple and cult) to shape the life of Jews who are not baptized, preserving them as a people until they are baptized. It does not further shape the life of baptized Jews, however, except in the same way that it shapes the life of baptized Gentiles; viz., by virtue of that which it supplies for messianic fulfillment and transformation.[23]

2. Because God wills to preserve the Jewish people as such, and because Jewish Christians continue to belong to that people—to Israel according to the flesh as well as to Israel according to the Spirit—the Mosaic form of the covenant should continue to shape even baptized Jews in a manner distinct from baptized Gentiles, albeit not in any fashion that effectively divides them from the latter.[24]

22. "New" (חדש) means also "renewed," though the renewal effected by Christ's exodus is a much more dramatic and far-reaching renewal than that effected in the Mosaic exodus. Cf. Irenaeus, *Haer.* 4.34.1.

23. It supplies much: the moral law is the basis for the law of liberty; the Mosaic liturgical calendar for the Christian; various ceremonial or purity laws for baptism and other sacraments or sacramentals; the juridical laws for much canon and even civil law; the Old Testament for the New, the Jewish lectionary for the Christian, the synagogue service for Christian gatherings. That baptized Jews have an advantage in the appropriation of this foundation is certainly true, and that they may appropriate it in ways their Gentile brethren do not is allowed. Which is to say, their religious heritage may shape them in unique ways—through an extended set of sacramentals, for example—but it does not shape them salvifically, and they can lay claim to no unique sacraments. For all has been taken up and transformed by Christ and is available equally to Jew and Gentile.

24. Neither requires circumcision, though both require baptism. The Jew, however, requires circumcision for the purpose of identification as a Jew. Mutatis mutandis, the same

Nota bene: While many who fit this category (particularly B.2) reject the supersessionist label, what they are really rejecting is hard supersessionism. Again, it is simply not possible within Christian orthodoxy to deny that the old covenant is taken up and transformed by the new;[25] and outside Christian orthodoxy it is possible only to be a hard supersessionist or an anti-supersessionist. Since the latter also comes in different forms, it will be useful to include it in our taxonomy.

C. Anti-Supersessionism

Anti-supersessionism regards the old and new covenants as coexistent in one of the following ways:

1. The new covenant is a more perfect form of the old covenant, an alteration or mutation that is operative within it, not alongside it or in place of it. The old covenant remains in force; the "new" covenant simply redirects it from within to the fulfillment accomplished by Jesus. On the basis of the achievements of Jesus, it is a covenant in which Gentiles may now participate, as Gentiles, in a new way, with their own distinct covenantal arrangements.

2. The new covenant is complementary to the old rather than an alteration of the old. There are two parallel covenants, in other words, one applying to Jews who do not believe in Jesus and one applying to anyone, Jew or Gentile, who does believe in Jesus. The believing Jew participates in both, while the believing Gentile participates in the latter only. As regards the believing Jew, there are two possibilities: either (a) he must live according to Torah and may live according to

---

can be said of other markers of Jewish identity: they show respect for the old covenant and for membership in the people whose covenant it was and, outside of Christ, still is; but inside Christ they are no longer regarded even as boundary markers, much less as having salvific import, for all that is already contained in baptism. They may distinguish, but they do not separate. Those whose view belongs here, under B.2, do not disagree fundamentally with those whose view belongs under B.1; they do allow a greater role for the Jewish Christian qua Jewish.

25. *Lumen Gentium* 9 (DEC 2:855) says that Christ called together "from Jews and gentiles a people which would be bound together in unity not according to the flesh but in the Spirit, and which would be the new people of God" (*ex Iudaeis ac gentibus plebem vocans, quae non secundum carnem sed in Spiritu ad unitatem coalesceret, essetque novus populus Dei*); that all that took place in the choosing and sanctifying of the people of Israel through the old covenant took place "as a preparation and a figure of that new and perfect covenant which was to be struck with Christ." If this remains a form of what Soulen calls "economic" supersessionism, so be it; in this form, it is simply Christian orthodoxy.

Jewish custom, or (b) he ought to live according to both Torah and Jewish custom.[26]

3. There is no new covenant, at least not for Jews, of the kind that Christians imagine. The Christian "new covenant" is, at its best, a complementary Gentile way of talking about and exercising faith in the God of Israel. From a Jewish perspective, it is a defective form of faith in God, yet one providentially employed by God. It may expect divine correction at the end of the age, as well as its own appropriate reward. What the blessing of the nations will look like when the Messiah comes is a matter of speculation.[27]

Nota bene: The first two options are symbiotic, each implying the other. C.1 start from the side of the Jews, C.2 from the side of the Gentiles. Both are regarded by the third with suspicion, for both are subversive of Judaism. The first tries to co-opt it for Jesus and the second insists at least that there is a proper Jewish form of Christianity—that Jews who follow Jesus are still, in their own way, legitimately Jewish.[28]

26. Both possibilities, and the second especially, violate B.2's exception clause by inviting or instructing baptized Jews to live in a fashion incompatible with Christianity. C.2, in positing "two 'separate but equal' parallel paths to salvation," is referred to by Schoeman (*Salvation Is from the Jews*, 352f.) as "a new and perhaps even more pernicious error" than hard supersessionism.

27. Thus David Novak, for one, though he thinks Christians, to be consistent, must themselves be soft supersessionists, not anti-supersessionists. Christians who suppose the new covenant to be a strictly Gentile affair are too obviously Marcionite to merit serious consideration by either Jews or Christians. As for Jews who reject all Christian talk of a new covenant as ipso facto anti-Semitic and inimical to Judaism, their view also is much too extreme.

28. Novak's own taxonomy may now be compared with mine. He also begins with covenants rather than with peoples, proposing three basic options: The new covenant is an extension of the old (a Jewish view which in the spirit of Jeremiah looks to the future), an addition to the old (a view such as early Jewish Christians may have held), or a replacement for the old (the later Christian view). The latter two are distinct forms of Christian supersessionism, one being soft and the other hard. The hard asserts that "the old covenant is dead: the Jews by their sins, most prominently of rejecting Jesus as the Messiah, have forfeited any covenantal status." The soft "does not assert that God terminated the covenant of Exodus-Sinai with the Jewish people. Rather, it asserts that Jesus came to fulfill the promise of the old covenant, first for those Jews already initiated into the covenant, who then accepted his messiahhood as that covenant's fulfillment. And, it asserts that Jesus came to both initiate and fulfill the promise of the covenant for those Gentiles whose sole connection to the covenant is through him. Hence, in this kind of supersessionism, those Jews who do not accept Jesus' messiahhood are still part of the covenant in the sense of 'what God has put together let no man put asunder'" ("The Covenant in Rabbinic Thought," in *Two Faiths, One Covenant?*, ed. E. Korn and J. Pawlikowski [Lanham, MD: Rowman & Littlefield, 2004], 66). Such differences as there are between these taxonomies can be put down to the fact that his, unlike mine, is directed toward relations between Christians and Jews, on which see also his "Edith Stein, Apostate Saint," *First Things* (October 1999): 15–17; cf. Matthew Levering, *Jewish-Christian Dialogue and the Life of Wisdom* (London: Continuum, 2010).

Now, to be sure, all these categories are somewhat fluid. It is not unusual to encounter those who attempt a bit of mixing and matching.[29] Invariably, however, they make mistakes in doing so, mistakes we shall try to avoid when observing the moments of truth that may be found even in the first or the third. We have already said that the first and the third (A and C.1–2) will not do, precisely because they are eschatologically flawed. That is why they try to talk about peoples first and covenants second, as if there were a people, in the biblical sense, without a covenant! That is why they turn out to be injurious in practice and debilitating for the Church's mission, the one tending quite openly to anti-Semitism (the gospel is not for the Jew at all, since the Jew is not worthy of it) and the other, ironically, to a kind of closet anti-Semitism (the gospel is for the Jew last, not first, if indeed the Jew can benefit from it). And how are they eschatologically flawed? By failing to reckon with the eucharistic tension introduced into the *saeculum* by the ascension of Jesus; by trying instead to interpret salvation history, the history of the Abrahamic covenant, in strictly linear terms—terms that treat Israel, as the community of the old covenant, and the Church, as the community of the new, as if they were essentially the same sort of thing.[30] Hence they do not know what to say

29. This may be done with more or less sophistication—more, in the case of Karl Barth, who regards the people of Israel as continuing to serve divine purposes, yet called to join the Church and believe in its Christ, revealing within the Church both the depth of human need and the greatness of divine mercy. Whether they like it or not, this calling will be fulfilled, if much more happily inside the Church than outside it (see *CD* 2.2:259ff.). But what does it mean to fulfill it inside the Church, precisely as Jews? Barth is less than clear, and a case can be made for placing him in either B.1 or B.2. Yet such clarity as he does provide shows traces of hard supersessionism in that the role he assigns Jews, whether inside or outside, is a witness first of all to the divine "no," even if the divine "no" itself is never anything but a witness to the divine "yes" in Jesus Christ.

30. This seems to affect adversely Marshall's analysis in "Christ and Israel," at 340ff. In attempting to resolve the problem generated by the fact that God both wills the people of Israel to persist until the end and wills all people to adhere to Christ—otherwise put, that God seems both to will and not to will the practice of Judaism—he contrasts a "thoroughly eschatological approach" with a more "chastened or tempered" one. The former, without positing "two discreet saving covenants," reserves the salvation of the Jews to the end of the age and rules out any present mission to Jews; but this seems both to exclude them from the benefits of Christ and his sacraments and to render their Torah observance paradoxical, if not sinful—what once was good is no longer good, though it remains necessary for them. The latter focuses on their halakhic anticipation of the Messiah, and hence on their implicit unity with the Church (per *CCC* 840), which already enjoys eucharistic unity with him. This Marshall thinks better, though it requires exceptionalism: for the Jewish people, God does not intend direct participation in the sacramental economy; and this, he acknowledges, has its own apparent incoherence. He does not remark on the difficulty posed by Jews who convert, nor does he return to Paul's claim that the gospel is for the Jew first. What I still miss here is a proper reckoning with the fact that the Church, precisely as the eucharistic community, does not exist in the *saeculum* in a merely secular fashion, as Israel does. What he calls "thoroughly eschatological" I call merely futuristic.

about the new covenant in Christ except that it either abrogates the old entirely or reduplicates it for Gentiles. If they try to say something more sophisticated, or at all events more biblical, acknowledging that the new covenant actually brings Jew and Gentile together, they are compelled to present this togetherness simply as a kind of getting along for Christ's sake. And what does this do but leave the baptized Jew with a double or even a triple burden: fulfilling Torah, living according to Jewish customs, and being a model Christian as well, engaged in the liturgical, sacramental, canonical, social, and evangelical life of the (largely Gentile) Church?

Under the second rubric we cannot entirely evade this last difficulty, of course, which appears in B.2. If we could, it would not be necessary to continue. But soft supersessionism, whether its adherents realize it or not, puts the problem in a very different light. It is "soft" just because it relativizes arrangements belonging to this world to arrangements belonging to the world to come. Which means that it is both soft and hard at the same time. While it recognizes that the distinction between Jew and Gentile does not disappear during the *saeculum*, even in the Church, it not only alters the application of that distinction (as in the case of male and female, etc.) but it also refuses to project it (unlike the distinction between male and female) back into the order of creation or forward into the eschaton. About all of this there is more to say. But why *doesn't* the distinction disappear? Let us begin there.

It is relatively easy to see (only Manichaeans and their modern SOGI or LGBTQ counterparts don't) that the distinction between man and woman is still required in the present age, for both social and sacramental purposes. That distinction carries over even into the new creation, though marriage and reproduction and the domestic family do not.[31] But the Jew/Gentile distinction does not belong to the *ordo creationis* but to the *ordo salutis*. And hasn't its peculiar soteriological purpose already been served? In the renewed image-bearing humanity produced by Jesus and the Spirit, is it not redundant? Yes and no. Yes, because when the Christ has emerged from the womb of Israel and led the people of God in their new exodus safely to the kingdom of God, the difference between a clean and an unclean people is not a distinction between Jew and Gentile but between those who are in Christ and those who

---

31. See Douglas Farrow, *Nation of Bastards: Essays on the End of Marriage* (Toronto: BPS Books, 2007), 69ff. The exclusion of "male and female" from the list given in Col. 3:11, by the way, is likely deliberate. Though the immediate concern is with obligation to the moral law, which would suggest inclusion rather than exclusion—as in Gal. 3:28, where, conversely, Paul's concern is with liberty from the custodianship of the ceremonial law—the argument of the Colossians passage is focused on the new creation. And, *pace* Origen and Gregory of Nyssa, in the new creation there will be male and female, though there will not, in quite the same sense, be Greek and Jew.

are not. No, for two reasons. First, because one enters the kingdom of God as oneself, not as another. Jesus himself remains "the lion of the tribe of Judah, the root of David" and does not become some nondescript, universal man. Likewise with us, mutatis mutandis; when we are transformed and perfected and given a new name, we remain the subject of that transformation (Rev. 2:17). Do we live now as creatures of particular places, times, ethnicities, gifts, vocations, and experiences? Certainly, and these "accidents" of our history matter. Some indeed are more than accidents; they are constitutive of our being. So things will be very different in the kingdom of God, but not altogether different. There will be continuity as well as discontinuity, and this applies to ethnicity as to sex, for ethnicity has become implicated in sex.[32] Second, and more importantly, the distinction in question is by no means redundant in the present eucharistic life of the Church, for it is the offering of Jew and Gentile together that witnesses to the world that God in Christ has redeemed the human race in fulfillment of his promises to Abraham, which is not evidently the case either if they must worship separately or if, in their united worship, there is no room for the Jew qua Jew and the Gentile qua Gentile.

It is just here that B.2 seems to commend itself over B.1, so long as we do not understand B.2 as resorting, like C.2, to parallel covenants. To say that the Mosaic form of the covenant should continue to shape even baptized Jews in a manner distinct from baptized Gentiles, albeit not in any fashion that effectively divides them from the latter, is not to say that circumcision, Sabbath keeping, food laws, etc. retain their function as boundary markers for the people of God. They do not. Baptism and the Eucharist, celebrated in communion with the whole Church, provide the new boundary markers, as well as the very means of saving grace. Yet there are Jews within those new boundary markers—Jews before Gentiles—and they remain Jews. They are circumcised, and their children after them are circumcised, no longer as the sign of their salvation but as the sign of their belonging to the brethren of Jesus according to the flesh. That "we regard no one from a human point of view," not even Jesus, in whom all are a new creation, does not, in Paul's mind, negate the benefits of being kinsmen to Christ according to the flesh. Paul did not, as his enemies charged, "teach all the Jews who are among the Gentiles to forsake Moses, telling them not to circumcise their children or

---

32. "I myself am an Israelite, a descendent of Abraham, a member of the tribe of Benjamin," says Paul (Rom. 11:1). This distinction can be laid aside (Phil. 3:3ff.; cf. Gal. 6:15f.), but it is certainly not a defect to be removed. On the other hand, it is not an inalienable feature of creation, like being male or female. God did not make man Jew and Gentile, though he did make from one man every nation of men (Acts 17:26).

observe the customs."[33] He did, however, tell them that they were not under the law, that no one is saved by the works of the law, that circumcision in itself is no longer a sign of salvation. None of that negates the glory that belongs to those to whom the law and the promises were first given. This glory may be laid aside, counted but loss, for Christ's sake; but glory it is, the glory of the natural branches on the tree of life. And it is right and proper, though not strictly necessary, that the natural branches should be identified as such, because it reminds their Gentile brethren that there is a definite root and distinct trunk to that tree, apart from which no branch, natural or grafted, can hope to flourish or even to survive.

There is a problem here, to be sure. The topic of circumcision, curiously, has had a prominent place in magisterial discourse only in documents directed at Gentiles, but these *exclude* it from acceptable Christian practice, together with other rituals "whose main function was to foreshadow the coming Messiah," such as the sacrifice of animals or the celebration of Passover.[34] What

---

33. 2 Cor. 5:16; Acts 21:21; cf. Rom. 9:1–5. We cannot overlook Acts 21, which tells of "many thousands" of Jews in Jerusalem who had believed and who were "all zealous for the law," though we do not know in what relation they stood either to the Christian elders or to those who were provoked by Paul's enemies to riot in the temple. We cannot overlook the fact that the elders advised Paul to purify himself in a public way so that all would know that there was nothing to the rumor that he taught his converts to forsake Moses. We must acknowledge that they asked Paul to make clear that he himself was "walking in step, observing the law" (στοιχεῖς καὶ αὐτὸς τὸν νόμον φυλάσσων). Does this passage falsify what we are trying to say? The one really striking thing in Paul's several attempts at self-defense in the following chapters against the charge that he was "teaching men everywhere against the people and the law and this place" is that, while vigorously denying the charge, he makes no case that he himself is Torah observant. (We may leave aside that he *had* vigorously to deny it, because it was put before Felix in a way that framed him for *seditio*; see C. Kavin Rowe, *World Upside Down: Reading Acts in the Graeco-Roman Age* [Oxford: Oxford University Press, 2009], 71ff.). Paul claims only that he worships "the God of our fathers," that he believes "everything laid down by the law or written in the prophets," that he came "to bring to my nation alms and offerings," that he has shown respect for the temple, that the real point of dispute is "the resurrection of the dead," that he had seen Jesus and been commissioned by Jesus (Acts 24:10–21)—there is nothing about being himself under the law or obligated to the law and observant of the law since his encounter with Jesus. This cannot be an accident. That there were in Jerusalem many who, despite believing in Jesus, remained zealous for the law is not to be doubted. That Paul, who always took pains "to have a clear conscience toward God and toward men," had accommodated them with the same love that he had accommodated, or tried to accommodate, the synagogues of Asia Minor is not to be doubted either. But that he regarded himself as under the law—*that* cannot be made to accommodate either his reputation or his letters. It cannot account for the circumcision of Timothy, which was performed, not out of zeal for the law, but "because of the Jews" (16:3), that is, because of possible scandal in the synagogues Paul meant to visit before returning to Jerusalem (cf. Wright, *Paul and the Faithfulness of God*, 1434ff., esp. n. 113). And it cannot account for what he says afterward: "I bear them witness that they have a zeal for God, but it is not enlightened" (Rom. 10:2).

34. Benedict XIV, *EQP* 63. In *Messianic Kingdom of Israel*, 236f., Lawrence Feingold observes that the ceremonial law aims inter alia at separating Israel from the nations and that this

are we to say to this, beyond registering the fact that what *Cantate Domino* and *Ex quo primum* forbid is in more recent times permitted, both for natural reasons and to Jewish Catholics for what amount to religious reasons?[35] Shall we try to justify it on the basis that everyone is finally clear that it can be done, and is being done, "with the intention not of obeying the precepts of the old law, which has now been abrogated, but of respecting the new law of the Church"?[36] But that is hardly the case! We must rather reckon, I think, with these two facts: The documents in question did have Gentile practices in view primarily; though their logic certainly applies to Jews, it is worked out in a context in which Christian Jews are almost out of mind. And when they return to mind—as they do today, thanks be to God—they require of the Church a new and different awareness of their needs, which have changed, as have those of Gentiles. It is no longer a matter of trying to "remove all occasion of disagreement between Jewish and Gentile converts to Christ," neither is it a matter of instructing Jewish converts in the spiritual

---

separation, unlike moral separation, "is no longer fitting." The moral, the ceremonial, and the judicial law have all been taken up and in their different ways fulfilled by Christ, such that the latter two "are no longer in force," having been replaced by the liturgy and laws of the new covenant. He appeals first to *Mystici Corporis* 29f., where Pius XII teaches that the regimes of the old and new covenants were simultaneously operative in Christ until the transfer from the one to the other was completed in his passion. Feingold then goes back behind *Mystici* to *EQP*, arguing that this does not mean that it is unlawful to make use of the ceremonial precepts of Torah "where there is some utility in their observance" (238). Benedict, he suggests, saw at least some of the prohibitions of *Cantate Domino* (Eugene IV's Bull of Union with the Copts during the Council of Florence) as a prudential measure, much as *Cantate* itself saw the Council of Jerusalem as including prudential measures (cf. *EQP* 61). Benedict himself is clear that the Church has power to refuse permission to make use of the ceremonial precepts of the old covenant and the power also to grant permission, "for just and serious reasons," where intentions and circumstances have changed (§63; cf. 64, 67, 74). Now it is noteworthy, as intimated above, that *Cantate* is aimed primarily at Coptic, not Jewish, practices and that in *EQP* Benedict is addressing Greek bishops about their own local practices (which did not include circumcision). Moreover, both documents are recounting and applying the faith of the Church, not defining it, so it should not be supposed that they provide full and binding answers to the questions with which we are here concerned. But both do indeed exclude circumcision—*pace* Feingold, *Mystery of Israel and the Church*, 238n32—just as both make it clear that it cannot ever be a matter of treating as binding "the precepts of the old Law, which as everybody knows have been revoked by the coming of Christ" (*EQP* 59). Christians cannot act as if "the observance of legal ceremonies of the old law was being added to or retained alongside the new law and the gospel" (§60). Circumcision, presumably, is regarded as too difficult to isolate from that implication.

35. Permitted in practice rather than in theory. The CCC mentions circumcision only twice (§§527, 1150), as a prefiguration of baptism, and does not speak to the matter at all; neither does canon law.

36. A positive restatement of the principle contained in *EQP* 60 is provided at §67 (cf. 70): "Do everything with the intention not of obeying the precepts of the old Law, which has now been abrogated, but of respecting the new Law of the Church or canonical custom made strong by long and unbroken observance."

freedom of the religion of the new covenant.[37] Quite the reverse. It is a matter
of the Gentile learning again, in this neo-Marcionite and all too gnostic age
of ours, to respect the earthiness of his salvation and to embrace the Jew as
Jew; and of the Jew learning once again how to be both Jew and Christian,
while glorying as never before in the very freedom of which Paul spoke and
which he himself modeled.

Circumcision is one thing, however, and observing the whole ceremonial
law—or rather what remains of it after the demise of the temple—is another,
not to mention the dictates of rabbinic law. Sacrifice is no issue. Sacrifice
cannot be an issue, except for those who suppose that the principle of abrogation can be altogether abrogated. There is now but one sacrifice, Jesus,
and there is but one way of participating in that sacrifice, the Eucharist.[38]
But what is to be said of those markers that involve neither sacrifice nor a
sign in the body but rather a form of life? The first thing to be said here is
that the elder brethren—who, even before their Champion at last appeared,
had borne the burden and known the joy of wrestling with God, whatever
their weaknesses and failures as exposed by Torah and confessed through its
penitential provisions—have inherited in Torah, and developed from Torah,
patterns of life and prayer that testify powerfully to the goodness of God
and to the divine purposes for man. Sabbath keeping is a case in point; or,
rather, it is *the* case in point, since it is specified in the Ten Commandments
and belongs indeed to the first table of the moral law. Whatever can be said
of Shabbat can also be said, with still greater force, of what belongs only to
the ceremonial or juridical law.

Now, of Shabbat two things must be said: First, it has not been abrogated
but is being fulfilled by the ascended Christ in the new creation. Second, it

37. See *EQP* 61. "The first consideration," says Benedict, "is that the ceremonies of the Mosaic
Law were abrogated by the coming of Christ and that they can no longer be observed without
sin after the promulgation of the Gospel." If allowances were made in the first century or so
for certain ceremonial law-related demands on the Gentiles—notice that he does not speak of
what was still permitted or even expected of Jews in that regard—all was for the sake of peace
in the Church during a period of instruction. "And since this reason has long since vanished, its
consequence should also be said to have vanished." So also *Cantate:* "when the Christian religion
is so propagated that no carnal Jew appears in it, but all passing over to the Church, join in the
same rites and ceremonies of the Gospel, believing 'all things clean to the clean,' with the ending
of the cause for this apostolic prohibition, the effect also ended."

38. Were the Dome of the Rock miraculously to disappear and a new temple to be built,
no Christian could participate, without mortal sin, in an attempt to revive, in the form of sin
offerings, what Christ brought to an end. The temple is not like the land, something withdrawn
for a time and then returned. The land is the place in which *the* sacrifice has already been made
and in which the one who made it will again set his holy foot; the temple, on the other hand,
is no more, because it is no more needed. He himself is the temple.

appears in the *berit hadasha* in altered form as witness to its fulfillment; it appears as the Eucharist, celebrated especially on the first day of the week as the sacrament par excellence of the new creation. The Church's common eucharistic celebration cannot simply be added to Shabbat, since it *is* now Shabbat. Rather, the Jewish Christian family or community does well to celebrate the new Shabbat in a fashion that incorporates whatever can be incorporated of the old Shabbat, thus bearing witness to the rest of the Church, in their own way, what Shabbat is. The rest of the Church ought to receive that witness, reviving as far as possible the Shabbat sensibility that is so often lacking in a Gentile culture. But may a Christian Jew keep the old Shabbat as well, out of solidarity with non-Christian Jews? Certainly. Paul himself sometimes did. That is a missionary act, however, as it was for Paul. And it is necessary for the Christian to conduct it in a way that witnesses to the true Sabbath rest into which the gospel of Jesus Christ calls us and in the Eucharist already shares with us.[39]

As with the Sabbath, so with all the festivals prescribed in the Torah. The Christian liturgical year has been overlaid on the Jewish, taking up and transforming those festivals. It would not be appropriate, even were it permissible, for Jewish Christians to celebrate Pesach or Shavuot, say, as if they had not been superseded by the Triduum, Easter, and Pentecost celebrations of the Church; or to observe Yom Kippur in the fashion of non-Christian Jews, detached from its sacramental reconfiguration in penance/reconciliation and the Eucharist.[40] A Yom Kippur memorial, devised by and for Christian Jews, need

39. In Christ we are already participants in the new creation, as Justin tries to make clear in his account of the Eucharist: "Sunday is the day on which we all hold our common assembly, because it is the first day on which God, having wrought a change in the darkness and matter, made the world; and Jesus Christ our Saviour on the same day rose from the dead" (*First Apology* 67, ANF 1:186; cf. §61ff. and Rev. 1). To celebrate Shabbat with fellow Jews, as Paul regularly did in his mission to Jews, is one thing; to celebrate Shabbat as a Christian community another.

40. For all the refinements and modifications that have been made both to the theology and to the prudential judgments found in documents such as *Cantate*, this fact remains, just as the *extra nullus* remains: "The relationship between Jewish liturgy and Christian liturgy, but also their *differences in content*, are particularly evident in the great feasts of the liturgical year, such as Passover. Christians and Jews both celebrate the Passover. For Jews, it is the Passover of history, tending toward the future; for Christians, it is the Passover fulfilled in the death and Resurrection of Christ, though always in expectation of its definitive consummation" (CCC 1096, emphasis added). The same can be said of Yom Kippur, as a recent reflection by Rabbi Sacks ("The Challenge of Jewish Repentance," *Wall Street Journal*, 16–17 September 2017) may serve to remind us. "All we have to do," he says, "is to acknowledge our wrongs, apologize, make amends and resolve to behave better, and God forgives." While that sounds a great deal like the sacrament of reconciliation, there is no third party, no reconciler; there is no *mirifica commutatio* or wonderful exchange.

not run the risk of putting new wine into old wineskins, perhaps, so long as it pointed clear across the cycle of the liturgical year to Holy Week. This too could be a service, a pedagogical service, to the whole Church. But it is not possible to celebrate the old in the same way when the new has come. Nor is it necessary, even for Jewish Christians, to celebrate the old at all. For they have been released from the law by the Christ who fulfilled it on their behalf.

What, then, need be said of kosher and cleanliness laws? These, too, are fulfilled by Christ and returned to the Church in altered form. Anything can be eaten, by Jew or Gentile, but everything must be eaten with thanksgiving, with generosity, and with purity of heart. One may even eat food offered to idols, so long as one is not participating in idolatry or leading another to do so. There is still fasting and there is still feasting, but the conditions of fasting and feasting are changed. And above all there is the Eucharist, by means of which one is separated from the world but joined in table fellowship to fellow Christians, be they Jew or Gentile. So may the Christian Jew continue to keep kosher, if he wishes or if he finds it useful to the missionary enterprise? Yes and no. He cannot deny that God has declared all things clean, for the Jew as for the Gentile. But he can be a Jew to the Jews, for the sake of the Jews. He can fast, as he sees fit, from some food or all food. The Christian Jew, however, is no longer bound by kosher laws, even biblical kosher laws, for through baptism he has passed into union with Christ in the new creation. To say that he is bound is to deny him his liberty in Christ—unless perhaps it is to posit that Christ himself cannot eat what he wills, which is absurd.[41]

To say that the Mosaic form of the covenant should continue to shape even baptized Jews in a manner distinct from baptized Gentiles, albeit not in any fashion that effectively divides them from the latter, is not to say that the Christian Jew is like the non-Christian Jew except in the matter of table fellowship. That too is absurd; for it is this very matter of table fellowship, together with that of sacrifice, that demonstrates the Church's right of disposal over Mosaic

---

41. It will be replied that, while Jesus has passed from this world, we have not, but this is to miss the point that Jew and Gentile are united to one another and distinguished from the rest of humanity precisely because they are eucharistically situated with Christ in the heavenlies. The lengths to which anti-supersessionists will go in order to refuse this unity on are on display in David Rudolph's thesis that since Mark probably had a primarily Gentile audience in view, he quotes and glosses Jesus at 7:19 only to assure Gentiles that all foods are clean for *them*, not for Jews ("Jesus and the Food Laws," *Evangelical Quarterly* 74.4 [2002]: 291–311; cf. Gerald McDermott, *Israel Matters: Why Christian Must Think Differently about the People and the Land* [Grand Rapids: Brazos, 2017], 145n2). But Mark, we ought to recall, is constantly hinting that even the disciples are like the blind man of Bethsaida who saw men as trees walking (8:25). Their moment of clarity—a moment of clarity for all God's people—is given them by God when Peter declares, "You are the Christ" (8:29). And this is the Christ who makes all things clean.

law. It *is* to say that Jewish Christians, as those whose lives and communities have already been shaped by Torah, have not only the privilege but the duty to aid their Gentile brethren in grasping the way in which the *berit hadasha* takes up and transcends Torah. This they cannot do well either if they try to live the Torah as it was, thus effectively remaining aloof and sending mixed signals about the Torah's relevance to Gentile Christians, or if they simply become indistinguishable from Gentile Christians. It is also to say that Jewish Christians have not only the privilege but the duty to aid their non-Christian brethren to grasp how the gospel takes up and transcends Torah. This they cannot do well either, if they try to live the Torah as it was, merely adding Christian obligations to it rather than embracing the Christian liberty, or if they flaunt their Christian liberty in a way that makes a hearing from other Jews more difficult. But nothing makes it more difficult than presenting themselves as fully Torah observant when in fact they are not, should not be, and indeed cannot be.

One Body, Two Peoples?

To state plainly, in summary form, the position I am arguing: Jesus the Christ has renewed and refashioned the covenant between God and Israel, becoming "the pioneer and perfecter" of the faith and life of God's people. In doing so he has made room for Gentiles to be included qua Gentiles and for Jews and Gentiles to live together in a mutual life centered on the Eucharist. There is only one gospel, "to the Jew first and also to the Greek," only one new or renewed covenant for both, and only one Church comprising both.[42] All Jews are invited to and ought to receive that gospel, though where they do not yet grasp or receive it they remain bound by, and may remain aided by, the demands of the old covenant. Jews who do receive it and enter the Church are bound only by the demands of the new covenant, as are Gentiles. The distinction between Jew and Gentile is not thereby eliminated, any more than the distinction between man and woman is eliminated, though the relation between the two has fundamentally changed due to their common access to the grace of God. In this new relation Jews have the responsibility to teach messianic Gentiles how to appropriate the Old Testament and to show non-messianic Jews how to receive the New Testament. To this end, they may and (with the encouragement of the Church) ordinarily should maintain their identity as Jews by circumcision and by perpetuating inherited patterns of prayer and devotion and learning and living, insofar as these are conducive

42. "Abraham has *one* family, not two or more" (Wright, *Paul and the Faithfulness of God*, 1432; cf. Gal. 3; *Lumen Gentium* 9; *Nostra Aetate* 4).

to maturity and to effective mission through Christian refashioning, though never in such a way as to impinge on their common sacramental and liturgical life with Gentiles. It must always be clear, as Matthew Levering has argued, that the Jewishness of Jews is fulfilled via their sacramental union with Jesus, in whom the demands of Torah have already been met and reconfigured in the Spirit for the whole Church. If that is not clear, nothing is clear, except that fulfillment is being sought in something other or more than Jesus.

So: The Christian Jew is a Jew by virtue of being a physical descendent of Abraham, called to walk now according to the law of liberty in Jesus Christin and to live out of his inheritance in Christ of the promises made to Abraham, Moses, and David.[43] That he or she is thus a Jew in a Christian sense rather than in the common rabbinic sense must be granted. And what of Gentiles?

---

43. "Christian Jews and Gentiles now observe the Mosaic law by participating sacramentally in Christ's perfect obedience/enactment of the Torah on the Cross," argues Levering, leaning on Thomas's wonderful reply to the first objection at *ST* 3.47.2; that is, in "a Torah reconfigured around the Messiah" (Matthew Levering, "Aquinas and Supersessionism One More Time: A Response to Matthew A. Tapie's *Aquinas on Israel and the Church*," Pro Ecclesia 25.4 [2016]: 397n5, cf. 401f.). Participating sacramentally means participating also in the halakhic forms derived from Christ and the apostles. Levering insists, and I concur, that no Christian is bound to unreconfigured Torah or Jewish ritual and that those who incorporate elements of the latter cannot do so as an institutionally distinct body. He also insists, and again I concur, that Torah does not become obsolete, or the call to walk in it obsolete, both because it *is* reconfigured and one may walk in it through sacramental participation in the one body of Christ and because non-Christian Jews are still called to walk in it according to its old configuration on their way to walking in it in the new. I differ from Levering, however, at the point where he, like Marshall, worries that it is difficult to reconcile the idea "that the Jewish religion has become a mode of infidelity," which (Thomas is right) it has wherever it is set over against Christ and his Church, with "commitment to the permanence of Israel's election" (ibid., 411n34). It is precisely the "hardening in part" that holds these together, for it is, after all, only in part and only for a time (Rom. 10:1f.; 11:1ff.). And what is the hardening if not the stern mercy of God, who chooses, who calls, who equips with Torah, who restores to the path of Torah, but who for now does not grant the grace to see and believe, to grasp in all the Scriptures the things concerning his Christ? One ought to think here of a very long Emmaus road, of a journey that lasts for the afternoon of an age rather than of a day. Is it really so difficult to distinguish between those who, when the gospel was first preached, were slow to grasp its implications, even Peter himself lagging behind Paul; and those who refused to believe at all, becoming the resolute enemies of Peter and Paul, as of Jesus himself; and those who, when in later centuries they encountered the gospel in its Gentile milieu, encrusted as it often was with confusion or cruelty and inured as they were to the harsh sound of its call, simply knew not how to believe in Jesus yet continued against all the odds to cling to Torah? This *clinging* belongs to their election, the *knowing not how* to their hardening. And the hardening was not and is not unjust, given the defiant unbelief of those whom Jesus warned, "I tell you, the kingdom of God will be taken away from you and given to a nation producing the fruits of it" (Matt. 21:43). Yet if in that nation or ἔθνος "he is a Jew who is one inwardly," and if among the sons of Israel he is not necessarily a Jew who is one outwardly (Rom. 2:25–29), still the gifts and calling of God are irrevocable (Rom. 11:28–32). Those who keep Torah, even in the old way, know that, and they know it by the stern and patient mercy of God. They too are called by God, through the law and the gospel, to discover Jesus Christ. Some do and some don't, but many shall.

Through baptism they also have been joined to the very same Christ and become members of the same covenantal community. In that community they find their fulfillment in just the same way, and the companionship of their Jewish brethren helps them to do so. For from many ἔθνη there is to be one holy Abrahamic λαός, as the Church's Scriptures, doctrine, and prayers testify.

> O God, whose ancient wonders
> remain undimmed in splendor even in our day—
> for what you once bestowed on a single people,
> freeing them from Pharaoh's persecution
> by the power of your right hand
> now you bring about as the salvation of the nations
> through the waters of rebirth—
> grant, we pray, that the whole world
> may become children of Abraham
> and inherit the dignity of Israel's birthright.[44]

Gentile and Jew, then, must labor together in the Church for the day when the Messiah will be known to all. Far from excluding the evangelization of Jews, this means renewed emphasis on "to the Jew first," which means also restoring Jews to a place of honor in the Church and, as far as possible without obscuring the lordship of Jesus over all things and all people, outside it. This, let it be added, entails recognizing their right to their historic homeland, to which God has restored them, though it does not entail particular political or prudential judgments about that homeland. It also includes cooperation to the greatest degree possible with Jews who desire to be faithful to the Mosaic covenant and who do not deliberately denigrate Jesus.[45] It does not include muting the witness to Jesus. It remains a form, an open and generous form, of soft supersessionism, of the sort respected (though not accepted) by the likes of Novak, that is, by those who understand that neither Jews nor Christians can bypass the question of messianic identity.[46]

Against this, however, is arrayed not only the hyper-Protestant anti-supersessionism dismissed earlier but certain more compelling versions of

---

44. Roman Missal (prayer after the third reading on Easter).

45. Cf. Mark 9:40. McDermott, in chap. 6 of *Israel Matters*, gets the balance about right as regards the nation.

46. Cf. CCC 840: "When one considers the future, God's People of the Old Covenant and the new People of God tend towards similar goals: expectation of the coming (or the return) of the Messiah. But one awaits the return of the Messiah who died and rose from the dead and is recognized as Lord and Son of God; the other awaits the coming of a Messiah, whose features remain hidden till the end of time; and the latter waiting is accompanied by the drama of not knowing or of misunderstanding Christ Jesus."

the position described at C.1 and C.2, whose objections and alternatives must now be faced. We shall tackle the most developed of these, and the one that comes closest to B.2, namely, that of the messianic rabbi, Mark Kinzer, who, though hardly less revolutionary, is much more careful and respectful in his engagement with Catholicism. It is his view (a variant of C.1) that we have in mind when we inquire about the possibility of positing one body but two peoples.

Kinzer, to his merit, recognizes that the question of supersessionism goes simultaneously to the heart of christology and of ecclesiology. He wants to see an ecclesiological revolution based on a properly Jewish view of the Messiah and on the primacy of the *ecclesia ex circumcisione*. The *ecclesia ex circumcisione* is the firstfruits of Israel as it enters upon its promised destiny, while the *ecclesia ex gentibus* is the firstfruits of the Gentiles as they are joined to Israel and participate in its inheritance. In Kinzer's hands, this distinction, which is adopted from the Commission for Relations with the Jews,[47] is differently deployed, for it is governed by five principles:

1. the perpetual validity of God's covenant with the Jewish people;
2. the perpetual validity of the Jewish way of life rooted in the Torah as the enduring sign and instrument of that covenant;
3. the validity of Jewish religious tradition as the historical embodiment of the Jewish way of life rooted in the Torah;
4. the bilateral constitution of the *ekklesia*, consisting of distinct but united Jewish and Gentile expressions of Yeshua-faith;
5. the ecumenical imperative of the *ekklesia*, which entails bringing the redeemed nations of the world into solidarity with the people of Israel in anticipation of Israel's—and the world's—final redemption.

In this case, unlike that of Willitts, it is the first few principles that are problematic rather than the final one, though that too must be queried, together with other conclusions to which Kinzer is led, including rejection of "the traditional Christian missionary posture towards the Jewish people."[48]

---

47. "'The Gifts and the Calling of God are Irrevocable' (Rom 11:29): A Reflection on Theological Questions Pertaining to Catholic-Jewish Relations on the Occasion of the 50th Anniversary of *Nostra Aetate* (No.4)" (2015), §15: "In the early years of the Church, therefore, there were the so-called Jewish Christians and the Gentile Christians, the *ecclesia ex circumcisione* and the *ecclesia ex gentibus*, one Church originating from Judaism, the other from the Gentiles, who however together constituted the one and only Church of Jesus Christ."

48. See Mark S. Kinzer, *Postmissionary Messianic Judaism: Redefining Christian Engagement with the Jewish People* (Grand Rapids: Brazos, 2005), 264. At principle 5 he continues: "In short, we have argued for a *bilateral ecclesiology in solidarity with Israel that affirms Israel's covenant, Torah, and religious tradition.* According to this pattern, the Jewish ekklesia

The first three may be taken together. To speak of "the perpetual validity of God's covenant with the Jewish people" is not in itself problematic from a Catholic soft-supersessionist perspective, but what is meant by that? Kinzer indicates in principles 2 and 3 both that the Mosaic form of the covenant is perpetually valid and that the rabbinic translation of that form into a way of life suited for those who have lost land and temple is perpetually valid. That is a very different sense than we find either in the New Testament or in Church tradition, both of which understand the covenant itself to be fundamentally altered through the appearance of Christ, who possesses all things and places and who is himself the temple cornerstone. Jewish Christians, like Gentile Christians after them, are called to be built on this cornerstone into one living temple for the Spirit.[49] That temple or—to shift the metaphor, that city in which Christ is the temple—does not have a Jewish Quarter and several Gentile Quarters. It is a temple and a city from which the partition or dividing wall has been removed. Are Jewish Christians nonetheless called to treat "Jewish observance as a matter of covenant fidelity"?[50] No, they are called to live an observant Christian life as an act of covenant fidelity. They can and should do this as Jews, but not as Jews governed by a form of the covenant that has already been fulfilled and superseded, and certainly not as Jews lacking land or temple. Are they not rather to show fellow Jews what it means for the covenant to be fulfilled and superseded by messianic gifts and kingdom powers? And what are they to show Gentile brethren—that they should see themselves as "a multinational extension of the people of Israel"?[51] Again, no, at least not in Kinzer's sense. They are to show them what it is that the incarnate Son of God has fulfilled and transformed.

---

serves the wider Jewish community by constituting its eschatological firstfruits, sanctifying the whole and revealing the eschatological meaning of Jewish identity and destiny. It also serves the wider Jewish community by linking the redeemed of the nations to Israel's corporate life and spiritual heritage, thereby enabling Israel to fulfill its mission as a light to the nations" (ibid., italics original).

49. Eph. 2:11–22. One takes the point that "Judaism is not a religious artifact from biblical times but a dynamic way of life embodied in and transmitted by a living community" (ibid., 215). One is not thereby caught on the horns of a dilemma, however, such that one must affirm (without qualification?) either "the actual religious tradition of the Jewish people" or that "the divine purpose for the Jewish people . . . has been definitively thwarted."

50. Ibid., 16. This thesis is built (see 72f.) on what I regard, despite Kinzer's roll call of sympathetic exegetes, as an entirely specious syllogistic arrangement of Gal. 5:3 and 5:11 with 1 Cor. 7:17–20, an arrangement that turns Paul inside out.

51. The Church is "one reality subsisting in two forms" and consisting of "two corporate subcommunities, each with its own formal or informal governmental and communal structures." The Gentile form "is joined to an extended multinational commonwealth of Israel and can legitimately identify with Israel's history and destiny" without itself becoming Jewish (ibid., 152; cf. 15ff.).

The contrast thus drawn, we come to the fourth principle, about which more must be said. The Church is not bilaterally constituted, if by that is meant that there are two ecclesial traditions, each with its own "institutional framework in which that tradition can be developed and practically applied."[52] There is no salvific national or transnational reality made up of two distinct bodies. Nor is there a single body, the body of Christ, made up of two peoples who continue to be defined by distinct covenants. Rather, both are defined by the same covenant, which is how they come to be one body and one people. The Church is, however, bilaterally constituted insofar as it comprises Jew and Gentile, who are distinct in their approach to and appropriation of a common font and a common sacramental life. They are not distinct in that one is bound by two covenants and the other by just one. They are not distinct in that one has seven sacraments and the other twelve.[53] They are distinct rather in that one has been prepared by the older form of the covenant and the other has not—in that one has come into his own, and the other into what did not belong to him. The former has the advantage of the latter just there, which is what makes him instructive to the latter, like an elder brother. But he is certainly not instructive if he talks of the *ecclesia ex circumcisione* and the *ecclesia ex gentibus* as if they were two churches rather than one, living under different covenantal arrangements.[54]

Just here we arrive at the nub of the matter. To borrow a line from Athanasius, "From this one question the whole case on both sides may be determined, what is fitting to say," two covenants or one?[55] Are there, or are there not, multiple covenants (C.2) or covenantal arrangements (C.1) simultaneously in force in the Christian Church? The entire weight of Church tradition, from Paul to the present day, requires us to say that there are not. The covenant as renewed by Christ does not lie alongside the Mosaic covenant. It supersedes it. Anyone who is in Christ has a duty to acknowledge that. It supersedes it, not by adding faith in Jesus to faith in Moses but by inaugurating the kingdom of God and the world to come. Which does mean—since it pleases God to inaugurate his kingdom in a fashion that permits a missionary age, an age

---

52. Ibid., 24.

53. See Mark S. Kinzer, *Searching Her Own Mystery: Nostra Aetate, the Jewish People, and the Identity of the Church* (Eugene, OR: Wipf & Stock, 2015), 152ff. It is very difficult to square living under different covenantal arrangements with the positing of but one covenant. Two covenants or a bifurcated covenant: Is this not a distinction without a difference?

54. In fairness to Kinzer, the language of the "Reflection on Theological Questions Pertaining to Catholic-Jewish Relations" (quoted above at n. 47) leaves itself open to the notion that the *ecclesia ex* involves reduplication.

55. Athanasius, *Against the Arians* 1.3.9, NPNF[2] 4:311. Of course, the second form of the question reads "He was, or he was not?"

in which what is old, though it is always becoming obsolete, persists alongside what is new—that *outside* the Church the Mosaic covenant still bears
directly on Jews, albeit without having any force that is not christologically
precursive. (As Kinzer agrees, it never had any such force). To say, however,
that *inside* the Church it binds Jewish Christians as the proper form of their
covenant faithfulness is, and for a very long time has been, heretical. It is the
settled mind of the Church that Jesus Christ has fulfilled and transcended the
Mosaic form of the covenant and that he has introduced through his death
and resurrection a genuinely new form of covenantal life.

This the Council of Florence, in *Cantate Domino*, reaffirmed and made perfectly clear, though that document was not directed at the problem of messianic
Judaism. Of course it is not the Council of Florence that tends to occupy those
who make this claim, since as Protestants they question or deny its authority, but
rather the Jerusalem Council. Of the famous proto-council, it is said that Gentiles
were permitted to live for the most part—adherence to basic biblical morality
and separation from idolatry aside—as Gentiles, while it was presumed that Jews
would continue to live as Jews, keeping to the old patterns of Torah observance,
table fellowship with Gentiles excepted. What are we to make of that?[56]

The first point to be made is that the biblical record of the Jerusalem
Council is silent about how Jewish Christians were living or should live and
that the best clue to what the council had in mind is to be found in its context
in the book of Acts, where it constitutes the mainstay of Luke's apology for
the Pauline mission. And Luke is quite clear, as is Paul himself in his epistles,
that Paul, a Hebrew of the Hebrews, regards himself as free from the law and
actually behaves as such. Free from the law means dead to the law—beyond
its reach—and alive to God in Christ, in whom both the law and the promises
are fulfilled. It means that, for prudential reasons, he may recommend the
circumcision of a Jewish-born colleague like Timothy, but not that he must
recommend it. It means that he may keep kosher—though not at the expense
of table fellowship with Gentiles—but not that he must. It means that he may
celebrate feasts or undertake vows, but not that he must. And it means that
what he must not do is regard the law as the proper form and instrument of
salvation or as that which governs his existence.[57]

56. I mean besides the fact that it is quintessentially Protestant in its attempt to send the
Church back to the Bible as if the Church had all along got the Bible wrong, a point on which
I will remark further below.

57. The Council of Florence was not unaware of the Council of Jerusalem! But neither was
it prepared to countenance the inversion of Paul, the systematic corruption of Paul, on which
today's "messianic Judaism" depends. The Church, as *Cantate* says, "firmly believes, professes,
and teaches that the matter pertaining to the law of the Old Testament, of the Mosaic law,
which are divided into ceremonies, sacred rites, sacrifices, and sacraments, because they were

Any reading of Acts 15 that does not face these facts, or that tries to overcome them by turning Paul's "eschatological messianism" into a reason to defer the actual unity of the body of Christ to the world to come, is simply not adequate.[58] "Through the law I died to the law that I might live to God," says Paul. "You also have died to the law through the body of Christ"; you have been "cut loose from the law," and just so from condemnation.[59]

> Do you not know that all of us who have been baptized into Christ Jesus were baptized into his death? Therefore we have been buried with him by baptism into death, so that, just as Christ was raised from the dead by the glory of the Father, so we too might walk in newness of life. . . . But if we have died with Christ, we believe that we will also live with him. . . . The death he died, he died to sin, once for all; but the life he lives, he lives to God. So you also must consider yourselves dead to sin and alive to God in Christ Jesus. . . . For sin will have no dominion over you, since you are not under law but under grace.[60]

Paul's position before, during, and after the Jerusalem Council was that the baptized have passed with Jesus beyond the reach of the law, though they may still benefit from the law. The example he therefore determined to set was to make himself a Jew to the Jews in order to win the Jews, yet without acknowledging as binding any law but the law of liberty, the law of Christ, whom he proclaimed to both Jew and Gentile.[61] Is the law of Christ somehow

---

established to signify something in the future, although they were suited to the divine worship at that time, after our Lord's coming had been signified by them, ceased, and the sacraments of the New Testament began; and that whoever, even after the passion, placed hope in these matters of the law and submitted himself to them as necessary for salvation, as if faith in Christ could not save without them, sinned mortally. Yet it does not deny that after the passion of Christ up to the promulgation of the Gospel they could have been observed until they were believed to be in no way necessary for salvation" (DZ 712; cf. DEC 1:575f.).

58. The term "eschatological messianism" is Wright's (see *Paul and the Faithfulness of God*, 1426ff., 1440f.). It is a pity that Wright does not do a better job of treating the Jerusalem Council, for in other respects he has far the better of the argument. His opponents make the same mistake as Miroslav Volf does in *After Our Likeness: The Church as the Image of the Trinity*, Sacra Doctrina: Christian Theology for a Postmodern Age (Grand Rapids: Eerdmans, 1998), 264ff.; cf. my "Church, Ecumenism, and Eschatology," in *The Oxford Handbook of Eschatology*, ed. Jerry Walls (Oxford: Oxford University Press, 2008), 356.

59. From Gal. 2:19 and Rom. 7:4–6, trans. mine; at Rom. 7:6 the RSV has "discharged from the law, dead to that which held us captive."

60. Rom. 6:3–14. McDermott (*Israel Matters*, 64) attempts a contrast between being "under the law" and "in the law," positing that Paul understands himself to be both, without any differentiation in the meaning or configuration of "law"; but this interpolated category (ἔννομος) only displays the weakness of the case.

61. Here, in 1 Cor. 9:20–21, are the Pauline categories, which admit of neither a post-supersessionist nor a post-missionary perspective: "To the Jews I became as a Jew, in order to win Jews; to those under the law I became as one under the law—though not being myself

different for Jews and Gentiles? God forbid. The one baptism holds together Jew and Gentile as one new man under one new law, yet without collapsing the distinction between them, not merely because they are and can be different ethnicities but because Jews have all along been the carriers of the covenant and because God (as Rom. 9–11 makes clear) has unfinished business with Jews that is distinct from his unfinished business with Gentiles.

The second point to be made is that this reading, the reading determined to ignore what the Church was already beginning to learn about the fundamental change in the priesthood and hence in the law,[62] is a reading that assumes what Kinzer is trying to prove, viz., that the body of Christ comprises two peoples who can even be spoken of as two churches. The first of these peoples is derived from genealogical Israel—from Israel *kata sarka*, in Paul's language, which is at once an *ethnos* and a religion shaped by Torah. Kinzer calls it genealogical-Israel renewed, but we may call it Israel *kata pneuma*, so long as we understand that it is the very same *ethnos* and religion now determined by commitment to Jesus and his messianic work, which work has opened it in a fresh way to the Spirit and to a much fuller participation by God-fearing *goyim*.[63] These *goyim* are the second of the two peoples, viewed as an ecclesial partner to Israel *kata pneuma*. Where they are in view, reference

---

under the law—that I might win those under the law. To those outside the law I became as one outside the law—not being without law toward God but under the law of Christ—that I might win those outside the law" (trans. mine). On the ἔννομος Χριστοῦ ("within the law of Christ" or "lawful in Christ"), cf. Wright, *Paul and the Faithfulness of God*, 1442.

62. Kinzer (*Postmissionary Messianic Judaism*, 92ff.; *Searching Her Own Mystery*, 62ff.) tries his best to get around Heb. 7:12–14, 9:6–10, 10:8–18, 13:9, etc. In the first of the two books, he suggests that, just as the demise of the temple and its sacrificial system didn't prevent Jews from carrying on with the rest of the ceremonial law, so Hebrews has no thought of abandoning it. "The centralized worship institutions of Israel constituted a self-contained component of Torah that was not required for the continuance of Jewish life" (*Postmissionary Messianic Judaism*, 93) and, in any event, was important only in Jerusalem. In the second book, he tries to make the case that the priesthood of Jesus was not in competition with the Aaronic priesthood anyway; rather, as Melchizedekian, it was a distinctly kingly priesthood: "Hebrews recognizes, in accordance with Psalm 110, that Jesus' eternal priesthood is an aspect of his role as Israel's messianic king. His identity as Messiah is primary; his role as priest derives from and is dependent upon that primary identity. This conclusion supports our contention that Israel's national priesthood provides the essential background for Jesus' priesthood" (*Searching Her Own Mystery*, 63). Of Jesus as the mediator of a better covenant (12:24), distinct from that of Sinai, and of a change in the law connected to the change in priesthood (7:12), he doesn't speak in either book. Moreover, the destruction of the temple in AD 70 seems to be a "tragedy" of little theological import. The effect, if I may say so, is to make the reader wonder why the Christians to which the epistle is addressed required a warning not to revert to a life they hadn't left behind.

63. So long as they don't try to become Jews, but rather Gentile members of the commonwealth of Israel. On Kinzer's preference for "genealogical Israel" over Israel *kata sarka*, see *Searching Her Own Mystery*, 24. He does not use the κατὰ σάρκα / κατὰ πνεῦμα language I am

is usually made to the *ecclesia ex circumcisione*, which is properly the lead partner, and to the *ecclesia ex gentibus*, which has nevertheless become the much larger and predominant partner. Despite being united by the sacrament of baptism into one body, these remain two peoples, two churches, in a bilateral relationship.

Arguably, that makes three peoples in all, and even three churches, for Kinzer finds Jesus to be anonymously present in Israel *kata sarka* wherever it is Torah observant. But Israel *kata pneuma* mediates between Israel *kata sarka* and the *ecclesia ex gentibus*, sharing in different ways the nature of both, so perhaps it would be better to say that we have one active agent—Jesus, accompanied by his *ecclesia ex circumcisione*—operative in two peoples.[64] That the Gentiles are not in fact a people in the biblical sense, but rather many peoples, does not feature in Kinzer's analysis; nor is his concern with the relation between Jews and Gentiles generally. His focus is on mediation between the two posited *ecclesiae*. More precisely, he is making an attempt from the side of the *ecclesia ex circumcisione* to rethink baptism and the Eucharist, and the sacramental life as a whole, in a way that encourages the *ecclesia ex gentibus* to buy into the new construct—to engage in the revolution that arises from an "Israel" christology and ecclesiology, thus recognizing its need to allow the lead partner to lead.[65]

Unfortunately, this revolution begs the question, Are there really two *ecclesiae*, or is there only one? Are there two ecclesial covenants, or is there only one? We should not overlook the fact that Kinzer's construct—perhaps this is the most serious criticism to be brought against it—can succeed only by reversing the relation between Jesus and Torah. He quotes Benedict XVI, who wrote in traditional Pauline fashion that "the Torah of the Messiah is the Messiah, Jesus himself," to follow whom *is* "to keep the Torah, which has been fulfilled in him once and for all."[66] But Kinzer then appeals to Hans Herman

---

employing here. His own talk is of Israel and Israel renewed, "the people of God of the renewed covenant" (53; cf. 48f., 60).

64. Kinzer (ibid. 18f.) quotes Christian Rutishauser, SJ, to this effect. He thus moves from "two lungs" imagery to talk of two partner churches, with a third, hidden church in Judaism, which turns out to be a kind of anonymous Christianity.

65. Ibid. 8. In *Postmissionary Messianic Judaism* Kinzer laments the "crumbling of the ecclesiological bridge" (211) that is the *ecclesia ex circumcisione* under the weight of supersessionism. Jonathan Kaplan, in his synopsis of that book in *Kesher: A Journal of Messianic Judaism* 20 (Winter/Spring 2006), summarizes the recommendations for repair: "First, churches should revitalize efforts to increase respect for Judaism. Second, Jewish covenantal identity should be viewed as incumbent on Yeshua believers in the churches. Third, the Gentile ekklesia should expand efforts at dialogue with the Messianic Jewish movement."

66. I find it surprising that Cardinal Schönborn, in his preface, did not think to probe this matter at least a little, not to speak of Kinzer's tendentious reading of John XIII, John Paul II,

Henrix, joining him in the process of turning Benedict inside out: "Whoever obeys the Torah as a Jew and strives toward the goal 'to be an incarnation of the Torah,' walks on his or her way in a manner that, because of Jesus Christ's link with the Torah, Christians believe to be salvific communion with Christ as the Torah incarnate."[67] Here it is Torah, not Jesus and his cross, that becomes the unitive factor and the decisive criterion. This does not make sense of Christianity. It does make sense of Kinzer's covenantal dualism and of his call for Christian baptism to be rethought. Baptism has a "tragic history," he says, and requires a new trajectory, on which Gentiles will be summoned "to solidarity with the Jewish people" and Jews obligated "to a radical commitment to Jewish life—a Jewish life renewed in Jesus."[68] It also makes sense of Kinzer's remarkable claim (leaning now on Christian Rutishauser, SJ) that what has been called the Church is in fact just the *ecclesia ex gentibus* and as such not properly catholic. To be properly catholic it would have to include both the *ecclesia ex circumcisione* and Israel *kata sarka*; for "Jesus is as much the mystery hidden in the depths of the Jewish people and the Jewish way of life as he is the mystery of the ecclesia."[69]

Now, we ought not to deny that, if the Church is the koinonic body "of a resurrected Jew, it needs finally to come to terms with the people and tradition to which that Jew belongs."[70] Or that it must "read the New Covenant as a Jewish book," if it means to read it well. But do we have "good grounds for upholding the view that the New Testament as a whole treats Jewish practice

---

and especially Cardinal Lustiger, who always saw himself as a Jewish disciple of Jesus, yes, but who didn't live as one bound by written Torah, but only by the Torah in person, and who did not talk of two churches. With *Searching Her Own Mystery*, 12ff., cf. D'Costa, "What Does the Catholic Church Teach about Mission to the Jewish People?," 612; and Schoeman, *Salvation Is from the Jews*, 323ff.

67. This remark is quoted twice, at fuller length, and is said to "deserve serious consideration." Kinzer, *Searching Her Own Mystery*, 12f., 165f.; from Hans Herman Henrix, "The Son of God Became Human as a Jew: Implications of the Jewishness of Jesus for Christology," in *Christ Jesus and the Jewish People Today: New Explorations of Theological Interrelationships*, ed. Philip Cunningham et al. (Grand Rapids: Eerdmans, 2011), 114–43.

68. Kinzer, *Searching Her Own Mystery*, 101; cf. 104.

69. See ibid., 174f. "The relationship of mutual-indwelling that Jesus has with both communities creates the 'spiritual bond' that joins each to the other." Cf. 19: "Rutishauser acknowledges that the empirical Church as presently constituted—'as she is in fact'—is only 'the *ecclesia ex gentibus*, the Church out of the nations.' She is unable to offer prospective Jewish disciples of Jesus an environment in which they can fulfill their distinctive covenantal responsibilities as Jews, and so any deliberate 'mission to the Jews' from the Church 'cannot really be an option.' Yet, the Church still cannot be true to herself if she denies 'the universal importance of Jesus.' This is a dilemma indeed." The proposed resolution is to make the Church properly catholic by acknowledging the *ecclesia ex circumcisione* as the other partner.

70. Kinzer, *Postmissionary Messianic Judaism*, 25; cf. *Searching Her Own Mystery*, 8, 81, 235.

as obligatory for Jews"?[71] Do we have good grounds for positing two covenants or (which comes to the same thing) distinct covenantal arrangements? No, we do not, and Kinzer supplies none.[72] Those who come to God in Christ come to him either out of a covenant or without a covenant. But either way they enter through baptism into one and the same covenant: not the covenant with Moses, but the covenant with Abraham that in all its prior forms was preliminary to, and has been fulfilled and superseded by, the covenant in Christ. In that covenant, Jew and Gentile are fully equal partners. If for a time, the time of decision, they still have "their distinctive covenantal responsibilities," as the Jerusalem Council implies, this is not, as anti-supersessionists suppose, because the Jew is still bound by the law of Moses while the Gentile is not. The old is in force until the new has come, which eucharistically it has indeed.[73] In the Church, the category of God-fearer is gone; so is the category of those under the law. The only category is an eschatological category, the ἐν Χριστῷ category. One knows oneself to be a Jew or a Gentile, but one's identity and obligations are determined by no one but Christ and the Church of Christ. One knows Jesus himself to be a Jew, but one does not know him κατὰ σάρκα any longer, as a Jew still living under the law of Moses. Rather, one knows him κατὰ πνεῦμα as the founder of the new creation and the judge of the old. And despite what the rabbis say, it is Jesus, the Word made flesh, who is the blueprint of creation—he himself, not Torah, under which he too lived for a time because it was God's good purpose that he should live among sinners who were being taught to expect their salvation.[74] There the whole matter

71. Kinzer, *Postmissionary Messianic Judaism*, 95 et passim, where the meaning includes Jewish Christians.

72. His dedication notwithstanding, my own view is that he supplies only the construct, which can be sustained if and only if one accepts the premises and omits contrary texts and evidence. Things are different, of course, if we are looking beyond the Church and asking merely: "Can New Testament teaching be plausibly construed in such a way that it affirms the continuing covenantal significance of the Jewish people, even as it orders its life without explicit Yeshua-faith?" (ibid., 149). There is no need to dispute that.

73. Eucharistically: that is, really and actually, by transubstantiation, though not without mystery and anticipation of what is yet to come.

74. In *Theo-Drama: Theological Dramatic Theory*, vol. 3, *The Dramatis Personae: The Person in Christ*, trans. Graham Harrison (San Francisco: Ignatius, 1992), 361ff., Hans Urs von Balthasar wrestles with what Przywara referred to as the "primal rupture" in the people of God that takes place with the birth of the Church, in Israel's "yes" and its "no" to God. Balthasar notes that the remnant of Israel that enters the Church through faith belongs now to "eschatological time" and to a people that are a people only in a metaphorical sense. It "loses its earthly (reproductive) significance" (376). Here there is no more place "for the particularism that wants to bask in its own glory." To be the *people* of God it must be willing to be the people of *God* (391). That the rest of Israel "survives Christ and continues to exist in history beside the Church" is a mystery difficult to unlock, he says, though he has very interesting things to say of the salting and the secularizing effects of the Jewish people. I miss in Kinzer sensitivity to this problem.

rests, as the authors of the Gospel of John and of the Epistle to the Hebrews knew and expressed in their famous prologues, just as Paul himself knew.

And the council? This is the place to observe that Kinzer, having begun by misinterpreting the Second Vatican Council in a fashion that accords with his view of the Jerusalem Council, then makes the entirely expected Protestant move: Given their sorry history (there is no need to deny, and I do not, that it is sometimes sorry), Catholics cannot go back behind Vatican II except to go back to the Bible, which he himself will reread for them.[75] Kinzer's reading in *Searching Her Own Mystery* is rich and valuable, but it is also at key points mistaken, because tendentiously selective, like his reading of Church history. The Jerusalem Council is one of those key points. The fathers were right, and popes to the present day were right, to distinguish the abiding content of that council from its temporary or transitional content. The abiding content was the equality of Jew and Gentile in Christ and the need for Gentiles to acknowledge Christ, in deed as in word, by separating themselves from pagan worship and pagan immorality, yet without taking up the burden of the whole law of Moses. All this was directly stated. The temporary or transitional content was not stated but implied: in Jerusalem, while the old temple stood, there was need for Christian witness in its precincts; and in every synagogue in the empire, as in every Jewish home or quarter, there was need for Christian witness by Christian Jews, willing and able to live freely for Christ's sake in the pattern of life Jews had learned from Torah, while belonging primarily to that community of holy fear and joyful expectation that was the eucharistic community of the apostles. The mistakes made in later centuries were mistakes made through a failure to recognize that this was *still* required, despite the destruction of the old temple and just because of the ascendency of Christianity throughout the empire. These mistakes were sometimes grave mistakes. They were not codified, however, even at the Council of Florence, in a theological or dogmatic fashion but only in an equally temporal and transitional (though not equally justified) fashion. That after the Holocaust, and after the restoration of Jews to their homeland, they were more easily recognized as mistakes goes without saying. But their correction does not lie, as the anti-supersessionists would have it, in the theologically devastating error of telling Christians that there are two forms of the covenant simultaneously in force and that Jews are subject to both while Gentiles are

---

There seems rather to be a certain basking in the glory of the *ecclesia ex circumcisione*, perhaps even just a trace of the Kabbalistic notion that according to Balthasar "we frequently find in rabbinic texts" (396), that "God needs the people just as must as it needs him, and Israel is the primal foundation of the entire creation."

75. See Kinzer, *Searching Her Own Mystery*, 21f.

subject to but one. Whether this is construed as the privilege of the Jew or the bondage of the Jew makes no difference. It is rightly forbidden by Florence. It is a form, however sophisticated, of that "turning back" against which the author of Hebrews warned.

To show the essential continuity between Judaism and Christianity is not only an excellent thing but an essential thing, if the discontinuity is not glossed over. Kinzer does the former well, as does his main theological opponent, the prolific Matthew Levering. The latter, however, does not make the mistake of the former by refusing to recognize that the rabbinic tradition is not, in the last analysis, compatible with the teaching of the New Testament—a compatibility it never intended and still disavows.[76] Levering, for all his efforts to improve Christianity's dialogue with Judaism, understands that the Jewish "no" to Jesus, insofar as it informs Jewish religion, does indeed remain an obstacle to Christian affirmation of that religion; that Christians must distinguish between Jews and Judaism, as between adherents to any religion and the religion itself, even while holding Judaism dear to Christianity in all those ways that—unlike other religions—it informs Christianity itself, as a daughter of the same mother. Levering also knows that there can be no such thing as a post-missionary Christianity, that there is only a Christianity that always has a gospel that is for the Jew too, indeed, for the Jew first.[77]

Lawrence Feingold (himself a Jewish Christian) gets it right in volume 3 of *The Mystery of Israel and the Church* when he observes that the Mosaic law was never meant to be an end in itself and that the messianic kingdom established by Christ must now be catholic—and can be, because the baptized have all died to the law in order to live to God. "It is clear," he says, that in the kingdom of Christ even the Jew "can no longer be bound by a ceremonial law partially designed to separate Israel from the nations until the Messiah had come, as well as to prefigure His coming."[78] This does not mean that the Church simply replaces Israel as the people of God, though it does mean

---

76. Gavin D'Costa, in review of *Searching Her Own Mystery*, writes that insofar as "Kinzer is clear that Israel's only *telos* is her Messiah, Jesus Christ, and his rule," what we have here is "non-supersessionist theology that might not sound like good news to Jews" (*Nova et Vetera*, English ed., 15.3 [2017]: 945). To flip this coin over: What does Kinzer mean by "the apparent Jewish no to Yeshua is no obstacle to our accepting the legitimacy and value of Jewish religious tradition, just as the actual Christian no to Judaism and the Jewish people has not negated the riches of Christian tradition" (*Postmissionary Messianic Judaism*, 233)—that the no is *only* apparent and has nothing in common with the no that Jesus himself encountered?

77. He does not shy from the claim that "authentic Jewish identity, at the end of the day, is Christian identity" (Levering, "Aquinas and Supersessionism One More Time," 404, but see also 408n29).

78. Feingold, *Messianic Kingdom of Israel*, 219.

that the old covenant has become obsolete in the sense that it is not binding in the Church.[79] There is one new man in place of the two, precisely because Christ abolished in his flesh the law of commandments and ordinances, even if he did not deprive them of all utility in the present age. "The obligatory quality of those rites has passed away, but their prophetic, typological, and revelatory value remains."[80] Feingold rejects both any simplistic supersession of peoples *and* the notion of parallel covenants, offering, as far as I can tell, a sensible version of what in the taxonomy above was indicated at B.2: one body, one people, composed of Jews and Gentiles, often living differently but sharing here and now in the already established, though still coming, kingdom of Jesus Christ.

The True Glory of Israel

We began by attending to the surprises of the twentieth century: the horrible eruption of anti-Semitism in its most demonic form, the form given it by National Socialism; and the return of a remnant to Zion, at once tearful and joyful, where by the providence of God the earth has more than once opened its mouth and swallowed the river pouring from the mouth of the dragon to sweep them away. We did not attend to the fact that many theologians, Christian and Jewish, being greatly moved by the *Shoah* and, more generally, by the two world wars, succumbed to temptation and made the grave, indeed, the pernicious error of abandoning faith in the perfections of God that traditionally were called his aseity and impassibility. Biblical scholars and ecumenists and political theologians not infrequently followed suit, looking for ways to soften or even to mute the Church's confession of the glory of Jesus Christ insofar as that involved talk of his deity and of his lordship over all things. To speak of a suffering God, not as God-made-man but as God qua God, God in his eternal glory, became popular though it did not cease thereby to be heretical. To speak of a still-suffering Messiah, of Jesus the persecuted

79. Ibid. 231. This arrangement shows the inadequacy of Matthew Tapie's definition in *Aquinas on Israel and the Church* (Eugene, OR: Wipf & Stock, 2014), 23f., of which Levering ("Aquinas and Supersessionism," 399) is insufficiently critical: "Supersessionism is the Christian claim that with the advent of Christ, Jewish law is fulfilled and obsolete, with the result that God replaces Israel with the Church."

80. Feingold, *Messianic Kingdom of Israel*, 239. If they remain obligatory, as D'Costa points out in his review of Kinzer's *Searching Her Own Mystery*, the question arises as to whether the mystical unity between the Jewish and Gentile *ecclesiae* is "a visible unity, or . . . an invisible unity that amounts to a 'visible disunity.'" Is it governed by the Petrine ministry? Are the liturgies of messianic Jewish Christians to be regarded *de iure* as an authentic *lex orandi* with corresponding *lex credendi* implications?

Jew—persecuted now by those who portray him as in any way in conflict
with his own people!—likewise became popular.[81] And with this came an
all-out assault on supersessionism, an assault that often lacked the necessary
distinctions between a supersession of covenants, with its modifications of
both the law and the people, and a supersession of peoples as such.

That, too, though an intuition of a real problem, led to heresy, though it
also led to many useful insights into Scripture, tradition, and history. It led to
heresy, if not through a denial of the deity of Christ and of his two natures—in
short, through a return to Ebionite and Nestorian ideas, with a convenient
forgetfulness of the fact that these were the very ideas that give birth to Islam,
that great falsification of biblical religion, as also to the Enlightenment, an
equally great falsification, and through both to the tremendous persecution
of Jews and Christians we have witnessed in the past century—then through
a denial of his ascension to heavenly glory, to his seat at the right hand of the
Father, from whence he shall come to judge the quick and the dead. It was
forgotten that the scandal of the gospel, which always appears as foolishness
to the Greeks and a stumbling block to the Jews, is found equally in the cross
and in the resurrection, in the suffering and in the lordship, in the divinity
and in the humanity.

The Church is the sign of this scandal, a sign of contradiction, which cannot be embraced by Greeks or Jews without abandoning their resistance to
the very idea of the incarnation and to the narrative of the cross and resurrection. When one enters the Church, one enters a community that already
participates in the new creation. That new creation remains a provocation
to the old until the old itself is transformed and made new. And one of its
provocations is what we are calling the *pax Paulinica*, which is nothing of
course but the *pax Christi*:

> For he is our peace, who has made us both one, and has broken down the divid-
> ing wall of hostility, by abolishing in his flesh the law of commandments and
> ordinances, that he might create in himself one new man in place of the two,
> so making peace, and might reconcile us both to God in one body through the
> cross, thereby bringing the hostility to an end. And he came and preached peace
> to you who were far off and peace to those who were near; for through him we
> both have access in one Spirit to the Father. So then you are no longer strangers
> and sojourners, but you are fellow citizens with the saints and members of the

81. To Jürgen Moltmann a good deal is owed on both counts (cf. Farrow, "In the End Is the
Beginning," *Modern Theology* 14.3 [1998]: 425ff.). Tom Weinandy tried to provide an antidote
in *Does God Suffer?* (South Bend, IN: University of Notre Dame Press, 2000), but it is still
necessary to plead: St Anselm, *ora pro nobis*.

household of God, built upon the foundation of the apostles and prophets, Christ Jesus himself being the cornerstone, in whom the whole structure is joined together and grows into a holy temple in the Lord; in whom you also are built into it for a dwelling place of God in the Spirit. (Eph. 2:14–22)

The true glory of Israel is the Spirit of God, *dominus et vivificans*, and the man remade by the Spirit in the image of God. That man is man in Christ, and man in Christ is the man who shows forth the splendor of the Spirit, man crucified and risen with Christ and no longer under the dispensation of death.[82] It is immaterial whether he be Jew or Gentile, though Christ is a Jew and that is not immaterial. Which is to say, it is immaterial whether he is a grafted branch or a native branch, for there is only one tree from which both draw their life, and there is only one Church in which the Lord and Giver of life grants life.

Today this must be articulated anew, just as the aseity, the impassibility, the freedom of God must be articulated anew. In honor of the Jews, it should always be said, "to them belong the sonship, the glory, the covenants, the giving of the law, the worship, and the promises; to them belong the patriarchs, and of their race, according to the flesh, is the Christ, who is God over all, blessed for ever. Amen" (Rom. 9:4–5). Yet there is but one Church from Jews and Gentiles, not a church of Jews and a church of Gentiles.[83] There is but

---

82. 2 Cor. 3:1ff.; cf. Irenaeus, *Haer.* 5.9.3.

83. Erik Peterson's *Theological Tractates* contains in chapter 4 an exposition of Rom. 9–11 delivered in 1932, titled "The Church from Jews and Gentiles." Peterson notes Paul's provocative use at 9:5 of the Jewish benediction (which I have interpolated into the RSVCE translation above). He also notes Paul's clarity about the fact that "it is not fleshly descent . . . that makes for a true descendant of Abraham" (45f.). "One understands everything once one realizes that Paul's concern is to emphasize the difference between the spiritual and the natural order," and thus to revise the very concept of election. Yet "no power of this world will be able to eliminate Judaism," he insists, for God is still waiting for the Jews (52f.). That the Church is the Church *from* Jews and Gentiles—that a spiritual separation among Jews as well as among Gentiles is still taking place—belongs to the eschatological character of the age. One is struck in reading this work with the now alien forthrightness of it, and conversely with Peterson's refusal to let go, "even inside the Church," of the natural distinction between Jew and Gentile (61). But one is also struck by the fact that the divine *skandalon* of the cross is not as yet obscured by the demonic *skandalon* of the Holocaust (which incarnated, among other evils, the Nazi parody of natural descent). Peterson still sees clearly not only that the natural must be subordinated to the spiritual but that "Jewish Christians cannot make their claim to be the remnant on the basis of their fulfillment of the commandments of the Mosaic Law." He sees that God does indeed intend to make non-Christian Jews jealous of what their divine Spouse is doing for those Gentiles who believe (62f.). He also sees, however, that "the Jew who does not believe in Christ belongs nonetheless to the noble olive tree of God," while "the Gentile who loses his faith is nothing at all" and is likely to succumb "to a measure of barbarism and loss of substance that is impossible for Jews" (65). This has since proved true. Or rather, it is continuing to prove true, "in a fearful confirmation" of the words of Paul, and will do so until the second advent—before which, as

one vessel of mercy, "prepared beforehand for glory, even us whom he has called, not from the Jews only but also from the Gentiles" (Rom. 9:23–24). There is but one baptism, one Eucharist, and one confirmation for the one mission: to call all alike out of the old creation and into the new. For the present eschatological situation, in which the new overlaps the old, causing it to become obsolete because of the surpassing splendor that has overtaken it, is precisely a missionary situation. If that mission has for a long while been focused on the Gentiles—sometimes too narrowly focused, due to a certain hardness of heart among Christians—it is now time to focus it again on the Jews, in faith and hope that their "hardening in part" is about to be lifted. That need not be done at the expense of the Gentiles, and it may be done in an outsized way by Jewish Christians, but it will not be done effectively by those who regard themselves as under the law. It will be done, rather, by those who know themselves free from the law but obligated to Christ.

Augustine says, the Jews shall believe and Antichrist shall persecute, until Christ shall judge. But perhaps, as Thomas remarks in his commentary on Romans (Rom. 11:11ff.), the conversion of the Jews shall rekindle the faith of Gentiles: "For Gentiles are the believers who will grow lukewarm . . . or will fall away entirely, being deceived by Antichrist. These will be restored to their primitive fervor after the conversion of the Jews." Meanwhile, as Peterson testifies, "the mystery of the Church from Jews and Gentiles is the mystery of the divine mercy" (67).

9

The Gift of Fear

A Meditation on Hebrews

In many and various ways God spoke of old to our fathers by the prophets; but in these last days he has spoken to us by a Son, whom he appointed the heir of all things, through whom also he created the world. He reflects the glory of God and bears the very stamp of his nature, upholding the universe by his word of power. When he had made purification for sins, he sat down at the right hand of the Majesty on high, having become as much superior to angels as the name he has obtained is more excellent than theirs. For to what angel did God ever say, "Thou art my Son, today I have begotten thee"? Or again, "I will be to him a father, and he shall be to me a son"? And again, when he brings the first-born into the world, he says, "Let all God's angels worship him."

Hebrews 1:1–6

For you have not come to what may be touched, a blazing fire, and darkness, and gloom, and a tempest, and the sound of a trumpet, and a voice whose words made the hearers entreat that no further messages be spoken to them. For they could not endure the order that was given, "If even a beast touches the mountain, it shall be stoned." Indeed, so terrifying was the sight that Moses said, "I tremble with fear." But you have come to Mount Zion and to the city of the living God, the heavenly Jerusalem, and to innumerable angels in festal gathering, and to the assembly of the first-born who are enrolled in heaven, and to a judge who is God of all, and to the spirits of just men made perfect, and to Jesus, the mediator of a new covenant, and to the sprinkled blood that speaks more graciously than the blood of Abel.

See that you do not refuse him who is speaking. For if they did not escape when they refused him who warned them on earth, much less shall we escape if we reject him who warns from heaven. His voice then shook the earth; but now he has promised, "Yet once more I will shake not only the earth but also the heaven." This phrase, "Yet once more," indicates the removal of what is shaken, as of what has been made, in order that what cannot be shaken may remain. Therefore let us be grateful for receiving a kingdom that cannot be shaken, and thus let us offer to God acceptable worship, with reverence and awe; for our God is a consuming fire.

Hebrews 12:18–29

A Tract for Our Times

These are the opening and closing salvos that bracket the epistle to the Hebrews. Do they not bracket it off altogether from today's reader? Copernican man peers into the heavens with his giant telescopes and space probes. He sees grandeur and mystery—for every mystery he solves, another wondrously appears—but he sees no throne of God. He wonders, with Kant, about the eventual collapse of the heavens, and what kind of universe might emerge from that. He contemplates the possibility of parallel universes, or of numberless universes in succession. He wonders about aliens, but he does not believe in angels. He expects no purification of earth or heaven, in the sense that our author does. He does not even know what τὰ ἐπουράνια might mean and can make no sense of their cleansing. Consequently, he does not understand the shaking either of earth or of heaven, the shaking that has already begun. He expects no judgment, though he anticipates disaster. There is no fear of God before his eyes. He lacks what Thomas Aquinas calls "the gift of fear."[1] And Hebrews cannot speak to him unless it imparts that gift.

It is not as if he has no fear at all. He still has those instinctual fears that belong to his creatureliness and that tend, for the time being, to his self-preservation. This, as far as it goes, is a healthy fear that on some level supports the pursuit of good and the avoidance of evil. But because it is not accompa-

---

1. My title is taken from Aquinas, not from Gavin de Becker's 1997 bestseller, *The Gift of Fear: Survival Signals That Protect Us from Violence*. The latter, however, puts me in mind of Heb. 10:26–31, inviting the observation that a Society of Biblical Literature session under the rubric "Hebrews, Theology, and Ethics" can hardly avoid having a paper touching on the fact that, though God is not violent but just, just because he is just it is "a fearful thing" to fall into his hands after ignoring his "signals" and spurning his grace.

nied by a proper fear of God, it does not support the pursuit of good and the avoidance of evil as far as it ought. It does not prevent him, for example, from experimenting with the very building blocks of human life in his reprogenetic technologies or from contradicting his responsibility for self-preservation by the introduction of euthanasia regimes. That is because he has also the kind of fear that leads ultimately to despair, to what Kierkegaard calls "the sickness unto death." For not only does he not worship the Son, the King of Glory who upholds all things by the word of his power, he does not even acknowledge that his own life is a gift, of which he is the steward rather than the owner. And yet he knows deep down that he is incapable of perfecting or even sustaining that which he received and did not create. Even if he is a committed transhumanist, who fancies that his scientific and technological prowess will carry him, or his consciousness, across boundary after boundary, opening before him currently unimaginable vistas, he cannot be certain that it will not come in the end to emptiness and unimaginable loneliness and frustration, to a place where there is "weeping and gnashing of teeth," so to say, though there be no teeth to gnash. And if he is willing nevertheless to face this terrifying prospect, it is not because he is confident that God does not exist and that he has no other option. Kierkegaard is right: The real reason is that he not wish to find himself *before God*, or to find *himself* before God—the self that God intends for him. But he *will* find himself before God, one way or another. He will discover that "it is appointed for men to die once, and after that comes judgment" (Heb. 9:27). He will encounter the Son, seated upon his heavenly throne. And of this he is secretly afraid with a fear that is no gift, unless it be the gift of the serpent who sent him off down this path to ruin.[2]

Hebrews is not actually addressed to such a man, of course. It is addressed rather to first-century Jewish Christians who found themselves in a situation not unlike that of the generation of the great exodus: fearful of going forward into Canaan, uncertain about returning to Egypt. So why do I bring him up? Because what is sapping the strength of many Christians today is that they live with Copernican man, and they don't seem to know how to confront him with the gospel. Hence they are themselves slipping into a situation governed by the wrong kind of fear, which produces apathy and immobility. They are becoming hard of hearing where the things of God are concerned. They

2. Schleiermacher, in the wake of Copernicus and Kant, tried to reinvent religion in Romantic terms, regarding it, in Elie Kedourie's much-quoted misquote, as "the outcome neither of the fear of death, nor of the fear of God" (*Nationalism* [New York: Praeger, 1960], 26), but rather of a deep reverence for unity or wholeness. But this gambit was doomed to fail. Religion is indeed a product of the fear of death, which has clouded the longing for immortality proper to man, and of the fear of God. Fear of God is one thing, however, and godly fear another.

are inventing for themselves an ethics of accommodation that amounts to a shrinking back. They themselves cannot hear what Hebrews has to say to them—not because of its Jewish idiom but because of its foreign narrative and worldview. They do not know what to do with its emphasis on godly confidence, because they do not know what to do with its focus on godly fear.

Copernicus himself had no intention of landing us in such a situation, nor did Galileo, who died a son of the Church. Such men did not believe that their scientific breakthroughs would make it impossible to receive the message of Hebrews or any other Scripture.[3] They did not yet grasp the danger that heliocentrism might lead not only to the displacement of earth and of man from the center of creation but also to the displacement of the Creator himself, and so to the displacement of both divine and natural law from ethical discourse.[4] And it needn't have happened that way. It was not the Copernican revolution but the Cartesian-Kantian revolution which brought that about.

Kant, like other Enlightenment thinkers, sought for ways to preserve divine law *as* natural law, and natural law as a law of reason if not of created order. Yet he removed "everything empirical" from the sphere of ethics, and especially the voice of Scripture, if understood as making reference to real events.[5] Take the exodus, for example. To such men Israel's meeting with God at Sinai was as incomprehensible as the eucharistic meeting of the Church "with angels and archangels and the whole company of heaven." Neither facet of Hebrews 12, neither covenant to which it refers, made any sense to them. As for the centrality of the Son, that could be no more than a cipher for the

---

3. "Even in those propositions which are not matters of faith," wrote Galileo in his Letter to the Grand Duchess Christina, "this [biblical] authority ought to be preferred over that of all human writings which are supported only by bare assertions or probable arguments, and not set forth in a demonstrative way. This I hold to be necessary and proper to the same extent that divine wisdom surpasses all human judgment and conjecture" (https://sourcebooks.fordham .edu/halsall/mod/galileo-tuscany.asp).

4. Joseph Ratzinger recalls the judgment of the agnostic philosopher Paul K. Feyerabend, *Wider den Methodenzwang* (Frankfurt am Main: Suhrkamp, 1976), 206: "The Church at the time of Galileo kept much more closely to reason than did Galileo himself, and she took into consideration the ethical and social consequences of Galileo's teaching too. Her verdict against Galileo was rational and just, and the revision of this verdict can be justified only on grounds of what is politically opportune" (quoted by Ratzinger in *A Turning Point for Europe? The Church and Modernity in the Europe of Upheavals*, trans. Brian McNeil [San Francisco: Ignatius, 1994], 98). Ratzinger adds: "To my great surprise, when I was interviewed recently about the case of Galileo, I was not asked (for instance), why the Church had presumed to hinder the knowledge of the natural sciences but, quite to the contrary, why the Church had not taken up a clearer position against the disasters that were bound to result when Galileo opened Pandora's box."

5. Cf. my remarks at 194ff. of "Melchizedek and Modernity," in *The Epistle to the Hebrews and Christian Theology*, ed. R. Bauckham et al. (Grand Rapids: Eerdmans, 2009), with respect to Troeltsch's attempt to maintain this Kantian position as a canon of modern hermeneutics.

necessity of the mind's imposition of order on an essentially mysterious and ultimately unknowable external reality.

After long puzzlement over the equally impenetrable mystery of self-consciousness, post-Kantian man is now gravitating back toward pure materialism, uncertain whether there *is* a mind, much less a meaningful ethical discourse. Even those who cling to Kant's maxim that we must treat persons as ends, and never as means, have little to say about what kind of "end" the person might be, or what ends are proper to a person. The truth of the matter, as Alasdair MacIntyre and others have observed, is that coherent moral discourse, which depends on a much more robust teleology than modern man subscribes to, is no longer possible.[6] And we have seen this coming for some time. As one mid-nineteenth-century tract put it, echoing John Donne: "All clamoured for their rights, but none thought of their duties. 'There was no fear of God before their eyes'; hence, with them, the cohesion of the moral world was gone, and they had sunk into a state of anarchy."[7]

"There is no fear of God before their eyes"[8]—this is the fundamental challenge in ethics today. What is ethics without the fear of God? Among the pagans of old, right reason or natural law ethics was a form of the fear of God; so also the pursuit of justice.[9] Among the pagans of today, ethics and the pursuit of justice, where they still exist as meaningful pursuits, exist, at least in the public sphere, without reference to God at all. We are more concerned with

---

6. We might appeal in illustration to the present absurd protests on our campuses about so-called safe spaces, where questions about goodness, beauty, and truth must not be asked.

7. "The Murdered King," *Church of England Magazine* 49.2 (1860): 406. Donne's famous lines, from "An Anatomy of the World" (1611), stand in the background:

> Tis all in pieces, all coherence gone,
> All just Supply, and all Relation;
> Prince, subject, father, son, are things forgot,
> For every man alone thinks he hath got
> To be a Phoenix, and that then can be
> None of that kind, of which he is, but he.

8. Rom. 3:18, quoting Ps. 36:1; cf. Rom. 1:18ff.

9. Cicero, *De republica* 3.22: "True law is right reason in agreement with nature; it is of universal application, unchanging and everlasting; it summons to duty by its commands, and averts from wrongdoing by its prohibitions. . . . It is a sin to try to alter this law, nor is it allowable to repeal any part of it, and it is impossible to abolish it entirely. We cannot be freed from its obligations by senate or people, and we need not look outside ourselves for an expounder or interpreter of it. And there will not be different laws at Rome and at Athens, or different laws now and in the future, but one eternal and unchangeable law will be valid for all nations and at all times, and there will be one master and ruler, that is God, over us all, for he is the author of this law, its promulgator and its enforcing judge. Whoever is disobedient is fleeing from himself and denying his human nature, and by reason of this very fact he will suffer the worst punishment" (trans. Clinton W. Keyes, Loeb Classical Library [Cambridge, MA: Harvard University Press, 1928], 211; cf. *De Legibus* 2.9f.).

what we call, in a telling semantic twist, homophobia[10] than with the φόβος θεοῦ. Which is to say, we are ethically *theo*phobic, to deploy that same semantic perversion. Do we fear being charged with fear of homosexual man or woman? Certainly we fear being charged with the fear of God! Not surprisingly, we have begun to fear even the terms "man" or "woman," lest we be charged with "cisnormativity." The eclipse of the sense of God leads, as it must, to the eclipse of the sense of man.[11] Or again: We fear the pains of death; that is why we require euthanasia regimes, as the Supreme Court of Canada recently observed in *Carter*.[12] We do not fear the pains of hell, which neither that court nor yours would even think of considering. In other words, through fear of death we are still very much subject to bondage, just as Hebrews says, but we have no fear of God by which we may become subject to salvation.

Perhaps then Hebrews may serve after all as a tract for our times, but only if we permit it to remind us of the dialectics of fear. For fear can be a curse or fear can be a gift, depending on who or what is feared and whether the fear in question is regarded as a fear proper to man, enabling him to live as he ought to live.

Godly Fear and Godly Confidence

The dialectic of Hebrews has God as the proper object of fear, and fear of God as the foundation of godly confidence in human salvation. The note on which it begins is a sustained note of confidence, based on the enthronement of the Son, culminating in the claim that the very angels in heaven are now

10. As I have noted elsewhere, "The word, in its literal sense, refers to an entrenched fear or dislike of the male sex or, more generally, of human beings. The *Oxford English Dictionary* refers us to *Chambers's Journal* (5 June 1920): 'Her salient characteristic was contempt for the male sex as represented in the human biped. . . . The seeds of homophobia had been sown early.' By the early Seventies, however, in part under the influence of the Manhattan psychotherapist, George Weinberg, the word was being used to refer to any aversion in the general population to the persons or practices of the homosexual minority. This redefinition of the word was part of a deliberate attempt to turn the tables on those who believed that homosexual behaviour was itself related to an unhealthy aversion to so-called normal men or women. Indeed it appears that 'homophobia' and 'homophobic' were semantically retooled for one crucial purpose: to identify those who regarded homosexuality as a sign of psychological or moral difficulty as witnesses against themselves, that is, against their own mental or moral health" ("Sexual Politics and Language," *National Post*, 31 August 2001).

11. See John Paul II, *Evangelium vitae*, 21ff.

12. In *Carter v. Canada*, 2015 SCC 5 (1 S.C.R. 331), the Supreme Court argued that the prohibition of assisted suicide violates the principles of fundamental justice because it "has the effect of forcing some individuals to take their own lives prematurely, for fear that they would be incapable of doing so when they reached the point where suffering was intolerable." See further my *Desiring a Better Country: Forays in Political Theology* (Montreal: McGill-Queen's Unversity Press, 2015), 141n25.

ordered under the Son to the welfare of those who are to share in his everlasting kingdom (1:14). This, as you know, is followed immediately by the first warning passage, establishing the Sinai/Pentecost parallel that frames the entire homily and reappears in the literary crescendo that is chapter 12. In the wake of the ascension of Jesus and the ensuing distribution of the gifts of the Holy Spirit, the dignity and destiny of man—who, as that astute reader of Hebrews, Irenaeus, also insists, will surpass the angels in glory[13]—is revealed, not only for Israel, but for all the world to see. Or rather, it is announced for all to hear, and to what they hear they had best pay the closest possible attention (2:1).

Those who are paying attention must hold fast their "confidence and pride" (3:6) in demonstration of their readiness for the kingdom. The counterpoint that is heard throughout this section, readying readers for the high point, the main point, the κεφάλαιον, of chapter 8, instructs them to take care lest there be in them "an evil, unbelieving heart . . . hardened by the deceitfulness of sin" (3:12–13). They must fear lest in the end any of them be judged to have fallen short of the kingdom (4:1). They must not doubt that the Word of God, which orders the affairs of the universe, is capable also of "discerning the thoughts and intentions of the heart" (4:12). That is the lower register, so to say; the upper register is all notes of joy and confidence, through which the audience is invited to approach the one who sits on the throne and to find in him the great High Priest who, knowing their weaknesses, knows also how to dispense mercy and grace "to help in time of need" (4:14–16).

This pattern is repeated throughout Hebrews, with a dynamic that moves in both directions. Godly fear is the ground of godly confidence, and godly confidence the fuel of godly fear. At the climax of the homily we are exhorted: "Let us be grateful for receiving a kingdom that cannot be shaken, and thus let us offer to God acceptable worship, with reverence and awe; for our God is a consuming fire" (12:28–29). At Sinai it was "Stand back! Stand back!" Here it is "Draw near! Draw near! Behold the God who is a consuming fire, without yourself being consumed. For you have a mediator with God who is a better mediator than Moses, and you are sprinkled with the blood of a better sacrifice. You belong to a higher covenant, you share in a liturgy grounded in heaven itself."

I have outlined elsewhere the rhetorical structure of Hebrews, which I take to be an Ascension-Pentecost homily.[14] But when I think about its contribution to Christian ethics, it is the motif of godly fear that most impresses itself upon me. If we "desire a better country, that is, a heavenly one" (11:16), we need

---

13. *Haer.* 5.36.3.

14. Douglas Farrow, *Ascension and Ecclesia* (Grand Rapids: Eerdmans, 1999), 279 (reproduced in Farrow, "Melchizedek and Modernity," 286); cf. Farrow, *Ascension Theology* (London: T&T Clark, 2011), 11, 158.

godly fear to get there. If even on earth we desire a better country, we must seek an alternative to the ethos of secularism. But the only real alternative to the ethos of secularism is the ethos of fear—the only alternative to "theophobia" is εὐλαβείας, reverence, the φόβος θεοῦ.

Ethics concerns the art of living well, and the art of living well is one and the same with the pursuit of happiness, which all people want—or rather, with the *effective* pursuit of happiness, which means (though they know it not) the godly pursuit of God, who is Happiness itself. And this is the concern of Hebrews also, though it is not expressed in just these terms. What Hebrews makes altogether clear is that the godly pursuit of God, and of the better country that has God as its founder and builder, begins with the fear of God and not with the fear of man. When the homilist has reached his conclusion, he appends in chapter 13 his final instructions about what it means to live on earth as citizens of heaven. Twelve commands mark out the life lived before God with reverence and awe, twelve halachic directives establish the practical ethics of the people whose ethos is the fear of God:

1. *Let brotherly love continue.*
2. *Do not neglect to show hospitality to strangers*, for thereby some have entertained angels unawares.
3. *Remember those who are in prison*, as though in prison with them; and those who are ill-treated, since you also are in the body.
4. *Let marriage be held in honor among all*, and let the marriage bed be undefiled; for God will judge the immoral and adulterous.
5. *Keep your life free from the love of money*, and be content with what you have; for he has said, "I will never fail you nor forsake you."
6. *Remember your leaders . . . and imitate their faith*. Jesus Christ is the same yesterday, today and for ever.
7. *Do not be led away by diverse and strange teachings*; for it is well that the heart be strengthened by grace.
8. *Let us go forth to him outside the camp, bearing abuse for him*. For here we have no lasting city, but we seek the city which is to come.
9. *Through him then let us continually offer up a sacrifice of praise to God*.
10. *Do not neglect to do good and to share what you have*, for such sacrifices are pleasing to God.
11. *Obey your leaders and submit to them*; for they are keeping watch over your souls, as men who will have to give account.

12. *Pray for us, for we are sure that we have a clear conscience, desiring to act honorably in all things.*[15]

Now each of these warrants a homily in itself, whether or not it warrants an academic paper. But I want only to observe that after the fifth directive, Ἀφιλάργυρος ὁ τρόπος, appeal is made to Deuteronomy 31:6: "Be strong and of good courage, do not fear or be in dread of them: for it is the LORD your God who goes with you; he will not fail you or forsake you."[16] To which is added Psalm 118:6: "With the LORD on my side I do not fear. What can man do to me?" This appeal is obviously directed at more than the love of silver or the fear of penury, just as the assertion that is situated between the sixth and seventh directives—"Jesus Christ is the same yesterday, today and for ever"— does more than support the counsel to be true to tradition and to reject the false coinage of heresy. These in fact are the keynotes, already sounded in the prologue. They govern all twelve directives. They establish the fact that in all the affairs of this life one *ought* to fear God and *ought not* to fear anyone or anything but God. Only such a one will act honorably in all things.

When this is said, the final punctuating note is a direct appeal to God: "Now may the God of peace, who brought again from the dead our Lord Jesus, the great shepherd of the sheep, by the blood of the eternal covenant, equip you with everything good that you may do his will, working in you that which is pleasing in his sight, through Jesus Christ; to whom be glory for ever and ever. Amen" (13:20–21). Within this *everything good in Jesus Christ* is most certainly the gift of fear. For the ethics of Hebrews is situated from start to finish within the dialectic of godly confidence and godly fear. But we must say a further word about the nature and the repository of this gift, the gift of fear.

"A Fearful Thing" and the Fearful King

"Fear regards two objects," remarks Thomas at *ST* 3.7.6, "one of which is an evil causing terror; the other is that by whose power an evil can be inflicted, as we fear the king inasmuch as he has the power of putting to death." Both of these objects are in view in Hebrews. The first is evident at 10:27, for instance, which speaks of "a fearful prospect of judgment," which to the judged may well appear

15. Heb. 13:1–19. Ten of these have a justification attached; the other two are restatements of the two great commandments. Together they elaborate on 12:12–17, as the pursuit of that holiness "without which no one will see the Lord."

16. This of course is the very point at which Israel is being given a second chance—through a new generation under Joshua's command—to complete the exodus by entering and conquering Canaan.

as an "evil" causing terror, though in truth it is pure justice (cf. 13:4). The second is evident at 11:27, for example, where Moses, when leading the people out of Egypt, is said to do so "not being afraid of the anger of the king."[17] That whole chapter, as a panegyric to faith, is at the same time a great testimony to godly, as opposed to ungodly, fear. The two objects coincide at Hebrews 10:31, where we are reminded that "it is a fearful thing to fall into the hands of the living God."

It is the second object that most concerns us, but let us pause a moment with the first. The author considers it his duty to warn them, in no uncertain terms, that a fearful prospect awaits those who "refuse him who is speaking" (12:25). He looks to ancient history, to the Sinaitic ascent and descent of Moses, for help in reading recent history—the heavenly ascent and impending descent of Jesus. "For if they did not escape when they refused him who warned them on earth, much less shall we escape if we reject him who warns from heaven" (12:25; cf. Exod. 32). Judgment fell then; judgment, a fortiori, will fall now. Everything that can be shaken, whether on earth or in heaven, will be shaken—shaken out altogether, that the kingdom may come in its perfection and permanence. What exactly that means, we are not told. But we are told that anyone who is to be removed faces a fearful prospect.

The Church incorporated this teaching (which accords with that of Jesus when he warned on earth, especially in his Gehenna sayings) into a doctrine of heaven and hell; that is, into its teaching about the four last things, which takes its starting point from Hebrews 9:27–28: "And just as it is appointed for men to die once, and after that comes judgment, so Christ, having been offered once to bear the sins of many, will appear a second time, not to deal with sin but to save those who are eagerly waiting for him." The prospect of hell ought to cause terror, just as the prospect of entering the divine rest ought to cause great joy. For God is indeed a consuming fire, and every human being is made, in his or her beginning, to stand before God in the end; and so it shall be. Not that the fear of hell is proper to man, but to stand before God is proper to man. And to stand before God qua sinner—the impossible necessity—is necessarily to be consumed. The difference between purgatory and hell is only this: that in the one case the sin is consumed, and in the other the sinner; and the latter is indeed a terrifying prospect, while the former is a liberating prospect, a prospect at once fearful and joyful.

Now the fear of hell is not proper to man, any more than the fear of man is proper to man,[18] even if it belongs to man as sinner. The fear of God, however,

---

17. We must assume that this is the event referred to, for the first time Moses left Egypt he did so in fear of the king.

18. This is not to say that, apart from the fall, political organization of human society would be unnecessary or that the kingdom of God will not take the form of a *polis* or city in which will

is proper to man, and not just because God has the power, as Jesus says, to cast body and soul into hell.[19] God is to be feared for his preeminence. He is to be feared *as Jesus himself fears God*. Here is Aquinas in full:

[F]ear regards two objects, one of which is an evil causing terror; the other is that by whose power an evil can be inflicted, as we fear the king inasmuch as he has the power of putting to death. Now whoever can hurt would not be feared unless he had a certain greatness of might, to which resistance could not easily be offered; for what we easily repel we do not fear. And hence it is plain that no one is feared except for some pre-eminence. And in this way it is said that in Christ there was the fear of God, not indeed as it regards the evil of separation from God by fault, nor as it regards the evil of punishment for fault; but inasmuch as it regards the Divine pre-eminence, on account of which the soul of Christ, led by the Holy Spirit, was borne towards God in an act of reverence. Hence it is said that in all things "he was heard for his reverence" [εὐλαβείας, Heb. 5:7]. For Christ as man had this act of reverence towards God in a fuller sense and beyond all others. And hence Scripture attributes to Him the fulness of the fear of the Lord.[20]

Jesus is the living embodiment of this reverence. As Aquinas says, the gift of fear, like other gifts that perfect the native powers of the soul, exists preeminently in Jesus.[21] In answer to those who would deny this, he appeals first to Isaiah 11:3, "and he shall be filled with the spirit of the fear of the LORD"; then to Hebrews 5, parsing that passage by attributing the perfection of Jesus in the fear of God to the grace of the Holy Spirit. Jesus, who is led by the Spirit into the wilderness to be tempted, and into Gethsemane too, becomes the

---

exist a certain godly fear of godly men. It is to say that some distinction must be made—even if not Wycliffe's exactly (*Civil Lordship* 1.18, 40c)—"between natural, or evangelical, lordship and civil lordship" as we currently know it.

19. "But I will warn you whom to fear: fear him who, after he has killed, has power to cast into hell; yes, I tell you, fear him!" (Luke 12:5).

20. *ST* 3.7.6 (cf. 1–2.42.1). Aquinas argues that of the pair, hope and fear, Christ has the latter rather than the former: "[T]he nature of the gift of fear regards not that evil which fear is concerned with, but the pre-eminence of that goodness, viz. of God, by Whose power evil may be inflicted. On the other hand, hope, as a virtue, regards not only the author of good, but even the good itself, as far as it is not yet possessed. And hence to Christ, Who already possessed the perfect good of beatitude, we do not attribute the virtue of hope, but we do attribute the gift of fear" (ad 1). Hope, however, may also be viewed in more than one aspect; and if we regard hope, as I think we must, as an essential virtue of the creature even as perfected (1 Cor. 13:13), then of course we must also attribute it preeminently to Christ.

21. "[T]he gifts, properly, are certain perfections of the soul's powers, inasmuch as these have a natural aptitude to be moved by the Holy Ghost, according to Luke 4:1: 'And Jesus, being full of the Holy Ghost, returned from the Jordan, and was led by the Spirit into the desert.' Hence it is manifest that in Christ the gifts were in a pre-eminent degree" (*ST* 3.7.5).

pioneer and perfecter of our faith by enduring the discipline of sonship and so demonstrating the fear of the Lord. Thus does he open up the path to glory.[22]

Fear of the second object—that is, recognition of God in his preeminence—can exist in the subject in two ways. Even in *homo religiosus* it often exists in the wrong way. In Jesus Christ it exists as it ought to exist. Which is to say, it exists, not in a servile manner, but as an operation of liberty and love. Perfect love, says Aquinas, "casts out servile fear, which principally regards punishment; this kind of fear was not in Christ."[23] The kind of fear that was (and is) in Christ is the kind of fear that everyone needs to live the good life, for it binds us *to* God in such a way as to liberate us *for* God. As Irenaeus put it long ago: "The more extensive operation of liberty implies that a more complete subjection and affection towards our Liberator has been implanted with us."[24] Here, of course, Irenaeus has in view not only God but Jesus Christ, as does the author of Hebrews. We ought to fear Jesus Christ, our liberator, as we fear God, his liberator. Jesus Christ, rescued from death and placed at the right hand of God, shares the divine preeminence. He shares it because of who he is—the Son of God—and because of what he is—the great Priest-King whom God has set over man. The author of Hebrews is at great pains to show that true regard for Torah has been concretized as regard for this Priest-King, whose blood *is* the blood of the eternal covenant,[25] and that the great exodus that is presently under way—the journey to God's promised rest for the entire creation—is a matter of liturgical waiting upon him in reverent fear. Jesus is both the chief repository of the fear of God and himself a proper object of godly fear.

Communicating the Gift of Fear

Post-Copernican man hasn't been cultivated in the belief that "the fear of the LORD is the beginning of wisdom" (Prov. 9:10);[26] indeed, he has been taught just the opposite. He no longer knows that the godly fear of Jesus Christ (the

---

22. *ST* 3.7.6; cf. 1–2.111.3: "Now there are five effects of grace in us: of these, the first is, to heal the soul; the second, to desire good; the third, to carry into effect the good proposed; the fourth, to persevere in good; the fifth, to reach glory."

23. *ST* 3.7.6, ad 3 (cf. 1 John 4:18).

24. *Haer.* 4.13.3. See further my essay, "The Greater Operation of Liberty," in *Christianity and Constitutionalism: An Introduction*, ed. Nicholas Aroney and Ian Leigh, Cambridge Studies in Law and Christianity (Cambridge: Cambridge University Press, forthcoming).

25. From which it follows that he is raised by God from the dead (13:20) through himself and for himself, in an event that is the work of the entire Trinity.

26. Cf. Michael Gillespie, *The Theological Origins of Modernity* (Chicago: University of Chicago Press, 2008), 206.

genitive here being both subjective and objective) is natural to man as made *by* God and essential to man as made *for* God. Therefore his ethical discourse is empty and largely incoherent. Very complex explanations of that can be offered, and like some of you I am engaged in the attempt to offer them. But this very simple explanation is the one explanation that goes to the heart of the matter. It is the same explanation already offered pre-Copernican man, *mutatis mutandis*, by Paul in Romans 1, say, and by the author of Hebrews, because of course it is not ultimately Copernicanism or even Kantianism that is the problem.

The Austrian-American skeptic, Paul Feyerabend, suggested that the Church was not too *slow* to make peace with Copernicanism but rather too quick, since so many miseries have followed from the subsequent marginalization of human beings in the cosmic scheme of things.[27] In point of fact, the Church has continued its anthropocentrism unabashed (as is evident even in Francis's *Laudato si'*) and it is not for any doubt of heliocentrism or any other development of modern science. Post-Copernican man is using his evolving astronomy and cosmology as an excuse, just as he is using his Kantian doubts about metaphysics as an excuse. Morally speaking, he is simply not man enough. As Cicero lamented of Rome, "morality has perished through poverty of great men; a poverty for which we must not only assign a reason, but for the guilt of which we must answer as criminals charged with a capital crime."[28]

The poverty of great men and women—in both cases, theirs and ours—stems from a decided lack of εὐλαβείας. But ours is the greater crime and ours the greater guilt, because we have been introduced to the one who is the very repository of the fear of God, and we have averted our eyes from him and turned away. Our lack of εὐλαβείας cannot be addressed, in any case, by mere lament. It can be addressed only by proclaiming afresh, in word and deed and liturgical holiness, the gospel of Hebrews, which is also the gospel of Paul and of Acts; that is, the gospel of the ascension of Jesus Christ and of the gift of fear in the Holy Spirit. Ἐγίνετο δὲ πάσῃ ψυχῇ φόβος, "and fear came upon every soul" (Acts 2:43). In proclaiming this gospel to contemporary Western man, who seems inured to his poverty, we must always remember what he has forgotten: that the fear of God is entirely proper to man, and that proclaiming it is proclaiming to man his humanity and his only hope of glory.

---

27. See n. 4 above. This was a marginalization that Kant, as already observed, unsuccessfully resisted and so exacerbated.

28. As quoted by Augustine at *Civ.* 2.21, NPNF[1] 2:36.

Index